1-91

Dress in
eighteenth-century Europe
1715–1789

To Muriel, with best wishes

Aileen Ribeiro

Dress in
eighteenth-century Europe
1715–1789

AILEEN RIBEIRO

B. T. BATSFORD LTD · LONDON

First published 1984

© Aileen Ribeiro 1984

ISBN 0 7134 4650 1

Phototypeset by Keyspools Ltd,
Golborne, Lancs

Printed in Great Britain
by Butler & Tanner Ltd
Frome, Somerset

for the publishers,
B. T. Batsford Ltd
4 Fitzhardinge Street, London W1H 0AH

– *Frontispiece*
Two Dressing Rooms by D. Chodowiecki

Contents

List of illustrations, with acknowledgements

NOTE
Plates 26, 85, 88 and 91 are taken from the *Gallerie des Modes . . . 1778–1787*, intr. P. Cornu, Paris (1911–14)

Colour *(between pages 84 and 85)*

I   **La Declaration de l'Amour**, 1731
J. F. de Troy   Oil on canvas
BERLIN, CHARLOTTENBERG PALACE

II   **La Toilette**, 1742
F. Boucher   Oil on canvas
THYSSEN–BORNEMISZA COLLECTION, LUGANO,
SWITZERLAND

III   **The Tailor**
P. Longhi   Oil on canvas
GALLERIE DELL'ACCADEMIA, VENICE

IV   **A lady, possibly Mary Gunning,
Countess of Coventry**
J.-E. Liotard   Pastel on parchment mounted on
canvas
RIJKSMUSEUM, AMSTERDAM

V   **Madame de Pompadour**
F.-H. Drouais   Oil on canvas
NATIONAL GALLERY, LONDON

Acknowledgements

I would like to thank the many people in art galleries and museums both in the United Kingdom and abroad who helped me during the research for this book, and who, along with many private owners, provided me with photographs, which they kindly allowed me to reproduce.

The Leverhulme Trust Fund were most generous in giving me a Research Grant for travel, with which I was able to visit the following museums and art galleries:

In the United States: the Metropolitan Museum of Art, the Costume Institute, the Museum of the City of New York, the Brooklyn Museum, all in New York; the Museum of Fine Arts, Boston; the Yale Center for British Art, New Haven; the Smithsonian Institution, the National Gallery and the National Portrait Gallery, all in Washington D.C.; the J. Paul Getty Museum and the Los Angeles County Museum of Art, both in Los Angeles. In Belgium: the Musées d'Art et de Costume, Brussels. In the Netherlands: the Rijksmuseum, Amsterdam; the Nederlands Kostuummuseum, the Hague. In Germany: the Bayerisches Nationalmuseum, Munich. In France: the Musée de la Mode and the Musée des Arts Décoratifs, both in Paris. In Sweden: the Nationalmuseum, the Livrustkammaren, the Nordiska Museet and the Drottningholms Teatermuseum, all in Stockholm. In Austria: the Modesammlungen des historisches Museums at Schloss Hetzendorf, and the Museum für angewandte Kunst, both in Vienna.

Space precludes a list of individual members of staff from the institutions listed above; I hope they will take my thanks as read, not only for their professional help, but also for their hospitality. Other acknowledgements include the staff of the Witt Library at the Courtauld Institute for their customary help and efficiency, and Caroline Pilkington who typed the final draft of the book. Last, but certainly not least, I owe a debt of gratitude to Tim Auger at Batsford for his help and encouragement.

Introduction

C'est le siècle des lumières, de la maturité, et de la raison.

J. F. Sobry, 1786

The eighteenth century is a century of contrasts. To most of us, thinking idly about the period, the essence of eighteenth-century costume is the sophisticated urban dress – embroidered velvet coat and knee breeches, rustling silk taffeta dress over paniers, powdered hairstyles – that was France's great contribution to the world of fashion and civilized living, part of the 'douceur de vivre' recalled by Talleyrand as he was witnessing the break-up of this society which relied on layers of privilege and servitude to survive. In such a society based on obvious differences in wealth and status, we will be concentrating on the fashions set and worn by the upper classes in most of Europe, internationally recognized symbols of caste. But this kind of dress, and the more modest versions of it worn by the middle classes, involved only a small percentage of the population; the dress worn by the common people was in many cases a mixture of received fashions long since vanished from the wardrobe of the 'haut monde', allied to a basic functional costume which had not changed much for the past hundred years; indeed, in certain parts of Europe the peasants wore regional costume with striking local characteristics which went back to the late Middle Ages. Most people in Europe were locked into an agrarian system, earning their living from the land; although the Industrial Revolution began in England in the second half of the eighteenth century, its impact on society even in England was not profound until after the end of our period.[1]

To cast a brief look at Europe in the beginning of the eighteenth century is to see how far France had established itself as the leader of fashion. Blessed with a wealth of natural resources, and a diversity of climate and produce, including well-established textile industries, France had, at the beginning of the century, a large population of between eighteen and nineteen million people, only exceeded by the population of the Holy Roman Empire, although Russia (with a population of about fourteen million at the beginning of the century) had caught up with the French at the time of the French Revolution with approximately 25 million people. Compared to these figures, countries such as Spain and England, for example, had at the beginning of the century very small populations, around five million; by the end of the century England had about nine million, roughly twice as many as the United States of America where the first census taken in 1790 showed a still small population of about four million.

French pre-eminence in wealth and culture had been achieved under the firm rule of Louis XIV; although the last years of his reign were clouded by war, the basic strength of the economy ensured a relatively quick recovery, when power was transferred in 1715 to his five-year-old great-grandson, Louis XV. French power was visible, also, in Spain; since 1700 Spain had been ruled by a French king and grandson of Louis XIV, Philip V, who remained a Frenchman at heart, much of his foreign policy revolving around attempts to have himself considered heir to the French throne too (although this was forbidden by the Treaty of Utrecht, 1713), until the birth of the Dauphin (1729) put an end to such hopes. Although the King of Spain was himself uninterested in clothes, the court was quick to take advantage of the opening up of this hitherto remote country cut off (as the Iberian peninsula always has been, due to its geographical position) from events in the rest of Europe; a new court dress based on the French model was introduced, and French dominance of the arts generally was a feature of Spanish cultural life in the first half of the eighteenth century. Portugal, too, which in the eighteenth century was enjoying a kind of sleepy golden age outside the mainstream of European politics, was closely allied to Spain through royal marriages, and followed the Spanish trend towards the adoption of French styles in dress.

Perhaps the most striking effect of French fashions in all the arts was on the German states. Nothing is more confusing than trying to define 'Germany' in the eighteenth century. An English visitor in 1778 talked of 'a large country of Europe divided into several states and principalities'; in fact Germany consisted of more than three hundred sovereign states, some, like Brandenburg-Prussia, being large enough to have a viable government and economy, and others having as their only source of revenue the hiring out of mercenary troops in return for subsidies to England, France and Holland, involved in the European territorial struggles of the period. Some small states were made even smaller by the practice of subdivision within different lines of the same family; when Boswell visited Germany in 1764 he found, for example, two Brunswicks, two Anhalts and five duchies of Saxony, besides the Electorate. The main aim of many of the German rulers was to keep a brilliant court on the French model; all social life was concentrated at court, to the exclusion of any other section of society such as the professional or middle classes. In many cases the minor German princelings and their aristocracy were obsessed by rank and precedence, although their style of living might not have warranted such pride; Voltaire, in *Candide*, was only repeating a well-worn theme when he poked fun at the sister of Baron Thunderten-tronck, who refused to marry a worthy gentleman 'because he could only claim seventy-one quarterings, the rest of his family tree having suffered from the ravages to time', and because 'The Baron was one of the most influential noblemen in Westphalia, for his house had a door and several windows and his hall was actually draped with tapestry'.

It was in Germany also that relics of the past could be seen in the continuing of sumptuary legislation long after it had been phased out by the more forward-looking countries of western Europe. In addition, many of the old medieval trading towns kept to regional styles of dress, worn by the merchant oligarchies. Some of the larger German courts, such as those of the Wittelsbachs in Munich, and the Elector of Saxony in Dresden, were renowned for their ceremony, elegance and lavish entertainments. The Elector of Saxony was also ruler of Poland for most of the first half of the eighteenth century; the country did not, however,

see much of its rulers until in the later eighteenth century a native Polish king established a court life based on that at Versailles although Poland had by then become a semi-protectorate of Russia. Warsaw was a long way away from Paris, but there were long-standing traditional links between the two countries, cemented in 1725 by a marriage between the young Louis XV and the daughter of the dispossessed King of Poland, Stanislas Lesczynski.

Perhaps the most significant of the German states was Prussia, which under the rule of the Elector (later King) Frederick I, totally adopted the French taste which, according to his grandson Frederick the Great, 'regulated our kitchens, our furniture, our dress and every other kind of trifle which is subject to the tyrannical sway of fashion. ... A young gentleman was taken for a fool if he had not been some time at the court of Versailles'.[2] Even though in 1713 this Francophile king was replaced by a military martinet, Frederick William I, whose aim was to make Prussia self-sufficient in terms of a strong army, and who tried to enforce strict regulations regarding civil clothing, travellers noted that 'those of some rank go dress'd after the French Fashion'. Like most cultivated people in the middle of the eighteenth century, Frederick the Great's tastes were French; French was the lingua franca of Europe in this period, replacing Latin except in learning and law, and it was the language of courts and diplomacy. The German language and culture, which had suffered as a result of the Thirty Years War (1618–48), was not to recover until the very end of our period.

Much of the political history of Europe in the eighteenth century revolved around the rivalry between Prussia and Austria for ultimate supremacy within the German Empire. This title, in theory, belonged to Austria, for from the fifteenth century there had been a fairly well-established habit of choosing successive heads of the house of Habsburg, the reigning archdukes of Austria, as Holy Roman Emperor. This convention was effectively shattered in 1740 with Frederick the Great's cynical invasion of Austrian territory on the death of the Emperor Charles VI, and not until 1745 was the empire back in Habsburg hands, where it was to remain until extinguished by the armies of Napoleon in 1806.

In the early part of the eighteenth century much of Habsburg foreign policy was motivated by hostility towards France, through the loss of the Spanish connection; the court at Vienna was noted for its elaborate Spanish ceremonial and hauteur, and the wearing of Spanish court dress was obligatory. With the marriage of Maria Theresa in 1736 to the Archduke Francis of Lorraine (later Emperor), French influence came to the Austrian court, for by this time no court with any pretensions to status or culture could afford to ignore the styles emanating from Paris.

It was equally true of countries with an important past, like Holland, now gently stagnating under the benign rule of a burgher oligarchy, and countries previously on the periphery of Europe, but with an important future, like Russia. From the beginning of the eighteenth century Russia was pushed violently into the European limelight by Peter the Great, who forced his nobles to adopt the clothes of western Europe. He himself preferred plain cloth suits in the English style, but the Russian court with its love of flamboyance and an almost oriental splendour soon adopted French clothes, under a succession of Empresses noted for lavish spending and discerning patronage of all the arts of France. In Sweden, the most powerful of the Scandinavian countries, there had long been an alliance with France, which manifested itself in a brilliant display of French culture around the throne, reaching a peak in the last quarter of the century with the last great Swedish king, Gustavus III. It is important to stress, however, that by the time we reach these outer fringes of Europe, the gulf between a tiny élite at court and the mass of the rural peasantry would be emphasized by striking differences in dress.

Like Germany, Italy was just a geographical expression; in the Middle Ages and in the Renaissance it had been a fashion leader, and produced the best silks in Europe. For the whole of the eighteenth century, with no great fashion impulse, Italy fell into a kind of retirement, with conflicting influences at work depending on the vagaries of foreign rule, Austrian in the north of the country, and Spanish in the Kingdom of Naples and Sicily. Strong regional influences were dominant in Italian dress, in addition to sumptuary legislation which tried both to limit foreign styles and to regulate the clothing of the patrician classes in the old city states. Such sumptuary legislation was only partly effective, and by the second half of the eighteenth century, French fashions were widespread.

Compared to Italy, England gave the impression of a compact unity which had basically been untroubled by the accession of a new dynasty in 1714. By defeating the armies of Louis XIV, England had become a first-class power, a success she attributed partly to the relative freedom of her laws and institutions. Contemporaries, such as a German visitor, von Archenholz, in 1789, noted that England was 'so different from all other states of Europe in the forms of its government, in its laws, its customs, and in the sentiments and manners of its inhabitants'; the English rather self-consciously cultivated this difference, even viewing their clothes, in their relative simplicity of cut and fabric, as extensions of their hard-won liberties. Yet there was in the eighteenth century, as today, a curious ambivalence with regard to France; coupled with a dislike of French policies at home and abroad went the feeling that only the French possessed the secrets of haute couture and high fashion, particularly with regard to women's dress.

That contemporaries were aware of the value of French fashions as cultural propaganda is evidenced by an Italian writer, Caraccioli, whose *Voyage de la Raison en Europe* (1772) put forward the thesis that people in his lifetime had become more civilized and peaceful not just through the virtues of philosophers who ridiculed war, but through the unifying influence of French dress: 'que les modes même avoient contribué à cette heureuse metamorphose; qu'en prenant la frisure & l'habillement des François, on avoit insensiblement pris leur language, & que l'amenité qui leur est propre, sembloit donner le ton'.[3] Not only was dress a unifying factor but also a civilizing one in an age in which Reason was the prevailing goddess. When Baretti in Exeter in 1760 heard a sermon preached against dress, he indignantly wrote:

Dressing is one of the many things that increase the difference between the reasonable animal and the unreasonable, and anything, be it ever so small that increases that difference, is never much amiss. Extremes to be sure are extremes; and the variety of dressing may be carried so far as to be ridiculous; yet sinful it can scarcely ever be; therefore if I were a preacher, I would never bear hard upon this point, because I have observed that people well dressed have in general a kind of respect for themselves, and whoever respects himself, does a very good thing.[4]

By 1760 French standards in taste and fashion were universally adopted; France was not only exporting the actual styles of fashion, but the way of life in which this fashion played such an important part. The concept of 'society' as defined by the French had, from the end of the seventeenth century, meant the growth in the civilized relationships between the sexes, characterized by wit, elegance and style and was seen at its best in the salons in Paris, where groups of cultivated men and women discussed all that was new in matters of politics, society and the intellect. Unlike the court where rank alone counted, the salons admitted a wider range of people whose passport for entry could equally be a brilliant work in the realm of letters, or their membership of one of the great noble families. The credo of the salon was expressed by an English visitor to Paris in 1712, where he found that

'Civility is more study'd in France than in the Kingdom of China'.[5] Such civility in the seventeenth century was practised at court almost exclusively, among 'Persons of Quality', but in the eighteenth century the concept spread to a wider section of society, first to Paris and then, later in the century, to provincial towns. Madame de Staël, writing after the French Revolution (although her words could equally apply to the whole of the eighteenth century) defined the difference between the essence of society in Germany and that in France: 'La Bonne Compagnie, en Allemagne, c'est la cour; en France, c'étaient tous ceux qui pouvaient se mettre sur un pied d'égalité avec elle ...'.[6] The salon was a useful link between the court and the aristocracy; the French nobility, deprived in most cases of the substance of power in return for mere proximity to the sovereign and social advancement, turned to the cultivation of the arts of gracious living.

An integral part of the increased refinement of relationships between the sexes was due to the improvement in the status of women in France. Although they had no political importance (and no philosopher was prepared to make an improvement to their political status a central plank of his philosophy), they were expected to provide an intelligent and sophisticated visual adornment; as arbiters of taste and judgement they were expected to lay a greater emphasis on the role of dress and displaying the person to best advantage, essential ingredients of society. The impetus towards greater education for women crept forward slowly; more perceptibly, progress was made in marriage relationships, and one can see a gradual change from the essentially cynical mercenary compacts of the first half of the century to a growing feeling that the ideal should be mutual affection and respect, however imperfect the reality. At the same time there was a growing feeling that the lot of children should be improved; Rousseau's *Emile* (1762) led public feeling to the belief that children's physical and social needs (including clothing based on practicalities rather than on a display of rank and wealth) should be considered independently. The English were, as we shall see, pioneers in the liberation of children from many of the restrictions imposed on them by adults.

Rousseau based much of his work in this respect on that of the English philosopher John Locke; the writings of English philosophers of the later seventeenth century with regard to the liberty of the subject and individual freedom proved fruitful sources for the French philosophers of the eighteenth century. No truly original or revolutionary modes of thought characterize the eighteenth century until the French Revolution; for most of the period we see a re-statement of ideas that had first been promulgated in the seventeenth century, a time of religious unrest and civil upheaval which had undermined men's faith in the fundamentals of their society, had caused them to question prevailing values and to establish a new critical climate which taught people to rely on their own judgement. Pope's maxim that 'the proper study of mankind is Man', in itself a re-working of the Renaissance ideal, can be seen both in the feeling of enlightenment (that all problems could be solved by reason), and in the growing demands for greater justice in the treatment given to the less privileged sections of society. This can be seen particularly in the second half of the eighteenth century with the growth of 'sentiment' and humanitarianism so characteristic of the English philanthropists and philosophers who took over the intellectual leadership from France. Good taste in dress by the time of the French Revolution meant virtually middle-class taste, as simpler styles in plainer stuffs had become the accepted everyday costume.

New discoveries in science, applied to the textile industries, meant that by the end of the century there was a greater expectation of life among the lower classes through the greater availability of comfortable, washable clothing. These industrial inventions occurred during the second half of the eighteenth century in England, due not so much to the natural advantages of the country, but more to a new entrepreneurial spirit unhindered by the medieval restrictions which beset most other European countries. Accelerating industrial improvements had been noted from the early eighteenth century (and machines and factory systems from before then); Defoe in his *Tour thro' the whole Island of Great Britain* (1713) was proud of 'new discoveries in metals, mines, and minerals, new undertakings in trade, engines and manufactures, in a nation pushing and improving as we are'. Capitalism and free trade made the Industrial Revolution possible in England; its extension and impact on the rest of Europe, in the early nineteenth century, is beyond the scope of this study.

As in the rest of Europe, there was for a variety of reasons a remarkable increase in the population in the second half of the eighteenth century in England. It was perhaps more noted in England, where a combination of decline in many rural industries and the social effects of the enclosures of land led to a vast increase in the population of the cities; London was the largest city in Europe with a population of a million, and by the time of the French Revolution one-fifth of the population in England lived in the towns, compared to one-tenth of the French population, the nearest rivals to England with regard to urbanization. Tensions were the inevitable outcome as society tried to cope with such an influx; violence, never far from the surface, erupted on many occasions and threatened to destroy the fabric of society, based on an implicit acceptance of the rights and privileges of the upper classes. Contemporary writings are witness to the part played by dress in enforcing the status quo, with constant complaints about the usurpation of the kinds of dress thought to be the prerogative of one particular class. This was particularly so in open and fluid societies like England (and, to a lesser extent, France), where sumptuary legislation was no longer an aid to the distinguishing of class by means of dress. So, for example, a London newspaper reported in 1744 that 'every illiterate coxcomb who had made a fortune by sharping or shop-keeping will endeavour to mimic the great ones'. Such imitation would, according to an English visitor to Paris early in the century, contribute to 'the End of excessive Luxury, there being nothing that can make Noble Personages so much despise Gold Trimming, than to see it upon the Bodies of the lowest Men in the World'.[7] In fact, even with the finest dress in the world, the lower classes would look awkward, for they would not have the correct manner of wearing their clothes; the correct dress, elegantly worn with a kind of nebulous grace and even a carelessness of deportment was part of the seemingly effortless aristocratic superiority, as taught by the French, and admired from St Petersburg to Madrid.

Equally remarked on as a trait of English society from the middle of the century was the habit of some of the younger members of the nobility to adopt the clothes of the working classes. Lord Chesterfield, arbiter of English elegance, wrote to his son in 1748 that 'some of our young fellows affect the tremendous, and wear a great and fiercely cocked hat, an enormous sword, a short waistcoat, and a black cravat; others go in brown frocks, leather breeches, great oaken cudgels in their hands, their hats uncocked and their hair unpowdered, and imitate grooms, stage-coachmen and country bumpkins'.[8]

This was a forerunner of the mood for ostensibly 'democratic' clothing, which spread from England in the 1780s with a wave of Anglomania; in the years before the outbreak of civil violence by the Parisian mob, fashionable men had adopted dark workman-like colours and cloths, boots, unpowdered hair instead of a wig, and even pantaloons, the trousers which had been worn by working men and sailors throughout the eighteenth century. De Ségur, writing during the upheavals in France after the Revolution, remarked that during the 1780s the aristocracy had begun to dress like their valets, appearing in company in informal sporting clothing – 'en cessant de respecter le public, on oublia toutes nuances en société'.[9] Mercier, an avowed Republican himself, lamented the demise of French elegance; even politeness was out of fashion. For women the 1780s were also a decade of novelty; simple linen or cotton dresses anticipated the neo-classical mood of post-revolutionary France. In effect, of course, what started life as variations on working clothes were soon changed out of all semblance to the original in quality of cut, fabric and disposition of ornament. Yet even an intelligent man like Charles James Fox believed that 'the neglect of dress in people of fashion had contributed much to remove the barriers between them and the vulgar, and to propagate levelling and equalizing notions'.[10]

Dress has always been one of the most sensitive barometers testing the feeling of a period; not only does it reflect the dominant mood of society, but in some cases it can even appear to anticipate abrupt and revolutionary changes. The French Revolution did not cause the immediate introduction of wholly new garments, but it did accelerate the pace of change of clothes that was already in the pipeline. It is for this reason that this book ends with the French Revolution, which, to people who had lived before and during these momentous events, seemed like the end of the known world; it seemed to deal a mortal blow to a society based on privilege and the unbridgeable gulfs between classes. In retrospect, however, the upper classes were never in serious danger of losing their place as the dominant force in society, but the early events of the Revolution with its unleashing of long-suppressed violence, gave them a shock which they never quite forgot.

We begin with 1715, a date marking the beginning of a new period in France after the interminable reign of Louis XIV, and of a new feeling of freedom in society after the dead hand of tradition was lifted from a society dominated by a rigidly formal court. In 1715, the year after the beginning of a new dynasty in England, came the first test (with the Jacobite rebellion) of the stability of the new régime, a test which was successfully passed. France and England, old enemies and rivals both in the European and colonial spheres, dominate the history of dress in the eighteenth century, the former through the splendour of formal costume, and the latter, particularly in the second half of the century, through informal, outdoor and sporting costume.

For the first half of the century, fashion changes were more noticeable with regard to women's dress. The stately gowns with sweeping trains and bustles, decorated with baroque ornament, which dominated the court at Versailles, gave way at the beginning of the new reign to more informal, negligée gowns worn over the newly fashionable cone-shaped hoops, which seemed to float as the wearer moved, and which can be seen to greatest advantage in the paintings of Watteau and de Troy. A new lightness was also to be seen in textiles; alongside the heavy floral brocades of formal dress went plain light silks and painted silks from the East. Throughout the whole of the eighteenth century, the most fashionable silks came from France and from Lyons in particular; the French silk industry was supported by the state, an added boost to the development of the fashion industry in France. For the heavier silks such as velvet, Italy produced the best examples, which in the first half of the eighteenth century went to make the finest-quality men's suits; by the later period, however, with the trend towards lighter silks, and fine cloth, velvets were more and more limited to use as furnishing fabrics.

By the time that Louis XV achieved his majority, the supremacy of French women in the fashion world was undoubted; although he was too lazy to regulate on dress like his predecessor, Louis XV liked fashionable women around him. Of all his mistresses, Madame de Pompadour was the most influential in the dissemination of French taste and fashions; she was almost the personification of the playful, three-dimensional elegance of the rococo style in dress, arguably the most seductive clothing ever invented for women. In the second half of the eighteenth century, such frivolity in dress gave way to simpler styles, with an increasing use of linen and cotton, and a growing emphasis on more functional clothing for a more active life.

For most of the eighteenth century there were no profound changes in men's dress, for the basic format of three-piece suit and coat had been well established by the end of the previous century. The changes to be chronicled were, basically, the progress from the heavy, baroque fullness of material and cut to a slimmer silhouette, with a corresponding movement from heavy, decorated silks to lightweight silk or cloth with delicate ornamentation. Although formal embroidered clothes continued to be worn for court throughout the eighteenth century, by the last quarter of the period the new fashion impulse was towards English sporting clothing; the last pre-Revolutionary decade was dominated by the dress of the country. For both men and women, the second half of the eighteenth century was characterized by a growing dichotomy between formal and informal clothing.

The impetus towards change was accelerated by the newly established fashion magazines, which began to appear regularly from the early 1770s, first in England and France and then in Germany. Such magazines emphasize the way in which ceremonial and court dress had frozen into a kind of uniform; for court dress in particular, there is a valedictory feel to the almost icon-like splendour which could never occur again in the vastly different world of post-Revolutionary Europe. It might also be noted here (although the scope of the book precludes its discussion) that it was during the eighteenth century that military and naval uniforms were systematized; they had of course existed before, but in a rather haphazard way linked very often to the personal whim of a commanding officer. With the eighteenth century love of reason and order (and helped by the fact that warfare was endemic throughout the period, although no great territorial changes – the First Partition of Poland aside – were made until the French Revolution), such uniforms were for the first time established.

In the eighteenth century dress was not truly innovatory, but essentially a refinement of already existing styles. The part played by dress in the regulation and civilizing of behaviour was an essential part of Louis XIV's grand plan in the seventeenth century, to cope with what was in many ways a nasty, brutish and insolent aristocracy; 'Persons of Quality must now become Persons of Taste' was the guiding rule, and for many nobles a brilliance of style in dress became almost their *raison d'être*. The etiquette of dress which visibly demonstrated one's place in society was a tyranny gladly accepted by the ruling classes, for uniformity of taste could also encompass an individualism of approach. The contribution made by the eighteenth century was to add a freedom of expression and imagination to the aesthetic unity of the period which had already been conceived by 1700, by which time the rules of art, conduct and intellect had been codified. The unity of the arts, politics and sciences can best be seen in the work most typical of the eighteenth century, the *Encyclopédie* of Diderot and d'Alembert. Particularly from the middle of the century, a variety of tastes were allowed to be fashionable in all the arts, including dress; these included the exotic, the historical, the picturesque, and a taste for classical antiquity, all of which manifested themselves in dress, for the fancy-dress entertainments which were such an important aspect of social life, in portraiture, and in fashionable clothing.

The evidence for our knowledge of dress in the eighteenth century is vast; the pitfalls of approaching a period about which everyone has firm ideas are legion. I have chosen to concentrate not so much on the details of construction (enough clothing survives to make this a study best attempted in detail in a narrower context than the scope of this book), but on the range and variety of dress in Europe as a whole, and by looking through the eyes of contemporaries at what they considered to be the part played by dress in society. In a period in which there are no major changes in costume, contemporary works of art assume a greater importance – they are the words translated into style and movement – for they tell us how people moved and had their being, and how they saw themselves as they really were, or as they wished to be.

The eighteenth century is a feeling as well as a period of time; it is the last time in which taste and individuality in all the arts, including dress, reached a peak never since equalled, and which in its standards of craftsmanship was destroyed by the machine age and its concomitant uniformity.

1715–1740: The dominance of France

They invent every Day new Modes of Dressing, and weary of living in their own Country, you may see 'em sometimes gadding into . . . a World of different Countries . . .

of France, and City of Paris,

[handwritten note: Death of Louis XIV / Regent Philippe'du / d'Orléen ruler]

The year 1715 saw a dramatic change in the fortunes of the new ruler of France, the Regent Philippe, duc d'Orléans, who came to power on the death of Louis XIV, for the new king was a child of five. In the last few years of the old king's rule there had been a sense of gloom in public life, resulting from the demands made by the War of the Spanish Succession, and the personal disasters suffered by Louis XIV in the loss of his heirs. Although inheriting a national debt of 2000 million livres (much of it caused by the wars), the Regent also inherited the professional government system created by Louis XIV which, with slight changes, lasted until the French Revolution. Like his young ruler, the Regent was a man, in Saint-Simon's phrase, 'born bored', a boredom which doubtless led him to the self-indulgences which killed him at an early age, but also led to a highly cultivated court keen to patronize the best of the new in design and art. Women, including his many mistresses, began that female dominance of the court which was to continue under Louis XV and which contributed to the sophisticated development of the arts of fashion.

of the new regime was to court at Versailles and to f power in Paris, home of s were beginning to disseminate new artistic ideas. The Regency style, the forerunner of the rococo, was characterized by a sense of lightness and a playful exoticism seen in art, interior design and textiles, all of which reacted against the measured classicism and conformity of

th reign. Light colours and floating silks, w ing vogue for the informality of the ne e typical of women's dress in the early ei entury; indolence and sensuality were th of the new dispensation.

n changes do not occur overnight, and si vith these new fashion influences went a c f the old order with regard to formal d rticularly for men's dress, where a kind o heaviness in style and fabric continued w e eighteenth century.

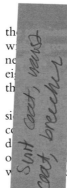

Men

Let us first look in detail at a fashionable man's wardrobe in 1715, bearing in mind that the main garments remained essentially the same in the period. The suit was the basic unit of the male wardrobe throughout the eighteenth century, composed of coat, waistcoat and breeches, usually, but not always, of the same fabric. The idea of the suit had originated in the 1660s, possibly influenced by oriental or theatrical modes but more probably deriving from the idea of the sleeved coat of the earlier seventeenth century worn with sleeveless jerkin and knee-breeches.

The tailoring of the coat in its early stages was still fairly crude; two fronts and two backs were sewn together with straight side seams stitched to just below the waist to leave room for the sword which hung from a sword-belt under the coat, the hilt coming through the side vent and the end point through a centre-back vent. It had no collar and was decorated with braid or metal lace or frogged clasps, and similar trimming outlined the horizontally flapped pockets set half way between the waist and the hem. By the beginning of our period the coat was tailored more tightly to the body; the French name 'justaucorps' can be literally translated as 'close to the body', and this tightness was empha-

1   **Portrait in tiles of an unknown man**

The relatively crude technique, relying on a
simplification of outline, conveys the exaggeratedly
heavy and stylized male dress of *c*.1715. The wig is huge,
with a conical peak and heavy side pieces, the coat is
waisted with reinforced side pleats, and the high-heeled
shoes with their turn-over tops are cut square across in
the front.

ABOVE RIGHT
2   **Sir Charles Haggerston**, 1714, by A. S. Belle

The passion for stylized contortion in dress can be seen in
the knotted wig and the cravat twisted into the
buttonhole *à la* Steinkirk.

sized by heavily stiffened side pleats, five or six in
number, which swung as the wearer walked. By the
end of the 1720s these side pleats, stiffened with
gummed linen (buckram) and interlined with wool
or horse-hair, were obviously comparable to the
huge hoops being worn by women; the *Mercure de
France* for March 1729 noted of the total effect: 'le
tout pour donner de la grace, dit on, & faire le
panier.'[1]

In line with the more complex tailoring, the front
edges of the coat swung slightly off the straight, the
tendency to curve in this way increasing as the
century progressed. *button*
buttoned just at the wa
and the fine lace cr
buttonholes were prominent pieces of jewellery,
they were often embroidered to match the embroidery on the coat.

Large, stiffened and decorated cuffs formed the
focal point for the wide sleeves; the flaring, turned-
back cuff which was open behind was that of more
formal suits and laste *cuffs* ✳
eighteenth century. In
century the most cha
cuff, keeping to the width of the sleeve, but coming
almost up to the elbow; in England this type of
cuffed sleeve was known as a 'boot-sleeve', and,
according to the novelist Henry Fielding, was
particularly useful as a re *waistcoats*
The waistcoat was cu
coat, but without the side
in the skirts. In the early
waistcoats had long sleeves, the upper sleeves often
matching the back of the garment, which, as it did

not show, was composed of coarse linen or cotton mixture fabric, but with a cuff matching in splendour the brocade or embroidery of the waistcoat front. In 1715 the waistcoat would be about the same length as the coat, that is knee-length, and with similar horizontal pockets; as the century progressed the waistcoat became shorter, and curved round at the front.

As for the final component of the suit, the breeches or culottes, these were in 1715 immensely full and baggy in the seat, sometimes being cut on the bias to stretch and give ease of movement. In an age in which, as the Vicar of Bray put it, 'moderate men looked big', to have 'bottom' had a meaning added to the usual one of solid dependency. These breeches were gathered into a waistband which could be adjusted by laces at the back or the sides; buttons closed the centre front and there were pockets, including a fob pocket in the waistband. Sometimes the breeches ended above the knee, when the stockings (usually of knitted, coloured silk, worsted or cotton) were rolled over the kneeband; this fashion lasted into the early 1730s, when it was replaced by slightly tighter breeches fastening firmly below the knee, but the earlier style lingered on into the 1750s in the dress of the elderly and conservative. Unlike the coat and waistcoat, the breeches were not decorated except for small buttons fastening the side seam open above the knee-band; the coat and waistcoat were so long in the early eighteenth century that the breeches did not show much beneath them and therefore, in an age in which visible show was important, they could be comfortable rather than elegant. For men it was a period of considerable ease and comfort, a time of well-fed gentlemen with slightly bulging eyes and florid complexions so familiar through the portraits of Kneller; by the middle of the century a new, slimmer silhouette made *embonpoint* increasingly unfashionable.

Throughout the eighteenth century, the coat was the focal point of attention, through the luxury and disposition of fabric and trimming. Decoration on the coat, in the form of braid, embroidery or lace, was applied down the centre fronts, the centre backs from the waist downwards, on and around the pockets, and on the cuffs. From about 1730, this decoration, usually heavy and three-dimensionally ornate, was woven in position on the coat lengths.

For formal and grand occasions embroidery would be heaped upon suits of brocade; to the modern eye the colours would seem very bright, but they were meant to be worn in the evenings when the candlelight caught the diamond buttons and reflected the glitter of gold and silver tissues, gold and silver lace and embroidery. In many cases,

the embroidery constituted the greatest expense; in 1740, for example, Frederick the Great, in the first year of his reign, before his legendary military prowess enabled him to wear a suit spartan in its simplicity, received from the court tailor a bill for a suit of which the fabric cost ten thalers, but the silver embroidery of which cost 85 thalers. The embroiderer Jean Pally sent, at the same time, a bill for silver embroidery costing 1000 thalers.[2]

In the early years of our period large floral silk brocades were worn for coat and breeches, but by the end of the second decade of the century, such large floral patterns were increasingly limited to the waistcoat. In the 1720s woven silks with small stylized floral designs were specially woven for men's suits, and the designs of these did not change much in the first half of the eighteenth century. By the end of the 1720s, it is possible to note the first faint shift in taste from elaborate woven patterns towards plain stuffs, often with subtle and understated colour combinations. At court in 1729 Mrs Delany saw the Prince of Wales 'in mouse-colour velvet turned up with scarlet and very richly trimmed with silver';[3] in the same year the *Mercure de France* told its readers that the winter colours were shades of tobacco, 'marron foncé', 'feuille morte', agate and grey.[4] By 1739 at the English court Mrs Delany found the men 'chiefly brown with gold or silver embroidery and rich waistcoats'.[5] Woven silk suits were usually lined with the lighter silks such as taffeta; for velvets, satin was used, and sometimes plush or fur in very cold climates.

For winter wear, the heaviness and richness of velvet was admired, the finest examples coming from Genoa. In 1736 the Hofrat (Court Councillor) Freiherr von Seckendorff listed in the *Frankfurter Intelligenzblatt* that the clothes stolen from him in transit from Bonn to Berlin included a black velvet suit, the coat lined with red velvet and the waistcoat lined with white taffeta, and also a coat and breeches of brown cut velvet, the coat lined with blue velvet, and with a waistcoat of blue satin decorated with silver.[6] From this, it can be seen that a fashionable wardrobe could comprise a three-piece suit made of the same fabric, and a suit consisting of coat and breeches of the same material with a waistcoat of contrasting fabric. This latter taste was to increase as the century wore on, with growing emphasis on the richness of the waistcoat, more of which was

3 **Charles III as a boy when Prince of the Asturias**, 1722, by J. Ranc

The heavily embroidered court coat is tightly waisted, and flares out into deep, lined side pleats.

revealed by the cutting away of the side of the coat.

Court waistcoats were sometimes decorated with fringes of silk, silver and gold thread and chenille in the first third of the eighteenth century; thereafter decoration on the waistcoat included sequins, and metal foils in various colours, as well as the ornate serpentine embroidery. In the first years of the century, waistcoats were sometimes made from 'bizarre' silks, silks of curious and fantastic patterns derived from the orient, and which were fashionable until *c.* 1720.[7] The exotic and imaginative effect of such silks also seemed to qualify them for dressing gowns, which were thought of as an oriental garment, and indeed were sometimes called Indian gowns; such designs beginning at the very end of the seventeenth century, were indicative of the restless and experimental phase in art and design at that period, reacting against the rigidity imposed by the late Baroque style, and which were sent whirling into action in the Regency due to a variety of fresh design impulses.

Such silks, with their elaborate and lengthy repeats, were very expensive; a roomful of fashionable gentlemen dressed in such exotic finery and laden with embroidery would serve to impress a visitor from out of town. Against the splendour of the French court, foreign visitors could either choose to vie with their hosts in luxury, or be the more noticed, often for political reasons, for the plainness of their attire. One such visitor, the Russian emperor Peter the Great, impressed Saint-Simon in 1716 with 'a simple linen collar, a brown and unpowdered wig falling short of his shoulders, a coat of plain material with gold buttons . . . neither gloves nor shirt ruffles. The star of his order was worn outside the coat, and the ribbon beneath. His coat was usually unbuttoned all the way down; his hat was always on a table, never on his head, not even out of doors'.[8] Saint-Simon, an indefatigable recorder of trifles and imagined slights, was quick to pick up the quintessentially Russian combination of richness and slovenliness which characterized their dress; he was amazed at the gold buttons on a plain cloth suit, and by the fact that for ease the Emperor did not, as the fashionable did, fasten his coat at the waist. He was impressed by the Russian ruler; less so by the unprepossessing King of Spain, Philip V, whom he found on a visit to Madrid in 1721 in a poor-quality suit of brown serge.[9]

The plainness of male attire was from the beginning of the eighteenth century a recognized feature of English dress, from the king downwards. Horace Walpole remembered as a small child being taken to kiss the hand of George I who wore 'a dark tye wig, a plain coat, waistcoat and breeches of snuff-coloured cloth with stockings of the same colour, and a blue ribband over all'.[10] A foreign visitor to England commented in 1722 that: 'The dress of the English is like the French but not so gaudy; they generally go plain but in the best cloths and stuffs . . . not but that they wear embroidery and laces on their cloathes on solemn days, but they dont make it their daily wear, as the French do.'[11] The main differences between the French and English man with regard to dress were thus stated early in our period, and these were to be the two most important influences on masculine clothing.

One of the earliest English influences to be felt was in the adoption of the frock coat, first appearing in the fashionable English wardrobe in the mid-1720s and on the Continent some ten years later. Like so many elements of masculine wear, the frock started life as a working-class garment, a loose coat with turned-down collar, sometimes made of fustian or coarse linen, a forerunner of the overall, to protect the clothes beneath. As adopted by gentlemen, it was first worn for hunting and shooting and other rural pursuits; it was cut on similar lines to the formal coat, but with no stiffened side pleats, and was made of woollen cloth. It had a small turned-down collar called a cape, and the sleeves either had small closed cuffs, or, for even greater ease of movement, decorative slits. Decoration in fact was minimal, often consisting of braid on the pockets and cuffs and down the centre fronts, sometimes with frogging or looped buttons. Originating from a garment worn to provide protection from the weather, some of the hunting frocks had fairly elaborate double-breasted fastenings, which fell back to form lapels. As such, the frock or jacket had been worn since the beginning of the century by European gentlemen for sport; the curiosity was to find this humble garment rising in the world. César de Saussure in the mid-1720s was amazed to see Englishmen in 'little coats called "frocks" without facings and without pleats, with a short cape above';[12] as late as 1733 a German visitor, Pöllnitz, was ready to link the lazy habits of the Englishman with his informal clothing: 'He rises late, puts on a Frock (which is a close-body'd Coat without Pockets or Plaits, and with strait Sleeves), and leaving his Sword at Home, takes his Cane and goes where he pleases.'[13]

For out-of-doors, the fashionable man had a choice of garments. The over-garment with the longest tradition was the cloak. Since the earliest recorded times, man wrapped a piece of material

4 Colonel George Douglas, 1727, by J. Smibert

The sitter wears a green damask nightgown and cap.

(either square or rectangular) round himself; by Roman times this had turned into a cloak made in the shape of a circle or segment of a circle. This heavy-weather-duty garment, wholly necessary for horse-rider or pedestrian, was worn throughout the eighteenth century by all classes in varying lengths; for the walker, a capacious cloak reached to calf-length, and for the horseman a shorter and more up-to-date version was worn. In the first half of the eighteenth century, in line with the gradual tailoring of clothing, a more fitted cloak called a 'roquelaure' was worn; this was a cape cut in three pieces, the side seams shaped to the shoulders.

Yet as the century progressed and public transport improved, so also did the civilized amenities of the city; as the streets became places where it was easier to walk, so did walking become a fashionable pursuit, and the 'surtout' or overcoat, originally a sturdy working garment, became a fashionable item at first in the Englishman's wardrobe, and then adopted by the rest of Europe. This took the form of a loose-fitting coat, with a back vent necessary for riding, and with a large collar which could be turned up in bad weather. According to Joseph Gay in *Trivia; or the Art of Walking the Streets of London*, published in 1716, the surtout was also called a greatcoat, joseph, or wrap-rascal, the last name indicating that one version was a wrapped gown similar to the dressing-gown. Although the *Mercure de France* of 1729–30 advised velvet surtouts, Gay advocated the wearing of kersey as the hardiest fabric for the English weather, and noted how essential a garment it was for his native climate:

That Garment best the Winter's Rage defends,
Whose shapeless Form in ample Plaits depends.[14]

The shape of the surtout did not change much until the last quarter of the century, when, taken up by the fashionable dandy, it became a tight-fitting, streamlined overcoat.

It has already been noted that although men's clothes were roomy in fit, they were uncomfortable in weight, both from linings (especially in the side pleats of the coat) and from the heaviness and rigidity of the surface decoration. From such cares, respite was needed, to be found in the loose gowns which had been worn since the end of the seventeenth century as a popular form of informal déshabillé. The nightgown was a long loose garment rather like a modern dressing-gown, with a wrap-over front, either held in place by the hand (a consciousness of clothes in the eighteenth century, their weight, texture and disposition is demonstrated in the way sitters are so often portrayed holding out their garments, or grasping them close to the body), or tying with a sash. Sometimes this

was called a 'morning-gown', according to Dr Johnson's *Dictionary*, for it could be worn informally in the morning before one was fully dressed for the day. The cut was similar to that of the kimono, which was basically two widths of material joined up the centre-back; the custom for wearing such gowns, often of expensive oriental fabrics, came from the Netherlands at the beginning of the seventeenth century and spread via the East India companies to the rest of Europe. Some came from Japan and many came from India; in fact in England they were known as 'Indian gowns', although by the early eighteenth century they were not necessarily made in India or of Indian material. A popular fabric in fact was chintz, originally of Indian origin, but imitated by the resourceful European printers. Such printed cottons were so popular in England in the early years of the eighteenth century that according to Defoe (1724) they were adversely affecting the trade of stuffs in Norwich, for long a home of the light wool and wool-mixture cloths which draped well for gowns.[15] A series of acts in England (1712, 1714 and 1721) prohibited the import and sale of all printed cottons including Indian goods, but the ingenious calico printers evaded the acts by printing on linen or mixed fabrics of linen warp and cotton weft, which was still allowed. Other materials used for these loose-fitting nightgowns were quilted cotton, wool, Scottish plaid, and various weights of silk, some being lined for winter use, or for protection from the frequent draughts which affected even the best houses. In the inventory of effects left by Frederick the Great (1786) was 'a blue wrapper, like a woman's, of satin, trimmed with rabbit-skin, which the King wore when he had the gout'.[16] Even warmer was the blue woollen damask gown worn by Jonathan Trumbull, governor of Connecticut, which is preserved in Hartford; a similar gown appears in the portrait of the governor painted by his son and dated 1778. The basic shape of these gowns changed little during the eighteenth century; most were full-length, but a French nightgown, the 'Apollon', of mid-thigh length, was briefly popular in the mid-eighteenth century.

A more formal nightgown was the 'banyan', a tight-fitting and double-breasted gown very often with elaborate cord or frogging fastenings; the length varied, but the most popular was a mid-calf length. The curious name derived from the name for a Hindu trader in the province of Gujerat, which came to be applied to the dress he was (erroneously) thought to wear. Some were in fact made to order, of the finest silks from India; others, made in Europe, were of local woollen cloths and silks. Very often, for extra warmth and formality when the banyan was left unfastened, matching waistcoat fronts were built into the gown; in 1772 the Duchess of Northumberland, on a pilgrimage to Voltaire at Ferney, saw the famous author in 'a long Banyan & Waistcoat of Brown Sattin with colour'd Flowers'.[17]

An impressive display of wealth and taste could be created by the nightgown. Among von Seckendorff's lost clothes in 1736 was a nightgown of red velvet lined with white fur; fine examples of damask and brocade which had been used for nightgowns were sometimes made into religious vestments – this was the case with the rich gown worn by the Emperor Franz Stephan of Austria on his deathbed (1765), made into a chasuble and given by his widow to the chapel of the castle in Innsbruck where he died.

Nightgowns figured largely in the male wardrobe; Peter the Great with his love of informality in clothing possessed a considerable number, of which 13 survive in the Hermitage Museum in Leningrad; all are made in the kimono style, the summer ones of silk and the winter ones of padded silk or cotton. Regular references occur to the purchase of nightgowns in the accounts of a Scottish gentleman, George Baillie of Mellerstain; many were bought in London where he spent part of the year as an M.P., and in Naples, as part of his Grand Tour of Europe in the early 1730s, he bought two nightgowns, one of velvet and one of armosin, both trimmed with gold loops and buttons.[18] Such grand gowns would have been used to receive visitors in the morning; surviving ones have sometimes matching caps or turbans to wear over shaven heads, many believing with Boswell that some kind of head-covering was necessary to keep out the damp and draughts, and to preserve the teeth.

The nightgown was a garment useful in a variety of climates. In the cool and unfashionable air of Amsterdam, a German visitor noted in the 1720s that the usual costume of the men was 'a Nightgown lined with Flannel, under which they are swaddled in three or four thick waistcoats', while the students in Leyden also preferred this informality of dress, making them look, he thought, like so many hospital patients.[19] In the 1730s, de Brosses, a French traveller in Venice, discovered that the Venetian patricians wore morning gowns and slippers, a costume that he himself adopted; 30 years later, Baretti visited Spain and found Spanish gentlemen constantly wearing 'cap, night-gown and slippers'.[20] Lightweight silks, cottons and linens made easy and comfortable gowns for hot climates and for colonies where the rules of etiquette could be relaxed. The nightgown's popularity is reflected in the numbers of portraits of sitters wearing such

5 **Captain Thomas Coram**, 1740, by W. Hogarth

The honest, unpretentious nature of the founder of the Foundling Hospital is reflected in his sober suit and functional capacious greatcoat.

garments; those artists in particular who did not want to be bothered by the minutiae of the suit and its decoration chose a gown for the possibilities of the drapery and for the air of agreeable negligence which the eighteenth century found so attractive.

A°. 1740

Come hither my Country Squire
Take Friendly Instructions from me.;
the Lords shall admire,
thy Taste in attire;
and the Ladies shall Languish
for thee.

a skimming dish hat provide.
with Little more brim then Lace.
nine hairs on a Side,
To a Pig=Tayl ty'd;
Will set of thy Jolly broad Face.

go get the a Footmans Frock,
a Cudgel quite up to thy nose;
the Frizz like a shock.
and plaister thy Block;
and Buckle thy shoes to thy Toes.
Such flaunting gallanting &c.

6 **'The Country Squire'**, 1740, from an album of drawings once the property of Horace Walpole.

7 **A Rake's Progress: Surrounded by Artists and Professors** (detail.) c.1733, by W. Hogarth

Standing next to the dancing master with his exaggeratedly fashionable costume and mincing pose, the Rake wears an elegant frogged banyan.

The shirt was an essential part of male clothing, a garment deriving from the Roman tunic in its basic rectangular form. In the eighteenth century, the shirt still conformed to the basic 'T' shape, but with the back slightly longer than the front, and with wide sleeves ending in a narrow wristband which fastened with a button. For formal occasions, a sleeve ruffle of fine lace, usually Flemish, was attached; some shirts had a plain front opening, but [others had a frill] ich grew larger [towards the end of the] 1720s. Shirts, [made of washable] material (they [served as] an all-purpose undergarment – even worn in bed by the poor), were quite costly if they were made of the finest linen which came from Holland; in 1740 an English country gentleman, Henry Purefoy, paid seven shillings an ell for what was called Dutch Holland, and only three shillings for a comparable amount of interior Irish Holland linen.

The body of the shirt was gathered into a [neckband] closed by linen-covered buttons, and [the neckwear of] the eighteenth [century can have] o better descrip[tion than that of] Randle Holme, whose *[Academy of Armory]* (1688) – a typically seventeenth-century mixture of fact and fiction with a superfluity of costume and heraldic detail – describes this kind of neckwear as 'a long Towel put about the Collar, and so tyed before with a Bow knot', a fashion which had been in use from the middle of the century. The two main ways of tying the cravat were to knot it at the front and let it hang straight down, or to twist the linen into a plait at the front and pass one end through a button hole to keep it in place. This latter method, called the 'steinkirk', was popularly supposed to derive from the battle of the same name (1692), when during the campaigns of Louis XIV some French soldiers, attacked unexpectedly, had only time to put their neckcloths on this way, instead of tying them in a formal bow. The steinkirk continued into the 1730s as a fashion kept to by elderly men, but the more fashionable cravat in the first ten years of our period hung straight down, described by an English visitor to France as 'spread about the Neck from whence they hang like Bologna-Sausages down to the Middle'.

At some point in the 1720s the cravat was replaced in fashionable wear by the stock, a made-up neckcloth fastening at the back. Sometimes this was a piece of muslin or lace gathered onto a stiffened band tying at the back of the neck, or it was simply the band itself fastening with a brooch or pin at the back, allowing the shirt ruffle to be seen.

The most typical, perhaps, of all the elements of male costume in the early eighteenth century was the wig, its high crown and profusion of curls adding to the gravitas imposed by the dignified heaviness of the clothing. This cumbersome and full-bottomed wig was beginning to pass out of common use by the end of the reign of Louis XIV, although it was retained by the learned professions in a less top-heavy form; the military campaigns of the War of Spanish Succession encouraged more manageable wigs. Such was the 'campaign wig', or 'perruque à marteaux', shorter than the huge periwig and with the hair divided into two locks hanging over each shoulder and with a long curl at the nape of the neck, which was in use until the middle of the century.

Another form of military wig in use in the early eighteenth century was the Ramillies wig with a single plait at the back of the head; this was particularly popular in the Prussia of Frederick William I, as being economical and neat. It was in fact popular among the military of all European nations throughout the whole of the eighteenth century, and passed in a truncated form into the early nineteenth.

By the early 1720s men were beginning to adopt the lighter tie-wigs, which were tied at the back with a black silk ribbon; in fact one of the first mentions of this style is in *The Guardian* of 1713, but it was not widely worn until a decade later. Alternatively, the hair could be tied back and enclosed in a small bag, called by the French a 'bourse', or 'crapaud', sometimes with a black silk ribbon coming from the bag to tie at the front in a bow, or with a brooch – this was called a 'solitaire', and was the usual style for formal occasions from about 1730, although for court balls a wig (or the natural hair) in long ringlets was *de rigueur*. For informal occasions, undress wigs were worn; these were usually 'bob wigs', made undivided into sections, but with all-over curl or frizz; the short bob came to just below the ears, the long bob to the shoulders. Formality also demanded that the wig be powdered with finely ground starch or wheat flour (sometimes perfumed) which was puffed on after the wig had been dressed with pomatum; a powder room was necessary in a gentleman's establishment so that his valet could retire with him, cover him in a powdering gown and puff the powder on his hair. For those men lucky enough to have thick and luxuriant hair, it was perfectly possible to be seen in company in this way, with the hair dressed and powdered in the style of the currently fashionable wig. Not until the 1740s, when hairstyles were more complex, close to the head and tightly curled, were all men of whatever class wearing wigs, even if they were not always of the finest hair.

8 An etching of a young man, 1725, from *Figures Françoises Nouvellement Inventées par Octavien*

The emphasis here is on trimming and accessories. Fringe trims the waistcoat, unbuttoned to the waist, thus revealing the plain shirt frill and the stock fastened with a brooch at the neck. The sword is a necessary mark of rank, but increasing gentility is reflected in the use of the cane hanging from the wrist by a looped ribbon.

The finest hair for wigs was in fact human hair, Diderot claiming in his *Encyclopédie* that the best came from beer-drinking countries such as Flanders. A rumour was current (as it had been from the middle of the seventeenth century when men had begun to wear wigs) that graves were robbed to provide hair; an anonymous author recording a trip to Paris in 1712 commented that 'the sepulchres and the Women furnish the finest ornament for the Heads of the Men'.[22] When French women (followed by other ladies in Europe) began to cut their hair in the 1720s, this was an obvious source for the wig-makers and added to the regular supplies from girls entering convents. Human hair, however, was

expensive and for those who could not afford it, horse-hair was a popular cheap alternative with the added advantage that it did not uncurl in the rain.

The wig was usually so imposing in the early years of the eighteenth century that the hat often appeared as an afterthought, not being worn on the high-piled wig because it would destroy the toupet, but being carried under the arm. Even when wigs were reduced in size, men continued to carry their hats (always black) in this way on formal occasions, a fashion which lasted throughout the eighteenth century; in the 1770s a hat, the so-called 'chapeau bras', was made specifically for this purpose and was not meant to be worn. For protection against the weather, for business and for those with no pretentions to elegance, hats were worn firmly on the head.

The most expensive hats were made of beaver-skins, which made an impermeable fabric; half-beavers, made by sticking beaver hair onto woollen felt, were considerably cheaper. Whatever the fabric, it had to be rigid enough to be shaped into the three-cornered style, which was the form of the formal hat through the eighteenth century; the brim was turned up (the contemporary word was 'cocked') on three sides to form a kind of triangle, with more or less equal sides. Slight inequalities in the length of the sides, the depth of the crown, or the angle at which the hat was cocked, created hats known to contemporaries by a variety of names, though to our eyes the distinctions are relatively small. Those wearing uncocked hats were either travelling in bad weather, or were members of the lower classes or young men-about-town deliberately setting out to shock their elders by adopting such uncouth attire. This latter attitude was more current in England than in the rest of Europe, as was, towards 1740, the vogue for jockey caps, round caps with peaks in front, which reflected the growing interest in racing.

The trimming of the three-cornered hat was more important than the relatively unchanging shape, the brim being usually edged with braid or lace, often with a feather fringe; the *Mercure de France* for October 1730 noted that the most fashionable hats were slightly smaller than of late and edged with *point d'Espagne* (a kind of metal braid), or gold or silver lace. Hats were fastened with a button and loop, which provided an opportunity for a display of precious stones; in 1729 Mrs Delany noted that George II's hat was 'buttoned up with prodigious fine diamonds' which matched the buttons on his blue velvet suit.[23]

At the other end of the body, the solidity of the footwear complemented the general heaviness of outline. Shoes were usually of leather with, at the beginning of our period, square blocked toes and high square heels; the uppers covered the foot, ending in square tongues rising high in front of the ankle. The sides were closed, and the shoes fastened by straps from the heel leathers, buckled in front over the tongues; red heels were widely worn at court and on formal occasions until the middle of the century. At the end of the 1720s the square toes were gradually being replaced by rounder toes, until by 1740 these were almost universal. The square toes, however, remained for some time in official and thus more conservative dress – 'square-toes' was slang for an old man, according to Grose's *Dictionary of the Vulgar Tongue* (1785).

Shoe buckles took various shapes; the most popular were small squares or oblongs until from the middle of the 1720s they gradually increased in size. For the rich attending court, shoe buckles were made of diamonds or silver; baser forms were of metal such as steel or pinchbeck, an alloy of copper and zinc imitating gold (named after a Fleet Street watchmaker who died in 1732). For the ballroom a lighter shoe with a lower heel was worn; this was called a pump and was even adopted out-of-doors by some of the more foppish men.

The arduous nature of travelling in the early eighteenth century demanded the wearing of boots; heavy jackboots which reached above the knees and with slightly spreading tops were also worn by the military. For hunting (and for the informal Englishman on his walks), jockey boots were worn; these were of softer leather, turned down at the top below the knee in a contrasting colour. Apart from the changeover from square to rounded toes, no real change took place in boots in the early eighteenth century. As it was thought rather eccentric in the early eighteenth century even for an Englishman to wear boots in town, a more usual form of leg-protector was the side-buttoning gaiter or spatter-dash, covering the knee to the ankle; the *Mercure de France* first noted these in the cold winter of 1729–30, advising that they should be made of the same colour and stuff as the suit, but for the less fashionable, the more functional leather or canvas were worn.

The eighteenth century is not, on the whole, an age for emphasis on male accessories; the hat played a minor role subservient to the wig, and gloves, of plain untrimmed leather in shades of tan or buff throughout the century, set off the fineness and delicacy of lace ruffles at the wrist.

A small number of men carried small muffs instead of gloves, these increasing in size in the 1730s, but the most usual accessories carried were swords and canes. The sword was not only a mark of gentility, but also necessary in a violent age; it continued to be worn even when, in the first decade of the eighteenth century, men began to carry canes, and it remained part of formal dress until the end of our period. The English were the first to abandon the sword (except for the most formal occasions) in preference to the cane, and de Saussure was surprised to see in 1726 that almost all men he met in the streets 'wear small round wigs, plain hats, and carry canes in their hands ... You will see rich merchants and gentlemen thus dressed and sometimes even noblemen of high rank.'[24] The canes were made with a tasselled loop so that they could be hung from a coat button; the cane heads were made of gold, silver, rock crystal, agate and other rare or exotic material. The traveller La Motraye bought on the Baltic coast in Courland in 1726 an amber 'Head for a Cane wherein was a Fly with Wings extended'.[25] Some men, careful of their health or adversely affected by the stench of the streets, carried canes with pomander tops; as a preventive against infection these were carried by doctors in the first half of the century.

Women

By the beginning of the eighteenth century, men had evolved a nearly perfect costume, a suit that did not need to vary in style whatever the occasion, but which could be distinguished through excellence of fabric and taste in decoration. In contrast, women's dress (as in the modern period generally) was at the same time far less international and far more complex. Opportunities for women to travel were limited to a tiny fraction of the upper classes, and while it has been said that French dress was the ideal at which many women aimed (and French court dress was almost universally adopted at all courts) there were enormous differences in the extent of attaining this goal; women showed a far greater diversity of clothing from country to country, from region to region and from class to class, than did men. Women were also limited by the nature of their sexual and social roles in society from evolving functional clothing; instead, they had the much more enjoyable task of channelling their creative intelligence and energy into 'new Modes of Dressings', which led, with increased rapidity of change as the century progressed, to the fashion industry dominated by France.

The complexity of women's dress and its regional variations, and the semantic difficulties attendant upon interpretation of the many confusing terms for various garments, make a study of female clothing in the eighteenth century infinitely more difficult than the relative simplicities of male clothing.

It is perhaps best to begin with the basic statement that for most of the eighteenth century, women's dress consisted of open and closed robes.

The commonest type of gown was the open robe, which consisted of a bodice and overskirt joined together, but with the skirt open in front to reveal an underskirt or 'petticoat' (the contemporary name until in the late 1780s the word 'skirt' took over); when the robe and petticoat were made of the same or complementary fabric as a basic unity, this was known as a 'suit'. The bodice, which was always joined to the open overskirt, was, in the first half of the century, open to reveal a 'stomacher' piece or an underbodice, often with elaborate embroidery or lace decoration; occasionally, for less show, a closed bodice was worn, pinning or lacing at the front or sides.

9 **Les Manteaux**, drawn and engraved by A. Hérisset, from *Recueil des Differentes Modes du Temps à Paris*, 1729

The formal manteau or mantua, worn over a wide pyramid hoop, is distinguished by the stylized back drapery.

The other main type of dress was the closed robe, made all in one piece, with the bodice fastened to the skirt by means of a front-fall opening, like a bib, which tied round the waist with the bodice then laced or pinned over it. This was a popular form of undress for the first half of the eighteenth century; by about 1750 it had vanished from the fashionable wardrobe (although it continued to be worn by the lower classes), until in the 1780s it re-emerged with the vogue for simple all-in-one dresses. Finally, there was a costume composed of a separate bodice or jacket and skirt; for the fashionable woman, this was very much a strictly informal attire, worn either in the privacy of the home or for country pursuits. It was, in fact, the costume worn by working women, and not until the 1780s did it really enter the fashionable wardrobe.

It is the open robe which dominates female dress throughout the eighteenth century and particularly in the first half. The bodice was edged with flat sewn-down revers, sometimes double, extended to the waist, and, in the second half of the century, to the hem; in England these were known as 'robings'. The stomacher, which filled in the gap between the

Les Manteaux

33

sides of the bodice, was a panel of triangular shape, stiffened and sometimes boned down the centre front, and decorated with embroidery or ribbons – one of the most popular types of decoration was a row of ribbon bows decreasing in size from the top to the bottom and known as 'échelles'; the stomacher was either pinned, or laced discreetly with eyelet holes beneath the robings, or had decorative lacings across the front. The sleeves were full and loosely fitting, ending in a wide cuff which was often stiffened; the most fashionable sleeve in the 1720s was the pagoda sleeve, with a wide flat cuff horizontally pleated to fit the bend of the arm.

The petticoat was always cut straight across without any gores, the fullness being pleated into the waist and tied by a drawstring, leaving holes at the sides so that women could reach their pockets, which were tied on a belt round their waist over the under-petticoat. When the petticoat was worn over a very wide hoop, the side fullness was gathered separately onto a tape; horizontal flounces of lace or of the same fabric as the skirt ('falbalas') were used as decoration.

The most usual word for the formal gown in the early eighteenth century was 'mantua' or 'manteau'. Like so much that was formal, it had originally been an informal, loosely fitting negligée gown, described by Randle Holme as popular in the 1670s, 'a kind of loose Garment' worn with 'Stiffe Bodies' or stays beneath. Like the male nightgown, the early mantua was made in the kimono 'T' shape, and draped to show the repeats of the large-patterned silks then in vogue; early examples that survive show loosely stitched wide back pleats, with a train lightly pinned up at the sides but still trailing on the ground. The author of *The Present State of*

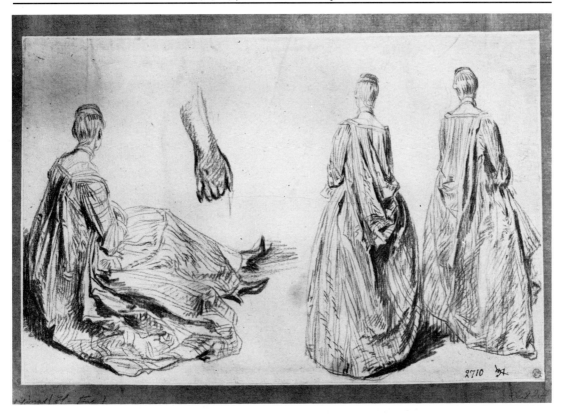

10   **A Tea-Party at Lord Harrington's**, 1730 (detail) by C. Phillips

The stiff, doll-like poses of the ladies are accentuated by their rigid bodice boning and tight-fitting formal mantuas. The most elaborate dress is that worn by Lady Betty Germain, a patterned silk trimmed with diamond buckles and bows.

11   **Studies of women's dress** by A. Watteau

No other artist has so successfully captured the refinement and elegance of the graceful floating sacque dress.

France (1712) noted how 'The Quality trail behind 'em a long Tail of Gold or Silk, with which they sweep the Churches and Gardens'.[26] At about this date the mantua lost its negligent appearance, and the train became more elaborately fitted at the back; although never itself boned (but worn over boned stays) it became tight-fitting at the waist. It gradually became a formal dress, being accepted at many European courts except for the grandest occasions; the elderly Madame, widow of Monsieur, brother of Louis XIV, sighed for the old days when the *grand habit* with its excessive bodice boning and massive train was ordinary court dress, but in spite of her strictures against the mantua, she had one 'so constructed that . . . all my underskirts are tied to the bodice with tabs, and my manteau is sewn onto it'[27] (1721). The English court adopted the mantua with enthusiasm; heavily embroidered, and with a cur-

tailed train sewn in place in addition to a detachable train which was sometimes added, and worn over the huge hoops of the early and mid-eighteenth century, it lumbers through the pages of the letters of Mrs Delany, that indefatigable recorder of court and social life in England. So universally was it adopted as the formal robe *par excellence* even outside court that the term for a dress-maker was 'mantua-maker', remaining so long after the style had ceased to be fashionable.

Yet the most characteristic dress of the early eighteenth century, and one that caught the eye of the artists with its graceful lines, was the 'sack' or 'sacque' dress. Like the mantua, it started life as an informal negligée, probably a dressing-gown; an early example, in Nuremberg, is a simple kimono shape of white linen with a quilted pattern, but made to put on over the head. The early sack dress (although there is an isolated reference in Pepys's *Diary* in 1668 to his wife's 'French gown called a sac') was usually called a 'contouche'; this name probably came from the Polish 'kontusz' (originally from the Turkish 'gontos'), a caftan-like garment with split or hanging sleeves, and in the shape of a cone, falling from neck to hem and being put on over the head. Its use to conceal increasing girth, for whatever reason, and its ease and grace made it immediately popular; Madame, in a famous letter dated 1721, stated that these 'robes battantes' (so called because of their bell shape) were originally invented by the old king's mistress, Madame de Montespan, to conceal her pregnancies.[28] Whether this was in fact true, this early form of the sack, made to hang full at the front, continued to be useful for pregnancies; Mrs Delany advised her pregnant sister in 1747 that they were 'easier and handsomer ... for a lady in your circumstances'.[29]

Although Madame insisted that ladies visiting her wore the formal *grand habit*, many ladies at court adopted the sack dress; the king was very young and there were few occasions at which the *grand habit* was compulsory. Early versions of the sack dress had loose pleats unstitched at the front or back; it was worn either with the front seamed from just below the waist, or it was completely open in front, revealing the petticoat. Gradually in the 1730s the back pleats became more formalized and set in two double box pleats, giving the graceful controlled fall so often referred to erroneously as a 'Watteau pleat' (the artist died in 1721), although as the most fashionable dress of the period, it was painted by a number of artists.

Another contemporary term for the sack was 'robe volante', implying the flowing, lilting movement so noticeable in the early negligée versions of the sack, which paradoxically attracted censure, for it was felt that the looseness of the shape hid a multitude of sins, and at the same time declared its origins in a garment suitable for the intimacy of the bedroom. For the playwright Marivaux, writing in the *Spectateur Français* in the 1720s, such negligée gowns were 'comme un honnête équivalent de la nudité même ... une abjuration simulée de coquetterie'.[30] Such a garment made of light floating taffeta or embroidered muslin was mentioned as being all the rage by the *Mercure de France* for March 1729: 'Les Robes volantes sont universellement en règne. On ne voit presque plus d'autre habit; on les a porte l'Été dernier, le plus grand nombre de taffetas blanc ou de couleur rose, surtout pour les jeunes personnes qui portoient aussi des robes de gaze ou de mousseline brodée sur un taffetas, dont la couleur paroît au travers'.[31] The *Mercure de France* also noted that large striped and floral patterns could be displayed to advantage on the vast areas of material needed for the sack, especially as worn over the hooped petticoat; such large brocades and damasks increased in popularity in the 1730s, as the sack gradually became more a formal gown, fitted into the waist and with the bodice cut separately from the skirt and seamed to it. At this point in the mid-1730s it was adopted by fashionable English ladies, happier with the security given by the more tailored cut than with the earlier loose-flowing gown. So typically French was the sack, however, that it was known all over Europe as the 'robe à la française'; conversely, the waisted gown deriving from the mantua became known in the second half of the century as the 'robe à l'anglaise'.

The sack, whether a formal trained garment or an informal kind of dressing-gown, dominated female dress for the first half of the eighteenth century. By the early 1730s it had become an open robe, a form it was to keep until its demise in the 1770s, worn with stomacher, robings on the bodice, and falbalas, or embroidery on the skirt. So comfortable, however, was the early loosely draped model that it continued to be worn, with front bow or button fastening, as a travelling garment until the middle of the century. One of the more popular versions of this was the 'andrienne' or 'adrienne' (named after a celebrated performance, in 1703, of Terence's popular comedy, Andria, in which the actress Marie Dancourt appeared in this kind of informal gown). Tightened up slightly and worn over stays with a small train and hoop, it entered the fashionable wardrobe of the Italian lady with its introduction in 1721 by the new Duchess of Modena, Charlotte-Agläe of Orléans, daughter of the Regent of France. Another version for the active lady was the 'robe retroussée dans les poches', where the fullness of the back material was caught up into the pocket holes of the skirt; it seems to have been especially popular with women whose pretensions to style were limited by their busier life – the middle classes and fashionable personal maids.

A dress with a similar origin to that of the sack was the 'wrapping gown', sometimes worn with a sash or pinned at the waist; like the sack, it had fullness at the back (where it was worn loose) and was put on over the stays, but with a modesty piece or tucker made of fine linen showing at the bosom. It was a flexible garment, which could be quite formal when worn as a closed gown over the hoops of the second decade of the century, but could also be worn by middle- and lower-class women over petticoats made of quilted linen or cotton, or embroidered wool. In the *Purefoy Letters* there are a number of references in the 1730s to such wrapping

12 La Déclaration de l'Amour, 1725, by
J. F. de Troy (detail)

Dress is a crucial part of such a *scène galante*, particularly
this voluminous, buttoned sacque with its tantalizing
lacing at the bosom, perfect for seduction.

gowns; in 1739 Henry Purefoy ordered from
London 'fine thick printed cotton enough to make
two wrappers for my Mother', which might have
been shortened versions worn over the 'neat white
quilted calico petticoat' which he ordered at the
same time.[32] Such wrapping gowns were fashionable until the late 1740s, and they continued to be
worn by other women for the rest of the century.

The female 'nightgown' also derived from the
dressing-gown; this is a confusing term, and in the
early years of the century may have referred to a
bedroom gown, as Lady Mary Wortley Montagu
describes in her *Town Eclogues* (1715) a lady in a
'night-gown fasten'd with a single pin'. As late as
1737, Queen Caroline of England, awakened at
Hampton Court by the news that the wife of the
Prince of Wales was in childbirth, and thinking that
the birth was taking place on the premises, cried out
'My God, my nightgown', but was told that this

dressing gown would not suffice as in fact the
princess was at St James's and the queen would need
her coaches too.[33] Yet by the early 1730s the
nightgown appears in a puzzling variety of guises,
made of rich and humble fabrics, and sometimes a
closed and sometimes an open gown. When closed,
it might have taken the form of a wrapping gown
securely pinned, or with an open bodice front, laced
over a handkerchief; it was frequently worn with an
apron of plain silk, calico, linen, or embroidered
muslin. In the 1720s Mrs Delany advised that for
country mourning a black nightgown was admis-
sible, but at the same time her letters of the period
note the purchase of nightgowns of 'gold coloured
tabby' (1729) and pink damask (1731); in 1734 the
inventory of Margaret Cavendish's wedding
clothes listed some nightgowns, including one of
'white lustring, embroidered all over the facings
and robings with silver and purple',[34] implying that
this was an open gown with costly embroidery (a
number of petticoats are listed, of calico and quilted
satin). By the end of the 1730s the nightgown was
usually worn as an open robe, tight-fitting at the
waist; it still kept the feeling of informality deriving
from its name, and was often worn in England with

a quilted petticoat and fine transparent apron. Whereas on the Continent most fashionable women wore the sack from the beginning of our period in preference to the tight-fitting night-gown, this latter garment was the favourite English wear, and was greatly to influence the development of the *robe à l'anglaise* in the last quarter of the century.

The trousseau of the Duchess of Portland in 1734, mentioned above, emphasized plain satins richly embroidered; her best suit was of 'white Padusoy richly imbroidered with gold and all coulers'. Rich three-dimensional embroideries in large floral designs, on silk, satin or velvet, decorated the dresses in which ladies in England were presented at court in the early eighteenth century; Mrs Delany in 1739 noted that Lady Huntingdon wore a gown of white satin with vases embroidered on the train, and with it a petticoat of black velvet embroidered with chenille, 'the pattern a large stone vase filled with ramping flowers that spread almost over a breadth of the petticoat from the bottom to the top . . . much properer for a stucco staircase than for the apparel of a lady'.[35]

Mary Granville, later Mrs Pendarves and later *Mrs Delany*, was born in 1700; her letters, full of information about the details of costume, are indispensable for the student of eighteenth-century dress, and her name figures largely in these pages. She was typical of her age, a mixture of courage and good nature tempered with a gentle malice, and with a sophisticated perception both of good taste and of the absurdities of fashion. Her letters chart the changing of textiles, styles and taste, particularly in the first half of the eighteenth century, and from them we can appreciate how difficult it is to make definitive statements about popular patterns when a variety of fabric and design was acceptable in any one period. Bright single colours as well as more subtle floral designs were popular in the 1720s and 1730s for the woven silks which made up the most fashionable dresses. Large-patterned damasks were widely worn in the early eighteenth century; in 1729 Mrs Delany bought a 'scarlet damask manteau and petticoat' and in the same year an English lady in Moscow, Mrs Ward, was also buying 'very handsome scarlet damask' to wear as a long-sleeved travelling gown over a fur petticoat. For the wedding in 1734 of the Hon. John Spencer with Lady Georgina Carteret, Mrs Delany detailed the dresses, many of which were damasks, and including 'a blue damask night-gown, and a white damask, the robings and facings embroidered with gold and flowers'.[36]

But of the woven silks, the brocades were the most expensive and showed the greatest variety of pattern and colour. From the first years of the eighteenth century, the floral patterns were either the heavy rather ornate baroque forms with silver or gold thread, or the more delicate and naturalistic depiction of flowers and foliage. In the 1720s small flower patterns of the 'meadow silk' type occur, and it is possibly one of these that Lady Lansdowne, writing from Paris in 1721, had in mind when she noted that 'there are very pretty silks come into fashion without gold or silver'. She might also have meant the newly popular 'lace pattern silks', with a notable asymmetrical movement created by lace motifs mingling with flowers; Mrs Delany paid £17 a yard for a French silk in 1729, 'the ground a dark grass green, brocaded in a running pattern like lace of white intermixt with festoons of flowers in faint colours'.[37] Light-coloured silks brocaded in silver were picked out by Mrs Delany at court in 1724; she particularly admired Lady Sunderland's dress which was 'the finest pale blue and pink, very richly flowered in a running pattern of silver frosted, and tissue with a little white', and Lady Carteret's 'pale straw lutestring . . . flowered with silver'.[38]

The decade of the 1730s was dominated by a return to the large heavy fruit-and-flower designs, but far more naturalistic than before. In Lyons, the centre of the silk industry, designers such as Jean Revel had developed a system by the mid-1730s of modelling in dark and light and dovetailing tones of colour, which meant that instead of just a surface pattern on the silk, three-dimensional forms could be represented with greater subtlety and almost overwhelming realism. Flowers in full bloom and gargantuan fruit were woven into huge repeats, as much as 28 inches or longer, suitable for the more structured dress with vast hoops of the later 1730s. Some of the inspiration for the large floral designs was from embroidery; for the wedding of Princess Anne of England to the Prince of Orange in 1734, the newspapers noted that the most fashionable silks 'were white paduasoys with large flowers of tulips, peonies, emmonies, carnations & in their proper colours some wove in the silk and some embroidered'.[39] Mrs Delany herself had chosen for the occasion a 'brocaded lutestring, white ground with great ramping flowers in shades of purples, reds and greens'.[40]

It is easy to forget that striped and plain silks were also popular in the 1720s and 1730s; very few plain silks survive in museum collections (they were not expensive enough to alter and keep, and many were given to servants or made into children's clothes), although they were liked by artists, for the opportunities they afforded to display virtuosity in the painting of light on the lustrous satins or shining taffetas. Plain silks were informal attire, suitable to be worn for taking tea, or playing cards, or just for sitting in a garden or on a terrace – all typical scenes depicted in the newly fashionable conversation piece.

Other stuffs popular for negligée gowns were painted silks from the East, or printed cottons, in spite of prohibitions against such fabrics in various countries to protect native silk industries. De Saussure in the mid-1720s noted how fond the English ladies were of 'cotton from the Indies', and the *Mercure de France* advised for summer 1729 'robes de toile de coton ou petit bazin des Indes blanc, tout uni ou brodé en soye & en laine de diverses couleurs'.[41]

Many of the large-patterned silks and the heavy plain silks were meant to be worn over hoops, that curious and essential component of female dress for a considerable part of the century. The originating country may have been either Germany or England, both countries renowned for extremes in fashion; in any case, the eighteenth-century hoop had as its predecessors the farthingale of the late sixteenth century and the stiffened bustle effect created by the back draping of the late-seventeenth-century mantua. The logical consequence of the weight of petticoats at the end of the seventeenth century was to wear a single-hooped underskirt which would be lighter and more comfortable, and would provide a more effective framework for the lightweight silks coming into fashion. The first hooped petticoats or 'paniers' (the French name derived from a type of basket under which chickens were kept) appeared at the French court in the last years of Louis XIV, although they had, since about 1710, been around in England; also from the earliest years of the century actresses on the French stage had been wearing (to accentuate their waists and give them an imposing presence) gum-starched petticoats called 'criardes', a name coming from the loud rustling noise which they made in movement.

The first hoops were roughly in the shape of a birdcage or rounded dome; the anonymous author of *The Art of Dress* (1717) attributed their inspiration to St Paul's Cathedral, and the French term was 'panier à coupole'. They were made of linen or stiffened canvas with rows of whalebone (wood was a cheaper alternative); the English hoops had eight tiers, the French usually five.

By the mid-1720s the hoop had assumed an oval shape, sometimes more than 11 feet in circumference, and by 1730 the front of the skirt was flattened by a system of cords inside, which made the hoop more manoeuvrable and more decent when the occupant sat down. As it flattened in the front, so it dramatically increased in width at the sides during the 1730s and 1740s, causing problems during movement (women had to go sideways through doors) and in a confined space.

Barbier's *Chronique de la Régence* noted that by the end of the 1720s women sitting in the theatre took up enormous amounts of room. In 1728 he reported that the queen, who herself preferred a modest hoop, was incommoded by the paniers of the princesses of the blood, whose right it was to sit next to her. The chief minister, Cardinal Fleury, took time off from matters of state to advise that there should be a spare armchair on either side of the queen to accommodate her skirt and those of the princesses. Yet this only served to cause a chain reaction; the princesses protested that they too should have chairs free on their side away from the queen, which then caused offence to the duchesses who were next in rank.[42] Barbier does not record how this was resolved; although the very large hoop disappeared some ten years later, the problem remained with the hoops which continued to be worn for court wear until the Revolution.

Although attracting more than its fair share of abuse – the *Mercure de France* of 1730 stated flatly that paniers were 'une mode outrée & hors de toute raison' – the fashion had by then caught on for all classes. The lilting swing of the hoop when elegantly worn (it was impossible to stride out: the correct way was to take tiny, gliding steps), although distorting the shape of the body, was highly attractive and gave a lightness of movement not possible with layers of heavy skirts. The swinging skirts gave a glimpse, really for the first time, of the ankle and shoe; raising the skirt to show the delicately embroidered stocking clocks or even the embroidered garters tying the hose above or below the knee had an almost sexual innuendo. The stockings were made of knitted cotton, silk, or worsted, the clocks either knitted in or embroidered; bright colours ensured their notice. The shoes, made of plain leather or of silk (sometimes brocade or damask, and decorated with gold or silver lace or fringe) had pointed toes and a sturdy heel with a height of two to three inches; in the 1730s the shoes became more rounded and generally more delicate, with slenderer heels, but retained the fastening of latchets buckled or tied over the instep. Such shoes were not meant for hard use, and many women wore out-of-doors an overshoe of matching material.

The correct shape was the all-important fashionable attribute in the eighteenth century, and more particularly in the first half, when the body was compressed into a somewhat unnatural form. Next to the skin was worn the shift or chemise, the main undergarment; for the fashionable woman this was made of fine Holland edged with plain linen or lace at the neck and sleeves; the sleeves were quite short and the frills attached to them were visible beneath the gown sleeve, until by the middle of the century they were replaced by sleeve ruffles tacked to the sleeve of the dress itself. Over the shift the stays were laced, either down the front or the back, and boned down the centre and side fronts to give the firm rigid line with raised bosom which was so fashionable in this period. It was impossible to imagine an existence without this reinforced structure, boned more or less according to the activity; there were stays for riding and even for pregnancy. The English, with their already noted fondness for the support of tight garments, wore stays which were appreciably higher, longer and tighter than those worn on the Continent, and these usually laced behind; the lines were already drawn between the more informal French with their low décolletage,

and the strait-laced English, when Pöllnitz in 1733 remarked on the latter:

Their gowns so close before, with strait Sleeves which don't reach beyond the Elbow, make them look as if they had no Shoulders nor Breasts. And what is worse than all, they have broad flat Rumps to their Gowns, and Hoop-Petticoats, narrow at the Top and monstrously wide at the Bottom. They are always laced, and 'tis as rare to see a Woman here without her Stays on, as it is to see one at Paris in a full Dress.[43]

The Englishwoman made her stay-hook an important accessory, either displayed on a châtelaine or hooked to the front of her bodice and used for suspending her watch chain.

The existence of a jacket-and-skirt style of dress for women has already been noted; such jackets could be fitted to the body and laced or fastened with hooks or eyes at the front – this was the French 'casaquin' – or they could be shortened versions of the tight-bodied gown, with robings and separate stomacher. Casaquins, furred *à la polonaise*, were worn for sleighing at Versailles in 1729 according to the *Mercure de France*. It was a similarly tight-fitting jacket that Catherine I of Russia wore, made of cloth of silver and with a petticoat trimmed with galloon, when she assisted in 1727 at the ceremony of benediction of the waters of the Neva.[44] Popular in France was the thigh-length jacket made like the sack dress with the fullness coming from the shoulders at the back. In most cases the sleeves followed the fashionable line, being full and with a winged cuff, but occasionally a working woman would wear a cuff slit at the wrist like that of the male frock coat.

Definitely adopted from the male wardrobe, first by the English lady and then by her sister in Europe, was the masculine suit adapted for the female riding costume. It consisted of a jacket, waistcoat and petticoat; the coat was usually of camlet, a coarse and closely woven worsted sometimes mixed with silk, and was cut on the lines of a man's coat, with back vent and side pleats and fastening left over right, as did the waistcoat. The waistcoat matched the coat with its gold or silver trimming, and was sometimes made with just the panels sewn to the coat lining. It was very often worn with male accessories such as the three-cornered hat or the jockey cap, and the lace cravat; in the early years of the eighteenth century women even wore long periwigs. From about 1730, women's riding habits copied details from the frock coat, such as the small turned-down collar and the closed or slit cuffs.

The riding habit, with its long sleeves and the extra warmth given by the waistcoat, proved an

13　**Study of a woman fencing** or Nicole in *Le Bourgeois Gentilhomme*, 1734, by F. Boucher. Boucher illustrated the complete works of Molière which were published in 1734

One of the jacket-and-skirt costumes thought suitable for a more active role, delightfully impractical though it appears; the tight-fitting jacket bodice fastens down the back and flares out over the hips, and the skirt is worn over the bell-hoop characteristic of the 1730s.

ideal travelling garment, though often attracting comment from Europeans unused to it. Lady Mary Wortley Montagu, always an eccentric dresser, astounded those she met in her journeys across Europe to Turkey in 1716/17 in her 'travelling habit which is a riding dress'; by the end of the 1730s people were more receptive, and Frances Hawes, eloping to France with Lord Vane in 1737, found Parisians impressed with her 'blue English riding habit trimmed with gold', until she 'metamorphosed' herself into a Frenchwoman, cut her hair, wore powder and a robe.[45]

The more usual wear for out-of-doors was the cloak; a modest woman would not wish to be seen much in the streets in the early eighteenth century, and the loose-fitting cloak, often hooded, was discreet and concealing and was in fact the only possible garment to be worn over the hoop. In the early years of the century it was the custom to walk masked; in France in 1712, women 'have the Priviledge of going maskt at all times, concealing or showing themselves when they please. With a Black-Velvet-Visor they go sometimes to Church as to a Ball or Play, unknown to God and their Husbands'.[46] This fashion continued for reasons of morality or modesty in Italy and Spain for at least the first half of the century; until about the same time it remained in the rest of Europe as a protection against the weather, and for those ravaged by smallpox. The author of *The Art of Dress* (1717) stated:

When for the Morning Air abroad you steal,
The Cloak of Camlet may your Charms conceal; . . .
That, with a Mask, is such a sure Disguise,
'Twould cheat an Argus, or a Spaniard's Eyes.[47]

For very bad weather, Gay's *Implements proper for female Walkers* in the streets of London in 1716 included umbrellas, which were regarded as effeminate for men, but necessary 'to guard from chilly Showr's the walking Maid'; he also mentioned pattens, overshoes made with wooden soles raised on iron rings, which protected the leather or fabric shoe from the mud.[48]

From about 1715 to the early 1730s, the cloak was very often full-length, and usually of camlet. Pöllnitz, whom we have already mentioned for his disparaging comments on the dress of Englishwomen, noted that: 'When they go out in a Deshabille, they commonly put on a camblet coat as long as their Petticoats, which is closed before, and on each side there's a Slit thro' which they put their Arms; they have withal a Hood of the same Stuff as the Cloak, which is tied under the Chin with a colour'd Ribband.'[49] By the early 1730s when Pöllnitz was visiting England, the long cloak was

gradually being reserved more for citizens' wives and daughters; the more fashionable cloaks were short, sometimes with hoods like the *capuchins*.

Short cloaks or mantles were necessary also not just for cold weather outdoors, but to cover the décolletage of everyday dress. These cloaks had a number of names; the *Mercure de France* for 1729 mentioned 'bagnolettes' which were hooded short cloaks made of satin in winter and muslin in summer, 'mantilles' of velvet, satin and ermine for winter, and 'palatines' (wide-shaped stoles or tippets falling in two ends at the front) of marten in winter, and in summer of blonde lace or fine muslin painted with butterflies and decorated with artificial flowers.[50]

At a humbler level, women kept their modesty and warmth by wearing a lace-edged handkerchief, a diagonally folded square of muslin or linen draped round the neck, with the ends knotted in front or secured under or over the stomacher. The size and shape remained unaltered throughout the first half of the century, but the lace changed with the fashion, from the heavy three-dimensional Ven-

14   Elizabeth Horton with her horse and groom, by W. Verelst

This portrait, dating probably from the early 1730s, shows the kind of fashionable riding costume – here of white satin trimmed with pink – which could be worn by Englishwomen both for riding and for travel.

etian needlepoint lace, looking like carved ivory, at the very beginning of our period, to the fine, supple, densely-patterned bobbin lace, such as Brussels, popular from the 1720s to the 1740s. Very often the lace on the handkerchief matched that on the sleeve ruffles and on the cap; as hairstyles became simpler, so the various forms of headwear assumed an increased importance, with women of all social classes wearing some form of head-covering in the first half of the eighteenth century.

With the change in dress which can be seen to have begun just prior to the death of Louis XIV, we have noted a movement of emphasis from the elaborately trained skirts to the lighter 'robe volante'. Similarly, the piled-up towers of hair decorated with wired lace caps, which formed a counterpoint to the heavy baroque costume, had been largely superseded by 1720, with small, neat hairstyles, either combed off the forehead into a knot at the back of the head, or closely curled. The elaborate tower headdresses which had been in vogue since the 1680s remained for some time for court wear and for the elderly. In 1716 Lady Mary Wortley Montagu noted in Vienna that the ladies at court 'build certain fabricks of Gause on their heads about a yard high consisting of 3 or 4 storys fortify'd with numberless yards of heavy riband', which, she said, they placed on a padded roll covered with a mixture of their own and false hair;[51] these were no doubt the 'frizled tours' that Lady Mary poked fun at in her *Town Eclogues* (1716) as being worn only by 'ancient matrons'. Already by 1711 Dean Swift remarked that at dinner with the Duchess of Grafton, she wore 'a great high headdress such as was in fashion fifteen years ago and looks like a mad woman in it'.[52] Such headdresses, known as 'commodes', were unwieldy structures prone to accidents; Saint-Simon recounted in 1719 that the elderly Marquise de Charlus, leaning forward at dinner, caught her towering headdress in the candle flame, and the gallant Archbishop of Rheims, thinking to save her by knocking her tower to the ground, received for his pains the lady's egg in his face.[53]

The hair dressed low first appeared worn by the wife of the English ambassador at Versailles in 1713; although the automatic reaction of the French court was to mock, the king was quite impressed, and soon the fashionable ladies followed suit.[54]

The commode was a linen cap with edgings of lace and layers of lace-edged pleats supported by a wire frame and with two long streamers called 'lappets' or 'barbes' made of lace, which either hung down or were pinned up. These lappets were retained in the simpler caps of the second decade of the eighteenth century, which were of linen with a frill of lace or muslin. By 1720 (although the long ringleted hair-style remained in England for a few more years), most fashionable French women curled their hair tightly to the head in the style known as 'tête de mouton'; the *Mercure de France* for 1730 advocated the use of false hair, 'boucles à la Medicis' for those women unwilling to frizz their own hair. In the 1720s caps became smaller and more delicate and began that complicated language of innuendo and allusion which was to distinguish the millinery trade throughout the century; caps were 'en dormeuse', 'avec désespoir', 'en négligé', 'en Papillon', 'en équivoque, dont les barbes sont retroussées', and so on.[55] An alternative and more formal hairdressing was a decoration of ribbons, silk lace and gauze flowers, worn with powdered hair; Lady Mary Wortley Montagu noted in 1718 that the French ladies powdered their hair so heavily that it looked like white wool, a startling contrast to the English, who, according to de Saussure (1726) did not curl or powder their hair and 'seldom wear ribbons or flowers, but little headdresses of cambric or of magnificent lace'.[56]

The English were renowned for their advocacy of caps and hats throughout the century; not until the 1730s did they belatedly adopt the French taste for curled hair with delicate rococo decorations, and many preferred the loosely waved 'Dutch' style with side curls and ringlets falling to the shoulders. A popular cap in the 1730s was the 'coif' or 'round-eared cap', which was somewhat like a bonnet, curving round the face to the level of the ears or below, with lappets either pinned on top or tied under the chin. The mob cap also hid much of the face, with side pieces which were either left hanging or tied under the chin. These plain caps retained their appeal for middle-class women and the more conservative throughout the century in most countries of Europe, some developing their own regional characteristics. Such caps were usually worn out-of-doors, under either hoods or the flat wide-brimmed hats which, made of silk or straw, were by 1730 a fashionable accessory.

CHAPTER TWO

Getting and spending

People, where they are not known, are generally honour'd according to their Cloaths and other Accoutrements they have about them; from the richness of them we judge of their Wealth, and by their ordering of them we guess at their understanding.

B. de Mandeville, *The Fable of the Bees*, 1714

No man is ignorant that a Taylor is the Person that makes our Cloaths; to some he not only makes their Dress, but, in some measure, may be said to make themselves. There are Numbers of Beings in and about this Metropolis who have no other identical Existence than what the Taylor, Milliner and Periwig-Maker bestow upon them. Strip them of these Distinctions, and they are quite a different Species of Beings; have no more Relation to their dressed selves, than they have to the Great Mogul, and are as insignificant in Society as Punch, deprived of his moving Wires, and hung up upon a Peg.

R. Campbell, *The London Tradesman*, 1747

The statement made by Maréchal in the 1780s that Paris 'par ses modes, est le maîtresse du monde' was true in fashionable society in the eighteenth century. Not only did Paris establish new modes, but it also had the best fabrics and accessories available in its shops – it was a Mecca for the fashion-conscious.

The clothing trade was still, at the beginning of the century, organized on medieval specialist lines. At the top were the mercers who sold the best silks and also the finest woollen stuffs; they were based in the rue Saint-Honoré and supplied the materials for the fashion industry. It was not surprising that the *marchands de modes*, the ancestors of the couturiers and suppliers of trimmings and accessories, also had their premises in this area. The drapers were situated in the rue de la Vieille-Draperie; they supplied the less valuable woollen materials, cottons and linens. Other suppliers to the fashion industry included the shoe-makers in the rue de la Cordonnerie, and the goldsmiths and jewellers in the quai des Orfèvres; in all, some 20 guilds specialized in various items of clothing, from fabrics to ribbons.

Already by the early years of the eighteenth century visitors were commenting on the large numbers of shops in Paris with their wide range of goods, although standards of display were fairly poor, with tiny windows and dark interiors. It was in fact easier to shop at the Lent fair in Saint-Germain 'in a great Place fill'd with Shops, where an infinite Number of Merchants set out all the finest and richest Goods that are made in this great City'.[1] By the end of the century the Lent Fair which lasted for three months in the winter, and the Saint-Laurent Fair which lasted for the same time in the early summer, were less fashionable and more patronized by provincial French people. To meet an increased demand for luxury goods, including those related to dress, in the second half of the century, many shops were transformed into handsomely decorated mirrored saloons, illuminated at night. The most fashionable shops in the 1780s were in the Palais Royal, built by the duc d'Orléans in 1782 in the grounds of his town palace; the arcades covered shops, coffee houses and promenades, where, according to a Russian visitor, 'all the riches of the world are displayed to the astonished eye ... all the inventions of luxury to embellish life'.[2]

Every large city in Europe showed enormous contrasts between parade and poverty, and, in an age in which illiteracy was the norm, a visual shorthand announced shops, services and occupations. The noise and commotion made by the street activities and the shop signs was more akin to an Arab city today than to the Paris or London we know. W. H. Pyne in *Wine and Walnuts* (1823)

remembered 70 years beforehand in London 'the thousand monster signs swinging and loudly creaking in a wintry wind, joining in concert with the multifarious wares suspended o'er the open shops';[3] shop signs included the universal pair of scissors for the tailor, for the hosier a pair of stockings, hats (in Rome a cardinal's hat) for the hatter, and so on. The London shop signs were taken down or placed against the sides of the shops in the 1760s, at about the same time that the old City gates were removed, and the fashionable populace gravitated towards the West End. But throughout the century those involved in the business of adorning the human body were recognizable through their trades:

Then the tailor was well known . . . whilst a stay-maker was distinct from he. A barber could be descried the full length of Cornhill . . . Each branch of business which a man pursued stood manifest either in his coat, hat or wig – his apron, sleeves, jacket or general gait . . . Never did a country lout newly dubbed a London porter after a month's sojournment midst the bustling scene accost a leather-parer for a perruquier, nor baker for a plaster-manufacturer, though all were, as the miller, white.[4]

Barbers, who spent Sunday mornings covered in powder from carrying wigs to their customers, were known, says Mercier in his *Tableau de Paris* of the 1780s, as 'merlans' or whitings.[5]

15 **The Curds and Whey Seller**, *c.*1730, attributed to B. Nebot

This unusual painting shows a seller of curds and whey sitting by the Little Conduit in Cheapside; in the background one can see a rare depiction of the range of street signs to be found in early-eighteenth-century London, including, on the left, a glover's. As a contrast to the blackened and ragged costume of the chimney sweeps (notice particularly the functional trousers), the curds-and-whey seller wears the clean and modestly fashionable dress of the self-respecting working girl. Her skirt is protected by a rough apron and her shoes by pattens; a characteristic of working-class costume is the headscarf tied under the straw hat – Boitard's studies of women in Covent Garden in the 1740s show a similar style.

16 **'Ein Friseur Perrücken'**, 1773, by D. Chodowiecki

The barber, running through the streets carrying dressed wigs to his customers, was a familiar sight of metropolitan life. Mercier in Paris, in the early 1780s, describes the way in which on Sunday mornings 'the streets are crowded with a swarm of barbers and hair-dressers, holding in one hand their curling-irons, in the other a ready-dressed perriwig, their clothes bepowdered from top to bottom' (*Tableau de Paris*).

OPPOSITE
17 **Exeter Exchange**, 1762, engraved after H. Gravelot

Exeter Exchange in the Strand was a fashionable shopping arcade, particularly noted, according to Strype's *Stow's London*, 1720, for its seamstresses, hosiers and milliners.

H Gravelot inven

le Mire Sculp

Ce visage vaut mieux que toutes vos chansons

OPPOSITE
18 **An Election: Canvassing for Votes** (detail),
*c.*1754, by W. Hogarth

In this detail of Hogarth's famous painting showing
various attempts at bribery during an election, the Tory
candidate wishing to impress two girls on the balcony
above buys for them items, including a purse, from the
tray of a bearded Jewish pedlar, while before him kneels
a porter wearing the belted smock and wide shovel hat
typical of his profession.

19 **A Fair in Berlin**, by D. Chodowiecki

Among the wide range of goods sold at this German fair
can be seen rolls of fabrics and second-hand clothes.

In London in the early eighteenth century, the
City contained the most fashionable shops; in the
mid-1720s de Saussure admired the shops along
Ludgate Hill with 'silken tissue of beautiful and
costly kinds being sold there', and at the Royal
Exchange, a kind of covered market, he saw 'booths
along either side covered with rich merchandise,
jewellery and other tempting wares'.[6] Fashionable
people had long patronized the mercers' shops in
Covent Garden, and this area remained a traditional
home of the fine specialist textiles. But it was
Oxford Street which in the 1780s became the
English equivalent of the Palais Royal; the shops,
open until ten in the evenings, dazzled the eye by
the novelty of the large expanse of glass window,
and were built 'with a little projection on to the
street so that they can be seen from three sides'.
Sophie von la Roche in 1786 admired the silk fabrics
and chintzes hanging in the windows, but most of
all the linen shops where anything could be bought
'from swaddling cloths to shrouds'.[7]

So much did Paris and London dominate the
retail clothing trade in the eighteenth century that
one is likely to forget that only a small proportion of
fashionable people were able to visit these capitals to
order clothes or to buy fabrics. Some provincial
cities, such as Bath, were able to provide a good
range of metropolitan goods for the local nobility,
but many people found distances too great for
regular visits to large towns. Some enterprising
merchants travelled with their goods to their
customers; in the 1760s an English traveller in
Prussia found that at a nobleman's house 'were
spread all sorts of mercery goods as silks, stuffs,
velvets, brocades', which were brought by a mercer
from Gustrow twice a year to save the ladies the
trouble of visiting his shop.[8] At a lower level of
society, pedlars (including many Jews distinguished
in some countries by coloured badges)[9] sold cheaper
textiles such as cottons, lace and millinery items;
travelling sometimes hundreds of miles, they passed
on changes in fashion as well as local news.

Specialist fairs were also sources of clothing
materials. Perhaps the most famous was held three
times a year at Leipzig, and was known for the
quality of its rich silks and gold and silver laces;
Goethe tells us that it was called 'klein Paris' for the
range of its luxury goods, and Lady Mary Wortley
Montagu was able in 1716 not only to buy liveries
for her servants but also 'gold stuffs for myselfe'. In
England, a number of fairs concentrated on the
wide variety of woollen goods for which the
country had long been famous, and which were
increasingly to dominate the market for men's
wear; in *A Tour Thro' the Whole Island of Great
Britain* (1724), Daniel Defoe noted that the most
famous fair was at Stourbridge, which was devoted
to the sale of woollen goods, including those from
Yorkshire. In Leeds, the Brigg market attracted
buyers from all over Europe, and by 1790 there
were two cloth halls established, one for white and
one for coloured cloths.

For most of our period, silks ruled the fashionable

wardrobe. Although there were other silk centres in France, such as Tours and Marseilles, the best silks came from Lyons, a city which had prospered under Louis XIV's great minister, Colbert; with state patronage and mounting prosperity, the silk trade was not unduly depressed by the wars at the end of the seventeenth century, and was free to expand with the opening of foreign markets granted by the Treaty of Utrecht in 1713. By 1768 there were 11,000 looms in Lyons, and over 100 pattern-drawers for new designs; as early as the beginning of the century there would appear to have been new silk patterns every year, and seasonal silks by the middle of the period. Design and its importance in the growing fashion industry was recognized as an art, and artists were in fact employed at the first school for silk design opened in Lyons in 1756. French silk-designers and weavers were sent all over Europe, notably to Spain and to Sweden, and the French influenced design through the settlements of Huguenot refugees in the Protestant Netherlands and Germany. Even in England where there was a flourishing silk industry in Spitalfields in London, the most famous designers such as Anna Maria Garthwaite (1690–1763) relied on French patterns, and snobbery in any case dictated that French silks were the most highly prized. Although many countries in Europe produced their own light silks of varying qualities, the best woven silks came from France; the only other country worth mentioning here is Italy which, apart from making the best velvets in Europe, also made lightweight silks of great quality, and enough figured silks for home consumption.

Clothes made from silk were expensive due to the cost of the silk and the yardages required. The raw silk needed to be imported (and even within one country there were often regional customs dues); mounting a draw loom to weave a new pattern was a long, expensive business and a weaver could weave only a few inches a day of a very complicated silk. A rich, flowered silk brocaded in gold might cost 70 shillings or more, a figured silk 20 shillings a yard, and a plain taffeta about 8 shillings. Although it is difficult to make useful comparisons, Peter Thornton (*Baroque and Rococo Silks*) reminds us that 'a prosperous merchant's house might be valued at about £500, while a lady's silk dress could cost anything from about £10 to £60' – and much more for a court dress.[10] Silks were very often ordered by the piece, of anything from 18 to 80 yards; large amounts were needed for suits and dresses and their repairs, as it was difficult to get exactly the same quality and colour again, especially if the fabric was imported. Walter Spencer-Stanhope, a member of the Macaroni Club, ordered

a suit from Paris in 1775 of plum-coloured silk embroidered in silver, but the English customs seized the breeches; after Stanhope had failed to get them back, an English tailor tried but failed to match the colour; the Parisian tailor sent another pair but even these were not the right shade, and the suit was abandoned.[11]

There was no uniformity of measurement, a fact which caused confusion to the importer and the customer. An English ell was 45 inches, a French ell about 43 French inches or about $46\frac{1}{2}$ English inches. Cotton and silk fabrics were usually half-an-ell wide, though the lighter silks such as taffeta might be wider; woollen fabrics could range from either a French or an English ell in width to 58 French inches wide. Therefore the amounts of material required depended on the width of the fabric, as well as the size of the person. The grander the dress, the greater the amount of stuff needed, and this was particularly true for the court dress, the *grand habit*, which required a vast hooped skirt often decorated with swags of material, and a train. In 1789, for example, at the presentation of the vicomtesse de Moges, the *marchande de modes* used 22 ells of black taffeta for the gown and 14 ells of striped gauze for the skirt decoration and the train;[12] Rose Bertin, the greatest of all the *marchandes de modes*, made for a presentation dress in 1786 a gown of black velvet, taking 19 ells at 380 livres, and a garniture of black gauze, spangles, and fringe with crystals at 800 livres; in some cases, the total sum for a court dress could run into many thousands of livres.[13] The huge mantua and skirt worn at court in Vienna in the middle of the eighteenth century took about 30 ells of silk at prices ranging from 32 to 40 florins the ell; in 1737 Mrs Delany found that she needed 16 yards for a court dress. For the sack dress or for any open robe with a matching skirt, the amounts ranged from 15 to 25 ells. The more shaped gowns of the last quarter of the period, worn without hoops, necessitated approximately 10 to 20 ells, depending on the amount of back draping. The invaluable pattern book of Barbara Johnson,[14] who kept an account of all her purchases of dress materials from the end of the 1740s to the end of the century, often attaching swatches of material and fashion plates to her records, illustrates the complexity of widths and the varying amounts of stuff needed as styles changed. In 1767 she needed 22 yards of lilac silk for a negligée at half an ell wide; ten years later, for an informal nightgown of blue and white striped lustring, $11\frac{1}{4}$ yards of the same width were needed, and in the following year a 'Devonshire brown Lutestring negligée' took 19 yards of material at three-quarters-of-an-ell wide. The most expensive dress listed in her album was a negligée of garnet-coloured paduasoy, taking 22 yards at 10 shillings the yard, but a modest sum compared to the amounts spent by others on court dress.

For men, amounts of material were not so large, and there were no huge variations in style which demanded widely differing yardages. By the 1780s, when a slimmer line was fashionable, 2 ells of material were needed for the knee breeches, and it was customary to order these in pairs as they wore out more quickly than the coat or waistcoat. About 5 ells was average for the coat, but it is difficult to gauge how much was needed for the waistcoat, for this was often ordered from pieces already prepared with the design embroidered on; in the 1780s white waistcoats were popular, and it was the custom to order these by the dozen.

The mercers were the all-powerful middle men between the silk weaver and the customer, and there were many complaints about their insolence to those they summed up as infrequent clients. In many cases they had close business links with the weavers, and they were able to indicate likely fashionable lines; they offered samples to the customers to take away for consultation with tailor or dressmaker, and they recommended currently modish styles and colours. Much of the economy of France was based on their prosperity and their reputation as arbiters of taste. Many foreign princes and princesses ordered their wedding clothes from Paris; the duchesse d'Orléans in 1706 was commissioned to choose the wedding trousseau for a Hanoverian princess and on showing this to the king, Louis XIV 'wish'd, for the sake of the Mercers of Paris, that there were more Princesses who could afford to make such Purchases'.

One of the most important silk merchants was a M. Barbier, who supplied silks to the French court; his letters in the Victoria and Albert Museum[15] show how closely he worked with his customers, discussing the best fabrics for certain garments, and marking his sample books for those who were not so confident of their own taste. Although the client chose the main fabric of a dress or suit, the choice of linings was left to the silk merchant. The skill and taste lay, for much of the century, in the choice of the fabric and decoration, and not with the tailor, whose status was low; it is possible that some of the more important silk merchants had tailors on the premises to advise on yardages and to cut the required lengths, even roughly to sew up the fabric for a foreign customer so that customs duties could be avoided. A merchant like Barbier, with such a distinguished clientèle, had to be very patient with regard to money (as did all those dealing with the nobility, who throughout history have felt that the

20 **Tailor's doll or shop model**, *c.*1780

This standing figure, of beeswax, 27$\frac{1}{2}$ inches high, shows off what the fashionable man wears in the early 1780s. The clothing, other than the breeches, is of contemporary fabric.

settlement of bills was the last priority), and a wide use of credit was the rule, for well-connected customers could bring in others. Madame du Barry was a customer of Rose Bertin for many years and brought her much business, but many of her debts were still unpaid when she was guillotined in 1793.

The basic fabric was only the beginning of a suit or dress, and the fashionable customer needed accessories and trimmings. By the middle of the century women's dress was increasingly dominated by decorative trimmings such as ribbons, lace, and silk flowers; such trimmings or 'agréments' were made and sold in special shops or warehouses in Paris. In 1767 Lady Mary Coke went shopping 'to one of the great Mercers. I wanted to buy all his Shop, but chose only one Gown, a very fine winter silk, which I carried immediately to the famous place where they make all the Trimmings, & bespoke one to sute it. They asked me ten louis d'ors, but I hope to have it for nine'.[16] By 'gown', Lady Mary meant enough fabric for a dress, which she might either have had made up in Paris with the trimming loosely stitched on, or brought home for her mantua-maker.

It was widely accepted that the law could be flouted with regard to the customs dues on imported materials such as lace and silks. The novelist

21 **The Tailor's Shop**, *c.*1749, by L. P. Boitard

In this drawing of the interior of a tailor's shop, the master tailor, in gown and slippers, measures a customer for a coat. Paper or cloth patterns are pinned to a wall, and in the background, the journeyman tailors assume the traditional cross-legged pose for their sewing.

OPPOSITE
22 **At the Dressmaker's**, by G. D. Tiepolo, 1791

The rather hoydenish customer, wearing chemise, back-lacing stays and short skirt, stands before the mirror while the dress-maker measures her sleeve. On the left sits the girl's mother or her chaperone, wearing the traditional Venetian *zendaletta* over her head.

Tobias Smollett noticed at Boulogne in 1765 that there were large numbers of English smugglers from Kent and Sussex with an impressive trade in 'ribbons, laces, linen and cambrics'.[17] A professional smuggler in his novel *Ferdinand, Count Fathom* (1753) was discovered; having been 'stripped of his upper garments, and even of his shirt, [he] appeared like the mummy of an AEgyptian king most curiously rolled up in bandages of rich figured gold shalloon that covered the skirts of four embroidered red waistcoats ... a considerable body of the same sort of merchandize

was found in his boots, breeches, hat, and between the buckram and the lining of his surtout'.[18]

Towns along the Kent coast were particularly suitable as depots where smuggled goods could be seen; in 1768 Lady Mary Coke visited Deal where she went to 'three of the houses that smuggle Indian goods. I saw several pieces of very pretty silks . . . tea and musline is extremely cheap'.[19] At this period, Indian muslins and painted silks from China were coming into fashion for women's dresses; they could not be made up in their country of origin and were therefore liable to import duty.

Having obtained fabric and trimming, clothes then had to be made up by the mantua-maker or the tailor. For men this was less of a problem, for styles changed fairly slowly and the relative simplicity and uniformity of men's wear ensured easy access to the fashionable line. For women, with their more restricted lives, it was more difficult to follow the fashions; at the beginning of the eighteenth century there were no regularly produced fashion magazines and one could not rely on returning travellers (especially male) to report accurately on the niceties of cut or trimming.

Many of the fashions, therefore, were transmitted via dolls in the early part of the century, dressed in the latest taste and sent out from Paris to the courts of Europe; two dolls were usually sent, one, in court dress, 'la grande Pandora', and the other in fashionable everyday clothing, 'la petite Pandora'. The dolls, dressed in the latest styles, were a popular sight in the rue Saint-Honoré; Mercier in a famous passage in his *Tableau de Paris* described how visitors were taken to see the

fameuse poupée, le mannequin précieux, affublée des modes les plus nouvelles, enfin le prototype inspirateur passe de Paris à Londres tous les mois, et va de-là répandre ses grâces dans toute l'Europe. Il va au Nord et au Midi: il pénetre à Constantinople et à Pétersbourg; et le pli qu'a donné une main françoise, se répete chez toutes les nations, humble observatrices du goût de la rue Saint-Honoré.[20]

The dolls, having been copied by the court dressmakers, were displayed in the windows of fashionable shops for ladies to examine. In Bologna in the 1730s the French visitor de Brosses noted with some exaggeration that the ladies there 'wear nothing but what comes from Paris', for 'they have large dolls sent to them daily, robed head to toe in the latest fashion'.[21] In Venice the doll called the 'piavola de Franza' was placed in the window of the *merceria* so that it could be examined in detail; the poet Algarotti described to his readers how the ladies, with rapt attention, noted all the details from the headdress to the petticoat:

Tu le vedresti a lei dinnanzi in frotte
L'Andrienne, la cuffia, le nastriere
L'immenso guardinfante a parte a parte
Notomizzare e sino addento e sotto
Spinger gli avidi sguardi al gonnellino.[22]

Although the most fashionable dolls were sent from France, other dolls were sent from England. The *Gentleman's Magazine* for 1751 reported that dolls dressed in the English style had been sent to the Empress Elizabeth of Russia. Such dolls, known in English as 'babies', were also sent to the American colonies, where English was the dominant cultural influence. The *New England Weekly Journal* for 2 July 1733 stated that at Boston (the main fashion centre in America) was to be seen at a mantua-maker's 'a Baby drest after the Newest Fashion of Mantuas and Night Gowns, & everything belonging to a dress. Lately arrived on Capt. White from London'; it would cost ladies five shillings to borrow the doll, and seven shillings if the mantua-maker attended them in their own homes.[23] The *Lady's Magazine* for 1773 remarked sarcastically on the 'contagion' of fashion transmitted from the court to the city and then to the country 'by means of dolls which are sent thither and in a short time the provincials . . . are dressed like the gaudy doll which is sent from Paris. I imagine I see the women of a village, at least those of the better sort, collected together about the newcomer examining it from head to foot and running in rapture from the sweet idol to their milliners or mantua-makers . . .'[24] This was not just moral indignation on the part of the *Lady's Magazine*, but perhaps irritation at the lingering practice of sending such dressed dolls when fashion plates were available, which could not only spread the newest styles to a wider section of the populace, but also far more speedily.

It was in fact in the *Lady's Magazine* in the early 1770s that there appeared the first regular production every month of the newest fashions, a black-and-white engraving, which could be coloured by the reader and sent to her mantua-maker with instructions for making up. Previous fashion magazines such as the *Mercure de France* (which originally began as the *Mercure Galant* in 1672) only issued fashion plates sporadically, as did the earlier editions of the *Lady's Magazine*. In addition, in the first half of the eighteenth century, a number of well-known artists and engravers produced collections of costume drawings and fashion plates. Some, like those of Watteau, were more preparatory sketches for paintings; others, such as Picart's *Diverses Modes Dessinées d'Après Nature* (1728), were engravings of

the dress currently worn by all sections of society in Holland and North Germany, and not a fashionable ideal to be followed (the purpose of a fashion plate proper). A rare and isolated example of a collection of fashion plates and accessories was that published by Hérisset in 1729 under the title of *Recueil des Differentes Modes du Temps à Paris*. In 1744, the French artist Gravelot published a collection of English fashion plates, which were instrumental in the spread of the more informal English styles.

The innovation introduced by the *Lady's Magazine* in 1770 was not just to have a monthly fashion plate but also a detailed descriptive text; the aim was to provide the most distant readers 'with every innovation that is made in the female dress' but to avoid the 'fleeting whimsies of depraved Elegance'. Like the *Gentleman's Magazine* (which began in 1731), the *Lady's Magazine* also carried society news, theatre reviews and informative articles on the intellectual topics of the day; increasingly, however, towards the end of our period, there was a greater emphasis on moral advice and serialized sentimental stories.

In France similar magazines were established in the 1780s, the most important being the *Cabinet des Modes* (later called the *Magazin des Modes Nouvelles Françaises et Anglaises*) from 1785–9. French and English fashion plates were copied all over Europe. The only other country producing fashion plates in the 1780s was Germany; Daniel Chodowiecki illustrated German fashion almanacs in this decade, and from Weimar in 1786 came the first important rival to the French and English magazines, the *Journal des Luxus und der Moden*.

Fashion was taken more seriously in France as an art and a source of economic prosperity, and well-known artists through their fashion illustrations helped to ensure French superiority in that refinement of taste and elegance of style which could be imitated but never surpassed. The most famous collection of fashion plates designed to point a moral or adorn a tale was that published by the artist Moreau le Jeune (originally in three parts – in 1775, 1777 and 1783) as the *Monument du Costume Physique et Moral de la fin du dix-huitième siècle ou Tableaux de la Vie* (1789). Augustin de Saint-Aubin and F. L. J. Watteau – great nephew of the famous artist – were among a number of illustrators to the superb *Gallerie des Modes et des Costumes Français*, a set of 342 coloured fashion plates published in 1778–87; most of the designs were taken from the *marchands de modes*, and some were, for the first time, named.

It was not surprising that the names of some of the most important fashionable tailors occurred in the *Gallerie des Modes*, for France was acknowledged as the centre for the best tailoring. Those with any taste or pretensions to style not only bought their fabrics in Paris, but had them made up by a French tailor. The Richelieu collection in the Bibliothèque Nationale in Paris contains samples of the sumptuous French fabrics (including, for example, chenille velvets brocaded in gold, at 140 and 150 livres the ell) made up for the King of Portugal in 1735. Even for humbler clothes, the quality of tailoring in Paris was supreme; Christian VII of Denmark ordered there in 1768 his hunting suits of blue and red broadcloth trimmed with gold braid. The cachet of French clothes was particularly striking in the first half of the century; in Fielding's novel *Joseph Andrews* (1742), the author poked fun at the ultra-fashionable Englishman Bellarmine whose praise of French tailoring was addressed to Leonora:

Yes Madam this Coat I assure you was made at Paris, and I defy the best English Taylor even to imitate it. There is not one of them can cut, Madam, they can't cut. If you observe how this Skirt is turned, and this Sleeve, a clumsy English Rascal can do nothing like it . . . I never trust anything more than a Great Coat to an Englishman . . . for myself I would see the dirty Island at the bottom of the Sea rather than wear a single Rag of English Work about me, and I am sure after you have made one Tour to Paris, you will be of the same Opinion with regard to your own Clothes.[25]

A gentleman of fashion, like Smollett's *Peregrine Pickle* (1751), had made in Paris 'several suits of cloaths suitable to the French mode'. Some French tailors even sent their servants to the places patronized by foreign gentlemen to get custom; John Russell, a young English painter, was accosted in 1739 in the Café Anglais by a person 'dressed in black velvet with a gold-laced hat, silver-hilted sword . . . ready to equip me à la mode de Paris'.[26]

Travelling on the Grand Tour was a useful way of adding to the wardrobe, particularly as there was a universal belief that clothes were cheaper out of one's native land. When Robert Adam went on the Grand Tour with his brother James in 1754 he bought at Lyons 'a gold Stuff Vest which I verily believe in London would cost 16 or 18 pounds but here does not amount to above $\frac{1}{3}$ of that sum. I am also getting one of the genteelest and richest embroidered Vests that I ever saw which will cost me at least £14 or £15 sterling'; in Genoa, the next stage of his trip, he proposed to buy a suit of black velvet with which he could wear all his waistcoats in turn.[27] If unable to visit Paris, gentlemen should, advised Lord Chesterfield, use the services of French tailors, established in all the major capitals of Europe.

The most important treatise on tailoring in the eighteenth century, *L'Art du Tailleur*, was written by de Garsault for the *Description des Arts et Métiers* (1769); it detailed the fairly crude systems for measuring the customer (with paper tape measure) and cutting out the fabric with paper patterns. Ideally, according to the *London Tradesman* (1747) the tailor 'must be a perfect Proteus, change Shapes as often as the Moon, and still find something new; He ought to have a quick Eye to steal the Cut of a Sleeve, the Pattern of a Flap, or the Shape of a good Trimming at a Glance . . .'[28] Much of his skill lay in hiding any deformity, so that the coat hung well, and 'the Cloaths sit easy in spite of a stiff Gait or awkward Air'. The cutting of the coat and waistcoat was much more important than that of the largely unseen breeches; the latter were usually cut by the tailor and then made up by the less-skilled breeches-maker. In addition, there were specialists makers of leather breeches, worn by the upper classes for riding, and by the lower classes for work; the philanthropist Francis Place was apprenticed to a leather-breeches maker in 1785 but by then the trade was decaying as working men turned to cheaper and washable cloths such as cotton cord.

Cloth, whether silk or wool, was expensive, and cost far more than the labour; tailors were very often in the vanguard of any radical movements to increase their standard of living. The journeyman tailors in London published in 1754 a breakdown of the cost of a suit; the twelve yards of velvet cost £1 4s. a yard, plus the cost of the linings, facings and buttons, but the tailor could only charge 2s. 6d. for each of the $7\frac{1}{2}$ days it took to complete.[29] Admittedly in England the quality of tailoring was not high; Henry Purefoy sent a letter to his local tailor in Oxfordshire in 1736 saying: 'The Gold laced wastcoat you made mee last year has done you no credit in the making, it gapes so intolerably before at the bottom when I button it at the wastbone of my breetches & everybody takes notice of it. As to my size I am partly the same bignesse as I was when in Town last, but you made the last cloaths a little too streight.'[30] It was not surprising, in view of the information – or lack of it – regarding size and fit, that complaints were made to the tailors. In the more remote areas of the countryside it was, paradoxically, easier to have more personal service; travelling tailors with their journeymen would visit their clients once or twice during the year, carrying news as well as their needles and thread, and they would also carry out repairs and alterations. Some households were provided with servants skilled at tailoring; Goethe's father, a well-off citizen of Frankfurt, chose men-servants who could tailor, so that clothes could be made for the family at home.

For most of the seventeenth century tailors made the clothing of men and women, but in 1675[31] the profession was divided into two branches; the 'maîtresses couturières', after an apprenticeship of three years, could make various female garments such as the loose *robes de chambre*, the petticoats and jackets, unboned gowns and bodices, underwear and children's clothing, including that of boys up to the age of eight years. In practice, couturières specialized in various branches of clothing. The tailoring of gowns reinforced with whalebone and the stays themselves were made by men in the first half of the century, as it required male strength to work the whalebone. As the stiff-bodied gowns became limited to court wear, the couturières took over the job of making all gowns and the lighter stays which were worn in the second half of the century; in 1776 they were allowed to make stays, corsets, paniers, and after 1789 all restrictions were lifted. Roughly the same pattern occurred in England (although dress-makers seem to have had little training), with men making the boned bodices until the boning became lighter, but with women, from the earliest period, making the court mantuas, because they were not boned; throughout the century, however, tailors kept the privilege of making female riding habits, which was not surprising, based as they were on the masculine suit.

From the second half of the eighteenth century, with the diminution of the size and richness of the fabric design, the trimming came to be all important, which was when the *marchands de modes* came into their own. An offshoot of the mercers' guild, they supplied and arranged the ribbons, lace and other forms of trimmings on gowns and hats (the latter becoming highly complicated confections by the 1770s), and also articles of dress that did not require fitting, such as mantles and scarves; everything 'qui sert à la parure et au luxe', according to the *Encyclopédie* (1765), was supplied by the *marchands de modes*, and in some cases they took over the work of the couturière, although in theory the dress was fitted by the dress-maker and then sent to the modiste for the trimmings. Much of the credit for this take-over bid by the modiste was due to the greatest *marchande de modes* of all, Rose Bertin, whose flair for publicity and ability to catch the popular mood made her the Ministre de la Mode in Paris.

Born in 1747 in Abbéville, she came to Paris aged 16 to work for a milliner; her early successes in designing toilettes for such leaders of fashion as the duchesse de Chartres encouraged her to open her own establishment in 1770, the Grand Mogul, in the rue Saint-Honoré, from where she furnished some of the dresses offered to the new Dauphine, Marie Antoinette. She was actually introduced to the Dauphine, probably by the royal hairdresser Léonard, in 1772, and soon became the most fashionable modiste in Paris. Much of her success was in devising witty and topical items for her royal and aristocratic clientèle. In 1774 the new king, Louis XVI, was vaccinated, and immediately Rose made a headdress, a 'pouf à l'innoculation',[31]

23   **The Coquette at her Toilet**, after G. Morland

This engraving, of the 1780s, shows a fashionable modiste in a printed cotton ensemble and black silk hooded scarf, showing a newly designed muslin cap to an interested customer. Such visits were an essential part of the morning toilette.

OPPOSITE

24   **'Une Marchande de Rubans au Palais Royal'**, Paris, by J. B. Mallet

The Palais Royal was famed for its arcade of luxury shops which included those specializing in accessories such as millinery and ribbons.

incorporating a rising sun and an olive-tree laden with fruit round which a serpent, representing Aesculapius, the god of medicine, was entwined; the success of Beaumarchais' play *The Marriage of Figaro* (first performed in 1784) inspired Rose to offer a dress *à la Suzanne*, comprising a tight-fitting bodice with a fichu worn with a white skirt and apron (a fashionable version of the tasteful dress of a lady's maid), and a *toque à la Suzanne* with white feathers and ribbons.

By the 1780s even royalty felt flattered to be accepted as Bertin customers; travelling to Europe in 1782 under the name of the comtesse du Nord, the Grand Duchess of Russia bought from Rose Bertin a number of dresses including, according to the Baroness d'Oberkirch, one of silk brocaded with velvet flowers, with an overskirt of lace interwoven with gold.[32] The baroness herself was given in May of that year a preview of the 30 or so headdresses which Rose had designed for that month; such was the fickleness of public taste that the fashionable modiste had always to be a step ahead of the current whim.

The importance of the *marchands de modes* was recognized in the reform carried through in 1776 by Louis XVI, when the irrational guild system was replaced by various corporations of arts and trades, among which was a new corporation called the Marchands de Modes, who were to be allowed to make court dresses (previously a male preserve) and to play a greater part in making ordinary dresses. Rose Bertin was made Master of the Corporation for the first year of its existence, and by virtue of this office dressed 'la grande Pandora' for its journeys to the courts of Europe.

Rose Bertin's fame and fortune reached their peak in the mid-1780s; from then on the fortunes of the queen, bound up with those of Rose, were on the decline. Not only were the relative simplicities of the more tailored English styles forcing out some of the more frivolous excesses of the French fashions (the Anglo-French commercial treaty of 1786 allowed great increases in imported English fabrics), but the queen was at last forced to see the financial abyss looming up and had to retrench on her expenses; she was only allowed 120,000 livres a

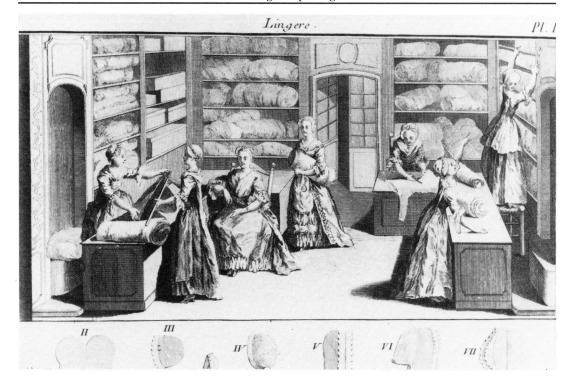

year, but in one year, 1786, she had spent 272,000, a considerable proportion of that finding its way to Rose Bertin. Although she continued to supply the queen, even in her imprisonment in the Temple during the revolutionary years, the great days were over; like the Vicar of Bray, Rose was a survivor under changing régimes; she spent the early years of the Revolution supplying aristocrats and republican sympathizers from her new shop in the rue de Richelieu, but she was prudent enough to have a business in London which she visited during the Terror and from where she sent out her fashion doll.

Rose Bertin was not the only modiste working for the French court and aristocracy; other names included a Mlle Mouillard (who seems to have worked for the royal children), a Mme Pompey and a M. Beaulard, whose main claim to fame was a coiffure of his own invention, called 'à ressort' or 'à la grand'mere', a bonnet fitted with springs so that the towering edifices of the 1770s and '80s could be lowered as occasion demanded.[33]

Mme Eloffe was another fashionable modiste working for the queen; her account book, dating from 1787 to 1790, demonstrates the simpler royal tastes for 'des robes de lingerie, de satin ou de taffetas de Florence de diverses couleurs', in contrast to the highly elaborate court presentation gowns. Her clients included the aristocracy, and artistic and literary ladies such as Vigée-Lebrun and Madame de

25 **'La Boutique d'une Lingère'**, 1771, from *L'Art de la Lingerie* by F. A. de Garsault

The seated customer is shown bolts of linen by smartly dressed assistants, while on the right one of the *couturière-lingère*'s apprentices cuts out a chemise.

26 **'Tailleur costumier essayant un cor à la mode'**, 1778, engraving after P.-T. Le Clère, from the *Gallerie des Modes*.

The fitting of such whaleboned corsets, themselves often works of engineering, seem to have required scrupulous attention from the stay-maker.

Staël – she even had the notorious chevalier d'Eon as a customer. Mme Eloffe was also one of the *couturières lingères* to the queen; the distinction between the goods supplied by the *marchand de modes* and those made by the *lingère* is not at all clear, for both dealt with lace and fine linen. According to de Garsault's *L'Art de la Lingerie* (1771), the *lingère* supplied the fabric and made the garments which were her speciality, such as shifts, shirts, caps, mourning linen for coifs and weepers, etc. The best linen came from Holland, and linen from all over the Netherlands was sent to Haarlem to be bleached. Cotton was supplied by the *lingère*, in particular for men's shirts, and so was the fine muslin from India which was fashionable not only for peignoirs and mantles, but increasingly in the early 1770s for dresses; linen laces were sold by the *lingère*, but not the gold or silver laces, which were sold by weight in specialist shops.

A great proportion of the work of the *couturière lingère* revolved around trousseaux and layettes. Items such as chemises, sleeve ruffles, pockets, peignoirs and caps were supplied by the dozen to the bride; in addition the *lingère* supplied the linen and lace trimmings for the stays and for the *corsets de nuit* (lightly boned stays worn at night), as well as the fine embroidered muslin *manteaux de lit*. Although lace was in the last quarter of the century no longer fashionable for the trimming of caps and sleeve ruffles (except for court dress), it continued to decorate night wear and the shoulder mantles worn by women in their boudoirs, and fine cottons and linens were worn for informal dresses; when in 1787 the marquise de la Tour du Pin was married, her trousseau, costing 45,000 livres,[34] consisted mainly of linen, lace and muslin gowns, and in the same year the bride of the baron de Montmorency spent, according to an English traveller, £25,000 on her trousseau which included a hundred dozen shifts.

The layette had to be prepared as soon as the bride

married; again, a fashionable mother-to-be ordered by the dozen her *chemises de couches*, open in front for feeding the baby, and numbers of muslin gowns and *manteaux de lit* for the period of convalescence.

Fine linen and lace demonstrated taste and wealth; the best lace came from the Austrian Netherlands and French Flanders, and travellers in those areas were often commissioned to bring back lace for their friends and relatives. Lady Mary Coke in 1767, at Spa, the fashionable watering place in the Austrian Netherlands, bought 'two . . . sutes of lace & a little Cloke of Brusselles lace'; a complete suit of lace comprised a cap (with optional lappets), ruffles and neckwear. Lady Mary also ordered eight guineas' worth of Holland for shifts; these would have been made up probably by her personal maid, for Lady Mary's ideas of grandeur would have precluded her from this task.[35] It was, however, customary for well-born ladies of the upper classes to make some of their own everyday underwear, and men's shirts; the latter were either plain or ruffled, and made by the dozen. Linen was usually bought in large quantities for the needs of the household, one of the tasks of young girls being to sew shirts and shifts.

In England there were less strict demarcation lines between suppliers of services and goods. The English equivalent of the *marchand de modes* was the milliner, who provided linen and lace and also every conceivable kind of made-up accessory, as described by the *London Tradesman* (1747):

The Milliner is concerned in making and providing the Ladies with Linen of all sorts, fit for Wearing Apparel, from the Holland Smock to the Tippet and Commode . . . the Milliner furnishes them with Holland, Cambrick, Lawn and Lace of all sorts and makes these Materials into Smocks, Aprons, Tippits, Handkerchiefs, Neckaties, Ruffles, Mobs, Caps, Dressed-Heads with as many Etceteras as would reach from Charing-Cross to the Royal Exchange.

They make up Cloaks, Manteels, Mantelets, Cheens and Capucheens, of Silk, Velvet, plain or brocaded and trim them with Silver and Gold Lace or Black Lace. They make up and sell Hats, Hoods, and Caps of all Sorts and Materials; they find them in Gloves, Muffs and Ribbons; they sell quilted Petticoats and Hoops of all Sizes . . . The Milliner . . . imports new Whims from Paris every Post . . . The most noted of them keep an Agent at Paris, who have nothing else to do but watch the Motions of the Fashions, and procure Intelligence of their Changes.[36]

Some provincial milliners also provided a making-up service for the fabrics sold in their shops.[37]

TAILLEUR COSTUMIER ESSAYANT UN COR A LA MODE.

In the first half of the eighteenth century in particular, the stay-maker was crucial to the fashionable tightly girt shape; this was usually a man (although 'Girls of Strength' could, according to the *London Tradesman*, be successful at making hooped petticoats) who 'takes the Lady's Shape as nicely as he can; if it is natural, and where it is not, he supplies the Deficiency; then he cuts out the Tabby and Canvas by the Shape in Quarters, which are given out to Women to be stitched'.[38] Usually a lady's measurements would be available at her dressmakers, but where the stay-maker 'is obliged by Art to mend a crooked Shape, to bolster up a fallen Hip or distorted Shoulder', he would usually, with whalebone bought from the haberdasher, visit her in her home. Specialized tradesmen were also needed at every court; they sold the quality 'Gold and Silver Lace, Gold and Silver Buttons, Shapes for Waistcoats, Lace and Network for Robeings and Women's Petticoats, Fringes, Bugles, Spangles, Plates for Embroidery . . . Gold and Silver Wire',[39] which gilded the lily of fashionable formal dress for most of the eighteenth century.

Professional embroiderers were needed at every court; they provided embroidery not only of gold and silver and silk, but coloured spangles, chenille, wool and even fur. For the grandest occasions precious stones were embroidered onto fabrics; in Saint-Aubin's *L'Art du Brodeur* (1770) the coat worn by the Dauphin for his wedding that year was embroidered with diamonds and that of the comte de Provence included opals in the border.[40] For the arrival in 1722 of the Infanta of Spain as his future bride (though the wedding never took place) the young king, Louis XV, held a ball at the Tuileries, where the guests dressed in cloth of gold or silver with embroidery to match;[41] the French were famed for the quality of their fine embroidery, their guild going back to the thirteenth century. Saint-Aubin claimed that after the French, the embroidery produced at Vienna was the next best, much of it made in the convents.

On a smaller scale, embroideresses worked for the English court; fine embroidery, *opus anglicanum*, had been an English art since at least the fourteenth century. Some of their work was recorded by Mrs Delany; at court in 1740 she admired the embroidery on the Duchess of Bedford's petticoat: 'the pattern was festoons of shells, coral, corn, cornflowers and sea-weeds, everything in different works of gold and silver except the flowers and coral'.[42]

Apart from the highly professional work of the court and trade embroiderers, much embroidery was done by ladies of gentle birth. In the first half of the century, embroidery in gold, silver and coloured silks was popular; in the 1740s Frederick the Great's sisters embroidered his waistcoats in silver, and in Richardson's novel *Clarissa* (1748) the heroine had herself embroidered the cuffs and robings of her primrose-coloured gown 'in a running pattern of violets and their leaves; the light in the flowers silver; gold in the leaves'.[43] From the beginning of the century women had embroidered their silk or linen aprons with white work or coloured silks; in the 1760s the round tambour frame was introduced from Turkey and eagerly taken up with the vogue for things oriental, the embroidery produced being used to decorate the fine muslin dresses which came to be popular.

It is difficult to assess how many ready-made garments were available to buy in the eighteenth century; they were probably the more informal items which required less fitting or could more easily be altered. For men, the most obvious garments to be bought ready-made were nightgowns and banyans; a trade card of 1764 from the Golden Lion in Tavistock Street informed customers that made-up 'Gentlemen's Banyans, Gowns and Caps' were available.[44] For the poorer classes, where fit was not so important, but economy of material was, a greater range of ready-made clothes could be bought; the trade card which Hogarth engraved in about 1730 for his sister's shop advertised for sale 'ye best and most Fashionable ready-made Frocks, suites of Fustian, Ticken and Holland, stript Dimmity and Flanel wastcoats, blue and canvas Frocks . . .'. For women, the early unstructured forms of mantua and nightgown were sometimes sold ready made; the *Spectator* of 9 June 1711 advertised ready-made gowns, several of them 'Japan'd Sattins', possibly mantuas.[45] Lady Mary Wortley Montagu asked her sister in Paris in the 1720s to send her 'a made-up Mantua and petticoat' and 'a night-gown ready-made', but this might have been to avoid the duty on unmade-up materials. Cloaks and mantles which needed no exact fit were, as we have seen, sold at the milliners along with the quilted or hooped petticoats and, in the second half of the century, loose-fitting sleeved coats, under various names, were advertised for sale in shops known as 'warehouses'.

It is virtually impossible to ascertain the proportion of income spent on clothes and the length of time they were expected to last. It is safe to say that clothes were expensive compared to the other costs of existence (eighteenth-century newspapers were full of advertisements offering rewards for stolen clothes), and except at the very top reaches of society, they were meant to last and were often altered.

The amounts spent on clothes by the princes of

Europe were astounding. The Empress Elizabeth of Russia seldom wore the same dress twice, and when she died in 1761, had 15,000 dresses in her wardrobe; Marie Antoinette with a yearly allowance of 120,000 livres usually ordered 36 formal and semi-formal dresses a year, and many more informal gowns. Some indication of the amounts of clothing purchased in the eighteenth century can be gained from trousseaux. The Archduchess Josepha of Austria, who married the King of Naples in 1767, had a trousseau costing 200,000 florins, which included 99 dresses made of rich silks with gold and silver lace, and according to Swinburne, £5000 was the average spent on a trousseau in France in the 1780s. Yet many trousseaux were more modest, even among princes; in 1748 the Countess Palatine, Frederica Sophia of Bayreuth, married Duke Karl Eugène of Württemberg, and her trousseau consisted merely of five rich robes, six informal gowns, and two negligées ornamented with Brabant lace.[46] In many cases the trousseau was the most complete wardrobe any woman possessed, and Mrs Piozzi in Rome in the 1780s commented that Italian women had for their weddings 'as many clothes as will last them seven years, for fashions do not change as often here as at London or Paris'.[47] Yet even in England a modest trousseau was the rule rather than the exception; when in 1748 Lady Frances Carteret married the Marquis of Tweeddale, Mrs Delany noted that she had six dresses including her wedding dress of flounced white satin with a silver trimming, and in 1756 the very wealthy Mrs Spencer had made 'four negligées, four nightgowns, four mantuas and petticoats'[48] – a very large number of clothes when the average for much of the century was four to six. Four to six also appears to have been the approximate number of suits a gentleman of fashion would order per year, but attendance at court or on occasions of spectacular splendour could double or treble this amount. It is also fair to say that some princes kept a meagre wardrobe; Frederick the Great's 'economy or carelessness or both, induce him to wear his cloaths as long as decency will permit; indeed sometimes rather longer. He is accustomed to order his breeches to be mended and his coat to be pieced under the arms'.[49] When Frederick died in 1786 his wardrobe comprised only some fur-lined cloaks, old uniforms, and 13 shirts, and it was sold for 400 thalers to a Jewish clothes dealer. And in the 1760s an English visitor noted that the Duke Frederick II of Mecklenburg-Schwerin 'has seldom more than one suit in wear throughout the year'.[50]

This attitude may explain why in museums there are relatively few male items of clothing; where suits exist they do so in many cases without the

Mary & Ann Hogarth
from the old Frock shop the corner of the Long Walk facing the Cloysters, Removed to ye Kings Arms joyning to ye Little Britain gate near Long Walk Sells ye best & most Fashionable Ready Made Frocks, suites of Fustian, Ticken & Holland, stript Dimmity & Flanel Waistcoats, blue & canvas Frocks & bluecoat Boys Dra. Likewise Fustians, Tickens, Hollands, white stript Dimitys white & stript Flanels in ye piece By Wholesale or Retale at Reasonable Rates.

27 **A trade card for Mary and Ann Hogarth,** by W. Hogarth (engraved by T. Cook)

Hogarth's apprenticeship to a silver-plate engraver enabled him to produce the often detailed and intricate shop interiors which were often used for trade cards or bill headings in the eighteenth century. This card, dating probably from the late 1720s, indicates the range of ready-made garments which were available to the lower classes of society. The sizing was virtually non-existent and the sewing was fairly crude, but this was a more acceptable alternative, perhaps, and sometimes cheaper than the buying of second-hand clothes.

breeches, which wore out more quickly than the coat or waistcoat. Smollett, visiting Paris in the early 1760s, noticed that the man of fashion changed his suit with the seasons; for spring and autumn he wore camlet trimmed with silver, for summer camlet lined with silk and for winter cloth of velvet laced with gold.[51] Changes occurred, as has been pointed out, not so much in cut but in fabric and decoration, changes more perceptible to contemporary commentators than to us. At about the time when Smollett was pouring scorn on what he considered the foppery of Frenchmen, a Swiss visitor to London remarked that

28 **View of the Castle of Königstein from the South,** *c.*1756–8 (detail), by B. Bellotto

As well as the clothes lines familiar to us, it was a well established practice to lay linen flat on the grass where it could be bleached by the sun.

OPPOSITE
29 **A sailor selling stockings**, by P. Sandby

A sailor stands before a slop-shop where a number of ready-made articles of clothing could be purchased.

a mode begins to be out of date at Paris just when it has been introduced at London by some English nobleman. The court and first-rate nobility immediately take it up; it is introduced about St James's by those that ape the manners of the court; and by the time it has reached the city, a contrary mode already prevails at Paris, where the English, bringing with them the obsolete mode, appear like the people of another world.[52]

Grosley here implies that it was only a matter of a few months before fashions changed noticeably, but this was (except for the faddish man of mode) an exaggeration. Small-patterned textiles, the usual wear for men's suits throughout the century, did not date as much as women's dress patterns; the character of the trimming was all-important, especially in the last quarter of the period, when plain suits were judged by the quality of their decoration. William Hickey, who had gone out to India in the later 1760s with a wardrobe of rich silk suits covered in lace, found on his return to England in 1780 that taste had changed, and so he took them off to the second-hand clothes dealers, who gave him 47 guineas – he had originally paid seven times that amount for them; he kept one 'full suit of beautiful velvet of four colours . . . and two others of those least ornamented with lace'.[53]

The relative rapidity of changes in silk designs meant that there was a greater turnover of dresses in the eighteenth century. The fashionable Parisienne, said Smollett, 'must have her taffeties for the summer, her flowered silks for the spring and autumn, her sattins and damasks for winter';[54] Casanova remarked that patterned silk stuffs halved in value after a year. Yet silks were expensive, and so, to give a new appearance to a dress, many were in fact altered in style. This refurbishing was easier later in the century, with the popularity of plain silks and lavish trimmings which could be removed. This happened even at the most exalted levels of society; Madame Eloffe's *Livre-Journal* of the later 1780s listed the many alterations and alternative trimmings to some of the French queen's dresses – in August 1787 alone, she re-made the sleeve trimming of a blue satin lévite, refurbished a 'robe turque' and retrimmed a lévite 'vert glacé violet uni en blonde et gaze'.[55]

One reason why the trimmings of a gown or suit were so important was that they were tangible signs of wealth which had to be renewed; silk gauze for example could not be washed because it lost its crispness, and the gold and silver lace tarnished and had to be removed, to be sold for melting down. The difficulties of keeping clothes clean were legion and included the hazards of street encounters (the mud thrown up by carriage wheels, the powder scattered by the barber racing along, to name but two), and human wear and tear – Casanova claimed that tinder inserted in the coat under the arm would reduce perspiration,[56] but this does not seem to have been greatly used. For women in particular, the shift afforded no real protection for the silk dress, which often rotted under the arms. Grosley in London in the later 1760s found terrible weather (and Londoners intolerant of 'our umbrellas of taffeta or waxed silk'), and 'swarms' of shops 'scouring, repairing and new furbishing' clothes ruined by the coal smoke.[57] Woollen clothes were scoured or cleaned with teazels and then pressed; fuller's earth was used to absorb grease from wool, and turpentine to remove stains. Another primitive form of dry cleaning was smoking with sulphur; in Smollett's last novel *Humphrey Clinker* (1771), the maid Win Jenkins, given a soiled yellow silk dress by her mistress, was advised by 'Mrs Drab, the manty-maker' that it would 'look very well when it is scowred and smoaked with sulfur'.[58] Light silks

could sometimes be washed – Win Jenkins used a mixture of vinegar, urine and stale beer – but they often lost their colour. One way of renewing clothes was to dye them but this was often responsible for rotting silks; in 1759 Mrs Washington sent her green sack to be dyed the same colour, but if it would not take the dye, then the dress was to be altered into a nightgown.[59] The quality of dyeing improved as the century progressed (and it was easier to dye the fashionable cottons and linens of the 1780s), and specialist dyers set up in major cities; Mark Thornhill Wade set up as a dyer in Soho in 1788 and his records indicate the extent to which people of all classes had their clothes dyed, the most popular colour being black for mourning.[60]

Clothes, if not exactly exchanged freely from one wearer to another, were cherished possessions to be handed on to relatives or friends. It was the custom for the aristocracy to give their clothes to their personal attendants, although these had to be worn altered. One of the perquisites of serving the Queen of France was to receive her cast-off clothes; the *dames d'atours*, the noble ladies of the Bedchamber, were given the court and full dresses, and the *femmes de chambre* were given the undress gowns.[61] These latter were usually sold to the second-hand clothes dealers in Paris, the *fripiers*, some of whom were rich enough to have shops in the rue Saint-Honoré.[62]

In a period before the manufacturers of clothing on a large scale for the mass of society, the part played by the dealer in second-hand clothes was very important. Many cities had a central area devoted to such a trade, convenient for the servants of the rich, who provided much of the stock from their masters and mistresses. In Rome the streets near the Piazza Navona were where second-hand clothes could be bought. In Paris, the place de Grève, according to Mercier in the 1780s, housed the Fair of the Holy Ghost, which specialized in the selling of women's and children's clothes. Second-hand wigs could be bought at the quai des Morfondus; in London there was a wig market in Rosemary Lane which dealt mainly in stolen wigs – one of the dangers of walking the streets of London was that 'sly boys', sitting in baskets on the shoulders of their confederates, would snatch the wigs off passers-by.

In London, the second-hand trade was divided into the poorer clothes sold on the east side of the City, and the better quality stuff in Covent Garden and Monmouth Street. Some shops sold a mixture of second-hand and ready-made goods, and some were specialists; the 'slop-shop' sold 'all kinds of Shirts, Jackets, Trousers, and other Wearing Apparel belonging to Sailors, ready made',[63] and other shops in the East End of London did a good trade in 'Negro Cloathing', light, cheap, ready-made clothes for the slave-trade. By the end of the period, in the North and Midlands of England, clubs were formed for providing clothes, promoted by the tradesmen supplying the articles in question, and paid for on a weeekly basis – an idea which lasted into the twentieth century in some industrial areas.

For the middle and professional classes, depending on their status and resources, their clothing was recognizably imitative of current fashion, and indeed, the plainness which they cultivated particularly with regard to men's dress in the 1770s and 1780s was to influence fashion in its turn at the end of the century. All those, both men and women, coming into contact with the upper classes and with sufficient financial resources, attempted to copy fashionable clothing with a mixture of native and imported fabrics, although at some remove and after a time-lag which varied from country to country. Some countries like England were more flexible with regard to the occasional crossing of class barriers in dress, and foreigners found it

difficult, for example, to distinguish serving maids from their mistresses; in France, too, the shop girls attracted admiration in their inexpensive versions of fashionable dress, and Mrs Adams, an American visitor to Paris in 1784, commented that the mantua-maker would appear in a silk gown and petticoat, even if she lived up five flights of stairs and ate only bread and water.[64]

For the majority of the population, reliance had to be placed on locally produced stuffs for clothing, for imported materials were prohibitive in price compared to the average wage. In the American

30   **The Distressed Poet**, *c.*1735 by W. Hogarth

The poet, wearing ill-fitting wig and striped morning gown, racks his brains for inspiration, while his wife mends his breeches; her hooded cloak hangs by the door. The stylish milkmaid, with flowers in her straw hat, and yoke over her shoulder, demands to be paid.

colonies, for example, during the wars of Independence, Mrs Adams noted that while a labourer earned 9 dollars a day, anything other than the cheapest homespun cloths could not be bought; imported linens cost 20 dollars a yard, ordinary calicoes were at 30 and 40 dollars, and the fine English broadcloths could cost as much as £40 a yard.[65]

Sir Frederick Eden, in the first real analysis of poverty in England, *The State of the Poor* (1797), found that there were considerable differences between the rural and the urban poor, and between north and south. In the north of England he found that most articles of dress were made in the home, of locally woven materials; this was a continuation of the custom noted by Defoe in the early eighteenth century when he found nearly every house in some of the Yorkshire villages such as Halifax weaving their own kersey or shalloon. The custom of wearing home-made stuff was not in fact limited to the lowest classes; in 1740, Richardson's heroine Pamela, when deciding to return home to her parents, considerably chastened after her attempts at gentility had only encouraged the advances of Mr B., 'bought of Farmer Nichol's wife and daughters a good sad-coloured stuff, of their own spinning, enough to make me a gown and two petticoats',[66] and some years later, Mrs Delany found a poor clergyman using the fleeces given him by his parishioners to clothe himself and his family. This clergyman's customary dress (when at home) was 'a coarse blue frock trimmed with black horn buttons, a checked shirt, a leather strap about his neck for a stock, a coarse apron, and a pair of great heavy wooden-soled shoes plated with iron to preserve them'.[67] For the poor, colours were usually dark for economy, very often the natural greyish-brown of woollen mixture cloths, and the white linen was replaced by the more practical checked or coloured shirts. Visitors to Spain and Portugal noted the almost universal dark brown linen/woollen cloths worn by the poor; much of this was woven in the houses of correction in the major cities such as Barcelona.

The stuffs woven and worn by the rural poor, either in their homes or by itinerant weavers, were usually of hard-wearing but coarse quality, producing a kind of uniformity of clothing in small communities which was a contrast to the more varied clothing found in towns. Nugent, in the 1760s at Groningen, found the peasants 'all uniformly clad in dark brown frize coats' and the women in black coarse cloth or linsey-woolsey, a mixture of linen and wool; at about the same time the Duchess of Northumberland saw poor people near Antwerp, the men in frocks of harden lined with swanskin, striped linsey-woolsey waistcoats and breeches and grey yarn stockings, and the women in jackets made of snuff-coloured frieze and blue petticoats of matching material. While much of the home-made clothing of the rural poor was in shades of buff or brown, some checked and striped fabrics were produced for aprons, handkerchiefs and jackets. In the 1780s visitors to Norway found the peasants weaving their own stone-coloured cloth and 'a kind of stuff like a Scotch plaid'. Plaids or checks were widely used for men's morning gowns; they were cheap, did not show wear and tear as would a fashionable silk gown, and enabled the suit to be kept for best.[68]

Although on the whole men wore clothes which resembled fairly closely fashionable dress, there were some garments such as knee-length tunics, smocks (worn in the country and for heavy work in cities), and trousers which were worn for reasons of practicality. These trousers took various forms according to the climate. In Russia they were sometimes made of fur, usually sheepskin, and worn under 'a short wide Coat without plaits, which wraps over ... round the waist',[69] or they consisted of bandages of flannel or wool tied round the legs; in the 1780s an English visitor to Spain saw the Basques in leg-coverings of black wool fastened with tapes. Trousers of linen or cotton were made for hot weather and tropical climates; the inventories of the poor whites living in the southern states of North America, for example, included jackets, waistcoats and trousers of locally produced light cotton and cottonade, a heavy coarse twilled cotton fabric widely used for work clothes.[70]

There were immense variations on footwear (or lack of it) for the rural poor; some wore strips of cloth, others cord sandals, and many wore wooden clogs. Good-quality footwear worn even by the poor was one of the many features noted by visitors to England throughout the eighteenth century. To a Swedish visitor, Pehr Kalm, visiting England in 1748, the country seemed a paradise for women: it appeared to him that they did not work as he was surprised not to see them working in the fields; in fact England was unique in Europe in that there was no true peasant class, and foreigners who mainly travelled in the south of England found it hard to distinguish between town and country women. According to Mme du Bocage in 1750, 'the poorest country girls drink tea, have bodices of chintz, straw hats upon their heads and scarlet cloaks on their shoulders';[71] this was echoed by Smollett in his novel *Sir Lancelot Greaves* (1762), where similar girls appeared 'in their best apparel, their white hose and clean short dimity petticoats, their gawdy gowns of printed cotton'.[72]

These were probably unmarried girls, possibly domestic servants, with some pretensions to fashionable status. Generally the range of clothing worn by poor women, particularly in towns, was greater than that worn by men, and more subject to regional variations. The basic wardrobe for a working woman comprised a shift, stays, thick hard-wearing petticoat, and a jacket. Francis Place, writing in 1824, recalled the working costume of 'the wives of journeymen tradesmen and shop-keepers' who

either wore leather stays or what were called full-boned stays . . . These were never washed although worn day by day for years. The wives and grown daughters of tradesmen . . . wore petticoats of camblet lined with dyed linen stuffed with wool and horsehair and quilted. These were also worn day by day till they were rotten . . . Formerly the women young and old were seen emptying their pails or pans at the doors or washing on stools in the street in the summer time without gowns on their backs or handkerchiefs on their necks, their leather stays half-laced and black as the door posts, their black coarse worsted stockings and striped linsey-woolsey petticoats standing alone with dirt.[73]

Since much of the dress was made of non-washable materials, it was important to keep linen – shifts, caps and handkerchiefs – clean, a matter of pride with many working women. A common hazard in the poorer streets of cities was to stumble into ropes of drying linen crossing the streets; this happened to Keysler, a German traveller in Rome in 1729, and it seems to have been a universal practice in hot climates to dry clothes in this way, the sun also acting as a bleach. For many very poor women with only one chemise or handkerchief, cleanliness was a problem; Mercier's *Tableau de Paris* of the 1780s described them rising at 4 a.m. so that the linen could be washed in the river near the Pont Neuf before work.

Over the shift a pair of stays was worn, sometimes of leather, and sometimes of canvas boned with reeds (when whalebone could not be afforded). The thick skirt, often quilted or made of flannel, provided warmth and durability; hoops were not usually worn because they wore out the fabric above them. Regional variations showed, particularly in the jackets worn. The fashionable tight-fitting versions, the Italian 'carmagnola' and the French 'casaquin' were comfortable and attractive, made of a variety of materials; similar tight-fitting padded jackets were worn in the north of Europe. A very popular working jacket in the second half of the century was the 'caraco' of three-quarter length and made tight-waisted or with a loose sack-back. A version of this mid-thigh jacket called the 'short-gown' had a cross-over front and was perhaps the most usual working jacket, deriving possibly from the informal fur or fabric-lined Dutch short gowns of the later seventeenth century. With the Dutch and German immigrants it came to North America,[74] the most popular fabrics being linens and cottons in checks and stripes, and the printed calicoes including the blue resist prints called 'indianas' in the Spanish areas, possibly denoting an oriental design origin. With such wrap-over gowns women wore aprons, the colour and fabric denoting status – white linen for upper servants, blue or brown sacking or similar coarse material for those involved in hard physical work. The studies made by Boitard of the working women in Covent Garden in the 1740s show that for really menial work there could be little pretence at any fashionable style; women wore scarves tied under hats, padded linen rolls to carry head loads, short skirts with patterned aprons and even cast-off male clothing such as coats and heavy leather shoes.

For all wage-earners, clothing took a considerable proportion of their income. At the end of our period in England, *very roughly* the average weekly wage for a labourer was 10s to 15s; women could earn as little as 3s for the poorest domestic work. Eden found that the prices paid for second-hand clothes were high in relation to income – 13s for a 'good foul weather coat' which would last two years, stout breeches to last one year at 3s 9d, and a shirt of dowlas (a strong cotton) cost 4s 6d; for women, a common stuff gown cost 6s 6d, a linsey-woolsey petticoat 4s 6d, the cheapest kind of cloak which would last two years also cost 4s 6d, and a pair of stays lasting six years were 6s.[75]

Those really poor, described by Defoe as 'the miserable that really pinch and suffer want', often wore several layers of clothing both to keep warm and to keep all their hard-earned wardrobe together. In Richard Cobb's survey of the clothing worn by suicides in Paris as recorded by the Basse-Geôle de la Seine for the late 1790s, he found this particularly applied to men; they wore as many as three pairs of breeches or trousers and several waistcoats. The suit was rarely mentioned, being an item beyond the reach of the really poor, their clothing gathered as it was item by item from the second-hand stalls.[76]

In England the beginnings of the Industrial Revolution ensured the glimmerings of improvement in the clothing worn by the poor classes at the end of the eighteenth century. The 1780s saw a series of inventions, based on earlier experiments, which rendered possible the large-scale production of

31 **'La Balayeuse'**, engraved after E. Bouchardon, from *Le Cris de Paris* (Third Series), 1738

The caraco with loose sack-back, worn with a striped skirt of mixed stuff, and with a coarse apron pinned over the bodice, forms almost a kind of working-class uniform in France.

textiles; developments in the production of cotton in particular, fostered by colonial trade, made cheap printed and plain materials available to a wider section of society. According to Francis Place, writing in the early nineteenth century, the great increase in the use of such washable cloths contributed to greater health and longevity. They were cheaper than the second-hand clothes, most of which 'are now sent abroad to Holland and Germany and some few to North America'. Few were needed in the independent United States, for the new inventions, very often brought over by English entrepreneurs, were enthusiastically taken up to make the country virtually self-sufficient in all but the most expensive fabrics such as high-quality silks and wools.

CHAPTER THREE

Wider Europe

This is the utility of travelling, when by contracting a familiarity at any place, you get into the inside of it, and see it in its undress. That is the only way of knowing the customs, the manners, and all the little characteristical peculiarities that distinguish one place from another.

Lord Chesterfield

So far, we have looked at fashions mainly in France and England, where the main factor in their introduction was the working of a completely free market in which no sumptuary legislation determined the clothes that people could or could not wear. Such countries where fashion was a strong impulse had long been unified nation states, with growing urbanization and a central authoritative fashion centre. In other European countries with less cohesive political structures or more recent political and social unity, a greater variety of taste and culture was to be found. Goethe, a townsman himself and a product of a century in which uniformity was something of an ideal, deplored the excessive individualism that he found in the German states with their lack of what he called a 'general culture', that uniformity of taste allied to a breadth of outlook which he found admirable in France and England.

Yet Europe was still a basically rural society, with few cities containing more than 100,000 inhabitants, and all but the greatest lived very parochial lives. Within the word 'Europe' we can discover a multitude of societies on every level; they included the tight-knit and still basically medieval guild-dominated cities of some areas of Italy and Germany, the expanding international capitals like Paris and London, the huge feudal estates in Eastern Europe and tiny village communities regulating their lives by the strength of unwritten traditions. Whether in the management of the agrarian serf-

dom of much of Russia, the Balkans, southern Spain and southern Italy, the infant democracy of the English House of Commons or the rule of patrician merchant oligarchies in German or Italian city states, all societies were governed by small groups of men (and sometimes women) interlinked by family relationships and personal loyalties.

Even in a relatively advanced industrial society like that of England, town wear differed to some extent from that worn in the country, and this difference was magnified many times over in the remote areas of, say, central Europe or any place where comparatively static regional peasant costume existed alongside cities where French and English fashions were increasingly the norm. It is impossible to discuss dress in the eighteenth century without at least giving a token recognition to the great varieties of dress which lie outside the general chronology of high fashion, although it is emphasized that only a small fraction of the range of dress seen at any one time in Europe can be mentioned in a book of this extent.

At the top level of society, people attempted on the whole to wear fashionable clothing derived from France, although this was in many cases in opposition to the desire of princes who wished to protect infant textile industries from foreign competition, and their subjects from the supposedly corrupting influences of foreign clothing. In Germany, there were a small number of important states like Saxony where rulers followed French tastes, magnificently embellishing their courts. At the other extreme, in Prussia, Frederick William I from the time of his accession in 1713 began to put into practice his views on martial simplicity in clothing. In fact the needs of the army were put first; the export of wool was prohibited so that the country could clothe its soldiers, and by 1725 Prussia was even exporting woollen cloth to the

32   The Interior of the Royal Exchange, 1777, by J. Chapman and P. J. de Loutherbourg

This was a meeting place for merchants from all over Europe and the East; those characterized by their costume include, on the right, a Jewish merchant with beard and huge cloak; in the centre, a Pole with knee-length caftan and trousers; and on the left, in the background, a Dutchman with round, baggy breeches and hands in his pockets.

Russian army (a monopoly that had once been English). This could be achieved because regulations were put into effect, as Frederick the Great tells us in his memoirs, limiting the amount of cloth in a coat to three yards. The king himself would have found this no hardship, for he was 'a decided enemy to gaudy dresses and new fashions; and while yet a boy, he had vowed vengeance against French wigs and gold brocade dresses, so they still continue to be objects of his displeasure'. This attitude was partly derived from a reaction against the Francophile tastes of his father, but also from a desire for economy; his wife and daughters commonly wore locally produced serge on all but the grandest occasions. The king himself 'till 1719 . . .

dressed sometimes in plain clothes, at others in uniform; in the following years he was scarcely ever seen but in the uniform of Colonel of the regiment of Potsdam grenadiers, blue turned up with red, yellow waistcoat and breeches, white linen gaiters with brass buttons and square toed shoes. Everything was made to fit very tight'.[1] Such was his hatred of anything French that when in the summer of 1730 the Crown Prince of Prussia made an abortive attempt to flee the country, the king, reported the English ambassador, sent him two suits cut in the French style 'to remind the Prince of his intended absconding to France which had rendered him unworthy to wear the uniform of a Prussian officer'. After a reconciliation the next year the king signalled his forgiveness by ordering his son a coat made in the Prussian style, which was, presumably, the very tight fit with military trimmings notably influenced by army uniform.[2] On state occasions, female members of the royal family were embarrassed at the lack of grandeur at court; when in 1728 the King of Poland and Elector of Saxony came with a magnificent entourage to seek the hand in marriage of the Princess Royal of Prussia, the intended bride was ashamed at the regimental air given by the Prussians' short coats which 'could not

Namen	Spanier	Frantzos	Wälsch	Teutscher	Engerländer	Schwöd	Polack	Unger	Muskawith	Türk oder Griech
Sitten	Hochmüetig	Leichtsinnig	Hinderhaltig	Offenherzig	Wohl Gestalt	Starck und Groß	Bäurisch	Untreu	boßhafft	Wie das Übrige weder
Natur und Eigenschaft	Wunderbarlich	Sehr gesprächig	Und Eifersichtig	Gantz Guet	Lieb-reich	Grausam	Hochwilder	Aller Grausambst	Guet Ungerisch	Zum Teüfel
Verstand	Klug un Weis	Fürsichtig	Scharffsinnig	Witzig	Anmuethig	Hartnäctig	Gering Achtent	Nochweniger	Gar Nichts	Oben Hluß
deren Eigenschaften	Männlich	Kindisch	Wie der will	Über Allmit	Weiblich	Unerkendlich	Mittlmäßig	Bluthbegirig	Unentlichrob	Zärt-lich
Wissenschaft	schrifftgelehrt	In Kriegssachen	Geistlichen Rechte	Weltlichen Rechte	Well Weis	Freuen Künsten	In Underschidlichensprachen	Ladeinischersprach	Krichischersprache	Politicus
Tracht der Kleidung	Ehrbaar	Unbeständig	Ehrsam	Macht alles Nach	Französischeart	Von Löder	Lang Röckig	Viel Färbig	Mit böltzen	Weiber Urt
Untugent	Hoffärtig	Betrügerisch	Geitzlichtig	Verschwenderisch	Unruhig	Überglauberisch	Praller	Veräther	Hartterätherisch	Veräterischer
Lieben	Ehr lob und Ruem	Den Krieg	Das Gold	Den Trunck	Die Wohllust	Köstlichespeisen	Den Adl	Die Aufruhr	Den Prügl	Selbst eigne Lieb
Krankheiten	Verstopfung	An Ligner	Un böser leüch	An bodogra	Verschwindsucht	Der Wassersucht	Den durchbruch	Un der freis	An Reichen	An Schwachheit
Ihr Land	Ist fruchtbaar	Wohlgearbeith	Und Wohllistig	Guet	Fruchtbaar	Bergig	Waldich	Und gott Reich	Voller Eiß	Ein Liebreiches
Krigs Tugente	Groß Müethig	Arglistig	Fürsichtig	Unüberwindlich	Ein See Held	Unuerzacht	In Ungestiml	Aufriererisch	Miesamb	Gar faul
Gottesdienst	Der aller beste	Guet	Etwas besser	Noch Andächtiger	Veränderlich Wie der Mond	Eifrig Im Glauben	Glaubt Allerley	Unmüeßig	Am Abtrinniger	Zwen einsolcher
für Ihren herrn	Einen Monarchen	Eine König	Einen Vaterärch	Einen Käiser	bald den baldt jene	Freue Herrschaft	Einen Erwölden	Einen Unbeliebigen	Einen Freimiligen	Ein Thiran
Haben überfluß	An Früchten	An Waren	An Wein	An Geträid	An Schiff-Weid	An Ertz Gruben	An Böltzwerch	In Alten	An Immen	Und weichenlache
die Zeit vertreiben	Mit Spillen	Mit betrügen	Mit schwätzen	Mit Trincken	Mit Arbeiten	Mit Essen	Mit zancken	Mit Müeßiggehn	Mit schlaffen	Mit Kränkeln
Vergleichung mit den Thiern	Ein Älefanthen	Ein Fuchsen	Einen Luchsen	Einen Löben	Einem Pferd	Einen Ochsen	Einen Bern	Einem Wolffen	Ein Esel	Einer Katz
Ihr Leben Ende	In Böth	In Krieg	In Kloster	In Wein	In Wasser	Auf der Erd	Im Stall	beym Sawel	In schnee	In betrug

have served as fig-leaves to our first parents and so strait that they did not move for fear of rending them'.[3]

Although he had infinitely more cultivated tastes, Frederick the Great continued the Prussian practice of wearing uniform on most occasions. A French visitor found him early in his reign awkward in demeanour, unwilling to carry his hat beneath his arm, and so used to wearing boots that he found it difficult to walk in shoes;[4] like his father, out of uniform he appeared in dark blue, Boswell finding him in Berlin in 1764 in 'a suit of plain blue serge with a star' – the star was the Prussian order of the Black Eagle.

The Prussian rulers were in a hurry to impose order and uniformity on a fairly recently united and sprawling country, and distinctive regional fashions were not much remarked on by foreign visitors such as La Motraye, who noted in 1726 that 'those of some rank go dress'd after the French but in General after the German fashion, the single women wear white that Long Vail which covers the Body

33 Völkertafel
'Kurze Beschreibung der In Europa Befintlichen Völckern Und Ihren Aigenschafften'

This illustrated table, dating from the end of the eighteenth century, lists the qualities as well as the costume of various countries in Europe. The French, not surprisingly, are the most fashionable, a startling contrast to the archaically dressed Spaniard still in trunk hose, ruff and round feathered hat.

OPPOSITE
34 A Hanoverian Party on a Terrace, 1725, by P. Mercier

The participants display stiff English elegance in their dress, tightly boned mantuas for the women, and for the men plain untrimmed suits and rather square, ponderous periwigs.

from head to Foot. In Winter they wear a kind of short Cloak, such as that which has been since few years brought to Fashion in England, but Linned with Furs as in Poland'.[5] The long light cloak, covering the head and body like an Arab mantle and dating back to medieval times, was common to many parts of Germany and Holland; Thomas Nugent in Hamburg in 1766 found women of fashion 'generally veiled with black silk like the ladies in Flanders',[6] the veil being worn over their ordinary clothing.

Throughout the eighteenth century, the German states that prospered were the more flexible ones able to impose protectionist policies and rely on the skills of immigrant workers, particularly in the textile trades. The range of home-produced textiles in Germany was wide; they included woollen cloth in Prussia, cotton and linen goods in many South German cities, and silk production at Krefeld, Berlin and Hamburg. Nugent noted that on a visit to Hamburg there was a flourishing trade in the weaving of velvets, brocades and damasks, and the

manufacture of gold and silver lace. He found that the quality of the goods was high, but in his travels through a number of the German states he found that rich silks were still imported from France (though forbidden in Austria and Prussia)[7] due to 'the passion the German ladies have for French modes'. To be 'französich gekleidet' was the fashionable ideal for women; for the men, Nugent noted that 'those that live anything tolerably decent, would not go without English stuffs and calimancoes',[8] although these too were forbidden in Austria and Prussia.

At the beginning of the century, foreign visitors noted the effectiveness of sumptuary legislation in the conservative free towns. Lady Mary Wortley Montagu, travelling through Germany on her way to Constantinople in 1716, felt that laws regulating dress prevented 'that Excesse which ruins so many other Citys, and has a more agreable Effect to the Eye of a Stranger than our Fashions'; in Nuremberg she found that people knew their place and dressed neatly according to it, whereas 'under the Government of absolute Princes' there was no such ease and people tried to dress above their means; even 'people of Quality' were sometimes 'tawder'd out & beggarly', attempting to follow French fashions beyond their purse.[9] For the ruling burghers in the towns, the self-imposed costume was sometimes a sober version of fashionable dress some years behind the times; a black suit with a short cloak remained almost a uniform for many conservative men in the religious and moral air of many of the north German towns. In some towns, the officials wore

35 **'Habillemens de Leipsic'** by J. A. Rossmässler

Leipzig was a centre of fashion in the eighteenth century, so it is not surprising to find French influence in formal dress, and England perhaps being the inspiration for the walking costume at the bottom.

Habillemens de Leipsic.

black, sometimes trimmed with lace and with a ruff, in styles reminiscent of early-seventeenth-century Spanish costume. Dark colours, of a mixture of imported and local stuffs, characterized the dress of many middle-class women; Goethe, who was brought up in Frankfurt, described the burgher's wife wearing a black dress of English cloth, a brown cloth skirt, a black camlet bodice, a black cotton cape, and a crape cap.[10]

Sumptuary laws were meant to keep the lower classes, and particularly women, in their subservient place; the clothing worn was therefore kept far behind current fashion, and some of the headdresses in particular were of considerable antiquity. The uniformity of such dress also appealed; in Hamburg, Nugent noted that 'the servant maids all wear the same kind of uniform habit consisting of a petticoat and jacket of serge on week-days; and of cloth or slight silk on Sundays; a linnen cap close to their heads and no farther than their ears, with an edging or border of muslin, a linnen or silk handkerchief and they all wear black aprons'.[11]

In the more conservative towns of southern Germany, serving maids' dress was even more old-fashioned; in Ulm, a travelling Berliner, Friedrich Nikolai, found at the end of the century that they wore long pointed bodices trimmed with silver, and with ruffs, but these were increasingly reserved for special occasions such as church-going or christenings.[12] Even patrician ladies sometimes wore regional costume, particularly in cities which had a long tradition of individual style. In Strasbourg, for example, a former Imperial city but a quasi-autonomous French fief since 1681, many women wore, according to a Hanoverian visitor in 1729, 'rich hats, broad over their Foreheads, and terminating on each Side in a Pick of considerable length', and gowns with a 'Multiplicity of Plaits';[13] these pleated gowns were seen by Goethe when he came to Strasbourg in 1770, but they were only worn by the elderly, French fashions having almost universally triumphed.

In fact by this time there were only pockets of striking regional costume, kept more as tradition than law (the only sumptuary legislation taking place in the second half of the century was at the smaller courts, limiting the privileges of rank, such as the numbers of liveried servants or the displaying of coats-of-arms); such costumes were noted for their extravagance of decoration or eccentricities of head attire. A characteristic of peasant dress has always been a love of jewellery, in many cases as either portable wealth or dowry, and this often caught the eye of a commentator; in 1719 Baron Pöllnitz, visiting a church in Lower Bavaria, was amazed to find the local girls wearing pearl necklaces and gold chains – rows of gold or silver chains, a German fashion since the sixteenth century, were widely worn in Saxony and Bavaria. It was in Munich, the capital of Bavaria, that Mrs Piozzi saw in 1785 the women wearing a 'stiff gold-stuff cap, as round, and hard and as heavy as an old Japan China bason . . . clapped close round the head, the hair combed smooth out of sight, and a plaited border of lace to it made firm with double-sprigged wire'.[14] This also dated from the sixteenth century, like many regional headdresses; from an even earlier period may have derived the curious headwear seen by Nugent in Lübeck, where the women wore 'a kind of straw bonnet, or rather basket, which projects in such a manner that you cannot see their faces'.[15]

The country where sumptuary legislation was most successfully imposed was Switzerland; the local authorities in Basel, Berne and Zurich published – on average every four years – 'acts against pride and superfluity in clothing and also other excesses and luxuries'. The main reason was religious (Switzerland had become a nation partly through its religious struggles, and the Calvinist church was still a very powerful influence), and the fierce independence maintained by the Swiss in the face of events in the rest of Europe, which, paradoxically, helped to create a climate tolerant to refugees and the propagation of liberal ideas. In addition, by the middle of the century, the Swiss were large producers of textiles such as cotton, light silks (ribbons were a speciality), wool and linen. The laws encouraged people to wear locally produced linen for headdresses, collars and cuffs, instead of imports from the Netherlands.

A typical act was that passed in Berne in 1708, which forbade everyone to wear smooth or flowered velvet, satin or brocatelle, except for official dress; suits made entirely of damask were only to be worn on feast days and Sundays, as were light silk gown and suit linings. To keep abreast of the current fashion, the 1708 act legislated against the large wigs with high fore-tops, and those with knotted ends (campaign wigs); wigs of any sort were forbidden to those under twenty. To prevent women wearing the fashionably ornate skirts, frills and falbalas were forbidden, as were mantles decorated with ribbons and lace. Later regulations inevitably focused on hoops, but this was a case in which the fashion proved too strongly implanted for the legislators, for they admitted defeat in 1737 by saying that they should not be 'too large and wide'.[16]

The success of the laws can be seen in the number of prosecutions; in 1727 in Basel, 210 women were prosecuted, the majority servants who had wished

36 **Patrician girl from Strasbourg**, 1729, from *Eigentliche Vorstellung der Heiligen Strasburgische Mode . . .* 1731

This traditional costume with its peaked triangular hat and pleated skirt was worn by well-to-do girls in Strasbourg, for gala occasions and weddings.

to dress above their station, but the regulations limited also what could be worn by upper-class women. Those fortunate enough to live near the German borders, said Keysler in 1729, '. . . impatiently wait the return of Summer, in order to their visiting Zellerbad or Teinach, Seltze, Embs and other German Spaws, where they may indulge their gay Inclinations, free from the Restraints of the Laws of their Country'.[17]

Fewer cases were reported as the century progressed, but throughout our period, sobriety in dress was the most noted Swiss characteristic. As late as 1789 a Russian visitor to Switzerland found that laws still restricted the wearing of silk, laces and jewellery, and French fashions and cosmetics were unknown. In Zurich the men 'in general wore black coats and the women had a black woollen dress and wore hoods or veils'.[18] The regulations stipulated that black was to be worn by both sexes for church; women were to wear hoods of white linen, but after the middle of the century other forms of headdress made of black gauze or taffeta were to be seen. Servants who came to work in the cities were urged to retain their village dress for as long as possible, and this appears to have been complied with on the part of the women at least. The peasant girls' costume of dark gowns, red petticoats and jackets 'with a great superfluity of buttons' was worn with long plaited hair; Dr John Moore, travelling as tutor to the Duke of Hamilton in the late 1770s, found that the unmarried girls 'value themselves on the length of their hair, which they separate into two divisions and allow to hang at its full length braided with ribbons in the Ramillie fashion. After marriage these tresses are no longer permitted to hang down, but being twisted round the head in spiral lines are fixed at the crown with large silver pins'.[19] Both married and unmarried women wore straw hats decorated with ribbons. Although he found their dress on the whole attractive, except for the 'amazing number' of petticoats bunched up in a high waist, he could not say as much for the men, whose everyday dress consisted of black linen coat and waistcoat and linen breeches 'something like a sailor's trousers, but drawn together in plaits below the knees'[20] – these were virtually the trunk breeches of the late sixteenth century which had remained part of rural male dress along with the 'immense Beards' cultivated by some of the older men.

Outside the main fashion centres of Paris and, to a lesser extent, London, the most important capital city was Vienna, focal point for the varied nations – the German vassal states, Hungary, Bohemia and (after 1772) Poland – that made up the Habsburg territories and the Holy Roman Empire. With a treasury drained by mercenary alliances and frequent wars, successive rulers legislated to prevent the import of foreign textiles such as English woollen cloths (for there was a flourishing woollen industry, established by Flemish weavers, in Hungary). Foreign silks were also prohibited; a typical statute of 1749 permitted clothing to be worn trimmed with gold and silver lace or braid provided it was made within the boundaries of the Empire; this was later (1754) limited only to the upper classes, and in 1766 Maria Theresa freed all classes from sumptuary legislation. Vienna was itself noted for the quality of its luxury goods like fine embroidery, and, by the middle of the century, for fine silks. With the active participation of her son, the future Emperor Joseph II, the Empress Maria Theresa encouraged Italian and then French silk-weavers to work in the capital; the Austrian Florian Zeiss, who had studied in Paris,

Ein Frauenzimmer im Winter ausgehend
Demoiselle sortant en hiver.

37   **Young girl in winter costume**, engraving after K. Sperling, from *Kleidungs Arten in der Stadt Augsburg*, 1730

This is in essence a modest version of fashionable dress worn over a hoop, but with local features such as the emphasized front lacing and furred cap.

OPPOSITE
38   **'Swiss Landscape to represent the Peasants Dwellings and Manner of dressing'**, 1765, by S. H. Grimm

opened a drawing academy in 1758 in order to teach silk-designers. By 1765 when the revised edition of Savary's *Dictionnaire de Commerce* was published, silks of all qualities were listed as being produced in Vienna, and exported to all areas of the Empire, and even to Turkey.

The taste within the imperial family was for private simplicity; unless it was a gala day, the empress wore simple dresses, often of Viennese silk, and only black as a widow. Her son Joseph, an admirer of Frederick the Great, preferred a uniform

(ri/s Landschape to represent the Peasants Dwellings, and manner of dressing

— in his early years that of his regiment of Hungarian hussars, and later his own regiment of Light Cavalry. 'At home or on his travels he put on a simple dark-coloured dress-coat; in severe weather a green or dark blue frock-coat with a plain military cocked hat, boots and spurs'.[21] His attempts in the 1780s to achieve a healthy simplicity in women's dress by legislating against tight stays and paniers met with no success.

Within the Empire, Prague and Budapest had the status of semi-capital cities, and visitors commented on the mixture of quasi-fashionable clothing and the oriental elements such as fur trimming which characterized dress at all social levels in central Europe, due to the proximity of Turkish territory. Lady Mary Wortley Montagu on a visit to Prague in 1716 found aristocratic ladies imitating Viennese court fashions, with high decorated headdresses, excessively furbelowed petticoats, and huge hoops; later in the century Nugent found that these ladies had begun to adopt French taste, but that 'other women of the better sort wear furred caps like the Grecian women, long clokes with large necks, some of them of sattin lined with taffeta, and petticoats of

the same but very short'.[22] In 1786 Mrs Piozzi found ladies attending the opera in Prague cut an odd figure in their 'rich embroidered caps or bright pink and blue satin headdresses, with ermine or sable fronts, a heavy gold tassel hanging down from the left ear'.[23] She found that ladies dressed very richly, but wore no powder on their hair.

Even more influenced by Turkish elements in dress was Hungarian costume, its popularity and glamorous appeal extending beyond the confines of the country itself. The Hungarian hussar troops had helped to save Vienna from the Turks at the end of the seventeenth century, and came to the aid of the new Habsburg ruler Maria Theresa when in 1740 the Austrian territory of Silesia was seized by Frederick the Great. Maria Theresa was also Queen of Hungary; not only was she herself depicted in Hungarian coronation dress, but she also dressed her son Joseph in this costume, some of which survives. For men, the costume is worth describing in detail,[24] for it was to turn up not only as a popular masquerade dress, but also as an influence on informal fashionable clothing. It consisted of tight-fitting trousers with braided seams tucked into boots, a tunic ('dolman') with a slanting triangular flap below the belt fastened with a twisted sash, and a pelisse ('mente') lined or edged with fur and with a frogged or tassel fastening. Dressed in this exotic costume, the Hungarian nobility appear like so many glamorous Hollywood extras in the large painted group scenes depicting life at the Viennese court.

For the women, the tight-fitting dress, often of the finest French silk, fastening at the front with tiny jewelled buttons, and the tiny embroidered cap, was Turkish in detail. Lady Mary Wortley Montagu found it 'extreme becoming'; a fashionable lady wore 'a Gown of Scarlet Velvet lin'd and fac'd with Sables, made exact to her Shape and the Skirt falling to her Feet. The Sleeves are straight to their Arms and the Stays button'd before with 2 rows of little Buttons of gold, pearl or di'monds. On their Heads they wear a Cap embroder'd with a Tassel of Gold that hangs low on one side, lin'd with sable or some other fine fur'.[25] An alternative style was to wear a sleeveless gown, heavily boned and embroidered on the bodice, laced down the front, showing huge chemise sleeves trimmed with lace and divided into three puffs of material fastened by ribbons. This latter version was more akin to the so-called 'peasant' style of costume with which we are familiar, with its emphasis on the bodice and the decorative shift sleeves; it was a costume much favoured by middle-class women, although the fabrics used were usually not the rich imported stuffs. As in all countries in this area of Europe, the middle class was tiny and of no importance; visitors commented on the gulf between the dress worn by the ruling nobility, and that worn by the serfs. Keysler, a German visitor to Hungary in 1730, found that

the peasants and lower sort of people dress very meanly. Among the latter the men are very proud of a furr'd mantle. Most of the women wear boots, and many of them a long furred gown, and have a kind of shift of a very coarse linen next to their skin, with a girdle round it at the waist. Their head-dress is a piece of white linen with two lappets hanging down behind. Blue is the usual colour worn here by both sexes.[26]

Nothing much had changed by the time that Wraxall visited Hungary almost 50 years later when he saw that 'few of the women had any covering below the knee except boots', and the postillions who drove him in their 'black sheep skins with the wool outward . . . long moustachios and fur bonnets, gave them the appearance of tartars more than of Europeans'.[27]

Even greater was the disparity noted between the feudal magnates of Poland and the mass of the peasant population, a situation exacerbated by the tragedy of Polish politics, with an elective monarchy and, for much of the century, a foreign king resident in Dresden. A Polish king, Stanislas Poniatowski, elected to the throne in 1764, was a cultivated man with French taste, but his preference for 'idle amusements and Gallantry' (Wraxall's phrase) did not fit him to cope with the anarchic mosaic of different peoples and religions that made up Poland, rendering it an easy prey for gradual dismemberment. Wraxall, visiting Poland in 1778, was appalled by the dirt and poverty of the cities, many kept alive only by the artificial needs of an extravagant court; there was hardly any middle class, except for a few German merchants in the semi-German cities to the north, like Danzig. He also noted the air of indifferent despair after the First Partition of Poland (1772) which had deprived the country of one third of its territory. He found a semi-primitive country aristocracy 'living in a style

39 **Hungarian Nobleman in hussar costume**, engraved by J.-B. Haussart, from *Recueil de Cent Estampes Representant differentes Nations du Levant . . .* 1714

40   **A Polish family scene**, 1773, by
D. Chodowiecki

On the left is a good example of patrician Polish national dress, dominated by the caftan (*kontusz*) with its hanging sleeves. The other participants in the scene, including the priest on the far right, wear international fashionable dress.

almost royal amidst the ruins of their expiring country'; although French fashions were worn, and especially at court, many of the nobility wore their national dress and had even tried to pass a law obliging the king to wear it.[28]

The wearing of this national dress was partly a protest at the state of their country and also a part of a long tradition of semi-oriental splendour; for men, the basic garment was a long caftan ('kontusz'), fastened at the waist with a sash, usually of the striped silks woven near Warsaw, with hanging sleeves and the front edge cut to curve over to one side, worn over tight trousers. Like the Hungarian nobility, the Poles shaved their heads and wore large moustaches (a Turkish mode which made them almost unique in Europe, where facial hair was very much the exception). Wraxall again on the Polish gentleman found: 'His head, which he shaves, is covered with a large fur bonnet. He wears a sort of hussar's dress with long hanging sleeves, a sabre that reaches to the ground, and boots. His enormous moustachios complete the fierce singularity of his figure.'[29] The powerful magnates with their retinues of servants, some in Turkish caftans with hundreds of silver buttons and some in embroidered Hungarian dolmans, were typified in the person of Karol Radziwill, Prince Palatine of Vilna, who wore

a short pomegranate-coloured kontusz, with vest and trimmings of an amaranth hue, a silver girdle embroidered with amaranths, a sword on a sheath of costly fur, yellow boots soled with silver, the whole surmounted by a mantle (zupan) of thick grey cloth lined with fur, and fastened round the neck by a silver Radziwill eagle. His roomy pantaloons were fastened round his body by a sort of apron, so that his kontusz might not be dirtied. Stuck at the back of his shaven head, and leaving his ears uncovered in the coldest weather, was a carmine cap trimmed with black lambskin. He wore felt shoes over his boots.[30]

Wraxall found the women's long gowns edged with fur and tied round the waist with a sash or girdle 'something Asiatic . . . which reminds me of

LE MARCHAND DE GATEAU.
*Dédiée à Mr. Chardin Peintre du Roi Conseiller et Trésorier
de son Académie Royale de Peinture et de Sculpture
Par son très Humble et très Obéissant Serviteur Le Prince*

41 **Title page** of J. B. Le Prince's *Première Suite de Cris
et divers Marchands de Petersbourg et de Moscou*, 1765

Le Prince was in Russia from 1758 to 1763, and the
several series of etchings that he produced are accurate
records of the costume. Here the peasant buying cakes
wears a voluminous shirt and baggy wide trousers which
are pushed into fur leg coverings wrapped around with
strips of cloth.

Greek or Turkish, more than French or German
modes'.[31] This dress, often with short fur-trimmed
oversleeves and decorated with frogging and tassels,
was a fashionable déshabillé with Austrian and
German princesses through the century, and in the
last quarter began to influence French and English
modes.

In contrast to the deliberate adoption in Poland of
national dress to preserve independence, if we turn
to Russia in the early eighteenth century the
opposite is the case; Peter the Great forced his
subjects to wear the western clothes he had seen on
his travels and which he himself wore. His edicts or
ukases against the wearing of Russian dress dated
from the end of the seventeenth century, when the
'general Habit which the Russes used to wear was a
long Vestment hanging down to the middle of the
Small of their Legs, gathered and laid in pleats upon

their Hips, little differing from the Habit of Wo-
mens Petticoats'.[32] This description comes from the
account of *The State of Russia under the Present Czar*
(1716) by Captain John Perry, who worked in Peter
the Great's service as a naval engineer; he was one of
that hardy band of foreign experts who were
employed in Russia throughout the eighteenth
century helping to bring the country into the
modern world, and whose published accounts of
their experiences in a country regarded as a kind of
barbaric Ultima Thule found ready ears in a Europe
fascinated by the immensity of contrasts to be found
within that huge empire. The nobility and the small
middle class, said Perry, were ordered to wear
'handsome Cloaths made after the English Fashion,
and to appear with Gold and Silver Trimming,
those that could afford it. And next he commanded
that a Pattern of Cloaths of the English Fashion
should be hung up at all the Gates of the City of
Moscow'.[33] Those daring to appear at court or to
enter the city in the old-style dress were to have
their coats cut off at the knees or to be fined (he
emphasized his point by mockery; when one of his
court jesters married in 1701, the courtiers were
made to wear the old-style Russian dress for the
crude wedding masquerade, which the Emperor
enjoyed). The long beards hanging down to the
chest were to be trimmed except for priests and
peasants, and those disobeying were to be fined 100
roubles a year. Perry noted that although there was
much complaint, most became reconciled to this
practice, although he found that some of his
workmen kept their shaved-off beards to be buried
in.

Peter the Great succeeded only too well in his
injunctions to his subjects to adopt 'Gold and Silver
Trimming' on their western suits. In 1714 Weber, a
German traveller in St Petersburg, was turned away
from a reception given by a Russian general for
wearing a plain untrimmed suit, and in 1732 the
English Resident at the Russian court noted that he
'never saw such heaps of gold and silver lace laid
upon cloth, and even gold and silver stuffs, as are
seen here',[34] many of the Russian nobles being
ruined by the expense of the changing fashions
where it was not unusual to pay £200 for a suit. By
the end of the reign of Peter, any dislike of the edicts
against Russian dress had been overcome, and the
nobles were quick to adopt what many considered
the excesses of Parisian styles without much taste or
elegance. The unsympathetic Lord Macartney
laughed at the Russians for their slavish acceptance
of French modes or dress and behaviour:

... in France it is the etiquette of fashion to begin
the spring season at Easter, and to mark it by dress;

76

the imitative Russian does the same and flings off his winter garments whilst the earth is covered with snow . . . At Petersburg a Russ gentleman of any fashion must have a Swiss also, or some tall fellow with a laced belt and hanger, which it seems are the indispensable accoutrements of a Parisian janitor.[35]

Lord Macartney, whose account of Russia was published in 1767, admitted that the production of textiles had increased enormously since the days of Peter the Great, who had established manufactories for linen and woollen cloth; by the middle of the century, in the reign of the Empress Elizabeth, imported raw silk was woven into 'velvets, paduasoys, tabbies, armazeens', and gold and silver lace was also produced, a sumptuary law of 1740 having failed to restrict this decoration on male clothing.[36]

Sumptuary edicts concentrated on male dress, where it was felt that imperial example needed force to back it up. Peter the Great had established assemblies on the western European model at St Petersburg, where noble ladies, dragged from their almost oriental seclusion into court and social life, could dance, converse, and play cards, dressed in English and French fashions. The traditional Russian costume, consisting of a chemise with long, very wide sleeves worn under a sleeveless tunic ('sarafan') with ornamental front closures and a band-like headdress ('kokoshnik') of precious stones and gold or silver thread, was described in the early years of the eighteenth century by an official of the Austrian embassy:

their shapes, unimprisoned by stays, are free to grow as nature bids, and are not of so neat and trim figure as those of other Europeans. They wear chemises interwoven with gold all through, the sleeves of which are plaited up in a marvellous way, being light and sometimes ten ells in length . . .

Their outer garments resemble those of Eastern women; they wear a cloak over their tunic. They often dress in handsome silks and furs, and earrings and rings are in general fashion among them. Matrons and widows cover the head with furs of price; maidens only wear a rich band round their forehead and go bareheaded with their locks floating upon their shoulders, and arranged with great elegance in artificial knots.[37]

With certain regional variations, this kind of dress was worn all over Russia by the women in the towns and the more prosperous country women; even aristocratic ladies residing on their estates continued to wear it, for it was only in the towns,

42 **'Paysanne Moscovitte dans son Habit simple'**, by J. B. Le Prince

Traditional Russian peasant costume (sometimes also worn on certain occasions by the middle classes) consists of the front-fastening tunic (*sarafan*) and the stiff curved headdress (*kokoshnik*).

Moscow and St Petersburg in particular, that western fashions were demanded. In any case the Russian climate demanded more practical clothes than Paris could dictate. In the 1720s an English lady, Mrs Ward, prepared for the Russian winter by adopting the native costume of a long-sleeved fur-trimmed gown called a '*foube*, or gown to travel in or to wear to any place where ceremony is not required'; for more formal occasions she wore a crimson velvet cloak lined with ermine and 'a broad fore-head cloth of black velvet lined with sattin, and a muffler under the chin, that is fastened to it on the temples, so that only eyes, mouth and nose are seen'.[38] To an English traveller[39] in Russia in 1789, the dress of the women reminded him of that worn by the Highland women, in particular the use of what he called the plaid, probably a woollen cloak in a checked pattern worn in the summer, although he admitted that 'the Russian women are . . . far more elegant and rich in their attire; nor is gold lace wanting to set off their charms'. He noticed the short jacket (often padded) worn by the poorer women, whereas those of higher class wore a silk cloak lined with fur. What he described as 'a napkin rolled about their head' was one of the great variety of linen headdresses (in winter of flannel) worn by many women of the lower classes which had charmed the French artist Le Prince when he had sketched them in the 1760s.

By the time that Catherine the Great became Empress (1762), the court nobility and the small but growing middle and professional classes had adopted completely the western style in clothing; French was the language at court and whole libraries and art collections were purchased from the west in a process so quick that Russia seemed almost in a frenzy to catch up with the 'culture' of the civilized nations of Europe. Yet, paradoxically, this was also a period when traditional Russian costumes returned to favour; they had lost their connotations of barbarism and could now be regarded as picturesque. In her later years, visitors found Catherine in either feminine versions of the dress uniforms of her various regiments, or, as Archdeacon Coxe found in the 1770s, 'according to her usual custom a Russian dress, namely a robe with a short train and a vest with sleeves reaching to the wrist, like a Polonaise'.[40] She was also fond of the loose-fitting 'sarafan' and a dark grey or mauve dress in the Livonian style with hanging sleeves. The Empress encouraged the wearing of Russian silks, but her attempts to introduce a Russian dress for court seem to have met with little success.

Livonia had been captured from the Swedes by Peter the Great, and Riga, the capital, was, next to St Petersburg, the greatest commercial centre in the Russian empire, relying heavily for its prosperity on the Baltic trade. Visitors described the dress there as being very close in style to traditional Russian costume; in 1774 Wraxall found the more fashionable women wearing sleeveless red silk gowns covered in gold lace, and on their heads pearl embroidered headdresses, costing in some cases many thousands of roubles.

For all classes, keeping warm in winter was a major preoccupation. The wise foreign traveller 'dressed in furs; a fur coat or pellice, boots lined with fur, and a cap resembling a muff . . . his hands cloathed with fur gloves are likewise thrust into a muff almost as large as a French jackboot';[41] Russians wore a range of furs from the fine sables worn by the nobility to the sheepskins of the poor. In remote Siberia, John Bell, a Scottish doctor journeying from St Petersburg to Peking in 1719–22, found both sexes in deerskin garments, the women in knee-length gown and buskins, and the

men in jacket and trousers, with extra protection given by a 'ruff made of the tails of squirrels to preserve the tips of the ears from the cold'.[42]

We have already seen that one of the basic working-class male garments was the functional pair of trousers. In Poland, Coxe had found in 1778 that in summer the peasants wore 'nothing but a shirt and drawers of white linen, without shoes or stockings'; continuing to Russia he saw a similar costume with the addition of 'sandals woven from strips of a pliant bark, and fastened by strings of the same materials which are afterwards twined round the legs and serve as garters to the woollen or flannel wrappers' worn for extra warmth; this was a costume uniformly worn all over the Russian territories.[43] The peasants, said Coxe, 'still universally retain their beards, their national dress, their original manners'; the beards were needed for warmth, and most wore the long shirt with wide sleeves belted over trousers in the summer, and in the winter 'the long swaddling coat either of skins or of coarse cloth lined with skins in winter, and in summer of cloth only', tied round the middle (buttons were too expensive) with a yellow or green sash.

It was a brave man who penetrated to those countries in the north of Europe which, according to Wraxall, retained 'the vestiges of Gothic ignorance' with 'not many charms to tempt the traveller'. Russia was interesting for its mixture of barbarism and civilization, astonishing the comte de Ségur, acting as French Minister Plenipotentiary at the Russian court from 1784 to 1789, for its combination of 'the manners of Asia and those of Europe, uncouth Scythians and polite Europeans!' Such surprising contrasts were not to be found in any other country, and certainly not in neighbouring Sweden, where already by the late 1760s an air of complacent self-sufficiency characterized society. Marshall in 1769 found that although small amounts of French silks and English woollen cloths were imported, the Swedes were able to manufacture their own medium-quality silks, and 'some gentlemen and nobles, through patriotism, wear Swedish cloth that is pretty fine',[44] although this was in fact more expensive than imported materials. The peasants in both Sweden and Norway were reasonably

---

43 Winter, by J. J. Horemans

This painting, one of a series of the four seasons, shows a good range of Dutch lower-class costume; the men wear either lumpish versions of semi-fashionable dress, or, as with the skater, traditional peasant dress with its tight-fitting doublet fastening with tiny buttons. The women wear short jackets and traditional frilled linen caps.

well-clad in cloth of their own making, a striking contrast to the situation in Poland and Russia. In Sweden, particularly in the second half of the eighteenth century, the court, dominated by French taste, was able to encourage (and produce) a wide range of fine and applied arts of the highest quality, comparable to those in France and England. In Denmark, there was no such centre of fashion; apart from a small royal circle and an aristocratic élite adopting French and English styles, the country remained provincial, with some German influence in dress. The last period of Danish influence and prosperity had been the early seventeenth century, and when Coxe visited Copenhagen in 1779 he remarked that the local costume reminded him of that worn by the Quakers in seventeenth-century Dutch paintings, the men in 'broad brimmed hats, black jackets, full glazed breeches of the same colour, loose at the knee and tied round the waist. The women were dressed chiefly in black jackets and petticoats, with a piece of blue glazed cloth bound on their heads'.[45]

Much regional costume evolved in periods of prosperity, and this was certainly the case in the Low Countries, where many of the styles were seventeenth-century in origin; in Holland in the 1760s an English traveller found that the peasants 'change their fashions as rarely as in Spain. With regard to the dress of the men, they have neither shape nor plaits [pleats], and their long pockets are set as high as their ribs; but that of the women is still more odd, their coats coming no lower than the middle of their legs and in North-Holland only to their knees'.[46] As a seafaring nation, many of the Dutch sailors and lower classes had adopted trousers 'wide enough to make some People a whole Suit', said Pöllnitz; in 1776 Parson Woodforde saw some Dutchmen at Yarmouth 'with monstrous large Trousers and with large wooden shoes'. When Mrs. Adams visited Holland in 1786 she noted that the clothing of the country women had not changed for 200 years, and they reminded her of the styles worn by the German and Dutch settlers in America: 'many of them wear black tammy aprons, thick quilted coats or russet skirts and small hoops ... Gold earrings are universally worn by them.'[47] Many Dutch women in fact kept to the seventeenth-century type of headdress; under a linen cap was a metal band crossing the top of the head with ear-irons at the side, from which the wealthier hung gold pendant jewels.

For a number of complex reasons to do with the early decay of feudalism and the demands made by a more flexible society, England had very little that could be called regional costume. The red cloaks of calimanco (a kind of hard-wearing glazed wool)

Habit of a Lady in the Highlands of Scotland in 1745.

Dame des Montagnes d'Ecosse.

44 **Habit of a Lady in the Highlands of Scotland** in 1745, engraved by T. Jefferys in *A Collection of the Dresses of Different Nations*, 1757

were worn by fashionable and working men in the country all over the British Isles, though by the end of the century they were more a working garment. Occasionally the garments had hoods, and they could vary in length. With the English settlers the hooded cloaks came to America; the imported cloaks were expensive (Anna Winslow in Boston paid £45 for a cloak and bonnet in 1772), and were probably restricted to the upper classes in the long-established and more cultivated colonies. In Virginia in 1773, Philip Fithian noted at church: 'Almost every Lady wears a red Cloak; and when they ride out they tie a red handkerchief over their Head and Face, so that whenever I saw a Lady, I thought she had the Tooth-Ach.'[48] We have already noted that stuffs in patterns of stripes and checks played an important part in working-class and regional costume; the distinctive Welsh dress worn by women consisted of a tall hat, black bodice or jacket and striped skirt of Welsh cloth, though the latter fabric was also worn for aprons and short gowns by working women in England.

In the Highlands of Scotland in the early eighteenth century, the 'plaid' was almost synonymous

with a checked pattern, although strictly speaking it
was a type of garment. Originally it was a long strip
of fabric which had to be pleated or kilted in
position on the man, the ends being thrown over
the shoulder and fastened with a brooch; the kilt
was later made as a separate garment, and the plaid
became the cloak (sometimes square, sometimes
like a long scarf) worn by both sexes. It was worn
by the gentry with matching trews, and also by
women; Edward Burt, who was employed in the
constructions of military roads in the Highlands,
noted: 'The Plaid is the Undress of the Ladies, and
to a genteel Woman, who adjusts it with a good
Air, is a becoming veil . . . It is made of silk or fine
worstead, chequered with various lively colours,
two breadths wide and three yards in length; it is
brought over the head and may hide or discover the
face according to the Wearer's fancy or occasion.'[49]

The colours of the plaids were ordered by area
and not by clan (the clan tartan system was very
much a product of the vogue for things Scottish in
the early nineteenth century); according to Miège's
fanciful view in his *The Present State of Great-Britain
and Ireland* (1715), 'the Colours they affect most are
Purple and Blue . . . a Dark-colour resembling that
of the Corps of the Heath, that they may not be
discover'd while they lie in the Heaths waiting for
their Game',[50] but brighter colours could be woven
to fancy, particularly for women's plaids, which
were usually worn over current fashionable dress. In
the early 1720s Daniel Defoe saw in Glasgow 'a
Manufacture of Plaiding, a stuff cross-strip'd with
yellow and red'; in various colours it was popular
for morning gowns and men's waistcoats. In 1747,
as a result of the Jacobite Rebellion, the use of
Highland dress was forbidden except for the Highland regiments; the prohibition lasted until 1782.
Smollett's novel *Humphrey Clinker* (1771) described
the misery felt by the

poor Highlanders . . . [who] are compelled to wear
breeches, a restraint which they cannot bear with
any degree of patience – indeed the majority wear
them, not in the proper place, but on poles or long
staves over their shoulders. They are even debarred
the use of their striped stuff called Tartane, which
was their own manufacture, prized by them above
all velvets, brocades and tissues of Europe and Asia.
They now lounge along in loose great coats of
coarse russet, equally mean and cumbersome and
betray manifest marks of dejection.[51]

The Lowland Scots wore English dress, as did most
of the Irish by the beginning of the eighteenth
century; paradoxically, while the English authorities only succeeded in Scotland in stirring up
feelings of patriotism through their banning of

Highland dress, in Ireland the death blow was given
to the traditional forms of Irish dress not by
proscription (which was virtually non-existent) but
by the gradual infiltration of London fashions via
Anglo-Irish society. Ireland even produced its own
silks, which well-connected people like Dean Swift,
and later Mrs Delany, tried to promote at the
English court; Swift in 1726 urged his correspondent Mrs Howard – one of the Women of the
Bedchamber to the Princess of Wales – to populariz-
ize the 'Irish silk plaid', and the princess did in fact
order some in 'purple, yellow and white silk'.[52] By
the middle of the century only the Irish remote
from towns wore the old dress, the men in 'little
Woollen Jackets, Breeches close to their Thighs and
over them a Mantle or Shagg Rugg deeply
fringed',[53] and the women in linen shifts (this was
sometimes the only everyday garment), woollen
dresses and, increasingly rarely, the shag-rug
mantle.

Although an increasing number of visitors found
their way to Scotland in the eighteenth century,
very few penetrated into Ireland, unless, like Swift,
they were virtually exiled there. Of all the countries
in Europe which combined a long tradition of
culture with a variety of regional customs, Italy was
the most popular and most visited country in
Europe. The Italians, said Viero in his *Costume Book*
(1783), were not only 'la Nazione più colta del
Mondo' but they lived in the garden of Europe,
blessed with a good climate, a fertile soil and
magnificent cities. Among their productions were
fine textiles; the northern cities like Milan and
Turin wove a wide range of silks from heavy satin
to fine gauzes, Genoa and Verona made high-
quality velvets, and a number of cities produced
various weights of woollen cloth. The peculiarities
of the Italian climate, with extremes of heat in
summer and cold in winter, demanded a greater
range of clothing than perhaps was common in the
more temperate countries of northern Europe; since
Italy was a major producer of luxury goods as well
as woollens, cotton and linen, Italian gentlemen in
particular were able to indulge in a love of finery
that appeared to outsiders one of their noted traits.
To Baretti, an Italian living in England, dress in his
native country appeared rich and luxurious compared to the austerities of his adopted land: 'Gentlemen throughout Italy in the hot months dress in the
thinnest silks, and use velvet in winter, besides cloth
of all sorts and colours, much laced or embroidered
if they can afford it, for they love finery as well as
the French. In winter likewise they line their coats
with costly furs; wear large muffs; and in many
parts adorn their hats with feathers.'[54] Yet although
the fabrics were rich, the styles were often plain;

Nugent summed it up at the beginning of his third volume of travels (which took place in the 1770s) by describing the dress of both men and women 'being a kind of medium between the stiff Spanish querpo and the fantastic French garb'.[55] By 'querpo' he meant the stiffly boned, tight-fitting style which affected Spanish dress, and to some extent that of the south of Italy where Spain was a dominant political and cultural influence. In the north of Italy generally, except for the distinctive patrician dress of cities like Venice and Genoa, men and women of the upper classes wore more restrained versions of French dress – usually not the very latest styles, for there was no enormously wealthy aristocracy as in France or England. Milan was probably closest to being a fashion centre, with a wide range of luxury fabrics available.

The city states of Italy had in many cases founded their wealth on trade in the Middle Ages, but by the beginning of our period the great merchant families had become aristocratic in taste and autocratic in rule. Nowhere was this more evident than in the rules regarding dress, particularly in Venice and Genoa, where officials regulated the magnificent clothes worn by the patricians. The costume worn by the Doge of Genoa was a soutane and robe of crimson satin (velvet in winter) with huge sleeves; the Doge of Venice wore purple, but when he appeared in public for the ceremonial occasions that made up much of Venetian life, he wore a white gown with a cloak of cloth of gold faced with ermine; Nugent described his traditional headwear as 'a purple cap, almost in the form of a mitre, which is encompassed with a border of gold plate, and rises behind almost in the shape of a horn'.[56] Official regulations demanded that on reaching the age of 20, Venetian patricians wore the *veste patrizia*, a kind of gown with huge sleeves in either black, red or violet according to rank and employment; senators usually wore red. The most usual everyday colour was black; Baretti tells us that in winter this gown was made of black wool bordered with ermine and tied with a silver clasp at the waist. 'His gown has large hanging sleeves. He wears likewise an enormous periwig, but no hat or cap though formerly a black cap was part of his dress. His summer dress is likewise black, open loose and shorter than that of the winter, with a silk coat under it made after an old fashion somewhat resembling what is called a Vandyke-dress.'[57] A noted characteristic of ceremonial and official dress is the incorporation of elements of antiquity conferring tradition and dignity; the silk 'Vandyke-dress' was a tunic cut in seventeenth-century style, a period that was popular for both servants' liveries (the Doge of Genoa's pages dressed in a kind of

early-seventeenth-century red velvet doublet and hose, with a shoulder cloak trimmed with gold lace and a plumed hat), and the robes of knightly orders.

The size of the sleeve was a mark of distinction; de Brosses, the first President of the Burgundian Parlement who visited Italy in the 1730s found that 'the higher his grade, the larger the sleeve. That of the Doge is as big as a lady's hoop'.[58] With his gown the patrician wore a periwig of enormous size, adopted from the fashion of 1709 by Doge Giovanni Correr, and kept for official dress. The patrician gown or toga was, by the second half of the eighteenth century, reserved for government and for formal receptions; for the latter occasions when dancing it was rather cumbersome; as a German visitor to Venice on the eve of the French Revolution reported, 'it really makes a most droll appearance'. Increasingly, the nobility tended to prefer the 'tabarro', a large round cloak with a turned back collar which was worn over ordinary dress.

Venetian noblewomen were governed both by traditional forms of clothing and by sumptuary laws. Over their everyday clothing they wore a kind of veil made of fine black silk sometimes edged with lace, and with an iron wire at the top so as not to disturb the hairstyle; this veil, called a 'zenda', 'zendale', or 'zendaletta', tied at the waist and was worn over the dress of black silk or velvet. Mrs Piozzi, visiting Venice in 1785, was charmed by this arrangement:

A skeleton wire upon the head such as we use to make up hats, throwing loosely over it a large piece of black mode or persian, so as to shade the face like a curtain, the front being trimmed with a very deep black lace or souflet gauze infinitely becoming. The thin silk that remains to be disposed of, they roll back so as to discover the bosom; fasten it with a puff before at the top of their stomacher, and once more rolling it back from the shape, tie it gracefully behind and let it hang in two long ends.[59]

Over the dress and veil, or as an alternative covering, women wore a knee-length cloak called a 'tabarrino', usually white or a light colour and sometimes embroidered in gold if worn by a recent bride. For there were sumptuary regulations (1707, 1709, 1732) forbidding all women, except unmarried girls and noblemen's wives in the first two years after marriage, to wear anything but black, and prohibiting gold and silver trimmings. According to Keysler who came to Venice in 1730, great numbers of persons 'offend against this law, that it is not strictly put into execution'; in fact the Venetian authorities wished to impress on foreigners the

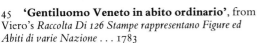

45 **'Gentiluomo Veneto in abito ordinario'**, from
Viero's *Raccolta Di 126 Stampe rappresentano Figure ed
Abiti di varie Nazione . . . 1783*

ABOVE RIGHT
46 **'Cittadina Veneziana in Cendale'**, from Viero's
*Raccolta Di 126 Stampe rappresentano Figure ed Abiti di
varie Nazione . . . 1783*

extent of luxury and affluence of the state. Many
visitors noticed a curious mixture of finery but with
no frenetic desire to keep up with the latest fashions;
the fashionable wardrobe of a Venetian lady in 1744
(taken from Molmenti's *History of Venice*) included
a 'black Patrician's mantle and petticoat, with
embroidery and lace . . . a Robe of black velvet', as
well as considerable numbers of sacks and other
gowns in plain silks or velvets, embroidered in gold
or silver.[61]

Other cities followed the lead of Venice in
insisting on black for the nobility. In Genoa, for
example, the nobleman wore black 'with a narrow
silk cloak hanging down his back; nor is his wig so
large as the Venetian's. He wears a plain hat,
generally under his arm. His lady dressed often in
colours; but her dress of ceremony is black silk or
black velvet according to the season'.[62] By law, the

wives of nobles were to wear coloured dresses for
only the year after marriage, but this was not strictly
observed, nor was the rule allowing jewellery to be
worn only six weeks before and six weeks after the
marriage.

The preponderance of black in many cities struck
the eyes of some observers, but the reasons for its
widescale adoption are not clear; it may possibly
derive from sixteenth- or seventeenth-century
Spanish influence, when black dye was hard to
achieve and the material correspondingly expensive. Yet in the eighteenth century black was popular
for all classes in Italy; it was worn by the nobility as
we have seen, and also by the middle classes, Goethe
observing in Verona in the 1780s that women of this
class wore the veste and *zendale* of black taffeta, a
costume suitable for those not devoted to cleanliness. In Rome, the men were often taken for abbés,
because they dressed solely in black; this was in
addition the dress worn at the papal court. At
Bologna, de Brosses found that the lower-class
women 'look like black phantoms as they cover
their bodies with black cotton shawls'.[63] Spanish
influence was particularly striking in the south of
Italy, in Naples and Sicily, in the first half of the
eighteenth century. The French traveller Labat who

visited Sicily in 1711 found fashionable ladies 'vétues à l'Espagnole . . . Elles ont toutes des voiles de soye noire sur la tête, & ne montrent qu'un oeil; mais c'est un oeil qui sçait parler à merveille'.[64] In the streets they were carefully chaperoned by lackeys dressed in the Spanish fashion with spectacles on their noses (the inexplicable fondness of Spaniards for spectacles amazed the rest of Europe), fiercely armed to protect their lady's honour and 'd'une manière qu'ils sembloient avoir étudiés sous Don Guichotte'. Most men of substance wore Spanish dress, black short doublet and breeches and the 'golilla', a plain standing wired collar introduced by Philip of Spain in the early 1620s; this continued as a kind of official costume for professional men until the end of the century. When the Englishman Swinburne visited the Kingdom of the Two Sicilies from 1770 to 1780, he discovered that although the upper-class women were now mainly following French fashions, for church and for the purposes of incognito they continued to wear the all-embracing cloak; the netted headdresses which were a feature of Spanish dress (and had been worn in southern Italy by all classes) were worn only by the lower classes, but this style was occasionally to be seen worn by a woman of fashion; so also was that of wearing two black silk petticoats, one pulled over the head, which Mrs Piozzi noted in Naples in the 1780s.

Greater extremes of poverty were to be seen in the south of Italy than in any other part of the country; in the very hot weather the children went naked, and visitors from northern Europe found the absence of adult underlinen as distressing as the sunburnt complexions of the women in an age in which whiteness was the norm. In Sicily the clothing was of poorer quality than on the mainland; the men wore rough serge breeches and waistcoats, with enormous cloaks. When the French traveller and artist Jean Houel visited Sicily at the end of the 1770s (his account is the most comprehensive in this period) he dressed like a Sicilian peasant[65] for ease of travelling, his hair in a net with ribbons, a turned-down hat (uncocked) and short boots. He noticed how Spanish influence remained in the types of cloaks worn by both sexes: the 'capotto', a vast cloak with a collar, and the 'palandrano', a cloak with a long pointed hood, both of these of black or dark brown wool. The women sometimes wore short mantles tying round the waist and falling down the back in a kind of tail.

We have already seen that the basic working costume for women throughout the eighteenth century comprised a shift, stays, petticoat and bodice. In very poor (or hot) countries women dispensed with the bodice, or wore the type with removeable sleeves, laced in at the shoulders.

In any society, distinctions are created by dress; in a relatively primitive peasant society where the monotony of agrarian life is punctuated by religious and secular feasts, holiday dress often assumes a great importance. It was the gala dress worn by the peasants on Sundays and holidays which many visitors to Italy found so attractive; the variety of costume displayed was enormous, some deriving from fashionable dress of the sixteenth and seventeenth centuries and much decorated with metal lace, semi-precious stones and embroidery. Mrs Piozzi found the holiday dress of the women in Naples in the 1780s to be 'a scarlet cloth petticoat with a broad gold lace at the bottom, a jacket open before, but charged with heavy ornaments and the head not unbecomingly dressed with an embroidered handkerchief from Turkey',[66] while the men appeared in 'thick blue velvet coats'. It was the variety of headdresses in particular that Mrs Piozzi found charming on a visit to north Italy in 1785; they ranged 'from the velvet cap, commonly a crimson one worn by the girls in Savoia, to the Piedmontese plait round the bodkin at Turin, and the odd kind of white wrapper used in the exterior provinces of the Genoese dominions'.[67]

A few years earlier Swinburne had visited Genoa, giving a fuller description of the headdress worn by the countrywomen there, who 'plait and twist their coal-black hair in a round upon the crown of their head; then fasten it together with a large silver or steel bodkin. The front is cropped and kept back with pomatum. In winter they wear a veil of white linen checked with red flowers, which they throw over their heads; it falls down to their hips, and some of them hide almost all their faces behind it'.[68] In many cities, sumptuary regulations prevented the wearing of rich jewellery made with precious stones, so countrywomen wore either starched muslin handkerchiefs (in Lucca they were arranged in turban shape), or straw hats with ribbons, as in Pisa or Florence. To Madame de Bocage in the mid-eighteenth century, the pretty country girls in Tuscany seemed like members of the chorus from the opera in Paris, and the description given some 30 years later by Mrs Piozzi conjures up the gracefulness of a costume drawing by Boquet, for they wore:

a very rich white silk petticoat exceedingly full and short, to shew her neat pink slipper and pretty ancle, her pink corps de robe and straps, with white silk lacing down the stomacher, puffed shift sleeves . . . with at least eight or nine bows of narrow pink ribbon, a lawn handkerchief trimmed with broad lace, put on somewhat coquettishly, and finishing

I **La Déclaration de l'Amour,** 1731
J.F. de Troy   Oil on canvas   BERLIN, CHARLOTTENBERG PALACE

II **La Toilette,** 1742
F. Boucher   Oil on canvas
THYSSEN-BORNEMISZA COLLECTION, LUGANO, SWITZERLAND

III **The Tailor**
P. Longhi   Oil on canvas
GALLERIE DELL'ACCADEMIA, VENICE

IV **A lady, possibly Mary Gunning, Countess of Coventry**
J. – E. Liotard   Pastel on parchment mounted on canvas   RIJKSMUSEUM, AMSTERDAM

V **Madame de Pompadour**
F. – H. Drouais   Oil on canvas   NATIONAL GALLERY, LONDON

in front with a nosegay . . . the hair is drawn away from the face, tight . . . under a red velvet cushion edged with gold, which gives the small Leghorn hat lined with green a pretty perking air.[69]

The peasant in Tuscany under a reasonably beneficent Habsburg regime were well-off, and were able to afford, said Mrs Piozzi, sets of garnet jewellery, for Italy was well supplied with the bright semiprecious stones which formed an important part of peasant decoration. In Naples, even the very poor women would not find it incongruous to be barefooted and yet wear the locally produced red, white and black coral, emeralds and cameos; in Rome a French visitor found in 1709 the poorer women wearing large necklaces of amber and matching pendant earrings; in the late 1740s while visiting Treviso, Casanova was attracted to a countrywoman who displayed more than 150 sequins' worth of gold pins and arrows fastening her plaits, in addition to a gold chain wound 20 times round her neck.

47　**'Contadina del Pian de Ripoli'**, from Viero's *Raccolta Di 126 Stampe rappresentano Figure ed Abiti di varie Nazione . . . 1783*

Contadina del Pian di Ripoli　　*Paisane du Plan de Ripoli*
Luogo presso Firenze.　　　*endroit pres Florence.*

Italy, in spite of its natural geographical advantages and its long traditions of design, was a chequerboard politically, where a number of independent states managed their affairs with greater or lesser efficiency, and if not achieving the greatest happiness of the greatest number, made important cultural contributions to the life of the country. Such an example was the Naples of Charles III (his accession took place there in 1734), where appalling poverty, superstition and a Spanish indolence went side by side with the rediscovery of much of our heritage of classical antiquities, and with major contemporary developments in architecture, painting and music.

Spain, a country that had had so much influence in earlier periods on the culture and dress of the rest of Europe, was by the eighteenth century no longer a dominant power. Its isolation was emphasized by the distinctive Spanish men's dress which had evolved in the early seventeenth century, Philip IV having banned French fashions from court in 1623. He had introduced a short tabbed doublet and narrow knee-breeches, a golilla collar starched and raised on a wire frame, and flat shoes without a high heel; other manifestations of Spanish dress recognized all over Europe included a ruff (as an alternative to the collar), a moustache, and spectacles, and above all, 'une gravité des plus grandes & une morgue des plus fières', noted the abbé Labat,[70] who, travelling in Spain in the first decade of the eighteenth century, found nearly all the men of quality wearing the traditional black suit and cloak in early-seventeenth-century style.

The cloak, also dating from the seventeenth century, was an essential part of Spanish dress, being worn by all classes. An English visitor to Spain in 1786–7 found how 'it is pleasing to see the genteel young Spaniard in his capa, which he throws into a thousand graceful forms, each remarkable for its peculiar ease and elegance, such as no foreigner can imitate'.[71] This cloak was usually brown, and remained as part of the dress of the upper classes when the rest of the Spanish dress was limited to court and official costume; Almaviva, a grandee of Spain in Beaumarchais' *The Barber of Seville* (1775) wore over his satin suit a 'grand manteau brun, ou cape espagnole'. In the second half of the century, the old costume disappeared except for official dress, and by the early 1760s an English clergyman, the Revd Clarke, regretted the fact that the Spanish 'have quitted that old dress, which looks so well on our English stage'; it had long been the costume of some of the popular *Commedia dell'Arte* characters. It remained, however, a popular masquerade costume. Dr Bartholo, Rosine's tutor in *The Barber of Seville*, wore, according to the stage directions, 'un

habit noir, court, boutonné, grand perruque, fraise & manchettes relevées',[72] but this was increasingly regarded as eccentrically conservative, especially when worn with a large wig.

In the early 1760s Baretti visited Spain to find that most men dressed in the French manner, with the addition of the Spanish cloak, and the sombrero, a 'hat with the flaps down', although this costume was frowned on by the authorities, for it disguised identity and concealed weapons. Another traditional feature of Spanish dress was the hair gathered up in a black net, observed by Arthur Young on his visit to Spain in 1787, worn by the middle classes and the well-off men with their French clothes. The colours of men's clothes were dark, often black, a sobriety seen at the highest levels with the Spanish kings. None were in any way leaders of fashion, preferring a sporting simplicity to French court grandeur. Charles III (1759–89), an ugly but appealing king who played a considerable part in restoring the artistic glories of Spain, was happiest in his hunting costume of plain grey cloth frock, leather breeches and boots; on gala days, according to Swinburne, 'a fine suit is hung upon his shoulders, but as he had an eye to his afternoon sport, and is a great economist of his time, the black breeches are worn to all coats'.[73] Baretti, in the 1760s, found that he preferred 'the fashion

48 'El Paseo de las Delicias en Madrid', by F. Bayeu

Promenading in the park in Madrid are these fashionably dressed Spaniards. Most of the men wear French dress, and one, in the background, the capacious, traditional Spanish cloak. Some of the women wear the mantilla which serves, as an English visitor said, as hood, cloak and veil.

that was used in his younger days, and he always appears impatient to undress, being never easy until he resumes his grey frock and leather waistcoat'.[74] The king's grey frock was made in Segovia, a long-established centre for the woollen trade which was based on the excellent wool produced by the Spanish merino sheep. Other textile industries made Spain self-sufficient; Valencia was the centre of the silk industry, with 5000 looms by the end of the 1780s, and light silks were made in Madrid and Barcelona; cotton also was woven in Barcelona (the raw material came from the Spanish colonies in America), and linen at Corunna. Spanish silks were exported to their own and to Portuguese colonies in South America, as was woollen cloth for these growing and important markets. But in spite of an appreciable increase in national prosperity in the second half of the eighteenth century, most foreign visitors were exasperated by the inability of the country to take up the possibilities offered by its range of natural resources, a failure they attributed to the inherent indolence of the people, for the peasants, said Swinburne, spent all their time 'wrapped up in a cloak, standing in rows against a wall, or dozing under a tree'.

Joseph Townsend, one of that breed of English travellers inspired by recent discoveries and improvements in agriculture and science, found it rough going in Spain ('a good constitution' was essential for the hazards of getting round the country) when he came there in the late 1780s. He found hardly any middle-class society, and a large gulf between the nobility and the poor. Like all visitors to Spain, he was attracted to the distinctive and seductive clothing worn by the women, in particular the 'mantilla', 'a kind of muslin shawl, covering both the head and shoulders, and serving the various purposes of the hood, of the cloak, of the veil',[75] which, used for flirtatious display, almost became an art form. At mass, the ladies wore their normal dress (this was French in taste) but with an extra black silk petticoat, the 'basquina', over the top. This fondness for layers of skirt coverings had been a characteristic of Spanish dress ever since the abbé Labat, in the early years of the century, noted how women had seven or eight skirts, the one covering their feet being called a 'garde pied', for a lady showing her foot to a man indicated her readiness to grant him further favours.

To foreign visitors the most striking costume was that worn by the lower-class people of fashion, the *majo* and the *maja*; Baretti was told that the *majo* was 'a low personage between the poissard of Paris and the city-spark of London … a low fellow who dresses sprucely, affects the walk of a gentleman, looks blunt and menacing and endeavours after dry wit, upon every occasion'. He goes on to describe the dress, which 'consists in the man of a tight waistcoat, tight breeches, white stockings, white shoes tied with a ribband instead of a buckle, the hair in a net of various colours, and a *montéra* over, instead of a hat. The *montéra* is a cap of black velvet, and of a particular cut which fits the head exactly and covers the ears'.[76] In Beaumarchais' *The Barber of Seville*, this was the costume worn by Figaro, the scheming valet with an eye to the main chance, and it remained for many years in the popular imagination as the epitome of Spanish dress.

The *maja* wore 'a tight jacket, so open before as to form two hanging flaps under the breast, something in the form of wings, with sleeves close to the fist, a short petticoat of any colour, a black apron, a striped handkerchief carefully covering the whole net, and the *montéra* exactly such as the man. The

seams of both dresses (male and female) are not sowed but kept together by interlacing ribbands'.[77] This was a popular dress for masquerades, and, by the 1780s, it had begun to influence the informal déshabillé of the Spanish aristocracy, following the general trend in costume in that decade of adopting picturesque versions of working-class dress.

As with all costume showing strong regional traits, the headdresses were both inventive and varied. A visitor to Cadiz in 1773 found that the ladies in the evening 'fixed glow-worms by threads to their hair, which had a luminous and pleasing effect'; in Aragon Baretti found old women wearing the *montéra*, and younger women with their hair netted; near Pamplona the hair was interwoven with coloured ribbons, and in Valencia it was fastened with a large silver pin. Usually the dress of the poorer women was made of a brown coarse woollen mixture, in jacket and skirt style, but in northern Castile in 1760 Baretti found a vestige of the old Spanish style which 'consists of a robe, generally brown, that runs close to the neck and wrists, with several cuts along the sleeves from the shoulder to the elbow and a broad girdle round the waist'.[78]

The most usual dress for the Spanish male peasant was a jacket and breeches of dark brown locally produced cloth; even the poorest, said Labat, possessed a cloak, which was needed for warmth and bedcovering. Whereas most poor men in the rest of Europe would wear a wig of some kind, in Spain, Labat noted, men grew their hair long, shaving it at the top in the form of a triangle (to distinguish it from the round clerical tonsure), a practice commended by doctors for health; they then bound it up into a net at the back.

In summer, the very poor wore linen trousers and waistcoats; their feet were clothed in what reminded Townsend of theatrical 'buskins … called by them *alpargates*, which are made of the esparto rush', tying round the legs with strings, and which lasted only two weeks. By the end of the eighteenth century some uniformity had set in to the dress of the poor, but in the more remote areas individual characteristics still ruled; Swinburne in the mid-1770s saw mountaineers in Barcelona with netted hair, a handkerchief tied round the neck, a short striped waistcoat, a red jacket with large silver bell-shaped buttons, blue and white striped breeches and a great-coat embroidered with white thread.

In Portugal, which had very close links with Spain, the costume worn was very similar. Women wore a version of the Spanish mantilla called a 'velo', made usually of fine black silk, over their richly embroidered dresses in the French mode; although there were sumptuary laws prohibiting

49 The Shop, by L. Paret

The shop specializes in luxury goods, including millinery items such as ribboned straw hats, carnival masks and lace – fine silk lace spills from paper on the right-hand side of the counter. A wealthy couple examines a selection of goods. The seated gentleman wears a silk embroidered suit in the French style; his coat, lined with sable, is trimmed with decorative frogged fastenings. His wife's dress is a mixture of international fashion and that of Spain; her fur-lined pelisse and black silk dress are acceptable mid-eighteenth century European costume, but the mantilla is typically Spanish as is the jewelled comb which she holds, worn on gala days in the high-piled coiffure. To the right stands her maid, also wearing a mantilla, which has fallen back to reveal her hair in the Spanish net.

'all ornaments of gold or silver lace or embroidery', these were usually ignored and dress (of both sexes) exhibited a greater luxury and opulence than in Spain. According to Baretti, who visited Portugal in 1760, the famous earthquake of 1755 had deprived many women of their clothing, 'and they dress as well as they can, and have no prevalent or national fashion'. The poorer women, however, had in some areas kept to the large wide sleeves of the early sixteenth century – a period when Portugal was prosperous and influential – and many showed variety in their headdresses, some of ribbons and some with real or artificial flowers. Both

men and women of the lower classes wore 'a kind of network silk purse over their hair, with a long tassel behind and a ribbon tied in a bow-knot over the forehead', according to one of the few published accounts of Portugal, written by Richard Twiss in 1772–3.[79] Twiss found, as many did in Spain, that the contrasts between rich and poor were striking. On the one hand he found an elegant aristocracy covered in the precious stones from their South American colonies, listening to the Italian opera at Belem or walking through the royal palace of Queluz, built and decorated in the French rococo taste; on the other hand a poor peasantry in dark, coarse cloaks and slouched hats – a vignette that stayed in Twiss's mind was a man in Lisbon selling the services of a baboon to pick out lice from the hair of the poor.

It is these contrasts that sum up the extremes and variety of costume which could be seen in eighteenth-century Europe, and which should be born in mind in any discussion of dress; much regional costume changed only very slowly, and at any given time one would find society built up of layers, consisting of the most recent fashions imported from France or England, middle-class versions with local adaptations demanded by custom and law, and the virtually static traditional dress in the more remote areas, where costume varied from village to village, so tightly knit were the small communities.

CHAPTER FOUR

1740–1770: The triumph of the rococo

The beauty of intricacy lies in contriving winding shapes ... as the modern lappet when it is brought before. Every part of dress that will admit of the application of this principle, has an air (as it is term'd) given to it thereby; and although it requires dexterity and taste to execute these windings well, we find them daily performed with success.

W. Hogarth, *The Analysis of Beauty*, 1753

This period encapsulates all that is graceful and elegant in clothing in the eighteenth century. It marks the change from the symmetry and geometric restraint of mid-eighteenth century costume to the ornamented breaking up of the surface of dress, which was such a feature of women's clothing in the middle of the period; dress moves from the sobriety of the classical to the lightness and wit of the rococo, but one must note that in the late 1760s there appeared the beginnings of the neo-classical movement in dress, the antithesis of the rococo. By about 1730 in France the *style Régence* had turned into the rococo, the full development taking place in the 1740s, although in England this did not really happen until the following decade.

Men

For men, too, mid-eighteenth-century costume was characterized by a retreat from the almost sculptural heaviness of cut and material which we noted in the earlier period, although fashions were slower to change; the classical uniformity of the suit was international. However, from about 1740 there was a definite decrease in the amount of stuff needed for the coat; the side pleats were reduced in size and there was a perceptible curving away of the front edge of the coat from just above the waist. With this slight narrowing of cut, men were increasingly reluctant to fasten the buttons of their coats at waist level, but the emphasis moved to buttoning at mid-chest; this allowed more of the waistcoat to be seen and also perhaps encouraged the gesture so typical of the 1740s, that of placing the hand through the waistcoat over the heart. From the end of the 1760s the side flare of the coat had virtually disappeared, and another change to be noted from the middle of the century was the placing of pockets higher up, just below the waist. From the 1740s the waistcoat really began its upwardly mobile career; in 1740 it was only a few inches shorter than the coat, but by the end of the decade the discrepancy had increased so that it was only mid-thigh length, and it, too, had begun to curve away from waist to hem. By the end of the 1740s, sleeved waistcoats were only worn by the older man or the valetudinarian, the side stiffening had gone, and, increasingly, the back part of the waistcoat was cut much shorter than the front; with the greater popularity of embroidery, men would often buy a pair of embroidered waistcoat fronts which would then be joined to a plain back section. From the middle of the century, a much greater range of waistcoats was available; they included the formal sleeveless waistcoat or 'gilet', and a much shorter sporting waistcoat, usually double-breasted and sometimes with an assymmetrical flap fastening. With this shortening and curving of coat and waistcoat, the breeches also had to tighten up for the new slimmer silhouette; fastening below the knee in a buckled or buttoned band, they were closer-fitting to the thigh, the *London Chronicle* of 1762 noting 'long Trowser-like Breeches'. From the middle of the century, the central front buttoning began to be replaced by a 'fall' or flap front, covering the front opening.

The total effect was to tighten up the rather heavy, triangular male figure; a smaller head (wigs tightly curled at the sides with the hair drawn off the face into a bag at the back) and neater outline with

fewer projections by way of reinforced side pleats and large cuffs was the fashionable line. From about 1750 cuffs were smaller and narrower; a popular style, particularly on the frock coat, was the cuff *à la marinière*, a small round cuff with slightly scalloped vertical flap edged with three to four buttons.

The idea current at the beginning of the century that 'to keep to the propriety of dress, the coat, waistcoat and breeches must be of the same piece' (the *Guardian*, 1713), was no longer widely held. It remained, however, the rule for the patterned flowered velvet suits which played a part in every gentleman's wardrobe for winter. When Boswell made his preparations for foreign travel in 1763, Lord Keith urged him to take for the more formal German courts 'against winter, a complete suit of worked flowered velvet, the buttons of velvet';[1] in the same year Lord Riverstone had made in Paris a suit of claret velvet, coat, waistcoat and breeches in a small stylized design, which still exists, with its bill (it cost him £27 10s 3d, with £2 5s 6d to have it carried duty-free) in Birmingham Museum and Art Gallery. Gradually the suit became the coat and breeches only, the waistcoat being made of different material, usually embroidered. On the Grand Tour in 1754 the Adam brothers in Genoa bought black velvet suits 'with which we can wear all our waistcoats by turn'. Very often the embroidery on the coat matched that on the waistcoat; in 1753 Mrs Delany admired at court the Duke of Portland's appearance in 'dark mouse-coloured velvet, embroidered with silver . . . the waistcoat Isabella satin embroidered the same as the coat'.[2] The elegant Bellarmine in *Joseph Andrews* (1742) admired himself in 'a cut Velvet Coat of Cinnamon Colour, lined with a Pink Satten embroidered all over with Gold; his Waistcoat, which was Cloth of Silver, was embroidered with Gold likewise'.[3]

By the end of the 1740s the suit could (except for court and formal wear) be made of three different colours and stuffs. In Smollett's *Roderick Random* (1748), the absurd Captain Whiffle appeared thus:

His coat, consisting of a pink-coloured silk lined with white, by the elegance of the cut retired backwards, as it were, to discover a white satin waistcoat embroidered with gold, unbuttoned at the upper part to display a brooch set with garnets that glittered in the breast of his shirt, which was of the finest cambric edged with right Mechlin. The knees of crimson velvet breeches scarcely descended so low as to meet his silk stockings, which arose without a spot or wrinkle on his meagre legs, from shoes of blue Meroquin, studded with diamond buckles that flamed forth rivals to the sun.[4]

The clothes themselves are not here held up to ridicule, but the *manner* in which the effeminate Captain wore them. In the same novel, the hero Roderick bought a new wardrobe in London, which consisted of:

five fashionable coats, full mounted, two of which were plain, one of cut velvet, one trimmed with gold, and another large plate buttons, the other of blue with gold binding; one waistcoat of gold brocade; one of blue satin embroidered with silver; one of green silk trimmed with broad figured gold lace; one of black silk with fringes; one of white satin, one of black cloth and one of scarlet; six pair of cloth breeches, one pair of crimson, and another of black velvet . . .[5]

At this period the fashionable man appeared like a bird of plumage in bright colours.

With formal dress, furs were an important addition both for luxury and warmth. They lined court suits in winter, the soft fine furs like ermine, squirrel and sable being the perfect complement to silk velvet and brocade. In 1740 Mrs Delany saw Lord Baltimore in 'light brown and silver, his coat lined quite throughout with ermine'; in 1745, for the wedding celebrations of the Dauphin, the marquis de Stainville wore a coat of cloth of silver lined with sable, the lining alone costing 50,000 livres. The degree of bulkiness created by a fur-lined suit was permissible in the mid-eighteenth century – when, incidentally, there were some very cold winters – but by the end of the 1760s the slimmer line of fashion limited furs to edgings; only the vulgar or the effete could wear, like the duc de Villars in 1769, 'a gold stuff coat lined and turn'd up with sable in gold tassels and loops, all his diamonds & a great sable muff'.[6]

When François Mazerac entered the service of James Boswell in September 1763, he listed the wardrobe of his new master; this began with the formal suits of one colour and then the individual coats, waistcoats and breeches. Boswell's favourite suit was of scarlet trimmed with gold lace; this he wore 'with white silk stockings, handsome pumps . . . silver and gold sword-knot, Barcelona handkerchief and elegant tooth-pick case' at a formal

50 **Duval de l'Epinoy**, by M. Q. La Tour

The sitter retains the rather conservative knotted wig, and the silk hose fastening over the breeches. The coat, of superb silver watered silk, is still stiffly reinforced at the side pleats, so that it echoes the width of the female hooped skirt of this period.

51 **Sir Edward Dering**, *c.*1759, by P. Batoni

One reason for the success of Batoni was his flattery of his aristocratic sitters, not just by his lovingly rendered depiction of luxury fabrics such as this sumptuous velvet gown lined with squirrel, but also in his use of accessories from classical antiquity to create an atmosphere of learning and leisure.

assembly in October, and in December 1764 he wore the coat and waistcoat with buckskin breeches and boots, a mixture of the rich and the fashionably sporting with which he hoped to impress Rousseau. Increasingly by the 1760s suits were being made of cloth; for summer Boswell was urged to buy 'fine camlet with a gold thread button but no lace' (camlet was a closely woven worsted sometimes mixed with silk). His wardrobe inventory included only one frock of brown stuff, but this may have been because Boswell was travelling to the more formal German courts where the frock was still mainly a sporting garment, and because his own personal taste was for a gaudy finery.

In England by the early 1750s the frock was the most common ordinary wear; when Peregrine Pickle, the hero of Smollett's novel of the same name (1751) met Emily he wore 'a genteel grey frock, trimmed with silver binding', and *The World*

(1753) noted at Newmarket that it was difficult to 'distinguish between his Grace and his Groom ... for a pair of boots and buckskin breeches, a fustian frock, with a leather belt about it, and a black velvet cap, is the common covering of the whole town'.[8] To an English visitor in Paris in 1753 the frock was synonymous with liberty; in his 'full-dressed Coat, with hellish long Skirts, which I had never been used to, I thought myself as much deprived of my Liberty, as if I had been in the Bastile; and I frequently sighed for my little loose Frock, which I look upon as an Emblem of our happy Constitution; for it lays a Man under no uneasy Restraint, but leaves it in his Power to do as he pleases'.[9]

Frocks were made of a range of materials, usually wool or wool mixtures; the *London Chronicle* of 1762 noted the popularity of red shag frocks, shag being a worsted fabric with a long pile like velvet. Linen or cotton frocks (or fustian, a cloth with a linen warp and cotton weft) were worn in summer, close relations to the working-man's smock from which they derived. By the end of the 1760s de Garsault's *L'Art du Tailleur* acknowledged the existence of 'la Fraque, espèce de Justaucorps Leger, nouvellement en usage',[10] but it was not truly fashionable until the 1770s outside England. With the shorter frock, a short waistcoat was worn, de Garsault's 'veston ... espèce de Veste moderne à basques courtes'.

When Boswell made his pilgrimage to Rousseau in 1764, it was winter, so 'above all I wore a greatcoat of green camlet lined with fox-skin fur, with the collar and cuffs of the same fur';[11] in this he was painted in Rome by Willison in 1765. This greatcoat, which we have already noted as being the staple out-of-doors garment, was increasingly important as a fashionable replacement for the coat, which was no longer ample enough to serve for travelling in bad weather. It took various forms, that worn by Boswell being made in the form of a nightgown with wrap-over front; the *London Chronicle* of 1762 found that 'very spruce smarts have no buttons nor holes upon the breast of these surtouts ... and their garments only wrap over their breasts like a morning gown'.[12] The most usual fastening was by buttoning to the waist; this was what the French called the 'redingote', the original overcoat with side seams worn when riding, and an alternative to the short, buttoned, circular cape. By the middle of the century the surtout was quite sophisticated in cut and trimming, with buttoned or turned-back cuffs, single or double-breasted fastening and often with more than one collar for extra warmth; it should, said *L'Art du Tailleur*, strictly speaking, be worn in the country but it was increasingly worn in town.

52 **An Englishman at Paris**, 1767, by H. Bunbury

The bluff Englishman dressed in his frock and carrying a sturdy cane is surrounded by exaggerated French types; the peasant in trousers and sabots, the well-fed monk, the effeminate hair-dresser carrying an umbrella or parasol, and the over-refined nobleman in his carriage, who wears a powdered bag wig and fine lace shirt ruffle.

But it was functional as well as fashionable. George Washington in 1759 ordered 'a New-market great-coat with a loose hood to it, made of Blew Drab or broadcloth . . . let it be made of such cloth as will turn a good shower of rain'.[13] In England, umbrellas for men (which had been introduced by Jonas Hanway in 1756) were regarded as effete and detrimental to the livelihood of the hackney coachmen; when John Macdonald brought a silk umbrella from Spain to England in 1778, people shouted 'Frenchman, why don't you get a coach?', and Francis Place remembered in his youth the coachmen 'lashing the peoples umbrellas with their whips as they drove away'.[14]

The elegance of the fashionable man in the middle years of the eighteenth century depended on total perfection from head to toe, not just in tailoring but in the tasteful use of accessories and even a discreet use of cosmetics. The ideal masculine face was smooth and clean-shaven (only a very few

soldiers, actors, and those leading a deliberately bohemian existence, wore beards or moustaches); the *Female Spectator* (1744) found it necessary to poke fun at the male predilection for scents, patches, lip salves, cold cream and rouge, cosmetics widely used in the upper reaches of society until the early nineteenth century.[15] Criticism occurred when cosmetics were too heavily applied or the pursuit of a soft white complexion was taken too far; Captain Whiffle, for example, wore a face mask and white gloves to protect his skin, and Catherine the Great told in her *Memoirs* of the Danish envoy at the Russian court in 1750, known as the 'white count on account of his complexion' which he nurtured by covering 'his face and hands with ointment before going to bed'. In an age in which a hearty intake of food and drink was the norm, a rubicund complexion was often the result; the author Grimm found it necessary to tone down his complexion with ceruse or white lead.

As the cut of the suit changed relatively slowly, the dressing of the hair or wig assumed greater importance. The *London Magazine* for 1753 gave some advice to *Monsieur à la Mode*:

Let a well frizzled wig be set off from his face;
With a bag quite in taste from Paris just come,
That was made and ty'd up by Monsieur Frisson;

With powder quite grey, his head is complete,
If dress'd in the fashion, no matter for wit . . .
Then a black solitaire his neck to adorn,
Like those of Versailles, by the courtiers there
worn.[16]

Wigs, according to the *London Chronicle* (1762) 'are
essential to every person's head, as lace is to their
cloaths'; although earlier in the century men could
have their own hair dressed with pomatum and then
powdered, by the 1740s all except the lowest classes
wore wigs of some kind. The most usually worn
wig was the bag-wig, with the side hair formed into
rigid rolls of curls; the French word 'boucle' came
to be the English 'buckle', and to keep the hair in
buckle meant to keep to the tightness of the roll, a
sign of a well-dressed wig. Frederick the Great, for
example, was notoriously indifferent about his
clothing and about his wig, which was 'dressed with
a single buckle on each side. From their being very
carelessly put up and unequally powdered, we may
naturally conclude that the friseur had been greatly
hurried in the execution of his office'.[17] The
number and type of side rolls to the wig varied,
with one being fashionable in the 1750s, and two
generally the rule in the 1760s; Beaumont's *Enciclo-
pédie Perruquière* (1767) has many names for very
similar styles. W. H. Pyne's father, a weaver, in the
1760s 'had three wigs; two were of the same
pattern, with two curls on each side; these were
everyday wigs, one of which Ned regularly
brought, nicely powdered, every morning when he
came to shave master and my uncle; the other he
took away to dress; the third was a Sunday wig: this
was carried off on the Friday and returned on
Saturday morning'.[18]

Wigs were an expensive item of the male
wardrobe, but so essential that every man with
tolerable claims to substance would have enough to
ensure that while one was on his head, others were
ready dressed. The best hair was human hair (which
sold at about £1 a pound), but it needed constant
dressing with pomatum to keep the curls and toupet
in place, and then had to be heated to retain the
style; wigs were heated in ovens, but hair on the
customer's head was twisted into curl papers and
curled with a hot iron. Cheaper wigs were made of
horsehair and goatshair (though the latter broke off
too easily); other materials included Edward Wortley Montagu's famous wig made of copper and iron
wire which Walpole admired in 1751, and Dr
Johnson's wig of worsted given to him in 1777 by
Mr Thrale, because it stayed longer in curl (for this
reason, wool wigs were widely worn by sailors on
long voyages).

Pomatum for the hair was often perfumed

53 **Three men at a café**, by E. Jeaurat

The greatcoat in the forefront of this drawing, with a
collar of contrasting colour, has to be capacious enough
to cover the flared coat beneath it.

54 **Jacques Cazotte**, by J.-B. Perroneau

This portrait encapsulates all the elegance of mid-
eighteenth century French costume, from the pink silk
of the suit, to the powdered and carefully dressed hair
with its single curving roll at the side and the back hair
gathered into a black silk bag, the ends of which are
brought round to the front *en solitaire*. Placing the hand
between the buttons of the waistcoat was not only an
approved gesture of elegance, but also serves to show off
the fine point lace of the shirt sleeve ruffle, and keep the
hat firmly in place beneath the arm.

(Rome was reputed to produce some of the best
quality), and so, often, was hair powder, made from
rice flour. The secret of a good barber or valet was
to spread the powder evenly; the gentleman sat in a
small closet, with a powdering jacket to protect
himself from the rain of powder; the comte de
Ségur in Vienna in 1789 found the old Count
Kaunitz keeping to the elaborate wig of his youth,
and to ensure that the powder was put on evenly,
'he proceeded to a closet destined for this purpose
between two rows of servants, who, armed with

large puffs, covered him with a cloud of hair powder'.[19] In the following year Karamzin, a Russian visitor to London, in order to have his hair dressed went to a barber, 'who having first unmercifully flayed my face, plaistered my head with flour and tallow. "Alas, I am no longer in Paris", I said to myself with a sigh, "where the powder-puff of the ingenious lively Rulet played like a gentle zephyr around my head and strewed it with a resplendent white aromatic rime"'.[20] The French made the best barbers and hairdressers, a fact picked out by the Master Peruke-makers of London in 1763, who found that 'swarms of French hair-dressers' were depriving them of their business, and that men were increasingly 'beginning to dress their own hair pernicious to their trade'. This custom was gradually to increase towards the end of the 1760s, in spite of the barbers' protests; some were able to impose their will on their customers, and the young Goethe, finishing his education in Strasbourg in 1770, was told firmly by a barber that his hair would never take a 'frisure' (i.e. dressing), and he had to cut it off and wear a wig. Even Dr Johnson, visiting Paris with the Thrales in 1775 and astonishing the French with his rusty suit and his habit of speaking Latin, found it worth while to make some sartorial effort and bought a French wig, which must have been better fitting than the 'little old shrivelled unpowdered wig' which he wore when Boswell first visited his chambers in the Temple in 1763.

The wig which he purchased in Paris was probably a bob wig, for this was the most usual undress wig worn by the middle classes and by older men generally in the middle decades of the century; the hair was curled or frizzed up all round, stopping short of the shoulder. The campaign wigs with locks of hair were worn into the 1750s by older men; in the 1760s they were very old-fashioned, and the young William Hickey's favourite term of abuse for anyone he regarded as out-of-date was 'a horrid perriwig bore'.

Some fashionable wigs in the 1760s copied those worn by the working classes; the best known was the 'scratch wig', which the *London Chronicle* called 'the Blood's skull covering', 'combed over the forehead untoupeed, to imitate a head of hair, because these gentlemen love to have everything natural about them'. They were the colour of natural hair, the wearer's own hair mingling with the false hair at the front, dressed with pomatum. Smollett saw them being worn in the streets of Paris in the mid-1760s, an early example of English 'sporting' fashions' being adopted by the French.

Grey or white powder was the finishing touch for formal wigs, but the bob wigs were usually unpowdered, the most popular colours being black and

shades of brown from the almost blonde to the very dark. Red hair was intensely disliked; when Roderick Random came from Scotland to London in 1748, one of his first purchases was 'a good handsome bob' which cost him 10s, for his red hair 'was sufficient to beget an antipathy against me in all mankind'. For those who wished to keep to their own hair and not to wear a wig (which was the obvious solution), the *Gentleman's Magazine* for 1770 published a recipe for making red hair black with a dye of black lead and ebony shavings.

An essential part of the outfit of a well-dressed man was the hat, increasingly carried under the arm as the hairstyle gradually rose in the 1760s. The three-cornered style remained in vogue throughout the middle years of the eighteenth century, with slight variations in size and type of brim or trimming, and often named after famous battles (Dettingen) or men of fashion (Nivernois). The Nivernois hat was named after the French ambassador to London in the 1760s; it had a low round crown and a very wide brim which was rolled over at the edges into a broad triangle. When William Hickey was in Madras in 1769 he attracted a great deal of attention when he wore this hat newly brought out from England, for it was small compared to the large hats worn out there. Although hats became smaller towards the end of the 1760s, the main differences in style related to the cocking of the brims; 'some have their hats open before like a Church-spout, or the tin scale they weigh flour in, some wear them rather sharper, like the nose of a greyhound', declared the *London Chronicle* of 1762, whereas Quakers made 'a point of their faith not to wear a button or loop tight-up; their Hats spread over their heads like a pent-house, and darken the outward man to signify they have the inward light'.[21]

The loop and button fastened the hat up at one side, and provided an opportunity for the display of wealth and taste, for at court diamonds and other precious stones were used for the button and also for the hat-clasp, which was sometimes pinned on. One of the most famous single diamonds was the one called the Regent, bought in 1717 and, according to Saint-Simon, 'the size of a greengage plum', which was worn as a hat button by the kings of France throughout the eighteenth century. The French kings also wore another famous diamond, the Sancy, as part of the epaulette holding the cordon bleu of the order of the Saint-Esprit. Orders were an important part of the male jewellery, for precious stones surrounded the badge and held the sash in place. On gala occasions royalty sparkled like the stars they wore; to an English visitor at the court of Spain in the 1770s, the men of the royal family

55 Portrait of Gustavus III of Sweden with his brothers, Charles, Duke of Sudermanie, later Charles XIII, and Frederick-Adolf, 1771, by A. Roslin

All the brothers wear richly embroidered court costume; that of Gustavus III on the left is the most lavish, and in addition he wears the insignia of the Orders of Seraphins, the Order of Vasa, and the Polish Order of L'Etoile.

glittered 'like the belt of the constellation of Orion'. When Keysler visited the Saxon royal treasury in Dresden in 1730 he was amazed by the stones that he saw, which included a diamond setting for an order of the Golden Fleece which had cost 200,000 thalers. He noted also 'a set of diamond buttons for a suit of cloaths, diamond buckles and cane heads, one of a diamond the size of a nutmeg'.[22] For the grandest occasions, suit buttons were made of diamonds, such as those noted on the coat of the Austrian ambassador in London by Lady Mary Coke in 1768,

which had cost him £7000; in the following year at Lyons she found that the duc de Villars even had his shirt buttons made of diamonds. Not only were suit seams covered with diamonds for occasions like royal marriages, but so were swords and canes. This was particularly the case in Russia, where the nobility 'were almost covered in diamonds' which formed 'their buttons, buckles, hilts of swords and epaulets'; in 1777 Catherine the Great gave Gustavus III not only the Alexander Nevsky order in brilliants, but a cane with a knob made of a single diamond worth 60,000 roubles.

Such lavish display was rarely seen in England, where more modest jewellery was the rule. Except at court, buttons were made of crystal or paste set in silver, gold or base-metal cups. Shoe buckles, which became larger in the 1740s, were very often made of materials such as steel, brass, pinchbeck and quartz, which could be worked into very elaborate designs; they suited the more delicate shoe with pointed toe and smaller, slightly lower heel. From the middle of the century, the growing feeling in England that too much glitter was vulgar restricted the acceptable use of precious stones to that in small stock or breeches buckles, or finger rings of brilliants.

Women

To many, the rococo, with its emphasis on the ornamental frivolity of dress and accessories, is the epitome of eighteenth-century elegance; its essential features were the love of surface decoration, a fondness for asymmetrical curvilinear forms, and an eroticism and succulence which can best be seen in the portraits by Boucher in the 1740s. To many contemporaries the rococo in art seemed a decadent working out of the essential lines of the baroque, but without its seriousness (the word itself, first used during the very different moral and artistic climate of the French Revolutionary years, was a term of abuse), very often degenerating into meaningless superfluity of form; already by the 1750s many artists felt that domestic virtues and public morality

should be upheld by art, which, as practised by Boucher (and the artists whom Clive Bell called 'upholsterers to the nobility and gentry') was often mere decoration. Certainly the rococo was a princely and urban art form, which demonstrated a kind of opulence in taste sympathetic to absolute rule; it was thus adopted by the wealthier German princes with their admiration of French culture and their own tradition (particularly in the south and in Austria) for the more extreme forms of the baroque, and it never quite got off the ground in the more democratic and tepid climate of England. Indeed, by the time that the rococo in terms of dress came to England in the 1750s, there was already a movement towards the more restrained and classical in art, which was itself to be taken up in costume in the 1760s.

In 1745 Madame de Pompadour commenced her reign as 'maîtresse en titre', and her fashion sense was dominant for the next decade; she summed up the elegance of the rococo which could so easily in a less practised wearer seem mere fussiness of dress and decoration. From 1752 her intimacy with the king ceased, but she continued to dominate the French court until her death in 1764, even in 1752 being made lady-in-waiting to the modest and retiring queen, with whom she had the good sense always to be on the best of terms.

The sack or *robe à la française*, usually worn over small side hoops, was the dress most typical of the period; to the English it was sometimes known as a 'negligée', a slightly confusing term as in fact it was gradually becoming more a formal gown, more fitted to the waist and with the bodice cut separately and seamed to the skirt. It was worn as an open robe (though the English kept to the closed version until the end of the 1740s), with stomacher pinned to the sides of the bodice; the robings were, from the middle of the 1740s, carried down to the hem, increasing in size and elaboration. From about 1740 the pleated cuff was replaced by sleeve flounces, increasing in number (often three at the end of the decade) and in size; these were cut to hang very

56 **A lady with a fan**, 1744, engraving after H. Gravelot

The cap with long lappets, and the mantua with folded-back train denote formal dress for an English lady at this period.

57 **Madame de Pompadour**, 1759, by F. Boucher

58 **The Brockman Family at Beachborough Manor**, *c.*1743–6 (detail), by E. Haytley

The ladies wear the relatively informal English nightgown, with kerchief and apron.

59 **La Marquise d'Aiguirandes**, 1759, by F. H. Drouais

At the height of the rococo period, even patterned silks like this striped and floral brocade are covered in three-dimensional trimmings – ribbons, ruffles and furbelows all decorated with metal lace.

short inside the bend of the arm, but long over the elbow. By the end of the 1740s this type of sleeve was also seen on the tighter-fitting gowns preferred by the English, such as the mantua and the night-gown. The mantua by the 1740s was worn in England at court, but the earlier style of skirt drapery with the train gathered to fall over the hips was no longer possible because of the huge square hoops of the period; the skirt of the gown was cut separate from the bodice in front and folded round to the back, and by the end of the 1740s the side pieces were removed, the back panel only being cut in one with the bodice, forming a train for court dress. The train was increasingly coming to be associated with formal court wear, and could in some cases be made totally separate from the dress, hooking on above the waist.

Although the sack dress was widely worn in England and Scotland (the Scottish ladies were sometimes quicker than the English to adopt French fashions), the English preferred a tighter-fitting open gown such as the nightgown, which was less formal for everyday than the mantua with its back draping; sometimes the bodice extended without a seam into the skirt, sometimes it was cut quite separately. It was a gown worn in the mornings, usually with a kerchief crossed over the bosom, an apron, and a quilted petticoat. It captivated Love-lace, who wrote to his friend Belford of Clarissa in

Richardson's novel of 1748:

Her morning-gown was a pale primrose-coloured paduasoy, the cuffs and robings curiously embroidered by the fingers of this ever-charming Arachne, in a running pattern of violets and their leaves; the light in the flowers silver; gold in the leaves . . . A white handkerchief concealed – O Belford! what still more inimitable beauties did it not conceal! . . . Her ruffles were the same as her mob. Her apron a flowered lawn. Her coat white satten, quilted.[23]

Lovelace admired the delicate floral embroidery which Clarissa had worked herself; this type of decoration was particularly to be seen in England and also in Italy, where ladies were slow to adopt

the three-dimensional ornamentation of the dress which was an essential part of the rococo, preferring a plainer surface on which to embroider the large flower designs in silk or wool which were popular. Embroidery must have been the inspiration for the fine botanical English Spitalfields silks of the 1740s; in 1742 Mrs Delany noted 'several very handsome flowered silks, shaded like embroidery'.[24] Any sense of the roroco in dress in England in this decade manifested itself through the serpentine lines of the delicate meandering floral designs on light grounds which were popular for woven silks, and which were exported in large quantities to the fashion-conscious Americans. Silks were lighter in the 1740s and 1750s (heavy damasks and huge flowered brocades were out of fashion except at court), and small flowers often twined round trellises or meandered by the side of stripes. Much use was made of design motifs such as ribbons, butterflies, garlands and feathers; in 1747 Mrs Delany at a royal birthday had a gown made of 'a flowered silk . . . a pale deer-coloured figured ground; the flowers, mostly purple, are mixed with white feathers'.[25]

Great ingenuity was used to cover the surface of the dress with padded robings and furbelows, ribbons, feathers, and garlands of artificial flowers. In 1746 Mrs Delany, attending a reception at Leicester House, the home of the Prince of Wales, found the Duchess of Portland in a gown of 'white satin, the petticoat ruffled, and robings and facings'; two years later she described the trousseau of Lady Frances Carteret, which included a dress of 'white, flounced, with a magnificent silver trimming all over the gown and petticoat'.[26] Such French styles with frills and furbelows were being worn in

England by the end of the 1740s and had reached Russia by 1750 where the young Catherine annoyed the Empress Elizabeth by adopting the new French dresses flounced all over and with zig-zag borders.

Mrs Delany was most censorious about what she called 'the tubs of hoops' which reached an enormous width in the mid-1740s in England, although they had, as Mrs Montagu was told by a friend returning from Paris in 1742, disappeared from French dress except at court. In 1741 an English painter found the ladies in Rome wearing a sack 'extended on each side by a hoop, not quite six yards wide'; by the middle of the 1740s the hoops had become huge pyramid shapes, which were to turn into squares at the end of the decade. Such extremes were bound to attract comment; a writer in the *British Magazine* of September 1746 was struck at Vauxhall by the appearance of a lady 'whose Paraphernalia fill'd up three Fourths of the Breadth of the principal Walk, and spread over almost an equal Space of Ground behind her; the Hoop extending to an enormous Distance on each Side, and a majestick Length of Sack trailing

60 Anastasia Ivanovna, Countess of Hessen-Homburg, Princess Trubetskoij, *c*.1758, by A. Roslin

Princess Troubetskoij's dress is completely in the French rococo taste, with its sacque style and multiplicity of trimmings, her powdered hair with jewelled pompon, and ruched silk necklace. She wears the Grand Order of St Catherine the Martyr, received in 1741 when she was Lady-in-Waiting to the Empress Elizabeth of Russia.

61 Study of a woman seen from behind, by T. Gainsborough

Dress was meant to be as attractive in retreat as in advance, which may explain the popularity of the sack dress; one of the most characteristic gestures of the eighteenth century is the curve of the arm, allowing for the display of treble sleeve ruffles, hoisting the dress slightly at the back. This had the additional advantage of revealing the ankle and the graceful curves of the high-heeled shoes.

behind, and doing the Office of a Broom on the gravel Walk'.[27]

By the 1750s fashionable English ladies had abandoned their large hoops either for small side hoops or none at all, causing their gowns to trail on the ground, more or less elegantly according to their style. In 1754 Mrs Delany could not help but admire the casual elegance of Lady Coventry who wore 'a black silk sack, made for a large hoop, which she wore without any, and it trailed a yard on the ground';[28] a few years later, Oliver Goldsmith derided a bourgeoise imitation of the fashionable style when he saw 'a fat lady in a lutestring trollopee . . . how she waddles along with her train two yards behind her'.[29] The trollopee was a particularly descriptive word for the sometimes slovenly appearance which such a trailing gown, without hoops, made to the eyes of those accustomed to the tautness of silk spread over an understructure; it could also mean the original 'contouche' style of sack which some preferred for comfort and convenience.

Flowers and floral designs dominated dress silks of the middle eighteenth century, becoming more delicate in the 1760s, when small flowers or bunches of flowers were mixed in with lace-like meanders or diaper frameworks, or compartmented by scrolls and fronds. Painted silks from China came to Europe by way of Indian depots, their beautifully observed, naturalistic flower patterns making them both expensive and fashionable; General Napier advertised in 1761 for the recovery of a stolen 'painted silk Negligée and Petticoat, the ground white, a running pattern of flowers and leaves, the edges of the leaves painted in silver, and the veins gold, with some birds and butterflies painted thereon'.[30]

Chinese influence showed also in chinoiserie textile designs; amusing and totally imaginary 'Chinese' landscapes with pagodas, parasols and mandarins were featured in the many pattern books published in the mid-eighteenth century, which also inspired designs for china, furnishings and wallpaper, and contributed to the vogue for all things Chinese so tellingly satirized by Goldsmith in *The Citizen of the World* (1762). Just as popular as the painted silks, and cheaper, were the printed cottons, often also with Chinese patterns, but versatile enough to imitate silk designs as well; they could be produced quickly to match the changing moods for allegorical designs, pastoral scenes or topical allusion. By the middle of the century many centres in Europe had begun to manufacture polychrome printed cottons of high quality, the most famous being the Jouy factory in France established in 1760. Printed linens and cottons featured increasingly for

62 **Portrait of a woman**, by J. G. Grooth

Painted silks, such as this one, allow for a freedom in design not possible for woven silks, and contribute to the elegant informality of this morning dress, with its delicate worked muslin sleeve ruffles. A touch of German provincialism can be seen, however, in the black silk kerchief worn round the neck and in the lace cap with pinned up lappets.

jackets and for dresses in the wardrobes of women of all classes; Madame de Pompadour's inventory of her clothes on her death (1764) included 'indiennes', some half-mourning toilettes in black and white,[31] and in the same year Barbara Johnson paid 3s a yard for eight yards of 'a Blue & White Copper-plate linnen' to make a 'Gown' (printing linen by copper-plate had been invented in the early 1750s, Mrs Delany observing the process in Ireland in 1752). Many of the references in Barbara Johnson's record book are to 'gowns' made of linen or cotton, which may be the informal gowns, some wrapping over and tying with a sash, which were, with the vogue for the oriental, becoming high fashion in the 1760s. Painted silks, printed fine cottons and embroidered muslins made both formal dresses (Madame de Pompadour's inventory recorded a robe and skirt of muslin embroidered with small silver bouquets[32]) and the loosely draped gowns with long sleeves

63 The Craymoyel Family, 1760, by
L. G. de Carmontelle

The proud father, dressed in semi-formal suit and bag
wig, holds the leading strings attached to the gown of
the child who wears on its head a feather-trimmed
bourrelet as a protection against falls. The mother's
hooded, sack-back Brunswick gown, has the
characteristic long sleeves broken at the elbow with a
double, pinked ruffle.

which appealed to artists inspired by the neo-
classical.

Another new fashion (although it had earlier
been seen in working-women's dress) was that for
long sleeves, which were first worn with informal
gowns and travelling dresses. A long-sleeved version of the sack, usually three-quarter-length and
with a high neck and a buttoned, unstiffened bodice,
was called a 'German habit' or a 'Brunswick', and
was widely worn in Germany since the mid-
century; the *London Magazine* for January 1764
noted that the going-away dress for Princess Augu-
sta was 'the German fashion, a scarlet silk buttoned
before, sleeves down to her wrists and with a sack
behind'. The early sleeves had a break at the elbow
with a ruffle (so ingrained was the eighteenth-
century notion of a natural break there), but the
sleeve of the later 1760s ended in a small ruched cuff.
In Barbara Johnson's pattern book a three-quarter-

length Brunswick ordered in 1768 had military
buttoned-back revers and was used as a garment for
out-of-doors; but later, in 1772, a Brunswick of
blue and white checked cotton was probably more
seen as an informal dress for the cool English
climate. As was customary with informal clothing,
the latest textile designs were used, the tiny spots,
checks and plain stripes anticipating the formal silk
designs of a decade later.

Also indicative of the change in mood from large
expanses of unbroken surface to the fragmented
surface of the rococo in dress was the popularity of
the jacket and petticoat style, which gradually rose
in the social scale during the middle years of the
eighteenth century. From the 1740s many women
wore jackets made with a sackback; they were worn
with a stomacher pinned on over a laced-up, boned
lining, but after *c.* 1750 the usual fastening was
front-buttoning. 'Nothing is so ravishing than an
easy dishabille', said the *Connoisseur* in 1754, referring to 'the short sacks (pet-en-lairs) and negligées'.
Such jackets were often worn out-of-doors; Horace
Walpole described his old enemy Lady Mary
Wortley Montagu in 1762 as wearing 'a kind of
horseman's riding coat, calling itself a pet-en-l'air,
made of a dark green (green I think it had been)
brocade with coloured and silver flowers and lined
with furs'.[33] But generally for out-of-doors the
riding habit, which had been thought so eccentric
when worn by English travellers to Europe in the
early years of the century, was widely worn until
the feminine versions of the greatcoat overtook it in
popularity. Sometimes the riding habit was a three-
piece suit in the traditional English style; the future
Catherine the Great as a fashion-conscious German
princess at the Russian court wore habits of silk
camlet (these were not very practical as the rain
made them shrink), one in particular 'of rich sky-
blue material with silver braid and crystal buttons
which looked exactly like diamonds. My black hat
had a string of diamonds round it'.[34] Princess Ulrica
of Prussia's travelling gown (when she married the
heir to the Swedish crown in 1744) was 'a rose
colord amazonian habit, trim'd with silver; the
lappels and vest were of sea green. She had on an
English hat of black velvet, adornd with a white
feather'.[35]

Many German princesses rode astride and dressed
like men; an English visitor to the court of
Mecklenburg Schwerin in 1766 found the riding
habit with cocked hat and bag-wig to be the
everyday dress of the ladies except on Sundays.
Breeches for hunting were worn in many countries
(except in England where the art of riding side-
saddle was cultivated); the inventory of Madame de
Pompadour contained 'culottes pour la chasse',

some of knitted wool or silk, which could alternatively and with more propriety be worn under a riding skirt (Casanova saw, in 1758, ladies skating on the ice in Amsterdam with black velvet drawers worn under short petticoats). The idea of the riding habit as a kind of uniform based on the male suit was replaced in England in the mid-eighteenth century by the riding jacket and skirt (this is probably what Barbara Johnson meant by a 'Riding dress' which she ordered in 1757, taking seven yards of brown fustian), or a riding coat called a 'joseph', usually green in colour. In Goldsmith's *Vicar of Wakefield* (1766) a large historical family group was to be painted, Olivia to be an Amazon 'in a green joseph richly laced with gold and with a whip in her hand'.[36]

Yet over the hoops and the fragile decorated surface of the dress a cloak was the most practical garment and also the most luxurious. To the young Catherine the Great, coming to Russia in 1744 from a penny-pinching court, Russian splendour seemed to be typified in her first present, a cloak of gold brocade lined with sable. Such full-length cloaks were lined with the most expensive soft furs such as squirrel and ermine; the fashionable beauty Lady Coventry attracted the attention of Mrs Delany in 1754 in her 'pink satin long cloke lined with ermine mixt with squirrel skins'. Shorter hooded cloaks were less sumptuous but more functional; to an out-of-town enquiry, Mrs Delany in 1755 described the pelisse as a cloak 'made of satin or velvet, black or any colour lined or trimmed with silk, satin or fur, with slits for the arms to come out'.[37] Summer cloaks had the hood and the edge of the cloak ruched with tiny pleats; popular fabrics were dark glazed cottons, linens and silks. Even indoors small shoulder mantles made of silk, lace or feathers were needed to protect the skin and cover the décolletage; in the 1750s black lace mantles were all the rage. They varied in shape from tiny shoulder capelets like large collars to the pelerine with front pendants crossed at the waist.

Not only was fur used to edge and line jackets and coats, but it was also used to line wrapping gowns; a 1744 Venetian trousseau included a wrapping gown of black velvet lined with marten and one of pale blue velvet lined with ermine and squirrel. However, its most rococo manifestation was for decoration on the dress; its fluffiness and the taste for sharp contrasts in fabrics (and sheer expensive impracticability) appealed to the fashionable lady, and from the 1740s it was turned into robings, petticoat bands, stomacher ornaments, tippets and necklaces. Although it is often stated that this fashion for fur trimming came from the Polish styles introduced by Louis XV's wife Maria Lesczynska in the mid-1720s, it is more likely that it was made popular by the involvement of the central European troops – and in particular the Hungarian hussars with their glamorous, fur-lined uniforms of Oriental origin – in the War of the Austrian Succession which began in 1740; in any case the French queen was no leader of fashion.[38] Fur was used not only to trim fashionable dresses, but for the heavy swag-like decorations on court gowns. Ermine, in particular, which had once been reserved just for royalty, was a popular trimming; in 1740 Mrs Delany saw a dress at court of dark green velvet trimmed with ermine and with an ermine petticoat which must have been monstrously heavy. By the end of the 1760s ermine was no longer a fashionable fur (soft white furs like fox and dyed rabbit were in vogue for edging pelisses) but it remained for the superfluity of ornament demanded at court; on one occasion in 1769 Mrs Montagu wore 'a corded blue tabby trimmed with Ermine which with fine lace and jewels makes a respectable figure and as I had the Ermine cost me little'.[39]

The middle years of the eighteenth century are years of show and splendour, very often superimposed on a lack of personal hygiene that we would find startling; ideas of cleanliness seem in many cases to have been honoured more in the breach than in the observance. A few, like Lord Chesterfield, regarded personal cleanliness as necessary for health and good manners, but many men would sympathize with Boswell who preferred to have 'a suit of clean linen every day' rather than to wash frequently, and consequently, according to the sculptor Nollekens, stank. Although towards the end of the eighteenth century, with the growing emphasis on plainer simplicity in dress, and the increased use of washable fabrics, the standard of hygiene improved, there was a general acknowledgement that cosmetics and perfumes were necessary to rectify the inadequacies of plumbing (only the grandest houses had built-in baths, and water supplies were erratic); ideas of health were also involved, for many felt that it was, for example, dangerous to wash the hair because it made the brain 'humid', and bran or ivory powder was used

64 Lady Mary Fox, later Baroness Holland, 1767, by P. Batoni

The sitter wears a travelling costume, a Brunswick gown of grey silk, comprising a fitted three-quarter-length hooded jacket and skirt. It is a practical yet feminine costume, with its ruched trimming, and striped ribbons which decorate the sleeves, the lace jabot and the small lace headdress.

instead. Sweet floral perfumes were worn by both sexes to cover the lack of cleanliness, and the smells of the streets.

Higher standards of physical cleanliness and appearance were expected of women throughout the century, and there was no shortage of advice on skin care and cosmetics. The perfect face typified eighteenth-century ideas of regularity and proportion, being an oval shape, with small straight nose, slightly rosy cheeks and lips, and a white complexion. 'The Face is the chief Seat of Beauty' stated Le Camus, the author of *Abdeker, or the Art of preserving Beauty* (1754), who proceeded to list cures for skin disorders and recipes to improve its whiteness; white paint or white lead (ceruse) were used, although the dangers of the latter were recognized by the middle of the century. By this time the thicker paint was no longer needed to cover the ravages of smallpox, and lighter face washes were used such as mercury water or rice water, which were safe enough to cover the neck and bosom. In addition, parasols shielded the skin from the sun, and masks protected it in bad weather. The face was as much a work of art as the costume, and as much time had to be spent on it to achieve the delicate enamelled effect that was admired in such leaders of fashion as Madame de Pompadour. With white skin, and the use of grey or white hair powder, rouge was necessary to give colour; red lead was mixed with carmine or vermilion to produce bright spots of colour on the cheeks. To appear natural was not the aim, said Casanova; he claimed that rouge emphasized the eyes and indicated an 'amorous fury'. The practice began in France, along with the use of hair powder, in the early years of the century; in Paris in 1739 John Russell found the women's faces made hideous by 'two globular spots . . . as fiery red as the orb of the sun when setting in a dusky evening'.[40] It continued to the Revolution, although after the middle of the century, it was worn at court and in the evenings only. The custom rapidly spread to other countries in spite of attacks on the grounds of health and morality. As early as

1723 Weber noted in Russia how it was a compliment to call a woman 'a red maid'; this must have looked rather startling with the black teeth to be seen in the early eighteenth century – the wife of the English Resident was visited in Moscow in 1729 by an admiral's wife, 'her teeth being dyed black and shining as if japanned'.[41] The Russian custom for dyeing the teeth had disappeared by the mid-eighteenth century, but rouging continued until the end of the period; the comte de Ségur, accompanying Catherine the Great on a provincial tour of Russia in the mid-1780s, described how at the end of every day the Empress was covered in red from the homage of local ladies.

Wherever French fashions reigned, so did rouge; thus it was widely worn at the German courts, and even at Vienna, although forbidden to the archduchesses and court ladies by Empress Maria Theresa. In England rouge was not much worn except on very formal occasions; Lord Glenbervie, an inveterate collector of gossip, noted how people remembered the 'extraordinary ugliness' of the young Queen Charlotte at the English court in 1761, a plainness emphasized by her lack of rouge and powder, which she remedied eventually by adopting the latter but never the former. Italian women on the whole preferred a pale complexion; in Venice in 1785 Mrs Piozzi commented that the rest of the fashionable world, influenced by the cult of naturalism and sentimentality, had caught up with Italian taste in the vogue for a pale face. To emphasize the whiteness of the skin, the eyes were sometimes made up with lamp black or the residue of burnt ivory shavings; false eyebrows were made of fur or mouse-skin. Another essential part of the female armoury (and worn too by men in the early eighteenth century) was the use of patches, made of 'black Taffety . . . cover'd with Gum Arabic'. This, too, was a French fashion, which could be taken to excess by the undiscriminating; the Russian ladies, said Weber in 1723, covered their faces in patches cut out in the shapes of trees and horses as well as the more usual suns, stars and moons.[42] The *Lady's Magazine* for 1759 stated that no woman should have more than one, 'or at the utmost one large patch and a little satellite stuck just by the greater planet'. The placing of the patch was a language of allusion; Le Camus said a patch 'at the exterior Angle of the Eye' was 'killing', and one 'in the midst of the Forehead, Majestic'; one in the middle of the cheek indicated gallantry, a patch near the lips the coquette, and one on the nose demonstrated daring.[43] Larger patches covered up the effects of venereal disease; the Germans called them 'Venusblumen', claiming that this fashion was also the result of French influence.

65 **Mme Grimod de la Reynière**, 1751, by M. Q. La Tour

The powdered hair, possibly a wig, is arranged in the tightly curled tête-de-mouton style. The sacque dress is of watered silk, and the separate lace stomacher bodice is front-fastening in the buttoned compère style. Notable aids to the elegant display of the hands are the fine painted fan and the embroidered knotting bag.

As the face could be changed by art, so too could the hair or wig. With the contrariness that affects human nature, southern women preferred blonde hair, while their northern sisters desired black above all. In Italy, for example, the ladies, said Nugent, 'affect yellow hair, as the Roman ladies and courtesans formerly did, and where nature denies them that colour (which it often does, their hair being generally black) they obtain it by art'.[44] The ladies in southern Italy used 'a lye of wood ashes' to turn their hair 'flaxen yellow'. In Venice they dyed their hair in the sun as they had for hundreds of years; the more affluent (or less successful at dyeing) bought wigs of pale blonde hair from the convents of the Austrian Netherlands. In *The Art of Dress* (1717) the anonymous author declared:

Not all your locks are equal in Renown,
Red yields to Fair, and Black excells the Brown.[45]

66 **Une boutique de fourrure**, 1765, from Diderot's Encyclopédie

The interior of the shop shows customers buying a fur muff; muffs in various sizes line the walls, and a fur-lined pelisse is displayed hanging up on the right.

Although a greater variety of hair colouring was permissible in the fashion centres of north and western Europe, black was the most admired. In 1746, the Empress Elizabeth, with the kind of autocratic whim which ran in the family of Peter the Great, ordered all her ladies to shave their heads and wear black perukes.[46] As late as 1775, the *Lady's Magazine* gave a recipe for dyeing yellow hair; elderberries and wine simmered together would 'in time' produce 'an agreeable black colour'. By the 1780s the uniformity of taste was breaking up; even red hair could be worn, and the changes could be rung with the use of red, blue and yellow powder, in addition to the grey or white powder which had been *de rigueur* for most of the century.

The French had taken the lead in the 1720s with regard to the cutting and curling of the hair, which by the early 1740s was universally adopted. Some cut their hair short and curled it, as did Maria Theresa for the first time in 1743, for her coronation in Prague; the following year in Russia the newly arrived Catherine persuaded her ladies to adopt the new style, which they did though protesting that they looked like 'tufted birds'.[47] In England this tête-de-mouton style had arrived in the 1720s; Mrs Delany described it in 1727 as 'curley-murley', a style suited 'to the young and handsome', but it did

not make much headway for another ten years, for many Englishwomen preferred a longer style curling down the neck. By *c.* 1740 the increasingly complicated small tight curls needed to be arranged by a male peruke-maker, thus beginning the masculine rule in the kingdom of female hairdressing which lasts to this day. Sometimes women wore a tête-de-mouton wig; 'you must cut off your Hair and get a little Periwig and a French Cap,' was the cry in Fielding's farce *Miss Lucy in Town* (1742), and the *Female Spectator* of 1744 described how an unfortunate lady, wearing a 'mischief-making hoop', tangled with a flock of sheep in the street, slipped in the rain, 'her gause cap half off her head in the scuffle, and her tête de mouton hanging down on one shoulder'.[48]

By the 1760s hair was still curled short to the head at the back and sides, but smoothed back off the forehead; by the middle of the decade the hair was rising, often combed over a roll at the front, and set with small roll curls at the side. Lady Sarah Lennox advised a friend in 1766: 'The hair must be powdered, curled with very small curls ... and neat, but it must be high before and give your head the look of a sugar loaf a little. The roots of the hair must be drawn straight up and not frizzed at all for half an inch.'[49] As the hair rose, artificial hair was needed to supplement the wearer's own. In 1766 the choleric novelist Smollett found the French women 'covered with a vast load of false hair, which is Frizzled on the forehead, so as exactly to resemble the wooly heads of the Guinea negroes'.[50] So complicated had hairdressing become that in 1768 the first manual, *L'Art de la Coiffure des Dames Françoises*, was published; the author Jean Legros in the following year opened an Academy of Hair in Paris where ladies' maids and valets could practise on hired models, and where the hairdressing was created for the dolls sent to the rest of Europe.

Caps and other hair ornaments were always considered as part of the total hairdressing. In the 1740s the linen cap edged with lace and with lappets was increasingly a middle-class fashion, although the lappets, made of lace, continued to be worn at court until the end of our period. Other popular caps in this decade included the pinner, a circular cap edged with ruffles of linen or lace, and the round-eared cap which curved rather like a bonnet to the level of the ears; from the mid-1740s there was a fashion for wiring the side frill of these caps – Mrs Delany called them 'vast winkers' – which corresponded to the width of the hooped skirt. The most chic of all indoor caps, popular from the 1730s to the 1780s, was the dormeuse or French night-cap, a version of the mob cap with a close-fitting crown decorated with a ribbon.

But for more formal occasions, tiny wired caps, also from France, were the height of fashion in the 1750s; these were made of lace (the heavier Brussels lace was replaced by the lighter French and Flemish needlepoint laces, with fine mesh ground), but most often of blonde, which was lace made of white silk near Chantilly. The fashionable style for 1754 was a butterfly; the *Oxford Gazette and Reading Mercury* published a verse entitled *A la Mode* (1754) in which the lady of fashion was urged:

Let your Cap be a butterfly, slightly hung on,
Like the Shell of a Lapwing just hatch'd, on her
    Crown.[51]

That same year Mrs Delany admired Lady Coventry's 'French cap that just covered the top of her head, of blond, and stood in the form of a butterfly with its wings not quite extended'.[52] The variety of caps in the 1750s and 1760s was enormous, some named after popular whims, others after contemporary characters or historical personages. Walpole in Paris in 1755 found a 'fureur des cabriolets' (this was a one-horse chaise currently the vogue amongst the fashionable): '... the men paint them on their waistcoats and have them embroidered for clocks on their stockings, and the women ... are now muffled up in great caps with round sides, in the form of, and scarce less than, the wheels of chaises.'[53] The *London Chronicle* of 1762, amongst a list of fashionable caps, mentioned the Ranelagh Mob of gauze which crossed under the chin, tying at the back of the neck, 'copied from the silk handkerchiefs which Market-women tie over their ears, roll about their throats, and then pin up to the nape of their necks'; also popular was the Mary Queen of Scots cap made of black gauze, with a peak in the front, and 'edged down the face with French beads'.[54] By the end of the 1760s, silk scarves, rolled up in turban shape, demonstrated the new vogue for Turkish styles which was beginning to enter informal fashionable dress.

But the height of rococo delicacy in headwear was achieved by a style introduced by Madame de Pompadour in the mid-1740s and called in England, where it appeared in 1748, the pompon; it consisted of a small spray of flowers, feathers or jewels placed either centrally or to one side of the head, and worn either on its own, or with a small cap. Hogarth in his *Analysis of Beauty* (1755) found that women of the best taste preferred 'a single feather, flower or jewel ... on one side of the head';[55] by the later 1760s, according to Lady Sarah Lennox, 'you must wear no cap, and only little, little flowers dab'd in on the left side; the only feather permitted is the black and white sultane'.[56] The most attractive pompons were made of jewels, sometimes *tremblant* on wires so that they quivered with the wearer's movements, like the one admired by Lady Jane Coke in 1752, 'a diamond bird with the wings stretched out, and in its beak held a diamond drop'.[57]

For jewellery was an intrinsic part of dress, particularly in the middle years of the eighteenth century. At court women glittered in jewels, which were worn not just in their hair, ears, arms and necks but also on the dress itself; the inventory made on the death in 1767 of the Dauphine Marie-Josèphe of Saxony listed two *grandes parures* of jewels, which included diamond girdles, sleeve and shoulder knots, stomacher brooches, and brooches for holding back the sides of the *grand habit*.[58] The petticoat was also covered in jewels, but the focal point of formal dress was the ornamentation of the stomacher made of precious stones, very often of diamonds; the stomacher was a series of interlocking brooches, frequently in bow or floral designs after the prevailing French rococo taste. For her wedding to George III in 1761, Queen Charlotte was given by her husband a stomacher of diamonds set in an openwork floral design of silver, and worth £70,000.

For those with limitless wealth, the clothes could drip with jewels; Russian empresses in particular liked a great show of precious stones sewn onto their court robes in addition to the formal parure and to the jewelled orders which were worn. When Peter the Great and his wife visited Berlin in 1717, the Czarina (a courtesy title as she had not yet been crowned), in a famous description by an appalled hostess, 'wore a dozen orders and as many portraits of saints and relics fastened to the facing of her gown; so that when she walked, the jumbling of all these orders and portraits one against the other, made a tinkling noise like a mule in harness'.[59] But by 1750 St Petersburg had 51 silversmiths and 15 goldsmiths, French and Swiss designers producing the rich and exotic jewelled objects (particularly with bright stones such as emeralds and rubies) which remained part of Russian taste until the end of the Romanov empire.

Above all, the bright glitter of diamonds was the most admired effect for the rich and fashionable, either as a brooch or necklace, or set against black ribbon at the neck. By the beginning of the eighteenth century technical advances had led to the brilliant-cut diamond, so extensively faceted as to reflect a maximum of light, creating fire and brilliance. In the 1720s fine-quality stones were coming from the newly discovered mines in Brazil (India had previously been the major source), and in *A Treatise on Diamonds and Pearls* (1750), the author, a well-known jeweller, headed a chapter: 'Of the superior worth of Diamonds over all other Jewels'.[60] Prices were high; Mrs Delany in 1756, describing a friend's wedding jewels which had cost £12,000, found that the necklace was 'most perfect brilliants, the middle stone worth a thousand pounds, set at the edge with small brilliants'.[61] Single stones made the popular pendeloque earrings worn by ladies of fashion, and Madame de Pompadour's inventory contained a pair valued at 22,000 livres; the other style of earring seen in formal portraits was the girandole, with three pear-shaped drops.

Diamonds and other precious stones were used as dress buttons, and to decorate hats; they edged watches and miniatures such as those exchanged within royal families. The Dauphine Marie-Josèphe had two bracelets with miniatures (one of Louis XV, and the other of her husband) edged with small brilliants and set in six rows of pearls; a similar design can be seen in Lawrence's portrait of Queen Charlotte of 1789–90 (London, National Gallery) Pearls were age-old symbols of love and fidelity, suitable for miniatures; they had been fashionable since the end of the sixteenth century, and in our period were most usually worn either as a single strand, or as a choker of many rows, but always fastened at the back with a bow or ribbon. For those who could not afford the real thing, imitation pearls made of wax (called in England French beads) were available.

The English were in the van of the movement towards simpler clothing, and preferred the less expensive and less ostentatious types of jewellery. Very often their jewellery comprised a simple brooch bow or pendant cross, or clip earrings called snaps; these jewels were often made of paste, which was glass cut and polished into gem-like forms, which could reflect colour from foils placed at the back. Paste was the invention of G. F. Stras, a Parisian jeweller who was well established in the quai des Orfèvres by the mid-1730s, leading a growing group of *bijoutiers-faussetiers*. Although French paste was the best quality for much of the eighteenth century, towards the end of the period many English ladies were buying native products, particularly the fine opaline paste made in Derbyshire.

Many of the prettiest rococo designs in jewellery were based on flowers; in Garrick and Colman's play *The Clandestine Marriage* (1766), a bride described to her sister her new brooch made in the shape of a bouquet 'of diamonds, and rubies and emeralds and topazes and amethysts – jewels of all colours, green, red, blue, yellow intermixt – the prettiest thing you ever saw in your life'. Fresh flowers were worn as nosegays, particularly at court, although keeping them fresh was a problem;

by the 1750s the French wore water-filled bosom-bottles, described by Walpole as 'a tin funnel covered with green ribband ... which the ladies wear to keep their bouquets fresh'.[62] They were adapted in the 1780s for the huge fashionable hairstyles; Baroness d'Oberkirch in 1782 wore fresh flowers in her hair in little flat bottles. Some women wore fresh flowers in the straw bergère hats, popular in England from the middle years of the century, and in France in the 1770s and 1780s when Marie Antoinette and her ladies played at rural simplicity. The best straw plait came from Leghorn, and the hats were made with a flat crown and wide brim, lined with silk and decorated with ribbons; chip hats were made of finely shaved willow or poplar, and were almost as popular for strolling in the parks, sometimes worn over a small linen cap. The correct dashing angle at which the hat was worn, particularly over the rising hairstyles of the late 1760s, was one of the distinguishing marks of the Englishwoman, Lady Mary Coke remarking, 'I never knew a foreigner that could tell how to put on an English hat.'

Accessories were an important part of dress and etiquette as well as a language suited to demonstrate good breeding and the more (or less) subtle aspects of courtship. Ribbons, for example, worn in knots at the bosom, waist and on the sleeves were, like patches, a language of gallantry. 'Knots below and knots above, Emblems of the tyes of love,' declared a poem in the *London Magazine* of 1755. Fans were also an aid to coquetry, to hide a lady's blushes (Madame de Genlis, writing a dictionary of etiquette in 1818, felt that one of the greatest changes in manners was the new immodesty of girls compared to the blushing timidity of her youth), and to keep the heat off the face; de Saussure in England in the 1720s found the ladies 'have but little talk, and the main conversation is the flutter of their fans'. These fans, in the scallop shape so typical of rococo ornament, were made in every medium – ivory, painted silk and paper, lace, etc.; there were fans for every occasion, for mourning and for marriage, and they were one of the earliest tourist souvenirs, for they could be painted or printed with picturesque landscapes and topical allusions, or they could depict pastoral and mythological scenes, some after famous paintings. Apart from a temporary fad in the middle of the 1740s for very large fans – the *Spectator* noted in 1744 that they were 'from three quarters of a foot to even two feet' in length – they were usually about eight or nine inches long. For ceremonial occasions they acted as offertory plates; the Baroness d'Oberkirch stated that it was etiquette at the court in France to give something to the Queen on an open fan (the only time a fan could be opened before her) but on the occasion when she tried to show Marie Antoinette a bracelet this way, she dropped it and had great difficulty bending in her court panier to retrieve it.

The difficulty with the many cosmetic and jewellery accessories – perfume flasks, stay hooks, patch boxes, mirrors, watches etc. – which a fashionable lady needed, was where to carry them. Some of the more decorative items were kept on a châtelaine worn at the waist; less wealthy women kept their handkerchiefs, keys and money in their pockets tied by tapes round the waist under the petticoat. But in the 1760s an alternative place to hold such lightweight impedimenta was a knotting bag, made of silk and with a drawstring top; knotting had been a popular pastime since the end of the seventeenth century, and the bags were used to hold the linen or silk thread which was knotted with a small shuttle into a decorative braid which could be sewn onto fabric and small textile objects. The shuttles themselves were often a kind of jewellery, made of gold, silver, crystal, mother-of-pearl, ivory etc.; knotting (like the previous rage for *parfilage*, called 'drizzling' in England – the unravelling of gold and silver braid from tassels, galloons and epaulettes for the metal content which was then sold) was not so much a constructive pastime, unless one was highly skilled like Mrs Delany, but a chance to show off the graceful attitudes of the hands, and to gossip with the pretence of work. Said Madame du Deffand, friend of Horace Walpole and hostess of a famous literary salon:

Vive le parfilage!
Plus de plaisir sans lui!
Cet important ouvrage
Chasse partout l'ennui
Tandis que l'on déchire
Et galons et rubans
L'on peut encore médire
Et déchirer les gens.

Knotting was a fashionable pastime at court and on many social occasions; Lady Mary Coke found ladies knotting at the opera in 1770, and although she herself did not knot, 'the bag is convenient for one's gloves and fan'.

Formality demanded, as it does today, that gloves were worn as part of fashionable dress; many portraits show sitters carrying rather than wearing gloves, for the beauty of the hands and arms consisted in their delicacy of shape and whiteness of skin. Gloves were on the whole rather plain in style, of light-coloured kid, cotton or silk; they were usually elbow-length, tying with ribbons above the bend of the arm, thus preserving delicate white skin. Sometimes summer gloves (made with open ends) and mittens were worn, often of printed linen, knitted silk or a fabric matching that of the dress, all these being supplied by the milliner. They were quite cheaply produced and available to most women; Pamela, in Richardson's novel, bought from a pedlar 'a pair of knitt mittens turned up with calico', which would possibly have been manufactured on the framework knitting machines established in the English Midlands, or imported from France or Italy. An equally stylish way of keeping the hands and wrists warm was the muff, small in size until the 1770s, and made of silk, feathers or fur. Small muffs or 'muffettees' came in pairs covering the hand and wrist, and made of velvet or fur; in Richardson's *Clarissa Harlowe* the besotted Lovelace admired Clarissa's 'black velvet glove-like muffs of her own invention'. A specifically Roman and Florentine skill was in the perfuming of gloves and muffs; they were impregnated with scent by being suspended over a brazier of burning coals on which aromatic gums were sprinkled, or they could be rubbed with oil of roses, or musked rose-water. Very often the fur muff made of squirrel or sable matched the fur tippet twisted round the neck; both were needed for the bare arms and décolletage which were part of fashionable dress in the mid-eighteenth century, but more for the sensuous contrasts of furs and textiles. Mrs Piozzi in Milan in 1785 found a typical mixture of finery and function in the green velvet bags, adorned with gold tassels and lined with furs, which the servants of women of rank carried for their mistresses to put their feet in at church or at the opera.

For much of the century, even when women wore trained gowns, the skirts were lifted slightly at the front, so that the shoe and ankle could be seen. From the middle years of our period, developments in knitting machines meant that more complex designs could be incorporated into stockings and by the end of the 1750s ribbed hose were widely worn, usually in white silk or cotton; the brighter colours, especially red and blue, were increasingly limited after *c.* 1740 to the lower classes. When, at about this time, Pamela received some of her late mistress's clothing, it included 'fine white cotton stockings, and three pair of fine silk ones', which were suitable for the fine silk dresses she was also given; but when she decided to equip herself in humbler style to return to her original station in life, 'two pairs of ordinary blue worsted hose ... make a smartish appearance, with two white clocks'.[63]

Pamela was given three pairs of fine silk shoes that had once belonged to her mistress, but we are not told if they matched the 'delicate green Mantea silk gown and coat' with which they came. Fabric shoes, made of damask, brocade or plain silk, and often trimmed with gold or silver braid, did not necessarily match the dress, except on more formal occasions; in 1771 Mrs Nollekens was married in a sack 'of the most expensive brocaded white silk, resembling net-work, enriched with small flowers', and her shoes were made of matching material with silver spangles and Bristol buckles.[64] Such fine shoes were not meant to be worn much out-of-doors, and the fashionable lady needed a variety of shoes, including leather ones for sturdy walking, and clogs for bad weather; a bill in the Heal Collection (British Museum) dated 1766 shows Lady Winterton paying 6s for a pair of 'black Calemanco Pumps', the same for a 'pair of Bath clogs', 4s for red Morocco clogs, and, most expensively at £1 11s 6d, 'Pink Sattin Pumps trim'd with a Silver Shape the heel and quarters Trim'd with silver Cox-combe and Brade'. Shoes were, by the 1740s, more delicate with a lower and slenderer curved heel, often decorated with jewellery or embroidery, an element of coquetry not missed by contemporaries, who were equally aware of the erotic aspects of the garters, tying above or below the knee, and which were often embroidered with mottoes of a slightly risqué kind – 'No Search' was a popular phrase. The backless mule – called a slipper – made of silk with embroidery or lace, familiar through the intimate scenes by Boucher of ladies at their toilettes, is perhaps the most characteristic shoe of the rococo, typifying the softness and sexual allure of this most feminine period in the history of dress.

CHAPTER FIVE

Dress and etiquette

Dress is a very foolish thing, and yet it is a very foolish thing for a man not to be well dressed according to his rank and way of life.

Lord Chesterfield

Johnson had a fancy that as a dramatic author his dress should be more gay than what he ordinarily wore; he therefore appeared behind the scenes and even in one of the side boxes in a scarlet waistcoat, with rich gold lace, and a gold laced hat. He humorously observed to Langton 'that when in that dress he could not treat people with the same ease as when in his usual plain clothes'. Dress, indeed, we must allow, has more effect even upon strong minds than one should suppose, without having had the experience of it.

Boswell's *Life of Johnson*

In any age the demands of social life and the exigencies of rank and status determine the type of clothing worn, and this was certainly true in the eighteenth century, when the art of dressing well was not just a part of good manners but a necessary prop to established society. This art and contemporary attitudes to it must be appreciated in a consideration of eighteenth-century costume.

For most of the century, where styles did not alter dramatically some means had to be found to identify those with good taste from those aspiring perhaps to reach a higher social position than was merited; this was particularly the case in countries like England and France, where, in theory, lack of sumptuary regulations should have led to greater social flexibility. In fact, although those with no position but with money to buy rich clothes were able to do so, they were held back by the ridicule of the upper classes whose tightly knit club repelled outsiders. Barbier, in his *Chronique de la Régence et du Règne de Louis XV*, recounts the scorn poured on the head of a M. Dodun, *contrôleur-général des finances*, who bought in 1725 a marquisate, and, celebrating his elevation to the ranks of the nobility, began to dress in suits covered in gold lace (galloon); unfortunately it was discovered that his grandfather had been a lackey, and a song was sung about Paris, the refrain being: 'Galonnez, galonnez, galonnez-moi, Car je suis bon gentilhomme.'[1] The moral was to dress in a way suitable to one's station in life. On the other hand, Pamela, the heroine of Richardson's famous novel of 1740, although of humble status (she was a personal maid to a lady of the gentry), found that by assiduous application of the social niceties of life – dress, deportment, conversation and so on – she was able to achieve her ambition of marrying into the family of her late mistress; her impenetrable virtue was not so attractive to the rakish Mr B. as his knowledge of her acceptability in his world, an acceptability gained through natural virtues and applied intelligence.

Clothes, as Richardson knew, were the visible emblems of social standing. When Pamela dressed in her home-spun gown and petticoat with a plain muslin tucker, instead of the cast-off fine silk gown and lace which she had been given from her mistress's wardrobe, Mr B. was literally unable to recognize his mother's maid, so accustomed was he to seeing her in clothes befitting a newly acquired gentility. This theme occurs time after time in novels and plays in the eighteenth century, with its opportunities for deceit and the comedy of manners; potential suitors mistake the mistress for the maid, and women can be tricked by their lovers dressing up in fancy costume.

Foreigners were instantly recognizable by their clothes and a wise traveller quickly assumed the camouflage of the country. In Russia in the 1720s, the English wife of the British Resident had to adopt Russian dress to stop the people commenting at her appearance; some 50 years later an English clergyman in Smolensk was greeted coldly by the local governor, for 'the plainness of our dresses had raised suspicion of our being tradesmen', but he was finally convinced that 'English gentlemen seldom wore lace on their clothes or swords in a journey'.[2] Travellers from England, where woollen cloth was widely worn by the middle of the century, were often stared at; this happened to Baretti in Lisbon in 1760 because he was not 'dress'd in silk like other gentlemen'. Goethe in Rome in 1787 found that 'the long clothes of the native of the north, his large buttons, his curious round hat, strike the fancy of the Romans'[3] who thought it was almost a masque costume, used as they were to the silk suit and the three-cornered hat.

In England in particular, and especially so in the first half of the century, an oafish chauvinism ruled the streets of London; 'When I first went to London,' said Baretti, 'I remember that a stranger could scarcely walk about with his hair in a bag without being affronted. Every porter and every street-walker would give a pull to his bag.'[4] The bag-wig was the most obvious token of rank; supporters of Lord George Gordon in 1780 attacked peers thought to be sympathetic to Catholic emancipation, and removed their wigs. The appellation 'French dog' greeted anyone dressed in French styles throughout the century; Decremps in London at the end of the 1780s found that mud was thrown at men wearing the *habit à la française*, a sword and a chapeau bras, whether they were English or foreign.

An awareness of the nuances of class in dress is not unique to England, but it certainly seems more highly developed, even today. In the eighteenth century, with its firm sense of caste, there were fierce attacks made on those who presumed to ape their betters, though whether these feelings were motivated by class betrayal or sheer envy is hard to tell. When, in Smollett's *Humphrey Clinker* (1771) the foolish maid Win Jenkins put on airs and dressed in 'faded lutestring, washed gauze and ribbons three times refreshed' with her 'frisure . . . like a pyramid, seven inches above the scalp', and her face 'primed and patched from the chin up to the eyes', and walked through the streets with a valet dressed in the cast-off finery of his master, with a sword and 'his hair in a great bag with a huge solitaire', the people 'had got information of their real character and hissed and hooted them'.[5] The custom was to remove trimmings and generally simplify the clothing given to servants by their masters and mistresses; Clarissa, feeling that she had not long to live, decided to give to her maid Mabell 'a brown lutestring gown, which, with some alterations to make it suitable to her degree, would a great while

serve her for Sunday wear'.[6] When Molly Seagrim, the gamekeeper's daughter in Fielding's *Tom Jones* (1749), was foolish enough to wear to church a sack, unaltered, given to her by Sophia Western, with a laced cap and a fan, a near-riot ensued as the local women tried to tear the gown off her back. Women, with their greater sense of place in society, and at the same time their awareness of changing fashions, found it hard to reconcile the two. To the Vicar of Wakefield, 'finery is very unbecoming in us, who want the means of decency', but this pursuit of finery was a lodestar for those who wished to be fashionable. In Goldsmith's *The Citizen of the World* (1762), Mr and Mrs Tibbs, a lower-class couple, visit Vauxhall, she in 'flimsy silk, dirty gauze . . . and a hat as big as an umbrella', and he in a coat 'trimmed with tarnished twist',[7] and yellowing stockings; the point was that the silk had to be of high quality, the gauze had to be new and clean (it did not wash), the trimmings on a coat had to be sparkling (ideally, the coat should be plain out-of-doors), and stockings white. Snobbery was a guiding factor, recognized early on in de Mandeville's *The Fable of the Bees* (1714) for the 'poorest Labourer's Wife . . . who scorns to wear a strong wholesome Frize . . . will starve herself and her Husband to purchase a second hand Gown and Petticoat, that cannot do half the Service, because, forsooth, it is more genteel'.[8] So fashion became a race; ladies of fashion, said de Mandeville, sent for mantua-makers 'so that they may have always new Modes ready to take up, as soon as those sawcy Cits shall begin to imitate those in being'.[9]

Although fashions were fairly slow to change in the eighteenth century, there was a heightened awareness of out-of-date styles, which, particularly with regard to women's dress, often bordered on the cruel. Dress fabrics, as we have seen, were expensive and were sometimes refurbished over decades; the elderly, unmarried Tabitha Bramble (the sister of the irascible Matthew, Smollett's alter ego in *Humphry Clinker*) insisted on dressing for formal occasions in 'the style of 1739', appearing at a reception 'in a full suit of damask so thick and heavy that the sight of it alone . . . was sufficient to draw drops of sweat from any man of ordinary imagin-

67 **'Before'**, 1736, engraved by W. Hogarth

In spite of her last-minute resistance, the girl has anticipated events by removing her heavily boned stays which lie on a chair. The two velvet patches, one large, one small by her eye, may also indicate an invitation; the rest of her battery of patches lie spilled on the floor at her feet.

ation'.[10] Large patterned silks were quite out of fashion in 1771, as were the 'scanty curls, lappet-head, deep triple ruffles and high stays' that she also wore.[11] Lady Mary Coke, one of that breed of eccentric lady travellers which seems peculiarly English, spent much of her time chasing fresh air and royalty on the Continent, astounding foreign courts with the hoops and sacks which she wore in the 1770s although they were well out-of-date;[12] her riding habit, said her niece Lady Louisa Stuart in 1782, was 'shining with so much gold, I am amazed the boys do not follow her'.

By the 1780s clothes covered in gold lace looked absurd. Mrs Piozzi in Munich in 1785 was astounded to see an old gentleman in a white coat, lined with red satin and 'laced all down with gold', as was the red waistcoat, which reminded her of 'the very coat my father went in to the old King's birthday five and thirty years ago'.[13] Goethe in Palermo in 1787 found Prince Pallagonia 'frizzled and powdered, with his hat under his arm, in a silken vest, with his sword by his side',[14] a startling sight when cloth had virtually replaced silk except at court, and the sword and chapeau bras were as obsolete as buckled shoes. The author, well-known and indeed famous then, was able to afford the latest fashions coming from France or England, but he remembered when, as a student in Leipzig (which was a centre for luxury and French styles) in the mid-1760s, he had been laughed at for the heavy, clumsy cut of his suits, made of cloth which had been bought many years ago for economy.

For women there was very much a sense of what was suitable for their age, 30 being the onset of middle age when the frivolities of fashion, such as pastel colours, feathers and flowers, should be abandoned. Those who failed to observe this rule were commented upon; the acid Princess Royal of Prussia remarked on her great-aunt in 1731 that 'she tricked herself off like a young person. She wore her hair in large curls with pink ribbands of a shade somewhat lighter than her face; and the stones of her jewels were of as many colours as the rainbow'.[15]

The correct arrangement of dress and accessories, and the borderline between richness and simplicity, was highly perplexing to the eighteenth-century woman, for there were many to judge and criticize. According to *The Art of Dress* (1717):

Oft have I seen a Mantua pinn'd amiss
Make people sneer and almost cause a Hiss;
For Knots ill-fancy'd, or a tawdry Gown,
Ill-natur'd Criticks, cry the Woman down.[16]

One of the purposes behind the eighteenth-century women's magazines was to teach the correct way to dress, through advice columns ('Always dress rather above your time of life than below it,' said the *Lady's Magazine* of 1783) and novelettes, where the heroine was always dressed in the best of taste. One example, from the *Lady's Magazine* of 1773, had a rich heiress over-dressed in a 'pink and silver sacque, stretched over a wider hoop than was reckoned genteel', and covered in diamonds; she discovered her sartorial errors when confronted with a lady in a simple untrimmed negligée without a hoop, spotted gauze for linen, and instead of jewellery, a 'bouquet or orange and myrtle sprigs, mixed with Indian pinks'.[17]

Although regularity of features was admired in the female face, it was even more important to achieve the correct shape in the figure, accentuated with carefully-chosen clothes and accessories. Distinctive personal charm and conscious powers of fascination were in fact often preferred to a regular beauty; the French, in particular, 'are gifted with such a knack of magnifying the Worth of Bagatelles and making much out of Nothing, that whatever they devise relative to the Ornament and setting off of their persons, is generally thought agreeable and becoming'.[18] In an age in which a Lovelace could go into raptures about his beloved's taste in dress and her bodily charms and not mention her face, there was a consciousness of the natural body shape which could be abruptly changed with the fashionable understructures, such as stays and hoops.

Full dress, though very splendid, made women inaccessible, and their virtue could best be undermined when wearing the loose, floating negligée styles, which to many commentators smacked of indecency. A French periodical, *La Bagatelle* (1718), found that the new *robes volantes* gave women 'an air of coming pleasures' and their bodies 'freedom to expand and thicken'; a decree in Vienna (1728) stated that they could not be worn in church. Even when, by the middle of the century, the sack had become more fitted, there were still moralists in England who found it 'loose, and indecent ... calculated to hide any defects in the body'.[19] Yet even under a loose-fitting gown, women wore laced stays; lack of stays denoted a whore (the prostitutes in *Clarissa* wore a 'shocking dishabille, and without stays ... their gowns hanging trollopy'), or at least evidence of moral delinquency. For the stays were felt necessary to give support to the bust (lighter versions were worn at night), and to push the shoulders back; the shape of the bosom varied from the full protuberance of the early years of the century, to the flat effect, created by the stays laced high, of the middle years, and in the 1780s a pouter-pigeon look was fashionable, the natural bosom being eked out by layers of starched muslin

Taste A-La-Mode, 1745

Published According to Act of Parliament Sept. 12. 1745. Price 6.d.

68 **'Taste A-La-Mode'**, 1745, engraving after
L. P. Boitard

The enormously wide hooped skirts worn by the
fashionable female promenaders are ridiculed both for
their ungainly size and for their opportunities for
flirtatious invitation.

or even 'bosom friends' of wool or flannel. Stiffly
boned stays laced high up the bosom, which
contributed to the rigidity and antique appearance,
noted by foreigners, of Englishwomen in the early
eighteenth century, gave way by the 1760s to a
more natural shape, attributed by Grosley to the
newly fashionable country pursuits such as riding,
and also to the fact that young girls were not put in
'armour but in a lightly boned waistcoat' which
kept 'the body in a slight compression'.[20] High
lacing was a sign of the more modest middle class
throughout the century; in *Les Liaisons Dangereuses*
(1784) Présidente Tourvel, an attractive bourgeoise,
has 'a tolerable shape', but dressed without elegance,
with 'her stays up to her chin'.[21]

The stays, whether cut low or high, and the
hooped petticoat, presented a smooth taut appearance which was essential for formal dress. The
correct manipulation of the hoop, particularly
when it was very wide in the 1730s and 1740s, and
for court throughout the century (when the lady
had to move backwards from the royal presence),
was a sign of good breeding. The *Female Spectator*
of 1744, when hoops were huge, found women 'do
not walk, but straddle, and sometimes run with a
kind of frisk and jump, and throw their enormous
hoops almost in the faces of those who pass them
by'.[22] When hoops were flattened in front, there
was more decorum in movement (women could sit
down with more decency) but the excessive width
made women move sideways through doors, and sit
like puppets, with feet sticking out; the greater
negligence in dress with softer fabrics of the last
quarter of the century meant that for the first time
in the century, women were seen to have knees.

Men were also expected to demonstrate gentility
through their clothes, and in particular through the
accessories of formal elegance, the sword and the
chapeau bras. The sword was the traditional emblem of gentility, and was necessary to cope with
the violence that was part of life in the streets of any
city: '. . . all the World here wear Swords, and Paris
resembles the Utopia of Sir Thomas More, where

69 Portrait of a gentleman, *c.*1745, attributed to T. Hudson

The almost balletic stance, and the hand inserted in the waistcoat, are no doubt the work of the dancing master. This is formal, possibly court dress, with the lavishly trimmed brocade waistcoat, and chapeau bras.

they were not wearing a sword; the correct thing was to hold the hilt of the sword to prevent it entangling in the legs, or, worse still, in women's clothing, an occupational hazard at dances and polite assemblies and even in the street. Boswell, in Holland in 1763, wished Hogarth had been there to record the sight of a Dutchman in a blue night-gown, 'with a wig of amazing size and a sword at right-angles to his body'; not only should the sword have been held close to the side, but it was at this date properly worn only in full dress, along with the bag-wig and chapeau bras. The *London Magazine* of 1774 had great fun with those who did not know how to keep the black silk bag fixed to short hair, or to deal with the chapeau bras; 'a country boor' did not know which arm he was to put it under: '. . . sometimes he has it in his hand, sometimes in his mouth, and often betrayed a great inclination to put it on his head, concluding that it was a dammed troublesome, useless thing'.[25] Elegance of deport-ment was crucial for the man of fashion, and had to be taught by the dancing master; had Dr Johnson been so instructed, he might not have had his body in continual agitation, see-sawing up and down as Fanny Burney described it, but might have assumed the 'affected delicacy' of Horace Walpole, who entered a room 'chapeau-bras under his arm, or compressed between his hands, knees bent and feet on tiptoe, as if he were afraid of a wet floor'.[26]

Civilization was often only veneer-thin in a violent society, and dancing (at public assemblies established in fashionable towns all over Europe) helped people to participate in social functions, and to conduct themselves with gentility and without affectation. The dancing master was needed, said Lord Chesterfield to his lumpish son, 'not so much to teach you to dance, as to walk, dance and sit well', and for this purpose he employed Denoyer, a popular French dancing master of the 1740s who also taught at Westminster School, where the subject was as much an essential part of the syllabus as was Greek or Latin. In an age in which entry into company had to be performed like a minuet, with grace and elegance, men, said an English visitor to France, had to learn 'savoir vivre' which he defined thus: 'to make a Bow, enter a Room, or offer any Thing gracefully; to accost a Lady, or run over the Alphabet of Compliments with an Air of Facility and without the least Appearance of Bashfulness or Inexperience.'[27]

Minuets, allemandes and quadrilles were danced at court, but the most popular dances at assemblies were increasingly the so-called 'English' dances or country dances, where dancers ranged themselves opposite (i.e. 'contre') their partners in long lines. The aim, it was felt, of a civilized society was for the

there is no Distinction of Persons,' was the com-ment of an English visitor in the early eighteenth century.[23] As late as 1786 Sobry noted that all French gentlemen thought they had a right to wear a sword which it was difficult to make them renounce. In Bath in the early years of the century, Beau Nash fought hard to prevent swords being worn at the Assembly Rooms, and his influence helped to popularize the cane instead;[24] by the middle of our period in England, duels ceased to be such an important way of deciding quarrels, and, except on the most formal occasions, men no longer wore swords. Yet in countries where French in-fluence was paramount, where the nobility held on to this privilege, or where duelling remained in vogue, the sword continued to be worn. In Verona in 1786 the observant Goethe noted that men of rank swung their right arm as they walked, being accustomed to holding the left arm still, even when

70 The Mall in St James's Park, 1783 by
T. Gainsborough

This is the painting which Walpole aptly described as 'all
a-flutter like a lady's fan'. The floating layers of silk
gauze for the dresses emphasize the soft, rounded outline
of the fashionable lady. The dress can either trail on the
ground (on the left) or be fastened up (on the right) in
the jaunty triple loops of the polonaise.

sexes to dance together; a visitor to Edinburgh in
the mid-1770s found the men preferred their traditional dances which they performed 'with gestures so uncouth and a vivacity so hideous that you
would have thought they were acting some mid-
night ceremonies or enchanting the moon' (this was
before Sir Walter Scott had made Highland customs romantic), or when they did dance with
women, it was without looking at their partners,
and regarding it as 'a field of exercise'.[28] Dancing

masters found a ready audience for individual
lessons; a Mr Dukes of Cheapside, announcing his
services in the *Public Advertiser* of 17 October 1759,
emphasized that 'Grown Gentlemen or Ladies are
taught in so private a Manner as to be seen by none
but myself', successful pupils being 'fit to appear in
the genteelest Assemblies'. He also sold, for 10s 6d, a
book of instructions, one of the many manuals that
were produced throughout the century, which
taught dancing by numbers, men and women
practising before a mirror.

Dressing was a ritual as complicated as the
manoeuvres of the stately French dances, a rigid
dividing line being driven between formal and
informal dress. As formal dress was often rich and
uncomfortable, and took, in some cases, so long to
prepare, it was generally the custom to dress for
dinner time, the main meal of the day, which took
place at about 2 p.m., although often as late as 4 p.m.
by the end of the period. To Arthur Young in the
1780s, formal dressing was a nuisance which he

hoped would eventually take place in the evening:

What is a man good for after his silk breeches and stockings are on, his hat under his arm, and his head bien poudré. Can he botanize in a watered meadow? Can he clamber the rocks to mineralize? Can he farm with the peasant and the ploughman? He is in order for the conversation of the ladies . . . an excellent employment; but it is an employment that never relishes better than after a day spent in active toil or animated pursuit . . .[29]

When Pamela managed to capture Mr B., among the list of duties expected of her as his wife was 'to be dressed by dinner time . . . and whomsoever I bring home with me to my table, you'll be ready to receive them'. Lady Mary Coke tells us she was always dressed by 11.30 a.m., and Clarissa dressed after breakfast 'when I have no household employ-ments to prevent me'. For household tasks a skirt and jacket were often worn, the bodice being unboned for ease and comfort, or worn over a lightly boned and decoratively laced stomacher; for those not involved in the supervision of servants, a fashionable déshabillé or undress could be worn in the parks and gardens which every city possessed, and which were places to display the latest styles. In England, St James's Park and the Mall were places in which to be seen walking; Baron Bielfeld found the

71 **'Les Jardins de Benfica'**, 1785, by J. B. Pillement

These gardens provided a fashionable promenade for the citizens of Lisbon. The ladies have adopted French and English modes, with, in the background, the addition of wide, light shawls. Talking to two officers in the foreground is a fashionable lady wearing a polonaise, and with her ribboned cap tilting forwards over her high coiffure.

72 **'Le Lever'**, after P. Longhi

The sensual elements of the morning toilette, with its appreciative male audience, can be seen here as the lady is helped by her maid into her negligée du matin. The husband, or at least a man whose open shirt, loose gown, unbuttoned breeches and negligent hose indicate an intimacy with the central figure, has his patrician wig and gown on stands by the bed.

dress of the English ladies in the Mall 'extremely neat; instead of a large hoop, they have short pettycoats; their gowns are elegant but not gaudy; they have short cloaks trimd with lace and little hats either of straw or beaver, or els feathers in their hair'.[30] When dressed for the day, a hooped formal open robe would have been worn, suitable for all occasions except appearance at the opera, formal assembly, or court. In Paris people of fashion in the early eighteenth century loved the Tuileries gardens, where 'you may see display'd in Attire every thing that Extravagance can invent, the most tender and the most touching. The Ladies in Fashions ever new, with their Adjustments, their Ribbons, their Jewels, and agreeable Manner of dressing in Stuffs of Gold and Silver, declare the continual Applications of their Magnificence.'[31] Later, the gardens of the Palais Royal became the fashionable promenade.

In France, the morning toilette was a fine art and a leisurely procedure at which friends could be present and business affairs discussed. Louise Fusil, in her *Souvenirs d'une Actrice* (1841) described how a lady of fashion on the eve of the French Revolution performed her toilette with an almost sexual lingering on its pleasures, reflected in the importance of underwear and negligée garments[32] (Chérubin in *The Marriage of Figaro* confessed to Suzanne his envy at her intimacy with the Countess Almaviva, 'l'habiller le matin et la déshabiller le soir, épingle à épingle'). On awakening, the fashionable lady rang for her maid who handed her a lace-trimmed *manteau de lit* for her early ablutions, after which she was dressed in a *negligée du matin*, a loose robe worn over chemise and stays. Then she was ready to

receive visitors in her cabinet de toilette; these could include men, and very often abbés, who acted the part of *cicisbei* and were always there with the latest news and gossip. It was then that her hair was done, either by a personal maid or a male hairdresser, and the finishing touches applied to the face; the French hairdresser, said Smollett in 1766, 'regulates the distribution of her patches and advises where to lay on the paint . . . If he sees a curl or even a single hair amiss, he produces his comb, his scissors and pomatum and sets it to rights.'[33] The light-hearted intimacy of the lingering toilette was an essential part of dressing in the eighteenth century; 'Une femme, pour être jolie, emploie plus de raffinement & de politique à sa toilette, qu'il n'y en a dans tous les cabinets de l'Europe,' stated the *Petite Dictionnaire de la Cour* (1788). By this time the art of undress was a witty and subtle language of its own; a *negligée de malade* (a muslin peignoir trimmed with lace) could, according to Louise Fusil, 'annoncer une indisposition, ou une convalescence, à inspirer enfin un grand intérêt'.[34]

Informality for men was the keynote for the early morning, and nightgowns could be worn at breakfast and in the street. When in 1750 Sir Thomas Bottle, Chancellor to the Prince of Wales, visited Cliveden, Walpole noted that he took with him 'a night-gown, cap and slippers of gold brocade in which he came down to breakfast the next morning'.[35] So popular was the nightgown for street wear, particularly for students, that in some university towns there were regulations against its use out-of-doors; in 1781, for example, the Count Palatine of Bayreuth had to issue an order that students and young men in the street should wear 'decent dress' and not slop around in gowns. It was permissible to wear the gown in male company, in coffee houses and for morning business meetings, but not before ladies, and Beau Nash had forbidden their wear in Bath.

We have seen that England was the first country which adopted the frock coat for morning undress. In this, and sometimes with his hair rolled up in paper clay rollers (which curled the hair before it was dressed by the barber), the fashionable Englishman walked in the park. In Fielding's *Joseph Andrews* (1742), a foppish young man described his day to the accompaniment of groans from Parson Adams: 'In the Morning I arose, took my great Stick and walked out in my green Frock with my Hair in Papers (a Groan from Adams) and sauntered about till Ten.'[36] From 2 p.m. to 4 p.m. was spent in dressing, then came two hours dining, followed by a number of visits and finally to the theatre; by the end of the century Englishmen had begun to form exclusive clubs which largely took the place of the

La petite Toilette.

earlier coffee houses, and where formal dress was required.

For men, the morning toilet was an occasion for business affairs as well as for formal dressing. Madame d'Epinay found her husband's mornings rather a trial; while he was being dressed by his valets-de-chambre, with lackeys and a secretary waiting for orders, and discussing business with his horse-dealer, an opera singer, and other callers, she had to deal with the creditors.[37] One of Retif de la Bretonne's moral and entertaining stories to illustrate life and manners in the late 1780s recounts the morning toilet of the marquis de L***, who receives his tailor while his hair is being done; although the tailor and his assistant dwell on the elegance of cut and the refinement of the embroidery on the suit which they have made, the marquis insists on alternative buttons, like those which he has seen worn by the Duke of F***, the alterations to take place within the hour.

In England, said Madame du Bocage in 1750, 'it is not thought necessary to dress except to appear at the Opera, or at the places where they are invited to dine'.[38] For the theatre and for formal entertainment, full dress was *de rigueur*; this consisted of a suit with matching coat and breeches, usually of silk and sometimes embroidered, and with an embroidered waistcoat, hair dressed with a bag at the back, chapeau bras and sword. At the opera, said J. T. Smith in his *Nollekens and his Times*, men wore 'swords and bags in full dress', and he particularly noted the artist Cosway, a well-known dandy, who appeared 'full dressed in his sword and bag with a small three cornered hat on the top of his powdered toupee and a mulberry silk coat profusely embroidered with scarlet strawberries';[39] by this time full dress was, according to the *Fashionable Magazine*, 'too antiquated for any other place than court' (1786). The court in England was 'the residence of dullness', according to foreign visitors; the nobility paid their respects at the levées and drawing-rooms (and in fact any well-dressed person could see the royal family even if they were not officially presented), but the real centres of fashion were aristocratic

assemblies, or fashionable watering-places such as Bath. On the Continent, and particularly in the smaller German states, the court was the sum of fashionable people. It regulated existence and organized entertainments such as hunting, dances, card assemblies, sleighing parties in winter, promenades in summer, the French theatre and the Italian opera. Choosing the correct dress for the day, and for the many functions at court, required care and attention. The Saxon minister Count Brühl

had at least 300 suits of clothes; each had a duplicate, as he did not choose that his dress should appear different in the afternoon from what it had been in the morning. A painting of each suit, with the particular cane and snuff-box belonging to it, was very accurately drawn in a large book, which was presented to his Excellency every morning by his valet-de-chambre, that he might fix upon the dress in which he wished to appear for the day.[40]

The greatest ritual of the formal toilette took place at court, where for most of the century monarchs and their families were on display, dressing, dining and undressing in public. The process of dressing (*lever*) and undressing (*coucher*) had become formalized in the reign of Louis XIV, a tradition that was continued by his heirs, for personal attendance on the monarch was a sign of political favour. Louis XV, although interested in dress, performed the boring ritual of the formal *lever* and *coucher* with a dignified indifference. Before the formal dressing in the morning, he received the queen, the royal children and the princes of the blood in bed for the *grandes entrées*; then his personal officers such as the Grand Master of the Wardrobe and the Gentlemen of the Bedchamber were allowed the *premières entrées* to watch him wash, shave and dress for the day. In the evening at the *grand coucher* he retired publicly in the bedroom that had once belonged to Louis XIV, afterwards dressing to return to his private suite or that of his current mistress; after a time he no longer kept up the pretence of taking off his clothes.

Louis XVI was far less interested in what he wore, but readier to comply with the custom; his own taste was for simplicity, but the Wardrobe ordered for him six full-dress suits a quarter, in addition to hunting suits, uniforms, and the *habits de cérémonie* supplied by Dargé, master-tailor in Paris. One of his pages, d'Hézecques, left an account[42] of his *lever* and *coucher*, occasions of formality mixed with touches of buffoonery, a tradition that had become totally meaningless. The king rose at 7 or 8, but as the formal *lever* did not take place until 11.30, he dressed in a simple grey or brown suit; then he had to undress, put on a morning gown, and leave his

73 **'La petite toilette'**, engraving after J. M. Moreau, from the *Monument du Costume Physique et Moral de la fin du dix-huitième siècle*, (1789)

While the nobleman's hair is being dressed (the assistant barber on the far right heats up the curling papers with tongs), the tailor with a new coat is received in audience. In the background stands the running footman, with his traditional feathered cap, ready to deliver messages from his master.

private apartments for the bedroom of ceremony, where those such as the princes of the blood and the knights of the Saint-Esprit watched him being dressed in shirt and stockings; the Grand Master of the Wardrobe put on the breeches, waistcoat and the cordon bleu of the Saint-Esprit, and then the coat (those lesser courtiers such as tutors, equerries, chaplains and even distinguished foreigners were by now present), and finally the two Masters of the Wardrobe gave him his handkerchief, hat, gloves and sword. His hair, which had been prepared on rising by his *valet-de-chambre barbier*, was then given the finishing touches and powdered. For the coucher there was an equally ceremonial disrobing; the holding of the sleeves of the coat as it was taken off was a particularly prized privilege, as was that of presenting the king with his nightshirt. When the robe was put on, the breeches were unbuttoned and fell to the ground, and 'thus attired, hardly able to walk so absurdly encumbered, he began to make the round of the circle' (i.e. to talk to those watching him) before the final stages of his undressing were completed in privacy.

The queen had an equally elaborate morning ritual, her morning toilette being, according to Madame Campan, her First Lady of the Bedchamber,[42] a 'chef-d'œuvre d'etiquette'. The public *lever* took place at noon, after the queen had had her hair dressed; the first lady of honour handed her water to wash her hands, and then her chemise (this was also an honour claimed by a princess of the blood if she were present, which led to squabbles which Marie Antoinette found tiresome). The Mistress of the Robes handed the Queen her petticoat and robe, and the accessories that went with it, then her handkerchief and gloves which were presented to her on a gold or silver salver. Later in her reign, the Queen abandoned the formal dressing in her bedchamber, because she preferred Rose Bertin to be with her while this took place (and the modiste, not being of noble blood, was not allowed at the *lever*), so, after having had her hair done, she withdrew to her private closet to dress.

Her expenditure on clothes was huge; officially, said Madame de Campan in her memoirs, she had every winter and summer 12 *grands habits*, 12 *robes parées* (formal robes with paniers) and 12 undress robes, all of which were discarded at the end of every season. There were as well informal muslin or linen gowns which were brought when required and which were, paradoxically, kept for several years, being re-trimmed if especially liked. Yet the 120,000 livres allowed by the government would not have covered the numbers of gowns ordered; in one year alone 172 were recorded, and in 1786 she earned the sobriquet of Madame Deficit, for spending more than twice what was allocated to her. Clothes had to be stage-managed so that the correct colours and accessories were matched, and a dress for a gala occasion was worn but once; every day the queen was presented with a book of samples of dress materials, from which she marked with a pin those she needed for the various functions of the day, which could include formal morning dress, an afternoon déshabillé and full dress for evening card or supper parties in the private apartments, as well as the *grands habits* for court presentations. The sample book for 1782 survives in the Archives Nationales,[44] with 78 surviving samples (some have vanished and the total might be over 100) from *grands habits*, *robes parées*, to *robes turques*, lévites and redingotes, but not including jackets, skirts, cloaks, mantles, the hundreds of other accessories or the intimate gowns of the boudoir. The book was then taken back to the wardrobe and all that was needed for the day was brought in large baskets covered in silk; the wardrobe woman who had the care of the linen brought in the *prêt du jour* which contained a daily supply of chemises and kerchiefs, and in the evening the *prêt de la nuit* for nightgown and cap.

Other courts in Europe used Versailles as a model, but although formal dressing in public was an accepted idea, many rulers were more modest in their ritual or reluctant to spent their time on such a restrictive etiquette. Philip V of Spain, for example, although French by birth, only spent 15 minutes dressing, for the main royal event was the toilette of the queen, who was the real ruler of the country. The *lever* and *coucher* of the Swedish king, Gustavus III, was based on Versailles,[44] the courtiers entering to see his formal dressing; once a week the royal couple dined in public and played cards in state, the afternoons being spent in reading and other entertainment, while the king occasionally embroidered belts and scarves for the ladies of the court. To Catherine the Great, the French pomp affected at the Swedish court was the sign of an effeminate ruler, and she herself late in her reign had evolved a toilette that was comfortable rather than glamorous. One of her secretaries, Adrian Gribovsky,[45] listed the events of her day, which began with a morning spent on affairs of state, dressed in a heavy white silk dress and crêpe cap, and a simple toilet at noon which consisted of wiping the face with iced water and having her hair dressed with small curls behind the ears and a cap pinned on, while a selected circle of visitors chatted to her; she then retired into her private bedroom and with the help of her ladies dressed for the day, usually in Livonian dress or another informal gown. Unlike the Empress Anna, who changed her dress six times a day, Catherine's tastes were simple, although for formal court occasions, French splendour and lavish jewellery were worn.

Perhaps the simplest court in relation to its size and importance was that of England. George I brought with him in 1714 a German staff (and two Turkish valets-de-chambre) who dispensed with the more formal dressing and undressing by sine-cured courtiers, though the right of putting on the shirt remained a privilege of the groom closest to the king. The Office of the Robes, under a Master and a Yeoman, provided official robes, mourning and liveries, as well as furnishing for state apartments; although George I was dressed by his personal body servants, both George II and George

III reverted to the original custom of being dressed by the Master and the Yeoman, but formal dressing was a simple affair without the squabbling for precedence that marred the French court.[46]

The queen's morning toilette was also simple in comparison to that of her French counterpart. The most famous account was provided by the novelist Fanny Burney, who was appointed Assistant Keeper to Queen Charlotte in 1786. She found it interesting but exhausting, for she had to be ready dressed by 7 a.m., when the queen would call her to help Mrs Thielky, her wardrobe woman: 'Mrs Thielky hands the things to me and I put them on. 'Tis fortunate for me I have not the handling them – I should never know which to take first, embarrassed as I am, and should run a prodigious risk of giving the gown before the hoop, and the fan before the neckerchief'.[47] Fanny then had to help prepare the formal dress for the queen, who dressed at 12.45 in the State Dressing Room; the queen's gown was removed, a loose peignoir put on while she had her hair dressed and powdered (she read the newspapers while this was being done), and the robe was presented by the Keeper of the Robes, Mrs Schwellenberg.

Courts had, from the earliest times, been sources of power and wealth, and magnets for the ambitious; in addition, they were arbiters of taste and culture. This was particularly so at the court in France, which was, in La Bruyère's phrase, the 'centre du goût et de la politesse', personified by the brilliance of the ruler. Under Louis XIV, a system of controlled admission to the court and the king was introduced, a complicated set of rules called 'les honneurs de la cour', which governed who could sit in the presence of the king and the royal family (and the kind of chairs they could sit on), who could dine or play cards in the royal apartments, assist at the *lever* and *coucher*, ride in the royal carriages, hunt with the king and be present at the *débotter*, i.e. when he returned from hunting. Under Louis XIV no man was not a *fils* or *petit-fils de France* could be admitted to the king's table, although on campaigns this was sometimes relaxed, but by the reign of Louis XV some favourites were admitted not by birth but as 'une faveur de choix', leading to the unedifying squabbles over trifles which marked the eighteenth-century French court.

For men, court dress consisted of 'des habits à grands paremens, brodés sur toutes les tailles'; cloths of gold and silver stuff, with embroidery in precious or semi-precious stones on the coat and waistcoat made up court formal dress of unparalleled splendour. With the suit went red-heeled shoes, which remained as distinctive a mark of the aristocracy as the bag-wig or the sword.

74 'Le Seigneur et la Dame de Cour', anon. engraving, from *Les Costumes François Representans Les differens Etats du Royaume, avec les Habillemens*, 1776

The nobleman wears court dress with the sash and badge of the Order of the Saint-Esprit. The lady is in the full *robe de cour*, or *grand habit*, with tightly boned bodice, hooped skirt, and train.

For women, rules for admission to court were stricter, as they had to prove a title of nobility reaching back to 1400, although there could be a dispensation for favourites; in any society the laws regulating the conduct of women have always been more rigid, and sharp eyes were constantly on the lookout for any infringement in court etiquette. For presentation at court women had to wear the *grand habit*, which was basically the fashionable dress of the 1670s, with short sleeves, heavily boned bodice, and elaborately draped train, but worn over a large hoop; with no alterations, this lasted until the French Revolution. 'Le grand habit de Cour', said *L'Art du Tailleur* (1769), 'consiste en un corps fermé, plein de baleines, & un bas de robe; le corps se couvre d'étoffe; le bas de robe se fait de mêmes étoffes, ainsi que le jupon'.[49] The *tailleur de corps* made the whaleboned bodice and the train ('bas de robe'), the *couturière* made the skirt, and the *marchande de mode* provided the elaborate trimmings which covered the dress, as well as the lace for the flounced sleeves and the lappets for the head. On the day of presentation, the dress had to be in black, with matching trimming ('agréments'), and a little tippet ('palatine') of black decorated with black ornaments ('pompoms') as were the lower sleeve bands ('bracelets noirs'); the following day the lady had to appear at court in a *grand habit* made of colours and covered in jewels. For the presentation of Madame de Villedueil in 1787, Madame Eloffe made her a dress in black and silver decorated with fringes and ribbons, with court sleeves and lappets of Alençon lace; for the next day she wore a dress of satin, white and pistachio-coloured and decorated with embroidered gauze, over a skirt of white crêpe.[50]

The presentation was often an ordeal, for the lady had to curtsy with a large hoop, and to kiss the hem of the queen's gown (having taken off her glove to do so); after a brief conversation, she then retired backwards, with three curtsies, having to cope not only with the huge hoop, but also the enormous train. This was where the services of a dancing master were so useful; when the marquise de la Tour du Pin was presented a few days after her marriage in 1787, she had lessons from M. Huart, who impersonated the queen at one moment, and then the actions of the lady who was being presented to her.[51] Not only did the boned bodice straps cut into the shoulders, but, according to the marquise, the weight of the dress made it impossible to raise the foot in heels three inches high, so the correct movement was to take little gliding steps, the lady with huge hoop looking like a ship in full sail. Not only did the train and hooped skirt take vast amounts of material (20 to 22 yards, according

to the comtesse de Genlis) but the decorations on the paniers, she said, were an indescribable sight *en masse*:

Leurs énormes paniers formoient un riche espalier, artistement couvert de perles, d'argent, d'or, de paillons de couleur et de pierreries. L'effet de toutes ces brillantes paniers réunies, ne peut de décrire. On portoit alors non-seulement des fleurs mais de fruits, des cerises, des groseilles, des fraises avec leurs fleurs. L'art imitoit ces fruits à s'y méprendre.[52]

The *grand habit* was not only worn for court presentations, but for ceremonial occasions such as the chapters of the order of the Saint-Esprit, baptisms and marriages of members of the royal family, and the *grands bals parés*, the court balls. From about 1783 the *grande robe à la française*, worn over a medium hoop, replaced the *grand habit* on all but the most formal occasions, being acceptable for services in the royal chapel, receptions, court mourning and when the court travelled to Marly or Fontainebleau.

With varying degrees of imitation, court dress at Versailles was followed by the rest of Europe, notably at the German courts and in Russia. In Italy, courts were fairly poor, and women did not wear the *grand habit*, except for the grandest occasions. Men wore black suits, though the style of wig varied from court to court; Boswell in Turin in 1765 hired a valet (their advice regarding individual court regulations was invaluable to the travellers to whom they hired themselves) who stated that the hair had to be dressed in a 'horse-tail', which Boswell, after abusing the fellow, complied with. It was also possible at court to wear a uniform; Casanova, having renounced the clerical profession, went to Bologna, (1745), where he wore a uniform invented by himself of 'white, the vest blue, a gold and silver shoulder knot and a sword knot of the same material . . . I procured a long sword, and with my cockade and wearing a long false pigtail, I sallied forth'.[53] When Boswell was in Dresden in 1764 he wished to attend the court, but was at first frustrated for it was in mourning and he did not have a black suit; eventually he decided to go as an army officer, but with his unerring talent for the wrong thing, chose a white cockade for his hat, a Jacobite emblem which was hardly tactful.

In England, private frugal tastes at court contrasted with public show. The *grand habit*, or the English version of it, the 'straight-bodied gown', was worn only by members of the royal family and on occasions of exceptional splendour such as royal marriages and coronations; most ladies at court wore the mantua with train, described by the

View of the COURT at St JAMES's with the Ceremony of introducing a Lady to her Majesty. — Noble sculp

75   View of the Court at St James's with the Ceremony of introducing a Lady to her Majesty, engraving by Noble

Although this engraving dates from the late 1770s or early 1780s, a period when in theory women at court are beginning to adopt the sack dress, here it is still the elaborately decorated tight-bodied gown or mantua, with the treble sleeve ruffles that etiquette demanded. Most ladies wear the long lace lappets pendant.

Magazine à la Mode of 1777 as 'a close body without pleats or robings; and a train descending from the waist, two and a half, or three yards long, and containing two breadths of silk . . . The stays are cut low before and shaped like a heart. The Hoop is French resembling the shape of a bell.' The queen's train, three yards in length, was borne by a page, but those of the other ladies were 'looped up to the left side of the hoop by a button and a loop at the end of which is a large tassel'.[54] Mrs Adams, an American in London in 1785, chose 'a white lutestring, covered and full trimmed with white crape, festooned with lilac ribbon and mock point lace over a hoop of enormous extent',[55] which she wore with treble ruffles, lace lappets and white plumes; as a staunch republican she found the ceremony tedious (guests stood in a circle while the king walked round to the right, the queen and princesses to the left) and the royal conversation limited.

From the early 1780s the customary court dress was the sack (it had for some years been no longer a part of high fashion), also worn over a large hoop and with treble ruffles; the novelist Fanny Burney noted a conversation in 1782 between two ladies complaining about the court dress required for the Duchess of Cumberland's Drawing Room: 'How disagreeable these sacques are! I am so incommoded with these nasty ruffles.'[56] The actress Sarah Siddons went with some trepidation to read to the king and queen at Buckingham House, wearing 'a Sacque or Negligée with a hoop, treble ruffles and Lappets, in which costume I felt not at all my ease';[57] the hoop, in fact, was to stay as part of court dress until 1820, looking increasingly odd as the waistline rose during the neo-classical period.

As we would expect in England, men's court dress was influenced by the move towards simplicity; by the end of the 1770s the French frock, which was more stylish and tighter-fitting than the English frock, and embroidered, was admitted at court, except for very solemn and grand occasions.

In Spain at the beginning of the eighteenth century, a French-dominated court meant that for women the *grand habit* was worn, with slight differences, such as a panel of lace worn as a background to the many orders which royal ladies and others wore on occasions of ceremony. Men continued to wear the slashed trunk hose and doublet with ruff, which had not changed since the end of the sixteenth century, but, by the end of our period, only for the most formal occasions, such as court investitures and receptions.

Spanish influence lingered in the dress worn by men at the court in Vienna;[58] this consisted of black doublet and breeches with a short black cloak, the whole decorated with lace, a hat turned up on one side and surmounted by a plume, red stockings and red shoes. On gala days, the king wore a Spanish suit either in gold or in black, the latter with 'small cuffs of purple embroidered with silver; his shoe ribbons are also embroidered, and he wears a red feather in his hat',[59] the only item of French clothing being the long periwig; the greatest ceremony took place at the court in Vienna, the Hofburg, but at the summer palaces of Laxenburg and Schönbrunn, French elegance was permitted. Maria Theresa, who preferred a bourgeois intimacy in her private life, to a large extent dispensed with Spanish formality in clothing, although some of the older courtiers adhered to it; in 1788 the marquis de Bouillé met the aged Count Kaunitz wearing the short Spanish mantle[60] which he kept to for warmth in winter, with the traditional black suit which he always wore with the star of the Toison d'Or, and the diamond star of the Order of St Stephen, established by Maria Theresa in 1764. Formal occasions were still, however, regulated by the movements of Spanish etiquette (even men had to curtsy to the empress) until Joseph II in 1780 abolished all surviving remnants of it; the only fixed gala day was New Year's day, the others to be as he was moved to call them, which was unsettling to a court used to the old ways.

For women, Spanish black remained for some years as part of Austrian court dress; Lady Mary Wortley Montagu in 1716 found ladies wearing black velvet gowns embroidered with gold and silver and worn over coloured skirts. By the middle of the century, trained sacks in the French style were worn; Lady Mary Coke found in 1770 that the only difference was that along with the black lace lappets, 'you are permitted to wear the ribbon of the colour of your robe & as many diamonds as you please'.[61]

To a large extent the power of a court depended on its formal splendour (only exceptional princes like Frederick the Great could afford to dispense with pomp); where a king was personally insignificant, ceremony acted as a rampart to royal authority. This was particularly true at the court of Louis XVI, where the king appeared gauche against the pomp of pageantry; one of his pages, d'Hézecques,

76 **Infanta Carlota Joaquina, Queen of Portugal**, by M. S. Maella

The portrait dates from the mid-1780s, at the time of her marriage to the future King João VI of Portugal, when she was ten years old. The heavily embroidered and fringed court dress with its long pointed bodice and attached train has with some minor variations in the shape of the bodice neckline, and the cut of the sleeve, been adopted from France.

77 **The Empress Maria Theresa and her family**, after M. van Meytens

The Empress, in ermine-lined robes of state, is enthroned with her husband Franz Stephan who wears the Spanish-influenced gala court costume of gold, covered with embroidery, lace and ribbons. On his mother's left hand stands the future Emperor Joseph II wearing the Order of the Golden Fleece; two of the younger princes wear Hungarian costume which was popular at the Austrian court.

writing in 1804, in echo of Figaro's famous state-ment about the basic equality of all men if accidents of birth were set aside, said: 'Dépouillez le prince de l'état qui l'environne, il ne sera plus aux yeux de la multitude, qu'un homme ordinaire.'[62]

Ceremonial costume reinforced the historic rights of monarchs and the privileges of aristocracy. Coronation costume could emphasize the religious and traditional base on which a prince governed; Louis XV for example wore in 1722 the violet mantle sewn with gold fleur-de-lys and lined with ermine over a violet silk tunic and dalmatic also sewn with gold fleur-de-lys, religious vestments which dated in style from the early Middle Ages. In 1772 Gustavus III of Sweden deliberately strength-ened a somewhat shaky historical continuity when he designed for his coronation tunic[63] a copy of that worn by his predecessor, Karl XI, in the late seventeenth century, under a mantle of purple velvet lined with ermine and embroidered with crowns in gold thread and pearls. Imperial splen-dour also marked the coronation costume of Cath-erine II of Russia (1762), a gown of silver silk embroidered with eagles, and the customary purple velvet mantle (which had been made in Paris for the coronation of Catherine I in 1724) encrusted with hundreds of double-headed gold eagles.

The ceremonial processions and investitures of knightly orders formed an important part of court display, from the black embroidered with gold flames of the Saint-Esprit, to the gold-embroidered crimson habits of the Toison d'Or. A prince's standing was also demonstrated by the appearance of his envoys at foreign courts, and by the splendour of his liveries. As French ambassador to Vienna in 1725, the duc de Richelieu entered in state in regal style with 69 carriages, the horses of his own carriage being shod in silver, and surrounded by running footmen in red velvet covered in silver braid and fringes, 12 pages on horseback in red and silver, and 50 foot valets in scarlet embroidered in purple and silver galloon.

Richelieu knew that he had to make a considerable effort to impress the court in a city used to a wide range of glamorous uniforms and exotic liveries. For in Vienna,[64] a visitor could see the German guard in red with facings of black velvet, embroidered in gold, the Galician guard in Polish cavalry costume, and the Hungarian guard in scarlet hussar uniform; in addition, many of the magnates who made up the Austrian empire had large contingents of heyducks (liveried personal servants, originally Hungarian or Polish) dressed in Turkish caftans covered in gold or silver lace or embroidery. Joseph II followed the German fondness for wearing uniform as an alternative to court dress; this demonstrated independence from France and could also be as rich as the *habit à la française* when worn with diamond encrusted orders.

By the second half of the eighteenth century, many courts had begun to develop personal liveries exclusive to the royal family and their circle. These very often began as uniforms to be worn at royal places away from the main court centre; in France, for example, Louis XV instituted a 'uniforme des petits châteaux', of green braided with gold, to be worn by his intimate circle (later, each royal château required a uniform of a different colour), and at Madame de Pompadour's château of Bellevue[65] she invented in 1750 a livery which for men was a purple, gold-embroidered suit lined with white satin, with a waistcoat of grey-white embroidered in purple and gold, and for women a dress of grey-white silk with the same gold and purple embroidery. This was, in fact, almost as expensive as court wear, for although the marquise donated the material, the guests had to pay for the costly embroidery, and equip their valets in the correct livery of green cloth with gold braid. At other summer courts or hunting palaces, similar liveries were worn; at Laxenburg Maria Theresa introduced a red cloth frock with green waistcoat and golden tassels, and for women a red gown with gold trimming; at Nymphenburg (the summer palace of

the Bavarian royal family) guests were to wear a uniform of green and white, and at Oranienbaum (a Russian royal hunting lodge) in the 1750s men wore a blue coat with grey breeches and women a blue gown with grey petticoat.

In England in 1778 George III introduced the Windsor uniform[66] of blue with red collar and cuffs and gold braid; by this date blue and red were fashionable uniform colours as well as being used for servants' liveries, and made popular hunting and riding outfits (in 1779 the queen and princesses were wearing riding habits of blue faced and turned up with red). The Windsor uniform as worn by a small royal circle was very plain compared to the more lavish European styles, but it occasionally inspired elaborate feminine versions for special occasions; one such was a ball given at Windsor to celebrate the king's recovery from his illness in 1789, when ladies wore 'a Garter blue body trimmed with a scarlet and gold edge, the stomacher white, laced with gold cord, the sleeves white with a crêpe festoon on the shoulders, tied up with gold tassels, a

78 **Queen Maria Lesczynska**, 1740, by L. Tocqué

The queen wears her ermine-lined coronation mantle embroidered with fleurs-de-lis, over the *grand habit*; the bodice is trimmed with gold lace and a huge stomacher brooch with pendant pearls. Attached to her powdered hair can be seen the false ringlets which were customarily worn for coronations. The tout ensemble indicates her rank rather than her dress in 1740, for her marriage took place some years earlier.

79 **Gustavus III in coronation costume**, 1777, by A. Roslin

scarlet and gold band round the arm. The petticoat was white crêpe with a flounce trimmed at top and bottom with a white and gold fringe, and the same of scarlet and gold.'[67]

The year 1778 also saw the decision by Gustavus III to introduce a comprehensive court uniform, which was to encompass not only the royal households, but all government officials, legal and military officers, university and medical staffs, etc. The uniforms were based on early-seventeenth-century styles, arising perhaps out of the king's admiration for the fashionable Henri IV styles to be currently seen at the French court or his recall of a period when Sweden was a dominant power in Europe; the king had a collection of costumes from the reign of Gustavus Adolphus of the early seventeenth century which had inspired the court theatricals in which he took part as author, actor and designer. An English visitor in 1784 found the women at court wearing black dresses with puffed and slashed sleeves, red sash and central rosette:

The dress of the men resembles the old Spanish, and consists of a short coat, or jacket, a waistcoat, a cloak, a hat with a feather à la Henry IV, a sash round the waist, a sword, large and full breeches, and roses in the shoes; the cloak is of black cloth edged with red satin; the coat or jacket and breeches are also black, ornamented with red stripes and buttons; the waistcoat, the sash, the pinks at the knees, and roses for the shoes, are of red sattin.[68]

For more formal occasions, there was a uniform of white and red, and a gala costume of pale blue and white, trimmed with braid, the latter favoured by the royal family, although, said Archdeacon Coxe,

TEMPERANCE enjoying a Frugal Meal.

the king 'while he has limited his subjects to particular colours, assumes the liberty of varying his own dress with all the tints of the rainbow'.

In any examination of the etiquette of dress, we must look at weddings, for in royal circles, they cemented international alliances, as well as demonstrating courtly splendour. A queen as bride wore the *grand habit* covered with jewels, and the purple velvet state mantle; in 1725 the new French queen, said La Motraye, had 'the Fore-Sides of her Stays and of her Petticoat shinn'd with divers pretious Stones', and her 'Royal Mantel was of Purple-Velvet spread with gold Flower de Luces, linn'd with Ermine'.[69] When in 1761 Princess Charlotte of Mecklenberg-Strelitz came to England to be the bride of George III, she was married in the court 'stiffen-body'd Gown' of 'Silver Tissue, embroidered & trimmed with Silver, on her head a little Cap of purple Velvet quite covered with Diamonds, a Diamond Aigrette in the form of a Crown, 3 dropt Diamond Earrings, Diamond Necklace, Diamond Sprigs of Flowers in her Sleeves and to clasp back her Robe, a diamond Stomacher, her purple Velvet Mantle was laced with Gold and lined with Ermine'[70] (she wore the same dress for her coronation). At coronations it was the custom for royal ladies and peeresses to wear false ringlets, and this continued for royal brides (the origin was probably in the long hair worn by brides on their wedding day); the Princess Royal of Prussia

80 Portrait of a nobleman in the costume of the Order of the Saint-Esprit, 1732, by J.-M. Nattier

It would be impossible to imagine a more sumptuous costume in the eighteenth century than the lavishly trimmed ceremonial dress of this knightly order. The silver, ribboned trunk hose, the short black cloak and the feathered hat derive from the fashionable dress of the seventeenth century, for nearly all official or ceremonial dress is in part the fossilized dress of the past. The page, dressed in the royal red livery, gathers up the huge train embroidered with interlaced knots, fleur-de-lis and flames.

ABOVE RIGHT

81 'Temperance enjoying a frugal meal', 1792, by J. Gillray

A caricature of the frugal habits of George III and his consort, this shows the king wearing the Windsor uniform.

in 1731 was compelled to wear 'the royal crown . . . with four and twenty locks as thick as my arm . . . I could not hold my head up, it was too weak to sustain such a weight. My robe was of a very rich silver brocade, with a Brussells gold lace and my train was twelve yards long. I had well nigh died under this attire.'[71] As weddings were state occasions, the bride and groom were ceremonially conducted to the state bed, where the formal undressing took place in public; dynastic considerations outweighed royal privacy. Etiquette also demanded that a foreign royal bride should be disrobed on the borders of her future country, and dressed anew from head to foot in the clothes of her new kingdom; it was a symbolic gesture of commitment to the interests and loyalties of her adopted state.

Royal brides and grooms could, in the early eighteenth century, wear colours and gold; Louis XV wore gold brocade with diamond buttons for his wedding in 1725, and in 1734 Princess Anne of England married in 'a manteau and petticoat, white damask with the finest embroidery of flowers intermixed in their various colours'. By the middle of the century white with gold or white with silver was the rule; in Denmark, Christian VII's wedding suit (1766) was cloth of silver with gold embroidery, and in 1744 Princess Sophie of Anhalt-Zerbst (the future Catherine the Great) was ordered by the Empress Elizabeth, who was determined to follow the customs of Versailles, to wear a French dress of cloth of silver, embroidered in silver and with a cloak of silver lace. In the Livrustkammaren in Stockholm is the wedding dress worn by Princess Sophia Magdelena of Denmark, the bride of Gustavus III of Sweden, on her marriage in 1766; the dress, a French *robe de cour* (and possibly ordered in France), is white and silver damask brocaded with sprays of roses. The style, with separate boned bodice, train and petticoat worn over a huge hoop, is identical to her coronation dress which is also preserved; the fabric, a silver brocade with gold crowns, was designed by Rehn and woven by a French weaver, Peyron, who had settled in Stockholm in 1740, and it was originally woven for the coronation of Queen Louisa Ulrica in 1751.

The idea of a gown reserved for just the wedding ceremony was a nineteenth-century notion, when clothes, comparatively speaking, were cheaper. In the eighteenth century even the most richly elaborate dress (except for the *grand habit*) had to serve more than one occasion. In England, brides were often presented at court in their wedding dress, and, particularly in the first half of the century, a heavily embroidered mantua would be suitable, later to be replaced by a sack dress. In the eighteenth century,

emphasis was laid more on the pre-marriage financial settlement than on the actual ceremony; the marquise de la Tour du Pin, for example, tells us in her memoirs more about the white gauze gown that she wore at the signing of the marriage articles, than about the robe of white crape with Brussels lace that she wore for her wedding in 1787. This was because the first dress was the latest fashion, the chemise gown, tied round the waist with a blue silk ribbon; the wedding dress was more conservative in style.[72]

Weddings were very often private affairs, taking

place in the afternoon or evening; in England the 1753 Marriage Act stated that weddings should take place in church, but even after that date licences for private weddings could be obtained, for many, like Fanny Burney in 1768, believed that a public display at church was an affront to the sensibilities of the bride – 'I'm sure I trembled for the bride. Oh, what a gauntlet for any woman of delicacy to run.'[73] Modesty and informality were important aspects of the bride's attire; Walpole's niece Maria married Lord Waldegrave in 1759 'in a white and silver

82 **A conversation at Drottningholm**, by P. Hilleström

All the courtiers in this salon of the Swedish summer palace are shown wearing the court uniform devised by Gustavus III, who is seated to the left on a sofa.

night-gown with a hat very much pulled over her face',[74] and in the anonymous novel *Harcourt* (1780), the bride wore a negligée of white lustring with flounces of embroidered gauze, a short apron and a chip hat. White and silver were in the second half of the century the customary colours for upper-class brides, but more licence was granted to their grooms. Earl Ferrers, on his way to Tyburn in 1760 to be executed for the murder of his steward, wore his wedding suit of white and silver, but men could also wear other light colours; Mr B. wore a blue paduasoy waistcoat, a 'pearl-coloured fine cloth, with gold buttons and button-holes and lined with white silk',[75] and Lord Stormont in 1776 chose 'embroideries with foils upon Brown Cloath, and lined with couleur de paille, with a waistcoat paille embroidered with gold and foils'.[76] Lower down the social scale, the bride's dress was often her best and had to last; Mrs Primrose, wife of the Vicar of Wakefield, chose her gown 'not for a fine glossy surface, but such qualities as would wear well'; the sculptor Nollekens' bride wore in 1771 'a sacque and petticoat of the most expensive brocaded white silk, resembling network, enriched with small flowers, which displayed in the variation of the folds, a most delicate shade of pink';[77] the groom himself wore a suit bought in Rome of 'Pourpre de Pape', probably the only formal suit which he possessed during his life, and which survived at his death in 1823.

As in all centuries before our own, death was an ever-present fact of life, to be prepared for and to be accorded an important place in the rituals of society. It is sometimes hard to imagine how dismal and widespread full mourning could be, with its depressing effect on trade, for court mourning had to be observed for all reigning princes and sometimes their families. Barbier's journal in France records many times the protests of Parisian tradesmen and suppliers of luxury fabrics at the repeated orders for black. For example, in one short period, the Dauphine died in August 1746 so there was the customary six months' mourning, terminated in February by the festivities for the second marriage of the Dauphin; but in March 1747 the queen of Poland (mother of the French queen) died, and Louis XV decided that the whole court should wear 'un très grand deuil', even the army officers having to dress in black. This mourning, arriving only two months after the previous one, 'ruine totalement le commerce des marchands de soie, qui étoient déjà changés des habits de printemps et des taffetas de couleur'.[78] In some of the Italian states, which relied on the textile industries, mourning was limited by sumptuary legislation; the most important was Milan, which specified that six months was the

maximum length of time when black should be worn.

Court mourning was a sign of the international brotherhood of princes, and its diplomatic observance was necessary even when contending politics made this difficult; mourning was regulated less by the status of the deceased but more by their closeness in blood to the sovereign. It ranged from six months for a consort, to a few days for a minor princeling; in France in 1740 the court mourned three weeks for the Empress Anna of Russia, a similar period of time for the Emperor Charles VI, and in 1760 only two days for a mere Landegrave of Hesse-Cassel. In an age in which communications were poor, there could be occasional confusion; in 1748 the Grand Duchess of Tuscany died, the great-aunt of the Young Pretender, who had completed his mourning by the time the French court were officially informed, and he was to be seen conspicuous among the black-dressed courtiers at the theatre in his 'habit rouge brodé d'or'.[79]

The actual ceremonial of royal funerals, with formal lying-in-state, and the draping of apartments and mirrors with black, dated back to the Middle Ages. By the beginning of the eighteenth century, the medieval gown and hood had given way to a long cloak and hat adorned with black streamers; Baron Bielfeld attended the funeral in 1740 of the King of Prussia and found 'all the princes and noblemen were in the deepest mourning with trailing cloaks and long crapes in their hats'. Walpole, with an unfailing talent for finding something amusing on the most melancholy occasion, noted that on the death of George II (1760), the king's brother, the Duke of Cumberland, 'in a cloak of black cloth with a train five yards . . . felt himself weighed down, and turning round found it was the Duke of Newcastle standing upon his train to avoid the chill of the marble'.[80]

Purple was traditionally the colour worn by the sovereign for mourning, but otherwise the gloom was unrelieved; Mrs Delany found that the one topic of conversation in the pump-room in Bath was of the death of George II: '. . . the public mourning will make every place appear dismal till the eye is used to it.' Although the details of mourning varied from country to country, it generally graduated from the matt, untrimmed cloth of deep black, through black silk with touches of ornament, to shades of grey and white with black. Full mourning for men was the currently fashionable suit, of black cloth without buttons on pockets or sleeves, black sword, sword-belt and buckles, and black crape bands in the hat; linen was plain, sometimes edged with black, and 'weepers', white linen or muslin cuffs, were added to the coat,

83 **Maria Walpole, Lady Waldegrave**, *c.*1764, by T. Gainsborough

For second mourning, the fashionable Lady Waldegrave has followed current fashion, in her black silk sack trimmed on the sleeve with fly fringe, and with blonde lace for tippet and ruffles.

varying in size according to the stage of mourning. For second mourning, men could wear black silk (or dark grey frocks for undress), their linen could be fringed and swords and buckles could be silver.

Women's mourning was more complicated and extreme, particularly that of widows; their mourning generally followed current fashion, but for first mourning they wore the widow's cap and pleated white collar with a black veil. A large proportion of widows (particularly royalty) wore mourning for the rest of their lives. In 1716 Lady Mary Wortley Montagu in Vienna found the Dowager Empress with 'not the least bit of linnen to be seen; all black crape instead of it, the neck, ears and side of the face cover'd with a plaited piece of the same stuff; and the face that peeps out in the midst of it looks as if it were pillory'd'.[81] When the Empress Maria Theresa lost her husband (1765) she stayed in black for the rest of her life, Lady Mary Coke finding her

some years later 'still in deep mourning . . . Her own private apartment is hung with black Cloth, & in the room She sits in She has the pictures of the Emperor & all the Children she has lost.'[82] As with court mourning for men, the first stage was black woollen cloth, black accessories including a crape hood, and plain linen; then black silk, with fringed and embroidered muslin or net, and diamonds, with white or grey for undress wear.

As the prince was supposed to be a father to his people, there was, at least among the upper levels of society, widespread observance of mourning for members of ruling families, even though the prescribed stages might be omitted in favour of token black. De Saussure found in London in 1727 on the death of George I that 'nobles, gentlemen, officers, merchants and citizens' were in black; inevitably, however, the impact made on society further away from the immediate court was slighter. Court mourning abroad was an expected hazard for the gentleman on the Grand Tour; the British envoy in Dresden told Boswell 'never to be without a black coat, as so many accidents can happen'.

Personal family bereavements for those outside a court circle followed an equally hierarchic system. An ordinance in 1716 in France laid down the period of mourning which ranged from one year six weeks for a wife whose husband died (he mourned a wife for only six months), to two months for brother or sister and eight days for a distant cousin; widows wore black for the first year (they could not attend court for the first six months) and white for the last six weeks. Although many widows wore fashionable dress, some middle-class women wore a long-sleeved gown, with little or no trimming even when out of first mourning. There are constant references in the letters of Mrs Delany to her mourning preparations, not just for members of the royal family, but also relatives; for the death of her mother in 1747, both formal and informal mourning was needed: 'I think black bombazeen will do very well in a sack. I have one in a manteau and petticoat which I wear when in full dress, at home a dark grey poplin, and abroad, undrest, a dark grey watered tabby.'[83] In addition she put her housekeeper and personal maid into mourning; mourning for female servants consisted of black silk (if they were close to their mistress) or cloth, and for men a suit of black cloth or dark grey material. Parson Woodforde on the death of his father in 1771 gave to his servant 'a black crape hatband and buckles and a black broad cloth Coat and Waistcoat'; this was suitable for a clerical household, but many men wore for mourning just a black hatband and black gloves, relatively inexpensive items for those who could not afford full black.

CHAPTER SIX

1770–1789: Frivolity and freedom

De La Mode
Figurez-vous une infinité de Ministres, dont le règne ne s'étendoit pas au-delà d'un jour, & qui, chaque matin, changeroient à leur lever les habillments, les usages, les esprits, les moeurs, & meme les caractères de tout un peuple.

Mercier, *Tableau de Paris*, 1782

The last two decades before the French Revolution were years of transition, with a new informality in clothing an increasing contrast to the rich restrictions of full dress.

For men, the formal French suit with elaborate embroidery and equally decorated waistcoat was identified with an increasingly ossified court circle and the privileges of aristocracy. The *Fashionable Magazine* found by 1786 that 'gentlemen's full dress [was] too antiquated for any other place than court'; by then frock coats were the most widely worn, not just the English plain frock, but, more formally, the French version which was more elegantly cut and embroidered. Formality gave way to English 'country clothes' with their emphasis on sober simplicity of material and cut; finery was out and 'democratic' informality was in vogue.

In women's dress, two themes predominated. On the one hand there was a change in the female silhouette from the triangular rigidity imposed by boned stays and hooped petticoats, to a softer line where bulk was created by hip pads, bustles and layers of linen at the bosom, so that women, by the 1780s, looked like downy pigeons, this feeling emphasized by the popular white, blues and greys of fashionable clothing. On the other hand, in contrast to this billowing femininity, there was a growing emphasis on more functional dress; this included the adoption of masculine garments such as the greatcoat, which could be worn over the newly fashionable long-sleeved gowns. The most important new development in the 1780s was the extreme popularity of dresses made all in one piece and based on the chemise, which could be put on over the head; this was a revolutionary change from the dress into which, so to speak, the lady stepped sideways, and the chemise gown (which in various versions was to dominate the revolutionary period, and the Napoleonic aftermath) was the real ancestor of the dresses we wear today. The increased momentum of change and the almost frenzied adoption of every fashion whim was partly due to the enormous popularity of fashion magazines and considerably improved communications.

Men

This was the swan-song of the Ancien Régime, the last time that the formal French suit with its superbly decorated silk fabrics was the accepted dress for high society.

By the beginning of the 1770s, the coat was being cut quite narrow across the back; it began to curve away sharply at the sides, with a corresponding reduction in the reinforcement of the side pleats. By 1789 some coats were turned over at the sides, so that the back took the form of 'swallow-tails', and by this date many had their coats cut straight across at the waist, following the line of the fashionable sporting or informal waistcoat.

During the 1760s a small standing collar had been added to the formal coat, and this gradually increased in height, being embroidered to match the small cuffs, the pocket flaps and the side and back pleats. For court functions, the embroidery remained sumptuous and expensive; in May 1782, one of the coats ordered for Louis XVI was of lilac moiré silk, with silver and diamond embroidery costing 1400 livres. The sum of 78 livres was spent on the buttons of silver, diamonds, green and white spangles alone.[1] Buttons were increasingly *objets de*

84   **A Gentleman**, by A. von Maron

This portrait by an Austrian artist in Rome shows a fashionable tourist in the 1760s, in a gold-trimmed frock suit of the vivid red so popular in Italian male dress of this period; it seems to have been a popular choice, also, for foreigners on the Grand Tour who would have suits locally made.

ABOVE RIGHT
85   **'Jeune Officier en Habit de Zèbre'**, 1787, engraving after C-L. Desrais, from the *Gallerie des Modes et Costumes Français*

luxe, for the coat was cut away at the sides so much that it only met at chest level and then it fastened at the level of the third button down, with hooks and eyes; the buttons remained, jewelled, embroidered or enamelled with topographical, political or theatrical scenes, very large in the 1770s, a style set by the leader of fashion in France, the comte d'Artois, younger brother of Louis XVI.

At court and formal assemblies in England, suits were made of silk (and cloth, which was also acceptable provided it was trimmed as richly as silk), the colours varying with the season. For winter, either bright or dark colours were in vogue;

at the queen's birthday, in January 1777 there were, said the *Magazine à la Mode*,

many suits of velvet and cloth . . . trimmed with a rich appliqué, a term given to shapes of rich embroidery intermixed with gold and silver, and coloured spangles and foil, green, red and crimson . . . The plainer suits were Irish rateen lined with feathered velvet or sattin, of different colours from the coat, with gold spangled buttons . . . the plain suits were chiefly puce or flea colour, damson or chocolate lined with white, blue, green pink or rose-colour feathered velvets or sattins.[2]

For summer, the lighter silks were used with pale colours such as pink, light blue, buff and lilac; Walpole's summer visiting costume in the early 1770s was 'a lavender suit, the waistcoat embroidered with silver or tambour-work, ruffles and jabot of lace, partridge silk stockings'.[3] For woven silks, patterns were small stylized floral designs, or spots, stripes and chevrons; Mercier in Paris in 1787 found a popular source of inspiration was the king's zebra: '. . . coats and waistcoats imitate the handsome creature's markings as closely as they can. Men of all ages have gone into stripes from head to foot, even to their stockings.'[4]

The new fashionable male silhouette of the 1770s

was tall and slim, with short waistcoat and tighter-fitting breeches. The coat was made very tight across the back, with narrow sleeves that pulled the arms back; in a play called *The Pantheonites* (1773), an unhappy man complained of his French tailor that 'the French son of a cabbage has made sleeves as if I have no more giblets than a goose . . . I have no more use of my arms than an Egyptian mummy'.[5] And poor Henry Angelo at court in his summer suit of lilac poplin lined with yellow found to his embarrassment that the coat had split under the arms, which with presence of mind he covered with his chapeau bras, and then fled to his sedan chair.

Young men-about-town, such as the 'macaronis' in England and the 'élégants' in France, exaggerated their lean figures with striped suits and stockings, and their height with wigs where the toupet rose to six inches and more. The macaronis, latest in the long line of fashionable empty-headed young men, took their name in the 1760s from a dish they had tasted on their Italian grand tour; they formed a club, 'the members of which were supposed to be the standards of taste in polite learning, the fine arts and the genteel sciences; and fashion, amongst the other constituent parts of taste, became an object of their attention. But they soon proved, they had very little claim to any distinction, except in their external appearance.'[6] Their influence was out of proportion to their number, through the medium of society and fashion papers in the 1770s and because a few men of importance such as Charles James Fox helped to popularize their fashions in clubs such as Almacks. These fashions consisted of towering wigs with tiny hats, very tight coats (to achieve the fashionable unbroken line an inside pocket (1777) replaced the outside flapped pocket) with huge buttons, nosegays in their buttonholes and vast shoe buckles; inevitably they were a godsend to the first great age of caricature, particularly when artists could linger on the effeminate side of the costume, the parasols, the powder, the large muffs, the perfume, and the light colours, which were, except for court, becoming old-fashioned. The styles may have originated in France (possibly as a vain stemming of the flood of English outdoor fashions which were in the following decade to sweep all before them), but in England the frivolity and richness of macaroni clothes was attributed also the wealth of nabobs returning from India to England. William Hickey, who spent some years in India, described the transformation of a friend, where

Instead of the plain brown cloth suit we had last seen him in, with unpowdered hair and a single curl, we now beheld a furiously powdered and

PANTHEON MACARONI

86 **The Pantheon Macaroni**, 1773, by P. Dawe

The exaggerated styles of dress worn by the macaronis were popular masquerade costumes at places like the Pantheon in Oxford Street. A certain Lord P— at one masquerade (1773) wore a 'club of hair . . . of such a prodigious size, that it covered both his shoulders . . . his foretop was of an uncommon height, . . . and upon this amazing structure was placed a remarkable small hat . . . which he could not possibly reach without the help of his sword'.

OPPOSITE
87 **Sir Brooke Boothby**, 1781, by J. Wright

pomatumed head with six curls on each side, a little skimming dish of a hat . . . His coat was of a thick silk the colour sky blue and lined with crimson satin, the waistcoat and breeches also of crimson satin . . . The cut too was entirely different from anything we had seen, having a remarkable long waist to the coat with scarce any skirts.[7]

Ridiculous though many of the more exaggerated macaroni styles were, their emphasis on a slim figure helped to improve the quality of tailoring, and the shape of the average man. No longer, by the

1780s, could a moderately fashionable man be pot-bellied in baggy breeches, for, said the *Fashionable Magazine* (1786), they 'are made excessively high-waisted, long over the knees and to set very tight'; they had to be cut high, for by this time the waistcoat was 'exceedingly short', usually double-breasted and with 'small lappels'.[8] Braces or 'gallowses' (which before then had been limited to working men to keep up their often ill-fitting breeches or trousers) now entered the fashionable man's wardrobe and helped to hold up the breeches which could no longer cling to the hips for support.

The macaronis and their followers represented really the last gasp of the bright, highly decorative clothing which to many is so typical of the eighteenth century. The mood by the 1770s, and even more so in the following decade, was for 'the agreeable negligence in dress' typical of the English country gentleman. It was Dr Johnson in his 'rusty-brown' suit, rather than Oliver Goldsmith in his 'bloom-coloured coat' that fitted the mood of the last quarter of the century.[9]

Plain cloth frocks in either dark blue or black or buff, buff or leather breeches and boots had been, throughout the century, almost a uniform for the English gentleman, more content to live and work on his estates than to hover round a court looking for royal favour. A return to the supposed simplicities of country life had for long been advocated in the works of the French philosophers, who saw and admired what they thought was its highest expression in the relatively liberal climate of England. Many could find in the pleasant informality of country life and clothing a practical expression of their tentative movements towards democracy. Not for the first time was homespun equated with egalitarianism; when in 1789 Washington was inaugurated as President of the United States, he was careful to wear a suit of dark brown woollen cloth of American manufacture (though in 1793 aristocratic black velvet was deemed appropriate, with powdered hair in a bag).[10] Wright of Derby's portrait of Sir Brooke Boothby (1781) shows him lying somewhat uneasily in a wooded glade with a volume of Rousseau in his hand; he wears a sober brown cloth suit comprising frock coat, knee-breeches and double-breasted waistcoat, and plain linen. By the early 1780s plain linen had replaced lace, other than at court; fine, white, crisp linen made the neckcloths, sometimes stiffened, which were folded closely round the neck and buckled behind. An alternative form of neckwear from the mid-1780s was the cravat (a revival of an earlier fashion) which was a long muslin scarf, knotted in front, and known in France as a 'cravate à l'anglaise'.

The impetus which made many fashionable men on the Continent adopt English styles was the publication in Leipzig in 1774 of Goethe's *succès fou*, *The Sorrows of Young Werther*. Werther, the hero, was depicted in a romanticized version of English country clothing, dark blue coat, yellow waistcoat and buff breeches with boots; he was deliberately shown as a contrast to the aristocrats who spurned him, in their 'gothic dress' which 'made a still greater contrast to our modern coats'. When in 1740 Richardson's novel *Pamela* had appeared, this too was a runaway success, with foreign translations, imitations and parodies, but it made little if any impact on the readers' appearance; Goethe's novel, however, set a vogue for young men to dress *à la* Werther, for the mood of the moment, the beginnings of Sturm und Drang were already stirring the minds of young readers rebelling against the Augustan canons of reason and control. Werther, in fact, turns away from Homer to Ossian, whose poems he translates, and the end of the novel, with his suicide, even inspired imitators to follow suit out of pure sensibility of feeling.

The idea of the suit was breaking up, the *Gentleman's and London Magazine* (1777) noting that 'an entire suit of cloth is hardly ever seen except upon old people, physicians, apothecaries and lawyers'. William Hickey on his return to London in 1780 found that he needed a totally new wardrobe, so the tailor 'advised my having a dark green with gold binding, dark brown with the same, a plain blue, and for half-dress a Bon de Paris with gold frogs, all of which he spoke as being much worn and of the highest ton'.[11] These were dark-coloured frocks, some plain in the English style, the others trimmed in the French mode; the French took to the frock with enthusiasm (by 1778 Louis XVI was wearing one), and with typical ingenuity, produced different versions of it, including one with a sloping shawl collar, one *à la polonaise*, i.e. without a back vent, and so on. Dark blue and black were also popular colours for the frock, the latter being especially popular in France, giving, said commentators, an air of gloom to the streets in contrast to the natural gaiety of the French. In England by the early 1780s, most Englishmen wore 'a short white waistcoat, black breeches, white silk stockings, and a frock, generally of a very dark blue cloth which looks like black';[12] by the end of the decade a Russian visitor, Karamzin, found almost half the men in the streets wearing this dark blue, and even his ambassador wore a similar garment but with a small hair bag 'which distinguishes him from every other inhabitant of London'.[13]

Hickey's new wardrobe in 1780 included 'Rymer's for boots, Wagner for hats and Williams of Bond Street for leather breeches. In three days I was to come forth a proper Bond Street Lounger, a description of person then just coming into vogue.'[14] The full panoply of English sporting wear rightly included leather breeches or close-fitting

88 **Fraque à la Polonoise**, engraving after P-T Le Clère, from the *Gallerie des Modes et Costumes François, 1778–1787*

The newly fashionable slim male figure is accentuated by this frock with its braided seams and skimpily cut skirts.

OPPOSITE
89 **Mr and Mrs Thomas Coltman**, by J. Wright

Painted soon after their marriage in 1769, Mr and Mrs Coltman are shown in informal country costume. Seated side-saddle, Mrs Coltman wears a riding habit comprising matching jacket and skirt, and a buttoned waistcoat trimmed with braid. Mr Coltman wears a light riding frock and breeches, jockey boots and a waistcoat with frogging *à la* hussar.

tight trousers or pantaloons of stockinette, the latter being rare until the 1790s, but occasionally seen. As well as the frock, the buff breeches, the riding coat and the jockey cap, the French enthusiastically adopted English aristocratic sports like driving and racing, in a wave of Anglomania which, transmitted by the duc de Chartres (Philippe Egalité) who was a crony of the Prince of Wales, swept over Paris. The *Petit Dictionnaire de la Cour et de la Ville* (1788) commented sourly: 'Bientôt Paris sera tout Anglois. Habits, voitures, chevaux, bijoux, boissons, spectacles, jardins & morale, tout est à l'angloise. Nous avons pris de ce triste peuple le vauxhall, le club, les jocqueis, les fracs, le vishk, le punch, le spleen, & la fureur du suicide'.[15]

Hickey's newly-acquired London hat was probably a round hat with flat-topped crown and wide uncocked brim, which was originally a functional out-of-doors hat, taken up along with leather breeches by young bloods in the middle of the century. This round hat had, by the 1770s, replaced, except for court and formal assemblies, the three-cornered hat, though the latter was preferred by the more conservative and the professional and middle classes. Francis Place (born 1771) wore as a child a round hat with a gold band and tassel, although his father 'said none but thieves and persons who were ashamed to show their faces wore them'; yet for bad weather he too wore one 'covered with fine canvas and painted by himself'.[16] Although the formal three-cornered hat was black, other more fashionable hats, according to Mercier in the 1790s, could be coloured or white, the latter a popular choice for summer. Once the tyranny of the three-cornered hat was ended, hats assumed a variety of forms, some with brims turned high up in front and behind, some with high crowns, and some jockey caps.

But is was the footwear which distinguished the fashionable man in the north of Europe from his counterpart in hotter southern countries; Goethe in Verona in 1787 found the townspeople staring at his boots, which to Italians were purely for riding. The fashion for wearing soft leather jockey boots reaching to the knee and turned down at the top often with a contrasting colour had begun, as we noted, in the middle of the eighteenth century in England. They became by the 1770s fashionable for walking and for indoors, (even for polite assemblies, although frowned on), and so remained until the beginning of the next century: 'The number of walking jockies is very numerous and the rage for boots by no means over,' said the *Ipswich Journal* for June 1786. An alternative style in the 1780s was the hussar buskin, a calf-length boot dipped in front with a tassel at each side.

Formal occasions, however, demanded shoes and buckles (shoe strings or laces were in vogue for plain leather shoes from the mid-1780s); these buckles were large oblongs or ovals and a gentleman of fashion had vast numbers – the comtesse de Boigne visiting Mrs Fitzherbert in 1789 was astounded to see a large cupboard full of buckles belonging to the Prince of Wales, a different pair for every day of the year. At court precious stones were used, but increasingly cut steel in the English taste; this was what the *Petit Dictionnaire* meant when it referred to English jewels being all the rage in Paris in the 1780s. This cut steel (which could be faceted to a high degree of brilliance) made not only shoe and breeches buckles, but 'breloquets' (decorative chains hung with enamel plaques, intaglios and cameos which jangled as the dandy walked) and watches; there was a temporary fashion in the mid-1780s for two watches worn on either side of the waist, the false watch matching the real, and containing a mirror, a miniature or a vinaigrette. Cut steel also made suit and waistcoat buttons; for 'les habits de couleur sombre et sur les gilets de drap on ne porte guère que des boutons d'acier travaillé', said the *Magasin des Modes Nouvelles* of 1789.[17]

The overcoat or surtout had by the 1770s become a triumph of tailoring based on sober materials excellently cut (its apotheosis was to be achieved in later years under Beau Brummell); it was cut close to the body, with small cuffs and a variety of collar styles. The *Cabinet des Modes* for February 1787 stated that the most fashionable men were wearing 'un habit redingote de drap couleur de suie des cheminées de Londres', with scarlet collar and cuffs à la marinière; this was so close-fitting that it was worn straight over a waistcoat of grey satin and with boots and a 'chapeau-jockey'.[18] For very cold weather the fashion magazine recommended redingotes of plush which could be obtained from such specialists as Jubin at the Trois Mandarins in the arcades of the Palais Royal.

Surtouts could be plain and untrimmed; when in 1784 Gustavus III came to Paris (travelling under the name of the Count of Haga), he drove about the city streets dressed in a plain grey surtout, being mobbed by the crowd as 'the common's king' – perhaps another example of the equation made between simplicity of clothing and liberal accessibility to the sovereign. Some surtouts were made in the wrapping style which had been especially popular in the middle eighteenth century. When Mrs Piozzi was in Milan (1785) she saw the men in 'an odd sort of white riding coat, not buttoned together, but folded round their body after the fashion of the old Roman dress that one has seen in statues, and this they call Gaban'.[19] This is probably

90 **Portrait of a gentleman**, *c.* 1785, by F. Bayeu

With his formal pose and wig, this Spanish gentleman is dressed for winter in fur-lined coat; a fashionable touch is the wearing of two decorative chains suspended from the waist.

ABOVE RIGHT

91 **'Redingotte à trois colets'**, engraving after P-T. Le Clère, from the *Gallerie des Modes et Costumes Français, 1778–1787*

This triple-collared style of overcoat was all the rage in the 1780s both in London, from whence it was derived, and Paris. With it is worn a muslin cravat, *à l'anglaise*.

what Goethe wears in the famous portrait by Tischbein painted on his trip to Italy in 1786; after the romanticism of Werther, the author had turned away to classicism, the drapery of the gaban being particularly suitable for this classical mood as 'enveloped in a white mantle' he sits 'on a fallen obelisk viewing the ruins of the campagna di Roma'.[20] The most popular surtouts or greatcoats had collars of contrasting colours, sometimes more than one, an idea taken from the English coachmen, who wore, said Grosley, seeing them in the 1760s, 'an upper coat adorned with a long cape of two or three rows'. In 1775 Sir Joshua Reynolds's nephew in London chose a greatcoat of 'a light colour with a light green collar, made in the new fashion; the colour of the coat depends on one's own fancy, but the green capes are almost universal'.[21] In the 1780s, triple capes were the usual style both in London and Paris; in the latter capital a popular French version was the 'redingote à la lévite', with buttoned revers and the requisite three collars.

Although a convinced Republican, Mercier was first a patriot, and argued fiercely against the collared coats which to him were the epitome of a slovenly if easy-going English style; foreigners attending the House of Commons were astounded by the behaviour of M.P.'s, who came in dressed in boots and greatcoats, and lay on the benches eating nuts and oranges. Horace Walpole claimed that his good health and longevity was due to the fact that he never wore a greatcoat, though the real reason for his dislike of an overcoat might have been that it spoiled the line of his suit or the elegance of his gait. For such old-fashioned or conservative gentlemen the cloak continued to be worn, though it was increasingly in England being limited to professional men, army officers, and for funerals. In colder climates, however, fur-lined mantles were both necessary and luxurious; in Frederick the

147

92 **Goethe in the Roman campagna**, 1786 by
J. H. W. Tischbein

Goethe, in romantically pensive mood, 'on a fallen
obelisk viewing the ruins of the Campagna di Roma',
has chosen, to echo the classical mood, what an English
visitor called, 'an odd sort of white riding coat . . . folded
round [the] body after the fashion of the old Roman
dress that one has seen in statues'.

Great's inventory there were mantles of wolf-skin
and lynx lined with silk, and important visitors to
Russia were given fur pelisses – Gustavus III in St
Petersburg in 1777 had as a gift from Catherine the
Great one of blue fox.

Perhaps one of the greatest changes which demonstrated the new feelings of simplicity in men's
appearance was a rejection of the long-established
wig in favour of the natural hair. True, the
macaronis in the early 1770s had worn high powdered wigs, but this was the exception rather than
the rule, and from the end of the 1760s some men
had begun to wear their own hair either unpow-

dered, or dressed formally. In Fanny Burney's novel
Evelina (1778), a foolish young man of fashion was
urged after an accident (a monkey had bitten his ear)
to wear a wig. '"A wig?" repeated the affrighted
Mr Lovel, "I wear a wig? – no! not if you would
give me a thousand pounds an hour."'[22]

For court, the hair had to be dressed and then
powdered in stiff styles (with black silk bag at the
back); Henry Angelo in his *Reminiscences* (1775)
recalled how 'many a night (I then sported four
curls on each side), previous to going to bed, my
time has been long employed plaistering each curl
with a mixture of powder and pomatum; I then had
to roll them up separately preparatory to the
hairdresser's visit the next day to add his embellis-
ments . . . with maréchal powder'.[23] Paradoxically,
far more bother was needed to have the hair dressed
than to wear a wig; the *London Magazine* of 1772
had already commented unfavourably on 'the
plaistered pyramid of scented pomatum . . . those
immoveable buckles that destroy the grace of the
flowing curls', and even in the 1780s when the
rolled curls gave way to a more natural profusion of

curls, the fashionable look was still acquired by curl papers and grease to create the necessary bulk and width. The *Art of Hairdressing or the Gentleman's Director* by Alexander Stewart (1788) discusses the byzantine complexities of dressing and papering the hair ('a frise is put in the root of the curls') so that the fashionable frizz was achieved – this was a style known as 'à l'hérisson'; then it was powdered (a range of light colours was permissible). Even when, at the end of the 1780s, hairstyles were more natural and had lost the frizzed look in exchange for a more wind-blown appearance, powder continued to be used for formal wear; some men wore with their own hair a vestigial black silk bag, often with a fancy rosette, and sewn to the back of the coat collar. The proper bag-wig, like the hoops and the chapeau bras, remained as correct court wear into the nineteenth century, but the hair powder (except for the army, the church and some of the more learned professions) was abandoned in England in 1795 with the tax on powder; those who wished to pay to continue this privilege were called 'guinea-pigs' from the amount of tax they had to pay.

Women

Apart from the *robe de cour*, the most formal dress worn by fashionable women in the 1770s was the sack dress (it went out of fashion towards the end of the decade, except for at court). For formal occasions it demonstrated an *embarras de richesse*, stomacher, robings and petticoat being covered in padded furbelows, silk flowers, tassels, chenille trimmings; one such robe in silver, ordered by Madame du Barry from Rose Bertin in 1782, had large puffed pleats all down the front in Italian gauze edged with big ruchings of cut crape, a garland of silver rope placed over the puffs each separated by bunches of golden wheat-ears and fastenings in catkins of blue stones mixed with white pearls...' and the petticoat was flounced with Italian gauze with a decoration of fringe, gold corn-ears, shells and silver ropes.[24] A more modest version was worn at the English court, the Duchess of Cumberland appearing in 1773 in 'a full dress'd sack of Rose Colour'd Lutestring trimm'd with Point';[25] it was 'full dress'd' because the duchess wore not only point lace (which was out of fashion other than at court) but her diamonds.

To achieve a tight fit thought suitable for a formal gown, the bodice lining was laced at the back so that it fitted tightly under the flowing pleats. Less formally, the stomacher with its elaborate trimmings was replaced by a front-fastening bodice, hooked with an edge-to-edge closure. It was probably this kind of sack that the Duchess of Northumberland found Voltaire's 'niece', Madame

Denis, wearing in 1772, 'a sack of dark grounded chintz, brodée au tambour';[26] printed cotton was by this time an unusual fabric for a sack, though the combination probably continued in hot climates where even the most formal gowns needed to be washed. Occasionally the pleats were cut loose from the bodice at the back, forming a connecting bridge from the shoulders to the hips where the pleats again merged into the overskirt; this style was known as the 'robe à la piemontaise', the name deriving from a dress popularized by a fashionable actress in Lyons for the wedding of Madame Clothilde, the sister of Louis XVI, to the Prince of Piedmont in 1775.

By the 1770s the hoop, over which the sack was originally meant to be worn, had disappeared except for court; to create the soft bulk at the sides, very small paniers or hip pads were worn, or as an alternative, the excess skirt material of the overgown was fastened up with inside tapes, or loops and tassels. When the sack was worn at court, the sleeves had long double or treble flounces, but otherwise in the 1770s a small winged or round cuff could be seen, similar to those worn in the more popular *robes à l'anglaise*. The fitted gown had long been the favourite in England, and in the 1770s it had a new lease of life with a closed front fastening, worn usually over a skirt of a different colour. It was in a sense a hybrid gown, a marriage of the fitted mantua with the back pleats of the sack, but so reduced in size that they eventually became seams; the central section of the back bodice was sewn down with seams curved into the small of the back, extending without a waist seam into the skirt – this style was known as the 'fourreau back', and could even, by skilled seamstresses, be made from the sack dress. By the 1780s there was a complete division at the waist, and the skirt was set with tiny pleats into the bodice; these pleats (sometimes worn over small hip pads attached to the stays, or small crescent-shaped bustles, called 'rumps') created the side

OVERLEAF

93 Madame Adélaïde de France, daughter of Louis XV, by A. Labille-Guiard

Madame Adélaïde wears the formal sacque with embroidered robings; a similar star and floral design can be seen in the embroidery on the skirt. The wide, frizzed hairstyle supports an elaborate 'pouf' or confection of lace and ribbons.

94 A lady with a harp, by E.-L. Vigée-Lebrun

Stripes are the dominant design motif in this ensemble. This fashionable lady wears a striped silk *robe à l'anglaise*, and a striped silk gauze kerchief which crosses the bosom and fastens behind the waist.

95   **A Sea Shore**, 1776, by C. J. Vernet (detail)

In this detail from a fanciful Mediterranean scene, a man in hussar uniform points out to sea, while next to him stand two fashionable ladies, one showing from the back the looped-up polonaise skirt.

width and bounce which was so characteristic a feature of dress in this decade. The *robe à l'anglaise* was versatile enough to be regarded as a semi-formal ('half-dress') or informal gown, and is probably synonymous with the nightgown. Although it is difficult for us to disentangle contemporary terms, it would appear that the 'Italian nightgown' was more formal than the English version, which was usually of light silks or chintz and was often worn with an apron. Queen Charlotte liked both styles; Lady Mary Coke found her in 1769 in the park, walking 'in an English nightgown and a white apron', and some years later Mrs Delany admired her on a more formal occasion in 'an Italian nightgown of purple lutestring trimmed with silver gauze'. The English nightgown was a walking dress, but in the hands of a lady of fashion it could be fairly elaborate; Georgiana, Duchess of Devonshire, and her sister wore to Carlton House in 1785 'nightgowns of my invention. The body and sleeves black velvet bound with pink and fastened with silver buttons. The petycoat light pink and the skirt, apron and handkerchief crape bound with light pink, and large chip hats with feathers and pinks'.[27] The Italian nightgown very often had a train; the *Magazine à la Mode* said that for winter 1777 they were 'made with whalebone in the back to fit quite close to the stays', and with a very long train 'drawn up for walking'.[28] Very often the skirt had tapes inside so that it could be looped up to create the polonaise styles so popular in the 1770s and 1780s.

The name 'polonaise' or 'polonese' derives obviously from Polish styles – whether the fur trimming or the kilting up to one side of the skirt of the dress (a Polish fashion which came from Turkish costume), is not really clear. The 'polonese' in the mid-eighteenth century was a small hooded cloak trimmed with fur, but by the early 1770s the term usually referred to a dress where the back drapery of the overskirt was arranged (through tapes or rings sewn to inside seams) in three puffs of material, in varying lengths. There had, since the beginning of the eighteenth century, been various impromptu ways of lifting up the skirt of the overgown, a necessary feature of walking dress as worn by middle-class women in the streets of cities, but the polonaise, cut in four parts, two at the front and two at the back, was a fashionable version of this bourgeoise style. The petticoat was quite short at the end of the 1770s, and with the bunches of the polonaise overgrown, it created a bouncy bulkiness which was at the same time light, for the silks were the thinnest and the aprons which were often worn as part of the dress were of fine muslin or silk gauze. In the same way that the sack could be adapted for a jacket, so the half-polonaise was a shorter version of the dress, worn for travelling.

A characteristic feature of both the *robe à l'anglaise* and the polonaise was the bodice of the gown which closed at the top of the centre front and then sloped away to the sides, leaving a triangular gap with the base below, filled by a false waistcoat or 'zone' sewn to the lining of the inner sides of the bodice, laced, hooked or buttoned down the front. The sleeves were either three-quarter-length finished with a small double ruffle, or long to the wrist fastening there with a frill; according to the *Lady's Magazine* (1774), the Irish polonaise 'buttons down half the arm', but the other types of polonaise, Italian, French, etc., although identifiable to contemporaries, were probably only distinguished by slight differences in size of skirt puff or type of trimming.

The variety of fashionable dress in the 1770s and 1780s was immense, a confusion not helped by a host of names – some after aristocratic customers, or modish watering places such as Bath, or Spa, some following the mood for historic revivals and oriental fantasy (these were prevailing themes in dress in the years before the Revolution and are discussed in the following chapter) and some based on masculine garments such as the greatcoat.

But the style of dress which was to have the most profound influence on future developments in clothing was the gown known as the 'chemise à la reine', which derived its name from a controversial portrait by Vigée-Lebrun of Marie-Antoinette ex-

hibited at the Paris salon in 1783, and which depicted the queen in a simple white muslin gown rather reminiscent of a chemise or shift. The picture itself had to be withdrawn, but the attendant fuss helped to popularize a style of dress which had already been in the wardrobes of some fashionable women, including the French queen, for some years. The dress of white muslin with sleeves to the elbow or wrist, sometimes tied with ribbon, was put on over the head; it was gathered in on a drawstring round a low neckline, and the soft fullness was drawn in with a sash at the waist. Marie Antoinette preferred white dresses of Italian taffeta or muslin for the summer, and particularly at Marly or Petit Trianon; Soulavie in his *Mémoires Historiques et Politiques du Règne de Louis XVI* (1801) blamed the decline of the Lyons silk industry on the queen's taste for white muslin. It would have been unwise in 1801 to claim otherwise, but the queen was only following current taste, copying the simple tubes of white muslin which had for some time been worn by ladies on the plantations of the French West Indies; from the West Indies also came the indigo which blue-rinsed the muslin to a startling whiteness. Not only was taste moving towards the informal (all over Europe silk industries were feeling the pinch) but there was also the beginnings of a movement towards dress reform, a desire to free women from the restrictions of tight-lacing and clothes that did not reflect the natural body shape. Throughout the century there had been

96 **Queen Marie-Antoinette**, *c.*1783, after E.-L. Vigée-Lebrun

The Queen captures the pastoral mood with her straw hat, and her white muslin chemise gown, tied with a silk striped sash round the waist.

attacks on the damage done to women by their clothing, but this gathered momentum in the 1780s, especially in Germany. In 1783 the Emperor Joseph II tried to ban corsets and hoops; like most sumptuary legislation it was ineffectual (by the time such edicts became law, fashion has usually moved on), and they remained for court and formal dress. In 1785 Franz Ehrenberg, the publisher of the magazine *Frauenzimmer-Almanach* gave the artist Chodowiecki the task of designing a reform dress; the resulting gowns, very much in the classical Greek taste, were based on the simple chemise gown.

As soon as the French queen had made the chemise popular, it was taken up by ladies of fashion; Georgiana, Duchess of Devonshire, in 1784 'went to a concert in one of the muslin chemises with fine lace that the Queen of France gave me'.[29] Three years later (such was the increased change of fashion, and the comparative cheapness of the style), the *Lady's Magazine* noted 'all the Sex now, from 15 to 50 and upwards ... appear in their white muslin frocks with broad sashes'.[30]

The original chemise was pulled on over the head, but later versions had a front bib opening or were fastened with buttons or ribbons down the front; a popular English chemise (sometimes called the '"Perdita" chemise' after the actress Perdita Robinson) had a low neck with falling double collar with vandycked edge, and closed down the front with ribbon bows. The dress gradually became more complex, with a separate skirt and bodice, and a general tightening up at the waist.

A number of dresses in the 1780s derived from a mixture of sources – the neo-classical chemise gown, the oriental or theatrical styles, and the masculine greatcoat. The wrapping gown was given a new lease of life in this period, made of light material and fastened at the waist with a sash. Walpole saw one of these garments, newly named the 'lévite' (the name taken from the habits worn by actresses playing the Jewish priests in Racine's *Athalie*) on Lady Ossory in 1779 and exclaimed, 'where the deuce is the grace of a man's nightgown bound round with a belt?'[31] By the mid-1780s they had become more formal, often worn as an open

robe over a skirt, but retaining the sash and the simplicity of style and fabric; Vigée-Lebrun tells us in her Memoirs that Madame du Barry's favourite dresses when she was in her forties were lévites of cambric or white muslin. As well as disguising *embonpoint*, the lévite in its earlier form was a useful robe for pregnancy, the French queen herself favouring them in 1778. Other popular open robes which incorporated elements of the oriental were the 'circassiennes,' sometimes with a polonaise skirt, and with short sleeves trimmed with fur and decorated with tassels, and the 'robes à la turque', a name covering a multitude of meanings which ranged from the simple white robes with fringing and sash to a grand semi-formal gown; for 'la grande parure', said the *Cabinet de Modes* (1786), one could wear 'des Robes à la Turque de velours de differentes couleurs, doublées de satin'.[32]

One of Queen Charlotte's favourite gowns in the later 1780s, said Fanny Burney, was a 'dimity greatcoat', popular 'from the quickness with which they enable her to finish her toilette'.[33] This may have been a morning lévite gown, but it was more likely to have been an indoors version of the redingote or masculine greatcoat, a popular style of the 1780s. It could either close down the front with buttons, or, more usually, be worn open over a waistcoat; it sometimes adopted the caped collar of the male coat, and a fashionable feature was the large revers or lapels, very often a contrasting colour to the main body of the gown. The French wore it, very often made in silk, as a *robe à l'anglaise* made tightly fitting at the waist, the fullness flaring out at the back and over the hips. It was a fashionable walking dress for the mornings; the *Lady's Magazine* stated that for the summer of 1783 the most popular colour combinations were 'the Perdita's pearl colour with jonquil yellow facings, and the dark brown with a scarlet waistcoat'. In the same issue the editor published a letter from a tradesman complaining of his wife's predilection for the riding dress which she 'whips on ... as soon as she gets out of bed, sets down to breakfast in her beaver and goes to market in her boots', even though she had never mounted a horse in her life, and there were no redcoats in her family.

The masculine/military influence in women's clothing was particularly strong in the 1780s. We have seen that the greatcoat had been adopted from men's wear in the 1760s, when it was worn out-of-doors; in 1767 at Spa, the fashionable summer watering place in the Austrian Netherlands, Lady Mary Coke was extremely irritated when her maid forgot to pack her greatcoat, for she needed it as protection from the continual rain. When, in the 1770s, women began to wear long-sleeved dresses,

97 Lady Elizabeth Foster, 1786, by A. Kauffmann

This is another version of the chemise, with double falling collar, and three-quarter-length sleeves edged with a ruffle. A fashion increasingly popular in an age of growing sentimentality was to wear a jewelled miniature on a chain.

98 **Lady in a redingote**, fashion plate from the *Cabinet des Modes*, 1786

The caped collar of the masculine greatcoat is imitated in this fashionable tight-waisted redingote, the most popular outdoors garment of the 1780s. The design of spots on a plain ground is characteristic of silks of this decade.

ABOVE RIGHT

99 **'Caraco et jupon de mousseline rayée'**, anon. fashion plate from the *Cabinet des Modes*, 1786.

Ideally, says the accompanying text, this caraco and skirt of striped muslin is 'une toilette du matin', worn before one is ready to dress for the day, and suitable 'pour faire un tour de promenade avant midi'.

the greatcoat was an obvious choice for turning into a fashionable garment, worn with caped collar and lapels and fastening with large buttons like the man's coat. In the 1780s both the greatcoat and the riding habit (the latter by then comprising a jacket and skirt of matching material, with a satin waist-coat) were decorated with braid, frogs, loops and tassels, and fashionable ladies, like men, carried canes. Boots were the fashionable walking foot-wear; the *Ipswich Journal* (1786) noticed that: 'The ladies begin to wear morocco half-boots and Hussar riding habits.' According to the *Gentleman's Magazine* (1781), the unthinkable happened when ladies even began to wear breeches and watches on fobs tucked into their belts; this is a surprising statement, for although breeches were common riding wear on the Continent, and some men[34] in England had urged their use rather than 'silly and perilous modes' (i.e. riding habits with skirts), convention would have been outraged had they been worn in the

156

streets. But to many people, the times were out of joint, and the new freedom given to women by their adoption of masculine clothes caused a freedom of gait which the more conservative like Mrs Montagu found at best unappealing and at worst potentially immoral; in Bath in 1780 she found 'the misses waddle and straddle and strut and swagger about the streets here, one arm akimbo, the other swinging'.[35] The more natural look also demanded shoes with a low heel; no longer except for court did women look like galleons, with hoops and high heels and that curious tiupping walk that so many recalled as typical of the Ancien Régime.[36] Instead, dresses without hoops clung to the body and allowed its shape to be seen, and the new shoes gave women an unaccustomed freedom of movement.

Informality stretched out in the 1770s to include hitherto lowly garments such as the jacket and skirt, the staple wardrobe of the working woman throughout the century. The 'caraco', originally a short hip-length jacket with a sack back, first appeared as an informal toilette negligée at the end of the 1760s; by the 1770s it could be seen as a *déshabillé galant*, worn on the Champs Elysées. In England, the caraco was a close-fitting three-quarter-length jacket, the back sometimes longer than the front, usually worn closed and sometimes made of fashionable printed linen or cotton.

The most popular jackets by the end of the 1770s were worn open over the corsage, fastening at the centre front, sloping down at the sides and cut short to flare over the hips and back. The *Gentleman's and London Magazine* for February 1777 stated:

The most fashionable morning dress and home undress for all day is a dishabille which consists of a short jacket and petticoat. The coat is generally puckered round the bottom about a quarter of a yard deep, with gauze or the same silk. But the fur is more in vogue this month than any other trimming. The jacket is short, not above a quarter of a yard on the hip; it is neatly shaped in the back with four quarters; the front resembling the polonese, fastens at the top with two frogs and tassels. The waistcoat is generally ornamented with frogs and tassels.[37]

Small distinctions of style or trimming, or of the colour and fabric from which they were made, provided a variety of names – the 'pierrot', the 'juste à la suzanne' (this was white) to name just two – and these jackets, being newly popular, demonstrated the latest textiles and designs.

The 1770s and 1780s were periods of change in textile design, as well as marking the change from silks to cottons and linens. For woven silks, the large self-confident patterns that had dominated design for most of the century gave way to small flower patterns, spots and stripes. Only those conservative or middle-class ladies (whose outlay was limited, and whose silks had to last) kept to the large natural flowers; Mrs Nollekens, for example, had in 1771 as part of her trousseau 'a dress of lavender silk brocaded with white and enriched with bouquets of carnations, auriculas and jessamins the size of nature'.[38] Much more fashionable were stripes; Lady Stormont in 1776 wrote to Mary Graham that her 'birthday gown is to be Lilac with a little silver stripe', and a few years later Mrs Adams, visiting London and Paris, noted a wide use of the fine Chambéry gauze with satin stripes. The changing shape of women's gowns, with a newly narrow silhouette and long tight sleeves demanded tiny patterns; silks were ribbed to imitate stripes, they were patterned with spots, specks and random dots,[39] or with zodiac designs, and even imitated the new neo-classical motifs such as laurel wreaths and medallions which were so successfully being printed on linen and cotton. So desperate were the silk-weavers to keep their declining trade that by the end of the 1780s they were imitating printed cotton designs.

The 1770s showed a preference for strong colours. In 1775 puce was all the rage '... dos de puce or ventre de puce – the only colour that can be worn,' said Lady Spencer in a letter from Paris – all because of a chance remark made by the king to Marie-Antoinette about an item of dress, which was taken up by the fashionable modistes. Stripes of varying thicknesses were woven into silks, and printed onto linens, the latter also stamped and spotted, and decorated with copper-plate or wood-block designs. Barbara Johnson's account book has increasing references to chintzes and calicoes; in 1771 she had a 'purple and white copper-plate linnen Gown', and in 1776 a yellow spotted linen dress. The restrictions in England on the wearing of all-cotton printed fabrics were removed in 1774 – they had been unworkable for many years and ingenious manufacturers had found many ways to evade the strict letter of the law.

White was the colour of the 1780s, both for silks and, even more, for fine muslin. The Duchess of Devonshire in 1784 chose for a ball-dress 'an English night-gown of muslin with small silver sprigs and all white',[40] and even Queen Charlotte, usually conservative in her tastes, wore for the king's birthday in 1787 'a very beautiful dress, of a new manufacture of worked muslin, thin, fine and clear as the Chambéry gauze'.[41] Muslin could be embroidered with the tambour (introduced from Turkey in the 1760s and becoming a fashionable diversion) or painted; in 1784 J. T. Smith helped the

Misses Wyatt paint butterflies on a muslin dress.

To Mrs Adams in London in 1784 'everything [was] as light and thin as possible', the dress pleasing her best 'a delicate blue and white copper-plate calico with a blue lutestring skirt flounced, a muslin apron and a handkerchief'.[42] Whether this was because it reflected American styles (a French visitor had seen in Newhaven in 1788 the girls 'galloping boldly with an elegant hat on the head, a white apron, and a calico gown')[43] or was just admirable in its informality, the blue and white colour combination was *de rigueur* for the whole decade; subtle effects could also be created by wearing transparent muslin over coloured underskirts. Also noticeable was an excess of trimming; dresses were decorated with ribbons ('white ribbon in the Van-dyke style', noted Mrs Adams in the mid-1780s), floss silk and steel beads 'which are much in fashion and brought to such perfection as to resemble diamonds'. Sophie von la Roche, in England in 1786, admired the mixture of luxury and 'country informality' that she found in one dress of pink and white striped taffeta, with painted trailing roses on the hem, pearls on the seams and real roses in the straw hat. She was less taken with the sight of two ladies at the theatre with 'their neckerchiefs …

100 **The Remy family**, 1776, by J. Zick

Prominent in this predominantly middle-class musical conversation piece can be seen two ladies in the popular informal costume of flared jacket, and skirt of matching material.

101 **Madame Sorcy de Thélusson**, 1790, by J.-L. David

In this portrait with its revolutionary simplicity can be seen the beginning of the neo-classical style. The plain chemise has a simple drawstring round the neck, and the wide cashmere shawl is draped *à l'antique*.

puffed up so high that their noses were scarce visible, and their nosegays like large shrubs, large enough to conceal a person'.[44] For amplitude was in vogue in the 1780s, particularly at the bosom; *buffons* were large, diaphanous, sometimes starched handkerchiefs puffed up over the bust. Softness replaced crispness when lace gave way to silk gauze and muslin; the short silk mantles of the mid-eighteenth century gave way during the 1770s to the long scarf or stole, crossed over the bosom, and by the mid-1780s cashmere, 'more costly than silk, much lighter and also much warmer', was being

imported for the most expensive shawls.

Paradoxically, as some styles of dress were becoming simpler in cut and fabric, so hairstyles were increasing in height and complexity. From the beginning of the 1770s the hair on the forehead rose high, built up over pads; at the side were large stiff rolls placed diagonally, and at the back a wide flat loop of hair hung to the nape of the neck: the chignon. The height of the hairstyle sometimes exceeded the length of the face; the twelve-year-old Anna Winslow, sent from home in Nova Scotia to be 'finished' in Boston, proudly noted in her diary in 1772 that 'I mesur'd above an inch longer than I did downwards from the roots of my hair to the end of my chin'.[45] The gum (gum Arabic, pomatum, tallow or hog's grease) needed to keep the style in place, and the powder, made her 'head itch, & ach, & burn like anything', and to get the required bulk a 'cushion' of false hair included 'a Red Cow tail ... and horse-hair very coarse, and a little human hair of yellow hue'; the arrangement once concocted could not easily be disturbed, although it was dangerous to health and a source of endless satire. So full and tall was the hair that an English lady, Mrs

Fay, when attacked at Calcutta by the troops of Hyder Ali in 1779, was able to hide her own and her husband's watches in her hairstyle.[46]

By the middle 1770s the hair was enormously high, and, very often, covered with feathers, a fashion set in England by the Duchess of Devonshire (a shocked German visitor in 1775 found the most popular colours to be red, white and black, and they cost a guinea each), and in France by Marie Antoinette (though her mother Maria Theresa thought they were more suitable for actresses). Other forms of headcovering included jewels – the hair was gummed to such an extent that pins could be stuck there; the *Lady's Magazine* for July 1777 illustrated a hairstyle 'representing the hemisphere, interspersed with jewels representing stars'.

In the 1780s hair became very wide; the stiff side rolls unravelled to fall into a frizz of tiny curls and loose ringlets, but this slight disorder had to be equally carefully arranged, gummed and powdered, even when a seemingly nonchalant and natural air was aimed at. As hair flattened on top, so hats became more important; in the 1770s the hair had been so tall that very large and elaborate hats would have been impossible, and women concentrated on the decoration of the hair itself. To cover the hair out-of-doors a 'calash' was needed, a large hood built up on cane arches, sometimes quilted, and often collapsible so it could be more easily stored. The 1780s was the hat-maker's ideal decade, a period of enormous hats, covered with ribbons, tulle, feathers and flowers. Never was millinery more subject to the whims of the moment, whether political or fashionable; the first flight in a hot-air balloon from the Bois de Boulogne on 1 November 1783 inspired ballooning hats, 'poufs à la Montgolfier', and a grimmer event, the storming of the Bastille in 1789, produced 'bonnets à la Bastille', a strange flirting with danger; the same mood that, during the Terror, made some women adopt red ribbons round their necks in imitation of the mark made by the guillotine. Many of the most fashionable hats were made of straw, turned up at the side, lined with silk and covered with flowers; many were inspired by the countryside – Mercier in the early 1780s speaks of 'the English Park, the Windmill and the Grove ... Shepherds and Shepherdesses, the Huntsman in Covert', declaring his inability 'to fix a likeness of anything so fleeting'.[47] By the end of the 1780s the very large hats were on their way out – their last gasp was the 'lampshade' style with a curtain of lace all round the brim which sloped like a roof – and the magazines were describing smaller caps and turbans which were with their classical and exotic influences, to be the headwear for the revolutionary years and well into the nineteenth century.

Children

We have so far only looked at children's clothes in relation to those of adults, for, with some exceptions, the one was a miniature version of the other. But the word 'revolutionary' reminds us that it was in the third quarter of the eighteenth century that English ideas of sensible and functional clothing for children were gradually adopted by the rest of Europe. Many of the ideas regarding the education and general upbringing of children, popularized by eighteenth-century philosophers, had already been discussed by John Locke in his *Thoughts on Education* (1693); man, being born free, he said, should not have his limbs swaddled (this practice was on the wane in England by the middle of the eighteenth century, though still common in Europe), nor should he be confined by strait-lacing. Rousseau, in his *Emile* (1762), with the ardour of one who preaches rather than practises, enthusiastically popularized Locke's ideas, advocating breast-feeding, and a régime of loose-fitting clothes, cold water and fresh air for children from their earliest years. A few years later, Grosley noted how the English, even when not endowed with natural beauty, appeared lithe and healthy, the result of 'the free and easy manner in which the bodies of children of the present generation have been formed and the little use made of swaddling cloaths or constraint of any sort'.[48]

Babies of both sexes wore linen shirts, over which were worn stays, sometimes boned but very often corded or quilted; some reinforcement was necessary for the correct deportment which was so much a part of the eighteenth-century credo. Although the stiffened bodice was worn only for approximately the first year by boys, girls continued to wear some light form of reinforced bodice which kept the back flat by pushing back the shoulders; Mrs Delany strongly disapproved of the new front-buttoning gowns of the 1760s, for she felt they dragged the shoulders forward and spoilt the upright carriage which young girls were taught to observe.

At about a year old, the child was put into a short frock. Girls wore simple frocks of linen or muslin with a sash and fastening at the back, a linen cap or coif and an apron. Boys' frocks varied from the simple linen gown with a sash, to a more formal front-fastening gown, sometimes trimmed with frogging or braiding. When the child started to walk, leading strings, strips of material sewn to the back of the arm-holes, were needed, to control movement; it was at this age too that children wore head-protectors in the form of padded rolls (the English called them 'puddings', the French 'bourrelets'), for it was felt that the head was the most vulnerable part of the body and needed extra protection (this might explain the reluctance to wash the hair, and the universal practice of wearing a nightcap). Nollekens recalled that in his youth (he was born in 1737), 'I wore a pudding when I was a little boy ... This pudding consisted of a broad black silk band which went round the middle of the head, joined to two pieces of ribband crossing on the top of the head and then tied under the chin; so that by this most excellent contrivance children's heads were often preserved uninjured when they fell.'[49] In England such puddings were rarely worn in the later years of the century, but Madame de Genlis says that the practice continued in France until the revolution, except for the royal children, whose surroundings were well enough upholstered to prevent damage being caused by a fall. At the age of three or four the sexes went their separate ways with regard to clothing. Girls continued to wear the frock, but when greater formality was needed (generally for much of the eighteenth century, but particularly in the first half, upper-class parents did not see much of their children and their sometimes strained relationships were reflected in rather formal encounters) they were often put straight into adult styles. Wraxall on a visit to Vienna in 1779 found girls of seven or eight 'with powder, a high head, a Chignon and a hoop', such 'absurdities' being common in all countries other than England. In England, where family contacts were sometimes more relaxed, little girls wore either a simplified version of adult dress with boned back-fastening bodice and separate skirt, or, particularly by the 1760s, a white muslin gown and sash worn over a lightly boned corset; this was worn by girls up to their mid-teens, and of course anticipated the chemise dress of the 1780s, an early example of the young setting trends in dress. However, by the age of about twelve, girls were expected to begin to learn adult accomplishments such as dancing, and at such practice assemblies there was an opportunity to learn how to manage the intricacies of adult attire. Anna Winslow in Boston in 1772, aged twelve, attended a 'constitution' to learn dancing and good deportment, and proudly recorded in her diary her 'yellow coat, black bib & apron, black feathers on my head, my past comb, & all my past garnet marquesett & jet pins ... black collar round my neck, black mitts ... striped tucker and ruffels'.[50] Although this was her finest outfit it still included the childish bib and tucker, and the jewellery was imitation, paste and marcasite; Americans adopted English ideas on children's dress, and Abigail Adams, visiting France in the mid-1780s, was horrified at girls of seven being dressed like 20-year-

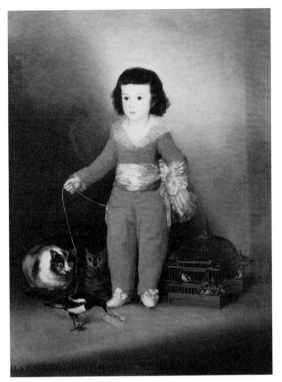

102 **Don Manuel Osorio de Zuñiga**, 1784, by F. Goya

A compromise between Spanish formality and the new, more relaxed and functional styles for children's wear can be seen in this little boy's red silk skeleton suit, fastened round the waist with a wide lace-trimmed silk sash.

olds. She echoed the feelings of Baretti, who commented in 1760 when in Portugal:

Here, as in France and Italy, they have the absurd custom of dressing their children too much. I hate to see a little girl with a tupee and a little sword at the side of a little boy ... In England, boys and girls, even when they are sons and daughters of Earls and Dukes are never made to look like dwarfish men and dwarfish women; and this may be the reason that England abounds less with fops and coquets than either France or Italy.[51]

Boys were breeched at the age of about four (although it could be as late as seven years). In Europe, and particularly at court, little boys were often put straight into adult styles, embroidered velvet suits, wigs and swords; even Mercier, fiercely anti-English in most respects, granted that the French way of dressing children was absurd (a boy of seven 'n'avoit ni poingts, ni bras, ni jambes, mais il savoit s'asseoir & danser le menuet') in comparison to the freedom granted in England. In some cases a compromise was reached between adult styles and childish behaviour; the Bayerisches National-museum in Munich has a boy's coat (for a child of about four) of red wool trimmed with silver braid and with two waistcoat fronts joined in so that from the front the child looked like a tiny adult; but turning to the back one notices not just leading strings, but the whole coat completely open, fasten-ing with hooks and eyes to the waist.[52]

In England it seems to have been the custom from early in the century for boys to wear easier-fitting coats, with the more functional slit cuff; instead of the formal stock or cravat, they wore a frilled shirt collar tied up high to the neck with a black ribbon. Compared to the Continent where quite small boys were put into wigs in the first half of the century, in England this was the exception rather than the rule; Lord Chesterfield in 1748 refused to allow his sixteen-year-old son (who had complained of head-aches) permission to cut his hair and wear a wig, for the latter, however well-made, was a 'disguise' and took away from the natural air which should be affected by the young.

From the 1760s foreign visitors to England admired the distinctive national informality in boys' dress (some of which must be attributed to the influence of sport both in and out of school), the frock suit with waistcoat cut straight across, shirt with open collar, and simply styled hair, left to grow naturally, and usually with a fringe. For the middle class or the prosperous artisan class, there was less of a gap between adult and boy, partly because of reliance on the second-hand trade, which prolonged the life of any style, and partly because new notions of a separate existence for children manifested through their clothing would have seemed a privileged fantasy in an age in which every member of a household had to contribute to the finances of the family. Francis Place, remembering his childhood in the 1770s, described the dress of the reasonably well-to-do apprentice boy as 'a cloth coat without any collar to it, and wide skirts ... single-breasted ... a waistcoat of the same material and a pair of sheepskin breeches, sometimes of a yellow, sometimes of a leaden colour, with four buttons at the knees ... sometimes the breeches were of cloth the same as the coat and waistcoat, worsted stockings, sometimes white cotton stoc-kings, shoes with buckles and a cocked hat'.[53] In fashionable terms this dress with its skirted coat and cocked hat was out-of-date for both adults and boys by the time that Place was wearing it, with the exception of the leather breeches, which were just

about to be taken up by young men such as William Hickey.

It was in this decade, the 1770s, that a new style for young boys took shape, and this was trousers, made in various forms from the baggy to the tight-fitting, from calf-length to ankle-length. Loose-fitting trousers had been worn for many years by sailors and peasants, and there are a few examples of upper-class boys in the middle years of the century wearing calf-length trousers, but with the new trend for informality in the 1770s, those worn by young boys foreshadowed the fashionable pan-taloons of the 1790s and early nineteenth century. With these new nether garments went a short jacket, sometimes double-breasted (the logical extension of the cut-away adult coat without its tails); by the end of the 1780s the shortened jacket (which anticipated the rising waist of a few years later) had the trousers buttoned on to it. This new garment, called the 'skeleton suit', was ideal for a young boy when he abandoned his childish frock; Mrs Papendiek described in 1790 the breeching of her four-year-old son:

A total change of dress it was then for a boy. The shirt was made like a man's except that the collar was large and frilled and turned over the jacket instead of being buttoned up. The jacket and trousers were of cloth, the latter being buttoned over the jacket and the trousers only to the ankle bone. Boots for children being then unknown they had gaiters which went over the end of the trousers, and these with strong shoes equipped them very properly for walking ...
Underwaistcoats and drawers were not then worn, so I had the linings of the trousers made separate which ensured proper cleanliness.[54]

By the end of the 1780s, the prevalence of English styles in children's dress was an accepted fact; even young princes, said the *Journal des Luxus und der Moden*, were being brought up under the principles first established by John Locke a century before. The short jacket and tight-fitting trousers, the open shirt collar and the long, casually arranged hair bespoke early-nineteenth-century Romanticism, the last flicker of male elegance before the black dreariness of the Victorian age (already presaged in the dark suits worn by English businessmen of the 1780s helping the Industrial Revolution on its way).

The simple white frocks worn by girls were worn also by women by the end of the 1780s; although the chemise gown as such came into fashion via a route other than as a child's dress, it too reflected new ideas of a natural informality which were to have a temporary sway over female dress during the revolutionary years.

Fantasy and fancy dress

I must tell you how fine the masquerade of last night was. There were five hundred persons, in the greatest variety of handsome and rich dress I ever saw . . . There were dozens of ugly Queens of Scots . . . the Princess of Wales was one, covered with diamonds, but did not take off her mask . . . Lady Conway was a charming Mary Stuart; Lord and Lady Euston, man and woman huzzars. But the finest and most charming masks were their Graces of Richmond, like Harry the Eighth and Jane Seymour, excessively rich and both so handsome . . . there were quantities of pretty Vandykes, and all kinds of old pictures walked out of their frames.

> H. Walpole, on a masquerade at Vauxhall, 1742

He therefore, who in his practice of portrait painting wishes to dignify his subject, which we will suppose to be a lady, will not paint her in the modern dress, the familiarity of which is sufficient to destroy all dignity. He . . . therefore dresses his figure something with the general air of the antique for the sake of dignity, and preserves something of the modern for the sake of likeness.

> Sir J. Reynolds, *Seventh Discourse*, 1776

'Avant tout . . . le XVIIIe siècle est un siècle de masques.' This statement, made by Pilon and Saisset in their book *Les Fêtes en Europe au XVIIIe Siècle* (1943) refers to the obvious fascination with masquerades and courtly *fêtes galantes* among the upper reaches of society in the eighteenth century. But no less an important part of this fondness for private theatricals and dressing up is reflected in the kind of portraiture through which people projected an image of fantasy, whether real or imaginary. Not only were people of every class used to colour and pageantry, whether at court balls or in the many official and religious processions that marked the

year, to an extent that we have lost, but in many of the portraits showing sitters in fancy dress, there is an almost Romantic interest in the exotic present and the historic past, partly at least influenced by carnival and masquerade, and which even inspired fashionable costume in the last quarter of the century.

Although in previous ages court masquerades were magnificent, they reached their apogee in the eighteenth century, along with the more democratic manifestations of the street carnival, from which the history of masking derives. 'The Italians', said Keysler, a German traveller in 1730, 'are excessively fond of masquerades', and the idea of the carnival began in Italy, although the custom of masking or disguise goes back into antiquity; blended with the lower-class theatrical masked mummeries went the Renaissance processional pageant, combining to form weeks of carnival festivity held just before the austerities of Lent. Each Italian city was *en fête* from the end of December to the start of Lent; the streets were decorated, pageants and tableaux vivants took place, private and public masked balls were held, regattas (in Venice), horse races (Rome and Florence) and firework displays were provided and the *commedia dell'arte* troupes performed their carefully impromptu stories to the crowds. The masquerade reached an art form most of all in Venice, from whence the rest of Europe took the all-embracing black silk gown, the 'domino' (possibly of ecclesiastical or oriental origin), whose ample folds made it an ideal garment for 'intrigues, trifling gallantries . . .' and disguised 'wanton syrens', according to Keysler. For the domino, like the mask and the three-cornered hat, was worn by both men and women, giving an androgynous effect which struck outsiders as curious and even gloomy, with so much black in a season of jollity; Madame du Bocage in Venice in the mid-eighteenth century found 'men and women wear the same sort of

103 Studies of carnival costume, by L. Carlevarijs

Unlike most patrician Venetians, these ordinary citizens have merely added the characteristic carnival mask, scarf and three-cornered hat to their everyday costume. Some element of disguise is, however, created by the use of (from left to right), a capacious cloak, the *zendaletta*, and the masculine coat which many Italian women wore as a surcoat.

OPPOSITE
104 The return from the Ridotto, engraved by G. Zompini, from *Le Arti che vanno per via nella Città di Venezia*, 1785 (the first edition was published in 1753)

Carnival costume was worn also to the theatres and in the Ridotto, the public gaming house in Venice. This fashionable couple being lighted home wear hat, scarf, mask and lace *mantellina* over their everyday dress.

clokes, hoods and hats, all black with white masks; so that, when they lie down in their black gondolas, as they frequently do, you may guess what sort of appearance they make'.[1] With the domino was worn a mask, either of black velvet ('moreta') or a white grotesque mask, the 'gnaga'; as masks only partly covered the face, a piece of black silk or lace, the 'bauta', was placed on the head and drawn across the lower jaw. When the three-cornered hat was placed on top of the head, the incognito was complete, and respected to the extent that those wearing black or white masks were admitted everywhere, even to the Ridotto, the public gaming house in Venice normally open only to patricians.

Venice above all was the city of masquing; not only at the carnival but at various other times of year, from October 5 to December 16, and on the many public holidays which made up the life of the city – the feast of San Marco, the election of the Doge or Procurator, and the ceremony of the Bucintoro, the wedding of Venice with the sea by the throwing of a ring into the harbour and an occasion for splendid regattas.

The upper classes usually wore the domino and mask, or occasionally the short net or lace cloak, the 'mantellina'; cloaks were so light and floating that

(although people's identity was preserved by their headcovering) 'their usual clothes, their hoops and even large nosegays . . . a quantity of precious stones and lace' could be observed. In any case, the prevailing aristocratic blackness was relieved by the costumes worn by the citizens, and by the coloured dominoes worn by foreign visitors (Venice in particular was used to welcoming royalty), for it

De notte, ora ai teatri, ora al Redutto
Son quel che col feral serve de lume;
E pur che i paga mi so andar per tutto.

whimsical dress. The coachmen ... generally affect some ridiculous display. Many of them chuse a woman's dress, and have their faces painted and adorned with patches ...

The peculiar dresses of every nation of the globe, and of every profession, besides all the fantastic characters usual at masquerades are to be seen on the Corso. Those of Harlequin and Pantaloon are in great vogue among the men. The citizens wives and daughters generally affect the pomp of women of quality; while their brothers, or other relatives, appear as train-bearers and attendants. In general they seem to delight in characters the most remote from their own. Young people assume the long beard, tottering step and other concomitants of old age; the aged chuse the bib and rattle of childhood; and the women of quality and women of the town appear in the character of country maidens, nuns and vestal virgins. All endeavour to support the assumed characters to the best of their ability; but none in my opinion succeed so well as those who represent children.[2]

In 1741, an English painter, John Russel, had found that the favourite costume of the women was male dress, 'the breeches, with gold clock'd stockings, shoes buckled to the toes, a laced coat and a hat cocked à la mode de Paris'[3] – dressing *en travesti* was a popular choice. It was noted by characters as diverse as Casanova and Goethe, the latter's famous account of the carnival in Rome in 1787 describing how the sexes changed clothes (some women even wearing uniform), raiding the second-hand clothes stalls for suitable costumes; some dressed as ghosts in white linen.

There was still a faint echo of Renaissance learning in some of the carnival entertainments. In Milan the masquerades were events organized by the members of the academics of gentlemen and artists, who wore their own uniforms with grotesque masks, and in Rome balls and pageants with classical, theatrical and exotic scenes were organized, very often by the famous noble families. Goethe attended a masked ball in the Aliberti theatre where he was impressed by the costumes and the masks 'taken from various art-epochs and imitating in a masterly way various statues preserved in Rome ... Egyptian Gods, Priestesses, Bacchus and Ariadne, the Tragic Muse, the Historical Muse ... Vestals'[4] – this was the period of the great antiquarian discoveries (the neo-classical artist Petitot was employed to design the costumes for a Roman tournament celebrating a royal marriage in the Duchy of Parma in 1769).

The carnival in Rome in 1763 had a number of pageant floats, that of the Colonnas with *commedia*

was an essential part of the Grand Tour to take part in the carnival at masquerade time. Foreign visitors often wore very elaborate coloured dominos with capes and huge sleeves; the egregious Baron Pöllnitz in Venice in 1730 was immediately recognizable by his 'scarlet Domino embroider'd with Silver', and was delighted to be accosted by two girls in St Marks'.

Most Italians opted for fancy dress, the most popular styles being characters from the *commedia dell'arte* (Casanova in Venice for the 1754 carnival chose for a masquerade a Pierrot costume of light calico), shepherds and shepherdesses, orientals, and the dress of the opposite sex – for a considerable amount of licence was allowed, a source of some complaint to visitors. Dr John Moore found Rome completely taken over for the carnival:

The citizens then appearing in the streets, masked, in the characters of Harlequins, Pantaloons, Punchinellos and all the fantastic variety of a masquerade. This humour spreads to men, women and children; descends to the lowest ranks and becomes universal. Even those who put on no mask and have no desire to remain unknown, reject their usual clothes and assume some

dell'arte characters representing the towns in Italy from which each had derived; the Orsini float represented a Hindu sacrifice, the 'priests' in turbans and the 'priestesses' in pink or blue silk with bare arms. The inhabitants of the floats pelted the crowds with sugar plums, which, according to Russel, were quite hard, and 'terribly discompose a well-powdered perruque'.

Some of the most popular themes were oriental, and some of the best organized were undertaken by the students of the French Academy in Rome; in 1735 they organized a *mascarade chinoise*, but their most famous effort (which was thought worth recording by one of the participants, J. M. Vien) was in 1748 when a Turkish procession travelled through the streets in triumphal cars, the students dressed as members of the court at Constantinople.[5] It was the great popularity of this cavalcade that inspired the carnival masquerade in Naples in 1778, 'representing the return of the Grand Signor from Mecca, all performed by the noblesse about Court, and the king's guards', the king and queen taking part too.[6] Italy was, of course, the most popular place for tourists in the eighteenth century, and we have a correspondingly large number of accounts of the splendour of carnival masquerades. But it was a practice common all over Europe, not just in Catholic countries where it was a last fling allowed

105 **The carnival in Rome**, by D. Allan

This is one of a series of drawings done by this Scottish artist in Rome in 1775. Romans and foreigners, dressed in a variety of fashionable and fancy dress, parade in the street, while pageant floats, exhibiting masquerade themes, drive by.

106 **'Le Repos Gracieux'**, by J.-A. Watteau

The popularity of the *Commedia dell'Arte* is manifested in the costumes of these two masqueraders, set in an Arcadian landscape. Elements of early-seventeenth-century dress, such as the doublet and the shoe roses occur in the traditional costume of ?Scaramouche, and his spiky ruff echoes that worn by Columbine, her black mask on the ground beside her.

by the church before Lent, but also in northern Protestant countries. Depending on the climate and on the tradition, masquerades revolved around the court, or they were more democratically open to a greater section of society, either in the streets or in the public pleasure gardens which most large cities possessed.

Masked balls were introduced into France in 1715, when the first was held at the Opéra; it was no accident that the new atmosphere of indulgence under the Regent was highly suitable for the spread of this form of intriguing and pleasurable entertainment – the phrase 'l'esprit de bal' came to be the fashionable jargon for the adventures and indiscretions carried on at masked balls. *Fêtes galantes*, rural masquerades immortalized by Watteau, Pater and Lancret, were occasions when courtly love and social graces were displayed, when courtiers dressed as shepherds and shepherdesses, or Harlequin and Columbine (the Italian players, after a long banishment, were allowed to return to France in 1716); the reality is hard to disentangle from the fantasy. But at times it appeared that the whole of the French court in the middle of the century was in masquerade. Not only were fashionable sitters painted as inhabitants of an Arcadian countryside, but the court, led by Madame de Pompadour, (who had to devise ways of amusing an easily bored king), performed in plays put on in her private theatre, le Théâtre des Petits Cabinets decorated by Boucher, who also helped with the costumes. Many of the plays were slight rococo pastorals in which the ladies in particular could appear in delightfully fashionable and frivolous versions of theatrical dress, with short skirts and bare arms. Madame de Pompadour

herself loved to dress up in private life; she could appear as 'une villageoise ... une gracieuse odalisque présentant du café à la turque ... une piquante espagnole ... un charmant page en travesti, ou même un Pierrot enfariné'.[7]

Louis XV loved attending the masquerades held at the Opéra, where the element of incognito, though present, was not sufficient to prevent him being mistaken for anyone other than the king; as a pilgrim, in 1739, he chose a costume of 'velour bleu ciselé, garni de boutons de diamans et doublé de satin blanc. Sa veste était d'une riche étoffe brodée d'or et il portait le Saint-Esprit en diamants'.[8]

Though the major cities in France, including Paris, held masked balls or street processions (Townsend in 1786 found in Paris that there were thousands in the streets, all masked, some in the clothes of the opposite sex, and many 'Popes, cardinals, monks, devils, courtiers, harlequins and lawyers, all mingled in one promiscuous crowd'),[9] the grandest balls were arranged for great court celebrations, such as royal marriages. When in 1745 the Dauphin was married to an Infanta of Spain, the Galerie des Glaces at Versailles provided the setting for a glittering masked ball; the French queen (who usually led a retired life), appeared in a dress studded with pearls and with the two crown diamonds, the Régent and the Sancy, and the Dauphin and his new wife came as a shepherd and shepherdess. Louis XV, along with seven attendant courtiers, came in the disguise of a yew tree clipped to the shape of a pillar, with a vase on top. It was at this masquerade that the king met Madame le Normand d'Etoiles, later the marquise de Pompadour (some thought her costume as Diana the huntress was apt), but they were publicly seen together at a masked ball given a few days later at the Hôtel de Ville, when both wore light silk dominoes as a disguise.

Although Marie Antoinette inspired a number of masquerades, Louis XVI lacked the necessary witty repartee and fondness for amorous intrigue which was the *sine qua non* of the masked ball, and which inevitably led to criticism of the queen when she was seen in such company at the Opéra.

In some countries where the court was not so much a leader of fashion, the masquerade was a more democratic process. In Holland, for example, the masquerades were held in May at the traditional fairs, or kermesses, which lasted a week, when all wore masks and fancy dress, even the nobility riding masked about the streets in chaises. In Spain, Baretti in the middle of the century found that at carnival time,[10] all the population attended the masquerades held twice a week in Madrid (an amphitheatre had been built by the king for these occasions, open to all, with the price of admission twenty reals, about

five shillings), and for dress 'everybody follows his own fancy' (although gold and silver were forbidden), some wearing the mask and domino, some the regional costumes of Spain, and some of the upper classes choosing the 'majo' and 'maja' styles (see Chapter III).

In England[11] the masquerade had been brought from Italy at the beginning of the eighteenth century, and set on a firm footing by a Swiss, Count Heidegger (later Master of the Revels to George II) at the Opera House in the Haymarket in 1708. This innovation fell on fertile ground, for not only had there long been a tradition for court masques (as there had been in many other countries) but there were well-established pleasure gardens so that all classes of society could take part in summer masquerades. There were thus splendid masquerades with musical entertainment at the theatres, which provided the kind of lavish spectacle which the English court was unwilling to arrange itself, and the pleasure gardens of Vauxhall and Ranelagh which, said Grosley, were more noted for their 'splendor and magnificence' than any other places in the kingdom. Vauxhall Gardens re-opened in 1732 (they had been in existence at the end of the seventeenth century, visited by Pepys, and found by Sir Roger de Coverley in 1712 to be 'a kind of Mahometan paradise', but shortly after they had

107 **'Décoration du Bal Masqué Donné par le Roy . . .**, 1745 (detail), engraving after C. N. Cochin the Elder

At this famous masked ball given in honour of the marriage of the Dauphin, the newly married couple can be seen in the centre dressed as a shepherd and shepherdess, and surrounded by crowds of masqueraders, some also dressed in pastoral costumes and others in the traditioal hooded domino. In the centre foreground can be seen the back view of a lady in jacket and wide hooped skirt, dressed as a pilgrim; her cape is trimmed with cockle-shells and she carries a staff.

OPPOSITE
108 **A View of the Canal, Chinese Building, Rotundo etc. in Ranelagh Gardens, with the Masquerade**, engraving after A. Canaletto

This is one of the many engravings of the masquerades held in 1749 to celebrate the Peace of Aix-la-Chapelle. A group of masqueraders – one can easily pick out such perennial favourites as Punch, Harlequin and a mixed bag of 'orientals' – strolls by the water in which is placed the 'Chinese Building'.

A View of the Canal, Chinese Building, Rotundo, &c. in RANELAGH GARDENS, with the MASQUERADE.

Vûe du Canal, du Bâtiment, Chinois, de la Rotunda, &c. des JARDINS de RANELAGH un jour de MASQUARADE.

been closed due to their unsavoury reputation); they were extended and improved with long vistas, lawns, fountains, statuary and temples, and even supper boxes in the Chinese style, and a 'Gothic' structure to house the orchestra. At Ranelagh Gardens in Chelsea, where the famous rotunda opened in 1742, there were also formal gardens, canals and 'Chinese' or 'Venetian' buildings. It was at Ranelagh in 1749 that a famous series of masquerades was held, celebrating the Peace of Aix-la-Chapelle which had, the previous year, ended the War of the Austrian Succession. One of the most extravagant of these events was 'a jubilee-masquerade in the Venetian manner' (the Venetian aspect seems to have consisted of a gondola 'adorned with flags and streamers and filled with music' on the canal); Walpole, whose comments on all the major English masquerades are an important source of information, found the gardens full of

masks and spread with tents ... In one quarter was a Maypole dressed with garlands and people dancing round it to a tabor and pipe and rustic music, all masked, as were all the various bands of music that were disposed in different parts of the garden; some like huntsmen with French horns, some like peasants, and a troop of harlequins and scaramouches in the little open temple on the

mount ... All round the outside of the amphi-theatre were shops, filled with Dresden china, japan &c and all the shopkeepers in mask.[12]

At a later masquerade some weeks later Walpole found the king enjoying himself 'in an old-fashioned English habit'; the Duke of Cumberland, victor of Culloden, had grown so fat that he reminded Walpole of a drunken captain in a Jacobean play[13] – the early-seventeenth-century costumes that many of the participants wore reflected English interest in this romantic period, further evidenced by the number of portraits in this style of dress which will be discussed later.

The English pleasure gardens were popular partly because of their accessibility, but mostly because of their amenities; they were quick to follow prevail-ing trends in taste, such as the mid-century love of chinoiserie (the only English interpretation of the rococo), and the later fondness for the neo-classical. A 'Chinese regatta' was held on the Thames in 1749, possibly inspired by a similar entertainment held in 1716 in Venice for the Elector of Saxony; *fêtes chinoises* were held in the Colisée, the Parisian imitation of Vauxhall, and at the Swedish summer palace of Drottningholm a 'Chinese' village was built for Queen Louisa Ulrica,[14] who even dressed her son, the future Gustavus III, as a Chinese prince, and his gentlemen as mandarins, thus inculcating a taste for the theatrical which was to have lasting effects. As well as buildings, gardens and follies, the Chinese taste was to be seen in Carlisle House in Soho, the fashionable place for winter masquerades in London in the 1760s; there Mrs Cornelys, an adventuress of dubious reputation (she had at one time been the mistress of Casanova) but with a sense of theatrical display, built a room for dancing, tea-rooms, a grotto and a 'Chinese Room ... so decorated as to afford the most enchanting coup d'oeil'. She arranged rural masquerades where whole suites of rooms were decorated with flowers, shrubs and trees, 'under whose embowering shade the masks will sup'. By the time that this description, taken from a newspaper of 1776, was published, Mrs Cornelys' masquerades were being eclipsed by those held in the Pantheon[16] in Oxford Street (this had opened in 1772 and was to Walpole 'so glorious a vision that I thought I was in the old Pantheon or in the Temples of Delphi or Ephesus'). The idea of *rus in urbe*, or the countryside indoors, was a popular theme for masked balls in places where the climate was unco-operative. In Russia, Mrs Ward attended a masquerade in 1734 (to celebrate the capture of Danzig) given at the Summer Palace on the banks of the Neva. The imperial family dined in a grotto under a pavilion of green silk supported by pillars round which twined flowers (in winter, the Winter Palace was heated so that orange trees and myrtles could bloom); the ladies were in 'stiffened bodied gowns of white gauze with silver flowers, their quilted petticoats were of different colours'.[17]

Arcadian themes had been popular since the Renaissance for court masques, and they provided a suitable source for the *fêtes champêtres* which many countries adopted in the eighteenth century, particularly in the second half of the period when 'picturesque' English landscaped gardens and the cult of open-air simplicity were in vogue; it was becoming the fashion, said Walpole in the 1770s, 'to make romances rather than balls'. A very expensive and elaborate *fête champêtre* was held in the grounds of Lord Stanley's house, The Oaks, near Epsom, in 1774;[18] a temporary amphitheatre, designed by Robert Adam, housed the guests, who were expected to dress in 'pastoral habits', although Lord Stanley and his fiancée chose to appear as Rubens and his wife, and, from the surviving illustrations, many interpreted the rural to include orientals and vandyke costumes. Some of the most lavish *fêtes champêtres* were held in Poland in this decade; Archdeacon Coxe attended one near Warsaw in 1778 where mock peasants' cottages were erected (this rather grates on our modern susceptibilities

when we consider the wretched state of the poor), along with Turkish tents, and the guests were entertained by dancers in Cossack and Polish costumes and by ladies 'in Grecian dresses of the most elegant simplicity'.[19]

In the same vein, there were courtly entertainments in Germany, called 'Wirtschaften', where the guests, dressed in the romanticized costumes of peasants, shepherds and shepherdesses, acted the verses of the court poet; one of Geothe's tasks when he was first employed by the court of Weimar in 1775 was to provide such entertainments.[20] In the Residenz in Munich, the Elector and Electress of Bavaria, dressed as village inn-keepers, received their guests who had driven from the summer palace of Nymphenburg dressed in peasant costume.[21] Regional costumes and pastoral themes provided the source for some of the rural masquerades popular in Vienna, many designed by Bertoli, who worked for the court from 1707 to 1743. During this period masquerades at carnival had been forbidden, but when Maria Theresa came to the throne, her own taste was for enjoyable public displays (though she became increasingly puritanical after the death of her husband in 1765). She organized sleighing parties in winter where the ladies, dressed in fur-trimmed velvets covered in diamonds, rode on gilded sledges shaped like swans, horses, griffins or unicorns. A popular court activity was the carrousel, a cavalry tournament where the riders performed elaborate equestrian dances, dressed in splendid, often exotic uniforms; one such was held in the winter riding school in 1743 to celebrate the recapture of Prague from the French, and Maria Theresa led the first quadrille on horseback, dressed in gold-embroidered purple, followed by her ladies in carriages.[22]

Masquerades were held at the opera house in Vienna, and at Schönbrunn, where in 1775 Dr Moore saw 4000 guests who watched a ballet danced by some of the imperial family and the nobility, 'all of them dressed in white silk fancy dresses trimmed with pink ribbons and blazing with diamonds'.[23] The Germans generally, said Moore, 'being so much harassed with ceremony and form ... are glad to seize every opportunity of assuming the masque and domino, that they may taste the pleasures of familiar conversation and social mirth'.[24] This was certainly so at the Austrian court, where Lady Mary Coke found in the 1770s that the popularity of the masquerade was unabated; light lustring dominos were the rule, decorated with ribbons (the emperor appeared in a white domino trimmed with gold), or an alternative dress for the ladies was a Polish costume 'made tight to the waist ... commonly of sattin trimmed with fur, and silver

109 A Tournament, 1778, by P. H. Hilleström

This painting of a carrousel held at Drottningholm Palace gives a good indication of the elaborate theatrical divertissements which were so much a part of Swedish court life under the cultivated Gustavus III. The king and his courtiers have adopted 'classical' costume, the king in a red-and-white Roman dress with ermine-lined mantle being received by 'Diana' (Duchess Hedvig Elisabet Charlotta) who wears a flower-trimmed version of fashionable costume and a crescent in her hair. The spectator courtiers are in the Swedish national costume, itself an amalgam of fashionable contemporary dress with elements of the Henri IV styles of the late sixteenth century. Walpole's comment that it was the fashion 'to make romances rather than balls' in the 1770s was particularly true of absolutist courts with unlimited funds to provide the kind of fantasy entertainments which were so popular. In this decade it is not surprising that fashionable dress itself was so strongly influenced by the historic past.

or gold'.[25] To Baron Bielfeld, the monotony of the court at Hanover was only lightened by the winter masquerades in the opera house and the summer masked balls held at Herrenhausen, where, seeing the white dominos walking down the lamp-lit allées, 'they gave the Gardens the appearance of the Elisian fields'. In Russia, masquerades had begun in the reign of Peter the Great, as part of his forcible westernizing policy; according to some commentators, they were more like burlesques than the elegant masked balls of other courts. La Motraye found when he went to court in 1719 that there was a masquerade to celebrate the taking of four Swedish men-of-war, and the Czar was dressed as a Dutch sailor, the Czarina and her ladies 'like country-women of Frizland and Zealand', 'and the rest in old Russian fashion ... & attended with a great number of Vizars in peculiar habits, some playing upon Instruments and others dancing as they march'd'.[26] By the 1770s masquerades were held twice a week in winter in St Petersburg, thousands attending at a time and the dresses a mixture of Russian regional costume or court dress under a domino; in the winter of 1778, Coxe found Catherine the Great dancing masquerade quadrilles with a number of partners dressed in such exotic costumes as Roman habits with diamond-studded helmets.

Many masquerades were theatrical in inspiration, some deriving directly from the staged *tableaux vivants* of the Renaissance; the Margravine of Bayreuth gave to her husband for his birthday in

1736 an entertainment where Mount Parnassus was erected: 'A very good singer whom I engaged represented Apollo; nine ladies magnificently attired, were the muses, and underneath Parnassus we had a theatre'[28] where the performers danced a ballet. Classical themes dominated some of the expensive tournament fêtes which seemed a particularly popular entertainment for absolute princes. Month-long celebrations occurred at the Bavarian court in 1722 for the marriage of the Electoral Prince to the Archduchess Maria Amelia; at one of the evening carrousels, the court dressed up as Greeks and Romans, in gold-embroidered costumes decorated with diamonds, for a mock tournament.[29] Such classical military combat was a particularly apt choice for the martial Prussian court; in August 1750 a fête was held at Potsdam in honour of a visit made by the king's favourite sister Fredericka Sophia Wilhelmina, when princes of the blood led contingents of courtiers dressed as Romans, Carthaginians, Greeks and Persians.[30] The entertainment was taken very seriously, and a month was spent in practising military manoeuvres, and the torchlight processions which, since medieval times, had been an important part of German court festivities. The costumes were distinguished more for their glamorous appearance than for accuracy, and were very similar to those worn for the courtly opera-ballet, light glittering fabrics with stiffened skirts, helmets, feathers and asymmetrically draped mantles. The Romans were distinguished by their feathered headdresses, gold cuirasses and gold-decorated blue mantles; the Carthaginians, imitating Moors, were clothed in black satin with feathered skirts and pearl collars and turbans of silver cloth and, they were led by the king's brother Frederick, dressed in a costume of cloth-of-silver, embroidered with a golden sun on the front, and in a tiger-skin cloak. The Greeks and the Persians proved more difficult to dress; the former wore a version of Roman dress with one-sided mantles edged with fringe, and the latter came in a kind of Turkish dress (some of them were called 'Janissaries' after the famous Turkish palace guard) in turbans; their leader wore a cloak of green satin lined with ermine over a tunic of silver brocaded with gold flowers, and a bonnet *à la Persanne*, a turban decorated with precious stones. After the ceremonial parades to music, the tournaments took place at barriers specially erected; later, masked balls were held, those taking part in the carrousel wearing the clothes they had worn for the tournaments. It was all very costly, with elaborate and contrived allegory, the kind of courtly entertainment with which an Olivier de la Marche in fifteenth-century Burgundy, or Inigo Jones in early Stuart England, would have instantly been familiar.

In Spain the mock battles with attendant processions were closely linked to the Moorish tradition; Swinburne in the mid-1770s described the *parejas*, 'a kind of dancing on horseback', where the courtiers 'arrayed in the ancient Spanish dress' tilted in the grounds of the royal palace of Aranjuez.[31] The ancient Spanish dress, which Baretti described in the 1760s as 'made fine with many ribbonds of various colours, with feathers on their hats', was also worn for bull-fighting both in Spain and Portugal.[32]

In the last quarter of the eighteenth century, the idea of the theatrically inspired tournament reached new heights of elaborate display; medieval themes, precursors of the rage for the 'Gothic' which had begun at this period and which were temporarily halted by the European wars, were to emerge in the early nineteenth century as a decisive cultural influence. Again, these could only be organized by courts oblivious to expense; in 1775 a medieval tournament was held at Choisy in honour of Marie Antoinette, in which knights in full armour jousted – first glimmerings of the *style troubadour*,[33] or the romantic harking back to the Middle Ages and the Renaissance. But the apogee of the fancy dress tournament came with Gustavus III of Sweden,[34] who wrote and acted in pageants with themes from recent (seventeenth-century) Swedish history (such as the court of Queen Christina), and the more distant past; one such fête was held in the grounds of Drottningholm in 1779, the theme being from the *chanson de geste*, *Amadis de Gaul*; Gustavus took the part of the enchanter Arcelaus, and the music was composed by Gluck. The king helped to design costumes and stage sets for plays performed at the court theatre in Gripsholm Castle, and it was ironic that he should have been shot at a masquerade in 1792 at the Stockholm Opera House that had been built at his expense and inspiration.

Masquerades celebrated occasions of national rejoicing but in many cases their full splendour

110 **Before the Masked Ball**, attributed to F. Fontebasso

Some of the most sumptuous masquerades were held by the Russian court in St Petersburg; this problematical painting (which has been attributed to a number of artists) may depict such an event. The men wear the generalized Central European dress, trimmed with fur and froggings, which was a staple, conventional masquerade costume of the period. The central, female figure wears a lavishly trimmed 'fancy dress', i.e. high fashion, with a superabundance of jewellery and such theatrical items as feathers, and glittering paste decorations on the gown.

could not be appreciated by the mass of the people, who were not admitted. What the populace could see were the civic and religious processions which formed an important part of everyday pageantry, and which were descended from medieval clerical and mercantile power. In Rome, for example, the richest entertainments were provided by the papal processions, attended by retainers in the deliberately archaic costumes of the previous century; in 1730 Pöllnitz saw Clement XII in his litter surrounded by pages 'in an antique Dress of white Sattin, with a great many red and silver'd Ribbands, and black cloaks lin'd with white and silver Mohair, and enriched with broad Gold Lace',[35] and accompanied by clerics, the Roman nobility, and drummers and trumpeters in red and gold.

City authorities provided much of their own pageantry; this ranged from the Lord Mayor's processions in London (with a cavalcade of City companies and a ceremonial progress up the Thames), to the staged *tableaux-vivants* with speeches and dances arranged by cities to welcome important events, such as those held by Strasbourg in 1744 to celebrate the recovery of Louis XV, who had fallen ill at Metz while on campaign. In Strasbourg the city companies formed themselves into battalions imitating the uniforms of the regiments of the French army; young boys dressed like the French king's Swiss Guard, in sixteenth-century costumes of blue camlet slashed with red, white muslin ruff and black hat with a white feather. An equal number of young girls wore their 'habits de cérémonie', with the traditional headdress of black velvet and lace, and there were young couples dressed as shepherds and shepherdesses in costumes of white taffeta, decorated with garlands of flowers and rose-coloured ribbons.[36]

It is in the eighteenth century that we get a last glimpse of the medieval *joyeuse entrée*, originally the formal acknowledgement by a city of the sovereignty of its prince but by this time merely an official if elaborate welcome. Strasbourg was in a special position in this respect, a former imperial city but with a certain degree of independence under French rule; it was there that foreign brides were welcomed to French territory, such as Marie-Josèphe of Saxony (1747) and Marie Antoinette (1770). On the latter occasion children dressed as shepherds and shepherdesses greeted the Austrian princess; Goethe saw the triumphal arches which traditionally decorated the city, and he saw the future French queen making her entry in a glass coach. In Spain, still behind the times, the king still formally entered his capital; in 1760 Charles III made a public entry into Madrid (where the balconies along the route were lined with people),

attended by his knights in old Spanish dress, and his guard 'in liveries of Moorish habits of silk, richly and elegantly ornamented with lace and embroidery'.[37]

It was no wonder that in such a climate where pageantry and masquerade were accepted parts of everyday existence, fancy dress played an important role. Dressing *en travesti* was part of this masquerade. For women there was a respectable operatic tradition of appearing as boys – Mozart's Cherubino in *The Marriage of Figaro* (1786) is the best example. And at masquerades male costume was very popular; the Empress Elizabeth of Russia in the 1740s organized masked balls called Metamorphoses, where men and women adopted the costume of the opposite sex – men in wide hooped dresses, and the empress herself in a robust selection of male clothing – as a cossack, or as a Dutch sailor.[38] We would not be surprised to find Casanova finding pleasure in changing clothes with his mistress for a masquerade, but it is slightly more startling to contemplate Goethe in 1775 attending a ball in a Savoyard dress given to him by the Duchess of Weimar.

Apart from a few notorious examples (and in spite of the attacks directed against the macaronis for their effeminacy) there was not much perceptible female influence on male costume in spite of the popularity of women's dress at masquerades. For women there have been, on the other hand, constant attacks on their propensity for borrowing from men's clothing, and this was true of the eighteenth century. When in 1728 Augustus the Strong of Saxony went to Berlin, accompanied by his daughter, she amazed the Prussian court with a large number of male outfits, some for dancing and some, as we would expect, for riding; we have already noted the masculine influence on the female riding habit and the great-coat. Later in this chapter we will be looking at other trends – historical and exotic – which played their part in fashionable costume and as fancy dress, although the subject is so vast (and the range of costumes so great) that only the major points can be mentioned.

It has already been noted to what an extent exotic and flamboyant liveries were worn at some of the German and central European courts. A royal marriage taking place at the Saxon court in 1719 included cavalcades of attendants in Saxon and Polish liveries, hussars, and 24 Moors 'dressed in Turkish habits' of scarlet edged with blue and feathered turbans.[40] These costumes were everyday wear in Saxony, which also ruled Poland, where, as we have seen, clothing was influenced by Turkey. By the middle of the century such exotic styles had made an impact all over Europe.[41]

The catalyst which popularized Hungarian hussar costume in England[41] was the sympathy caused when the Empress Maria Theresa enlisted the help of her Hungarian subjects against Frederick the Great's invasion of her territory in 1740; not only did English Catholics (who were refused commissions in the British army) fight in Austrian regiments, but fashionable men-about-town, according to the *Female Spectator*, swaggered about London 'like warriors for the Queen of Hungary'. No doubt they wore a version of hussar dress which had slight acquaintance with the original dolman, pelisse and fur-edged cap. At masquerades fashionable gentlemen turned up in what Thomas Jefferys described as 'the Modern Dress of a Hungarian Hussar ... rose-coloured Sattin trimmed with Silver', which was not very martial, but incorporated the frogged trimming which came to be synonymous with 'hussar'. The costume was further popularized by Garrick, when, for no conceivable reason except that it was in vogue, he wore it playing a twelfth-century ruler of Sicily, in Thomson's play *Tancred and Sigismunda* in 1745. Not only were servants put into hussar liveries (they were particularly if inappropriately worn by fashionable and highly prized negro servants), but children also wore them. Little hussars paraded the streets of Italian cities at carnival time, and even George III (who was later to disapprove of his sons' attendance at masquerades) attended a masque organized in 1769 by the governess of his two eldest sons 'in rich Hussar Habits of white satin embroidered with Gold & trimm'd with Sable'. Just as in the 1880s velvet Lord Fauntleroy suits adorned small boys, so from the middle of the eighteenth century 'Hussar Dresses' were advertised for sale; this jacket and calf-length trouser style was particularly suited to the new kind of boys' clothing pioneered by the English in the 1770s and 1780s. By the 1770s elements of hussar dress, notably the trimming and the fur, decorated men's coats. William Hickey (who put his Indian servant into a hussar livery) admired a particularly dashing friend in 1772: 'His dress then being a white coat, cut in the extremity of ton, lined with garter-blue satin, edged with ermine, and ornamented with rich silver frogs; waistcoat and breeches of the same blue satin, trimmed with silver twist à la hussar, and ermine edges.'[42] The Prince of Wales, the future George IV, loved fancy dress and uniforms, the two influences combining to create a fascination with hussar uniform, which was gradually being adopted by armies all over Europe. By the late 1780s, along with other fashion leaders, he was beginning to adopt the tight-fitting pantaloons and tasselled boots which were originally part of hussar costume.

Like many other princes, he loved to dress up in Turkish costume, a style of dress with long flowing robe/caftan and turban, which was not only 'very proper for a prince because it disguises well and has a commanding aspect',[43] but it also provided an opportunity to display jewelled ornaments and an exotic, if conventional, taste.

The influence of Turkey on the taste and culture of eighteenth-century Europe was immense. The Ottoman Empire, declining as a military power since the end of the seventeenth century, began to open out to western European travellers who had long been intrigued by the secret, autocratic and above all exotic court in Constantinople. Turkey had since the Middle Ages exported fine silks and embroideries to the west via Venice, and such trading links were further strengthened by the establishment of diplomatic facilities granted in particular to France, England and Holland by the beginning of the eighteenth century. At about that time, too, Turkish embassies appeared at European courts, a notable visit to France in 1721 inspiring artists, writers, interior designers and the theatre.

From the beginning of the century a number of foreign artists had settled in Constantinople, painting members of the merchant and diplomatic communities and their families, and an increasing number of young men who extended their Grand Tour to include the newly fashionable East. Perhaps the most famous was the artist J. B. Vanmour (who had worked in Turkey since the end of the seventeenth century), who was commissioned by the French ambassador, M. de Ferriol, to paint a series of scenes depicting the life and costumes of the Ottoman empire; these were engraved, and published in Paris in 1714 under the title *Recueil de Cent Estampes representant differentes Nations du Levant*. Their accuracy of detail and the quality of the design meant that this collection inspired artists throughout the eighteenth century to produce similar costume pieces, and a number of artists who had never been to Turkey, such as Aved, Cochin and Boucher (who illustrated one of the most popular works, Guer's *Moeurs et Usages des Turcs*, published in 1747), painted their sitters in the newly fashionable oriental dress. The Swiss artist Liotard (who himself dressed like a Turk for comfort and self-advertisement) painted sitters in Constantinople and in fashionable western European capitals, dressed *à la turque*..

Courtly entertainments were also inspired by Turkey, perhaps the most impressive *mise-en-scène* being at Dresden, where Augustus II in the early eighteenth century 'kept a kind of seraglio of the most beautiful females of his dominions'; the Saxon court, said a contemporary, 'was the seat of all pleasures; it might justly be styled the island of Cythera'.[44] There were Turkish gardens and portraits of court beauties in Turkish costume, Turkish entertainments were provided at court, where the Elector appeared as the Sultan; Keysler, the indefatigable Hanoverian traveller, saw in 1730 an astonishing array of 'rich habits' which belonged to the royal wardrobe, including many Turkish costumes which had been used at masquerades.[45] When in 1787 Catherine the Great visited the recently annexed Crimea, Potemkin designed in her honour a whole series of Turkish delights, banquets and regattas, dressed in his favourite costume of richly embroidered caftan and loose trousers. A prince's income was also needed for the party held in 1781 to celebrate the coming-of-age of William Beckford; Fonthill was transformed by the stage designer de Loutherbourg into a Turkish palace for three days of oriental entertainments.[46]

Anything oriental was in vogue for fancy dress; 'Turks pour'd by hundreds,' said a poem commemorating a masquerade held at the Haymarket Theatre in 1768 in honour of the visiting King of Denmark.[47] Also present on this occasion were the Duke of Northumberland 'in a Persian habit with a turban richly ornamented with diamonds ... Lord Clive in the dress of a Nabob very richly ornamented ... An East India director was dressed in the real habit of a Chinese Mandarin'. Some of the costumes were obviously brought back from eastern travels, some hired, and some no doubt made from the 'Indian' nightgowns which had for long been a staple item in the fashionable wardrobe; loose silk gowns often lined with fur were worn by European travellers to the East and worn by them in commemorative portraits.

Two years after the publication of the set of engravings after Vanmour, the most famous eighteenth-century traveller, Lady Mary Wortley Montagu, set off with her husband on an ambassadorial visit to Turkey. During her two years there she set herself to discover as much as possible about the life and customs of the Turks, the women in particular, whose relaxed and elegant clothing she compared to the 'slavery' suffered by Englishwomen with their tight-lacing and hooped skirts. Like previous male travellers, she found it convenient to dress *à la turque*, recording her clothing in great detail for her sister Lady Mar in Paris in 1717:

The first part of my dress is a pair of drawers, very full, that reach to my shoes and conceal the legs more modestly than your petticoats. They are of a thin rose-coloured damask, brocaded with silver flowers ... Over this hangs my smock, of a fine white silk gauze edged with embroidery. This

111 Lady Mary Wortley Montagu and her son (detail), attributed to J. B. Vanmour

Lady Mary wears a gold-coloured caftan tucked up into her jewelled girdle. The over-gown is a gold-embroidered blue curdee trimmed with ermine.

OPPOSITE
112 **Mlle Rosalie Duthé**, 1779, by E. Aubry

Western European etiquette and deportment do not allow this sitter to lounge like an odalisque on her sofa, but a moderately successful Turkish mise-en-scène, as to setting, pose and costume, is achieved. With regard to the dress, a compromise between East and West can be seen. The high-piled hair of the 1770s is trimmed with white feathers *à la mode*, but with a small black feather aigrette in the Turkish style, and a striped silk 'oriental' scarf. A similar, transparent silk covers the satin skirt, but the embroidered gown with short over-sleeves (possibly a circassian dress) is worn over a firmly structured, European, boned bodice.

smock has wide sleeves, hanging half-way down the arm, and is closed at the neck with a diamond button; but the shape and colour of the bosum are very well to be distinguished through it. The antery is a waistcoat made close to the shape, of white and gold damask, with very long sleeves falling back and fringed with deep gold fringe, and should have diamond or pearl buttons . . .

My caftan, of the same stuff with my drawers, is a robe exactly fitted to my shape, and reaching to my feet, with very long strait falling sleeves. Over this is my girdle, of about four fingers broad, which all that can afford it have entirely of diamonds or other precious stones . . . The curdee is a loose robe they throw off or put on according to the weather, being of a rich brocade (mine is green and gold) either lined with ermine or sables; the sleeves reach very little below the shoulders.[48]

With this dress noble Turkish ladies wore on their heads either a small velvet cap decorated with pearls or diamonds, or an embroidered silk handkerchief, or an aigrette of feathers or jewelled flowers.

Through these letters (which were circulated in manuscript before being published in 1763 and serialized in fashionable magazines thereafter) and a number of portraits, a vogue for Turkish fancy dress spread through England. It had an immediate appeal to a public ready for novelty; rich, glamorous, even erotic – to a later English traveller Turkish women's 'breasts are at full liberty under their Vest without any restraint of Stays or Boddice . . . in a word they are just as Nature has form'd them' – it was worn for masquerades and entered the vocabulary of the fashionable portrait-painter. The tremor of indecorum associated with it made it an ideal costume for the masquerade; the 1724 *Dialogue betwixt a Prude and a Coquet* describes a lady's surprise at her rival's choice of costume:

O Jesu – Coz – why this fantastick dress?
I fear some Frenzy does your Head possess;
That thus you sweep along a Turkish tail,
And let that Robe o'er Modesty prevail . . .
Why in this naughty Vestment are you seen?
Dress'd up for Love, with such an Air and Mien,
As if you wou'd commence Sultana Queen.[49]

At the King of Denmark's masquerade (1768), the Duchess of Richmond 'appeared as the Fatima described in Lady Mary Wortley Montagu's letters',[50] but the most admired dress was that of the Duchess of Ancaster in 'a robe of purple satin bordered with ermine'.[51] Turkish costumes came to mean all or any of the following: fur (usually ermine) trimming, a long gown or caftan (with short or hanging sleeves) one side of which was kilted up and held by an elaborately jewelled girdle over baggy trousers, and either a turban or asymmetrically placed aigrette of feathers or jewels.

For both masquerade-goers and artists there were a variety of sources which could be used; these included collections of engravings (such as Ferriol's), or records of famous masquerades such as the *Caravanne du Sultan à la Mecque* performed by the students of the French Academy in Rome in 1748 and depicted by one of the participants, J. M. Vien.[52] Both these sources were used in Thomas Jeffreys's masquerade pattern book of 1757, an important publication for the spread of certain fancy dress costumes. Turkish costumes were also popularized by fashionable plays with oriental themes (Mme Favart wore a genuine Turkish costume for her rôle in *Soliman* in 1767), and by well-known actresses; Liotard, as well as painting his sitters *à la turque*, also designed costumes, at least one for the actress Adrienne Lecouvreur at the request of her lover Maurice de Saxe.[53] Both the demi-monde and society ladies wished to appear in their portraits in Turkish costume; in 1755 Madame de Pompadour commissioned Carle van Loo to paint a series of portraits of her as a sultana for her chateau of Bellevue, and Liotard's clients included ladies as different as the beautiful Countess of Coventry and the Empress Maria Theresa.

In England the link between the masquerade and the popularity of 'oriental' fashionable dresses was clearly perceived by contemporaries; the *Magazine à la Mode* (1777) noted how far 'The dresses of our ladies have inclined very much to the Persian and Turkish, since the taste for masquerades as a fashion amusement has prevailed . . . The resemblance of the headdress and robe will be seen at first view, and it will be found that, with little or no alteration, an English lady, taken from one of our polite assemblies and conducted to Constantinople, would be properly dressed to appear before the Grand Signior.'[54]

During the 1760s the tambour frame was imported into western Europe from Turkey, to embroider the semi-transparent muslins used for dresses, turbans, and sashes, and from this time the number of 'oriental' gowns increased, though their exact meaning varied. The 'sultane' (a term used from the end of the seventeenth century) was a popular informal gown (Mrs Delany described a bride's trousseau in 1748 as containing a 'white satin sultane with embroidered robings of natural flowers . . . and a pink and white sprigged sultane'),[55] which was either tied back at the sides, or decorated with fur; the *Lady's Magazine* for 1783 noted that it was fashionably made of white lustring tied up at the sides, and in the following year the same magazine found that the currently fashionable 'Westmoreland sultane' was of 'boue de Paris' coloured satin trimmed with sable. Equally popular were 'circassians' (the name taken, said the *Gallerie des Modes*, from the grand Sultan's favourites in the seraglio), gowns decorated with tassels and fur, often with short sleeves. They could be quite informal; Mrs Montagu, attending a ball at the Mansion House in Newbury (1780) was upset to find a tailor's wife 'only dressed in a Circassian Robe and a Queen's night cap on her head'.[56] By the end of the 1780s there were even circassian corsets, which were lightly boned, and short, to accommodate the rising waist.

Some aspects of Turkish costume were approved of by artists who preferred the flow of drapery to the minutiae of fashion with all its trimmings. Angelica Kauffmann, for example, painting fashionable sitters in the 1770s, found that the modish oriental déshabillé of loose-fitting cross-over muslin gown, decorated with braid and fringe, with a sash, fitted in with her ideas about the simple styles of classical Greece. But to her friend Sir Joshua Reynolds, such 'eastern dresses', although rich and dignified, had 'a mock dignity in comparison with the simplicity of the antique'.[57]

Poor Reynolds had great trouble with the costume of his female sitters, for he had to contend not only with their desire to be painted in fashionable dress, but their choice of whatever was currently in vogue with regard to fancy dress; the resulting compromise costumes were often uneasy mixtures of the fashionable déshabillé and unreal drapery. The Duchess of Rutland, painted by Reynolds in 1781, had to try on eleven different dresses before the artist chose to paint her in a 'bedgown', a simple

113 **'Morning Amusement'**, by A. Kauffmann

This may be the painting referred to by Mrs Powys when she visited Stourhead in 1776, 'a lady in a white and gold Turkish habit working at a tambour'. The mood is one of exotic informality which in some ways anticipates later neo-classical styles. Embroidery done on the tambour frame was used both for masquerade and for fashionable dresses.

dress of white with a sash round the waist, which best accorded with his idea of a 'timeless' dress.[58] For the President of the Royal Academy, Greece and Rome were 'the fountains from whence have flowed all kinds of excellence ... We voluntarily add our approbation of every ornament that belonged to them, even to the fashion of their dress'.[59] He was not alone in his view, for from the 1760s the neo-classical was a theme popular with artists, partly as a reaction against what was seen as the over-decorative and meaningless prettiness of the rococo, and partly due to growing interest in published accounts of the classical discoveries at Herculaneum and Pompeii – it was the civilization of the Greeks in Italy which at this date inspired artists, and writers such as Winckelmann. Although in 1763 (the year that Winckelmann's *Geschichte der Kunst des Altertums* was published) Diderot was writing to Grimm that 'tout se fait aujourd'hui à la grecque', no such influence penetrated the world of fashion until the later 1780s, although artists such as Romney and Vigée-Lebrun had tried to persuade their sitters to adopt a classical costume of simple white gown (worn without stays or hoops), unpowdered hair and entwining scarves.[60] Vigée-Lebrun organized 'Grecian evenings' in the 1780s; a suitable Grecian dress could be achieved merely by adding a chaplet of flowers to her usual costume of white linen or muslin chemise, and her guests were lent draperies from her studio.[61] Until the waist rose appreciably in the 1790s, and the startling political developments in France caused parallels to be drawn between the heroic days of classical Greece and Rome, classical dress (other than on the stage where it had been worn intermittently throughout the eighteenth century, but especially in the 1780s) was no more than a self-conscious pose, or an artist's ideal.[62] In the former category, Lady Hamilton, seen by Goethe in 1787, had a Greek costume made for her by her husband in which, 'letting her hair loose, and taking a couple of shawls, she exhibits every variety of posture, expression and look'.[63] The artist J. W. Tischbein (who was later to publish four volumes of engravings taken from vases in Sir William Hamilton's collection) in Naples in 1789, admired the grace and beauty of Lady Charlotte Campbell, whom he likened to 'the swaying dancers of the paintings at Herculaneum', and he painted her in a white chemise with gold-embroidered gauze scarf, and white satin shoes also embroidered in gold.[64]

Certain mythological characters were popular for masquerades, such as the goddess Diana; the costume chosen could incorporate the classical with the ever-popular pastoral. White, however, was the only common factor in 'classical' or 'pastoral'

114 **Philippa Rooper, Lady Sunderlin**, 1788, by Sir J. Reynolds

This is some way removed from Turkish costume, but shows how aspects of Turkish dress have been incorporated into fashionable wear. The hanging sleeve has become a sleeve looped up with gold cord and fringed on the shoulders; the jewelled girdle is replaced by a fringed sash, and the turban by a bandeau.

OPPOSITE
115 **Lady Charlotte Campbell**, by J. W. Tischbein

This portrait of a noted beauty was painted in Naples in about 1789–90. In the artist's autobiography, he describes how her grace and beauty brought to life classical art, 'the lovely, youthful, fleeing figures on bas-reliefs and the swaying dancers of the paintings at Herculaneum'. For her costume, Tischbein has chosen the suitably classical white chemise, with rolled-up sleeves; an embroidered mantle is draped about her, and as a headdress Lady Charlotte wears a wreath of roses, an attribute of the goddess Aphrodite.

costumes; a 'Diana' masquerade costume noted in the *Covent Garden Magazine* (1773) was 'a short kind of jacket and petticoat of white gauze . . . and a small white turban of gauze striped with silver',[65] and some years earlier at the 'sylvan theatre' at Herrenhausen, the Princess of Hesse, said Bielfeld, 'was drest in the habit of a rural nymph, made of white sattin, and ornamented with Italian flowers. Her habit was made in the form of a vest, which finely marked her shape'.[66]

Flowers, floating scarves, tinsel trimming and feathers could be added to provide suitably romantic or pastoral costumes. In Richardson's novel *Sir Charles Grandison* (1753) the heroine Harriet Byron was most uneasy about her costume as an 'Arcadian Princess', which 'falls not in with any of my notions of the pastoral dress of Arcadia', for it comprised a white net cap with spangles and artificial flowers and a white feather, a blue satin waistcoat and skirt trimmed with silver braid and fringe, and 'a kind of scarf, of white Persian silk, which gathered at the top, is to be fastened to my shoulders, and fly loose behind me'; the only concession, she felt, was that 'I am not to have a hoop, for 'they wore not hoops in Arcadia'.[67]

Tight-fitting waistcoats or riding jackets (such as Olivia's 'green joseph' in *The Vicar of Wakefield*)

made popular rural costumes in the middle of the century; later, in the 1770s and 1780s the whole of fashionable informal dress was affected by a rather stylized simplicity, and the polonaise gowns with their bunched-up drapery and the white chemises with straw hats and flowers could make passable costumes for shepherdesses. Playing at rural simplicity was an eighteenth-century pastime; fashionable ladies queued up to be painted as milkmaids, dairymaids, hay-makers and shepherdesses. This vogue gathered popularity in the 1770s with new enthusiasm for the 'picturesque' in nature and its potential for both drama and simplicity. Gardens in the English style with carefully arranged wildness, and often hamlets with shepherds and shepherdesses, formed an essential part of many royal and princely courts; at the Petit Trianon Marie Antoinette could relax away from the formality of the palace of Versailles and with her intimate circle, dressed 'à la jardinière' or 'en belle fermière', could play in the miniature village with its lake and artificially aged farm buildings, dairy, barns and dovecots.

The classical past was far enough away in time for a multitude of fashionable interpretations in dress to occur, and the pastoral could be easily adapted from whatever was the current déshabillé. The vogue for fancy dress based on more recent historical periods is harder to fathom. In England, particularly, the range of historical costumes was enormous; in 1768 the Countess of Moira's masquerade guests included 'Vandykes, Hussars . . . Spaniards, ancient Frenchmen . . . the Rubens' wives, the Mary of Medici, the Isabella of Spain, Jane Seymour . . .'[68] Much of the interest in the fifteenth and sixteenth century was doubtless created by the popularity of stage plays with such themes; Rowe's play *Jane Shore* (1713) about the mistress of Edward IV, was performed throughout the eighteenth century, and probably inspired Lady Waldegrave's choice of masquerade costume in this role in 'a dress richly trimmed with beads and pearls' (1770). Tragic heroines are always popular, and at Lady Moira's masquerade the Jane Seymour costume consisted of 'a stiff bodice and farthingale with silver gauze beads and ermine made of black and white Persian'.[69]

Shakespearian characters from the history plays were frequent choice; Henry VIII and Anne Boleyn made a romantic pair (the play was a favourite of George II), and Anne Boleyn's costume was chosen by the blue-stocking Mrs Montagu for her portrait by the miniaturist Zincke in 1740. No doubt such interest in the past was also inculcated by the popularity of Salmon's Royal Wax-works, near Temple Bar, which displayed such tableaux as Henry VIII introducing Anne

Boleyn at court, and Charles I giving his blessing to his three children the day before his execution; a number of museums also displayed collections of historic costume.[70] Growing interest in the past (helped by the increased verisimilitude of stage costumes from the mid-eighteenth century onwards)[71] was furthered by scholarly research into the dress of the past, and a number of works which brought together engravings from a wide range of sources – fashion prints, Old Masters, and famous historical portraits. One such important publication was Thomas Jefferys's *A Collection of the Dresses of Different Nations both Ancient and Modern, and more particularly Old English Dresses after the designs of Holbein, Vandyke, Hollar and others,* which came out in two volumes in 1757 (with 240 plates) and a further two volumes in 1772 (also with 240 plates). Not only was this comprehensive collection a boon to the masquerader and shops selling or hiring fancy dress so that the costumes need 'no longer be a

116 **Design for a ball dress**, by C.-L. Desrais

This design, engraved for the *Gallerie des Modes*, shows the popular Henri IV costume which was worn at court balls in 1774–6 at the request of Marie-Antoinette, and made up by 'Sarrazin, Costumier de la Famille Royale'.

ABOVE LEFT
117 **The Hon. Mrs Graham**, 1777, by T. Gainsborough

118 **Lady Mary Coke**, 1762, by A. Ramsay

Lady Mary Coke, a somewhat eccentric traveller with, in Walpole's phrase, a 'Phrenzy for Royalty' (her voluminous diaries are full of the minutiae of court life on the Continent), is depicted here in a baroque setting, with both pose and costume inspired by Van Dyck, and holding a seventeenth-century theorbo. She had some pretensions as a blue-stocking (Walpole dedicated the second edition of his Gothic novel, *The Castle of Otranto*, 1765, to her), and a certain amount of historical accuracy can be seen in her dress which is copied from that worn in a number of portraits by Van Dyck of Queen Henrietta Maria in the 1630s.

torture to the invention', but it was also an invaluable source book for artists and their drapery painters. The emphasis in the title on sixteenth- and seventeenth-century artists was no accident. Walpole noted that for a masquerade to be given by the French ambassador in 1773, 'being antiquarians or historians, one is set to appear like the court of Henri Quatre', and the quadrilles were danced by a group of society ladies 'in blue satin with blond and collets montées à la reine Elizabeth'.[72] Raised collars, often with 'vandyked' lace edging, looped-up, often ruched overskirts, sleeves either slashed or decorated with ribbons, and feathered hats, characterized the dresses which were worn by many of Gainsborough's fashionable sitters in the 1770s and 1780s, and at the court of Marie-Antoinette. The French queen, helped by the royal tailor Sarrazin, popularized the Henri Quatre costume for court balls; she herself appeared as Gabrielle d'Estrées (mistress of Henri IV) in a dress of white and silver gauze with puffed slashed sleeves and a black hat with white feathers and diamonds, at a ball held in honour of the Grand Duke and Duchess of Russia in 1782.[73]

In England, no costume was more popular from the 1730s to the 1770s than that worn by Helena Fourment, Rubens's second wife, painted by the artist in the early 1630s, and for much of the eighteenth century in the collection of Sir Robert Walpole (it was sold to Catherine II of Russia, and now hangs in the Gulbenkian Museum in Lisbon); it was earlier in the century attributed to Van Dyck, although correctly identified by Thomas Jefferys in his 1757 collection of engravings. The dress of black silk with bunched-up overskirt, the open sleeves revealing the chemise and a gauzy over-sleeve tied with lilac ribbon, the asymmetrically placed jewelled chain looking over the shoulder from a central brooch, the raised collar, the hat fastened up to one side and adorned with white feathers – all these features from the original portrait were copied both in fancy costume for balls, and by a large number of artists. We have already seen at the fête champêtre held by Lord Stanley in 1774 that his fiancée Lady Betty Hamilton chose to appear in this costume; there were so many at Lady Moira's masquerade that they could not all be listed. The Duchess of Ancaster was painted in a 'Rubens's wife' dress that she wore for a masquerade at Ranelagh, but many other ladies merely wished to wear an artist's version of this dress, sometimes faithful to the original, or sometimes modified to suit the taste of the eighteenth century. The 'art historian' Vertue noted in 1732[74] that the painter Vanderbank had recently painted a portrait of his wife 'in a habit somewhat like a picture of Rubens' wife', and this idea, from being limited to an artistic circle, caught on with the fashionable world, primarily due to the drapery painters, and in particular to Joseph van Aken who worked in the 1730s and 1740s for such well-established artists as Hudson and Ramsay.[75] The more exact copies of the original dress date from the middle years of the eighteenth century, but by the 1770s although many of the essential features were still there, they had become subdued in the generalized romantic flavour of the period. Gainsborough's 'Hon. Mrs Graham' (1777), for example, wears a dress that is a successful blending of the Rubens's wife dress in style (overskirt, spiky collar, tied-up-ribbon sleeves and feathered hat) with fashionable fabrics such as white satin, ruched or puckered silk for the skirt and a hat of white satin edged with pearls; fashion had caught up the past, for the polonaise was another form of a draped overskirt, and the large hat with the feathers (called the 'Rubens hat' in the fashionable magazines) was the large picture hat of the 1780s.

The 'Rubens's wife' costume was only one of the many versions of Vandyke dress popular in the eighteenth century (it was, after all, from the same

119 **'L'Etude', by J.-H. Fragonard**

The influence of the early seventeenth century can be seen in this dress, with its sleeves of contrasting colour to the bodice, the tabbed shoulder-wings, and the baroque pendant jewel with attached pearl chain. The raised, lace-edged 'Medici' collar and 'Vandyke' cuffs indicate the extent of the penetration into fashionable dress of the Henri IV styles in France.

120 **Thomas William Coke, later First Earl of Leicester of the second creation**, 1774, by P. Batoni

This magnificent Vandyke costume of silvery white silk, embroidered in silver, dark pink cloak lined with ermine, and white silk hat trimmed with ostrich feathers, hints at the wealth and status of the sitter, whose handsome and fashionable appearance was often noted by his countrymen abroad. This is probably the costume which he wore to a masquerade given in Rome in 1773 by the Countess of Albany, the wife of the Young Pretender.

period as Van Dyck's painting career in England). At the beginning it seems to have been an English fad, noted by Walpole and others at masquerades as worn by both sexes: 'there were quantities of pretty Vandykes and all kinds of old pictures walked out of their frame,'[76] commented Walpole at a masquerade at Vauxhall (1742). Mrs Montagu had her picture painted in the masquerade costume she wore

at the jubilee masquerade at Ranelagh in 1749, 'my dress white satin, fine new point for tuckers, kerchief and ruffles, pearl necklace and earrings and pearls and diamonds on the head, and my hair curled after the Vandyke picture'[77] – it is not known which portrait of Henrietta Maria she meant. Most portraits of sitters in Vandyke dress adapted it to suit the fashionable style of long pointed waist and hooped skirt, but Ramsay's portrait of Lady Mary Coke (in a private Scottish collection) (1762) is a serious attempt to follow early-seventeenth-century fashion with its wide ribbon giving an impression of a high waist. Again through the offices of the drapery painter, the period of the greatest popularity of the Vandyke style was in the middle years of the period, when plain heavy silks and ringleted hairstyles echoed those of the 1630s. The *Lady's Magazine* for 1759 urged a return to the dress of this period with the 'short waste of our great-grandmothers' and the 'free dress of the hair', which was 'preferable to the prim and close curls we have adopted from the French'.[78]

Patriotism may have been one of the reasons why fashionable English dress should have been inspired by the early rather than the current French modes; but more important, probably, was a nostalgic hankering after a period just far enough distant in time to be romantic, but close enough to recall through literature (and in the theatre, where Vandyke dresses had been worn from the early eighteenth century) and the many portraits, copied both by professional and amateur artists. It was a great period, too, in Sweden, under the patriotic king Gustavus Adolphus, and, as we have seen, Vandyke dress formed the basis for the national costume adopted by Gustavus III.

But the success of the early seventeenth century as a theme for fancy-dress portraiture must be due not just to the English taste for the romantic and picturesque, with an appreciation of the subtlety of historical allusion, but also to the popularity of the masquerade. Many young men were recorded in their Vandyke masquerade suits, such as Viscount Powderham at his coming-of-age party in 1790; some on the Grand Tour in the 1760s and 1770s, may have taken with them a favourite Vandyke costume for the fashionable portraitist Batoni to copy in Rome. In addition, such costumes could easily be the stock-in-trade of certain artists; when Sylas Neville sat for a portrait in 1770 (to Sykes, a pupil of Hudson) he informed a correspondent that 'I am drawn in the Vandyke dress, the colour dark grey, sleeves and breast slashed with crimson', and he was gratified later to be told that 'two gentlemen have desired to be drawn in the same dress I am

drawn in'.[79] Some artists were especially expert in depicting early-seventeenth-century satin and lace; Zoffany painted the English royal family (1770) and the Grand Duke of Tuscany and his family (1776), all in Vandyke dress.

By the 1770s many fancy dress elements had entered fashionable costume; in 1774 Walpole wrote to Sir William Hamilton that, 'If you were to come over, you would find us a general masquerade. The macaronis, not content with producing new fashions every day, and who are great reformers, are going to restore the Vandyke dress'.[80] It is hard to estimate how far this was typical hyperbole on the part of Horace, or whether in fact the romantic fever which was dominating women's fashions had begun to affect male costume; certainly the lightness and delicacy of early Stuart costume would have appealed to the macaronis. It was also a period when adult costume was being influenced by new developments in children's clothes; some boys wore Vandyke suits for sport (and in particular for archery)[81] and some young men adopted this style as evidence perhaps of a precocious romantic 'sensibility', the forerunner of late-nineteenth-century aestheticism.

Many great artists had ambivalent attitudes towards fancy dress. Gainsborough, whose paintings sometimes achieve a sense of haunting melancholy typical of the work of Watteau, whom he so much admired, painted many of his young male sitters in a kind of composite Vandyke/Watteau/*commedia dell'arte* costume, but at the same time expressed his disapproval of 'the foolish custom of dressing people like Scaramouches'[82] (a character from the Italian comedy). On the subject of Vandyke dress, Reynolds noted in his *Discourse* of 1776 that: 'We all very well remember how common it was a few years ago for portraits to be drawn in this fantastic dress; and this custom is not yet entirely laid aside',[83] but he himself had attended masquerades, had even been painted in Vandyke dress (by Angelica Kauffmann in 1767), and knew the stubborn English preference for a familiar fancy dress rather than the 'timeless' classical allegories which he wished to promote.

'L'histoire des modes n'est pas si frivole qu'on le croit; elle est en partie celle des moeurs,' said Madame de Genlis; among fashions and the manners, the liking for dressing up, in fact and through the medium of the arts, is important in any consideration of the eighteenth century. It reflects a mood of optimistic romanticism, a sense of the attraction of the past and the exotic present, with no feeling of escape from the conventions of formal dress, but with an awareness of the possibilities of fantasy.

Conclusion

Paris is no longer what it was formerly. A threatening storm overcasts its horizon and darkens the splendour of this city, so magnificent formerly. Golden luxury, which resided here on its favorite spot, has covered its face with a sable veil, and has fled to distant regions.

N. M. Karamzin, 1790

Although one must avoid presenting the eighteenth century as the last flowering of the Ancien Régime, leading inexorably to the French Revolution, there is much to be said for ending a study of the period with the year 1789.

In May of that year, Louis XVI was forced to convoke the States General, the historical representatives of the French people, which had last met in 1614. No hint of any alteration in the status quo was expressed in the orders which were sent out by the marquis de Brezé, the grand Maître des Cérémonies de France, for the costume to be worn by the three Estates at the opening of the formal proceedings. The nobility wore black silk suits and cloaks embroidered with gold, white stockings, plumed hats in the style of Henri IV, and swords, the insignia of their rank. The costume of the Second Estate ranged from the simple soutane and 'manteau long et bonnet carré' of the parish clergy, to the scarlet and violet of cardinals and bishops. The Third Estate, which comprised half of the deputies and represented the vast majority of the population, wore plain black cloth suits and cloaks, untrimmed hats, black stockings and thick muslin cravats.

The States General spent almost two months arguing whether they were to vote by order, which would automatically have meant that the Third Estate would have been outvoted by the other two privileged orders; finally, on 17 June, the Third Estate seized power and proclaimed itself the National Assembly, setting in motion the gradual collapse of the old order.

Arthur Young was in Paris for the first historic meeting of the National Assembly; his account of the appearance of the newly powerful deputies reflected the links, which contemporaries had noted, between the discarding of the formal clothing of the old society and a brave new world of political freedom. 'Many of them', he noted, were without powder in their hair and some in boots; not above four or five were neatly dressed. How times are changed. When they had nothing better to attend to, the fashionable Parisians were correctness itself in all that pertained to the toilette, and were therefore thought a frivolous people; but now they have something of more importance than dress to occupy them, and the light airy character that was usually given them will have no foundation in truth.[1]

Yet the year 1789 saw a curious juxtaposition between the formal and the informal, between the present and the future. The court continued as before, with formal presentations, and the marquise de la Tour du Pin entertained at Versailles the members of the National Assembly in full dress, including Robespierre, nattily attired in an apple-green suit, with a carefully powdered white wig.[2]

It has been noted that no abrupt break in clothing marked the 1789 revolution. For women, the modes set in Paris continued to be as inconstant and expensive as if the storming of the Bastille had never taken place; for men, although the 'habit français' continued as formal wear, we have seen that from the 1780s a kind of informality in dress (noted by Young in 1789) had entered France and the rest of Europe from England. After that, no major changes in dress occurred until the mid-1790s. Nathaniel Wraxall, writing his memoirs in 1815, remembered that his first winter in London (1776–7) was a period 'which is now so distant, and the Manners, as well as the Inhabitants of the Metropolis have undergone since that Time so total a change, that they no longer preserve almost any similarity'. To him it was the year 1793, the year of the execution of the French monarchy and the 'Æra of Jacobinism' which brought with it 'Pantaloons, cropped Hair, and Shoe-strings ... the total abolition of Buckles and Ruffles ... the disuse of Hair-powder' for the men, and for the women the cutting of their hair and the wearing of a 'Drapery more suited to the Climate of Greece or of Italy than to the temperature of an Island situate in the fifty-first Degree of Latitude'.[3]

The events of 1789 not only quickened the pace of the change in clothing but also men's perceptions of the ways in which dress was linked to the rapidly changing face of politics; from 1789 onwards for the next few tumultuous years, continual change became a normal part of human existence, and contemporaries recognized that the break with the feudal tradition was final.

The Persian or Chinese philosopher, the *alter ego* of so many eighteenth-century writers, would have no difficulty in recognizing that the Europe of 1715 and that of 1789 were basically the same political and social entity. He would have agreed with the Frenchman J. F. Sobry, who, writing in 1786, emphasized how far clothing 'est mis au rang des choses publiques'; clothes played the most vital role in defining man and his part in society, to an extent which we cannot contemplate today. Every period has its drawbacks, and the potential for greater social and political fulfilment were unrealized for the mass of the population; however, the eighteenth century in its essentially urbane, civilized and moderate way attained a perfection never since achieved in all the decorative arts including dress. Anyone regretting its vanished grace would agree with Ben Jonson (talking of the Stuart masque) that: 'Only the envie was that it lasted not still, or (now it is past), cannot by imagination, much lesse description, be recovered to a part of that spirit it had in the gliding by.'

Notes

Introduction

1. G. Rudé (*Europe in the Eighteenth Century*, 1972) calculates that in the eighteenth century between 70 and 80 per cent of the population gained their living from the land.
2. *Memoirs of the House of Brandenburg From the Earliest Accounts to the Death of Frederick I, King of Prussia*, By the Hand of a Master (i.e. Frederick the Great), London 1751, p. 241. The author noted that under Frederick I, Berlin was the Athens of the North, but under Frederick William I, it became the Sparta.
3. L. A. de Caraccioli, *Voyage de la Raison en Europe*, Paris 1772, p. 420.
4. J. Baretti, *A Journey from London to Genoa, through England, Portugal, Spain and France*, 2 vols., London 1770, vol. I, p. 10.
5. *The Present State of the Court of France, and City of Paris, in a Letter from Monsieur M*** to the Honourable Matthew Prior*, London 1712, p. 43.
6. Quoted in W. H. Bruford, *Germany in the Eighteenth Century: The Social Background of the Literary Revival*, 1935, p. 48.
7. *The Present State of the Court of France, op. cit.*, p. 21.
8. *Letters of the Earl of Chesterfield to his son*, ed. C. Strachey, London 1901, I, p. 305–6.
9. J. A. de Ségur, 'Les femmes, leur condition et leur influence dans l'ordre social', 3 vols., Paris 1803, vol. III, p. 7.
10. Quoted in the *Diaries of Sylvester Douglas, Lord Glenbervie*, ed. F. Bickley, 1928, I, p. 39.

Chapter One

1. *Mercure de France*, Paris 1729, p. 619.
2. M. von Boehn, *Deutschland im 18 Jahrhundert*, Berlin 1921, II, p. 487.
3. *Autobiography and Correspondence of Mary Granville, Mrs Delany*, ed. Lady Llanover, London 1861–2, I, p. 193.
4. *Mercure de France, op. cit.*
5. Mrs Delany, *op. cit.*, II, p. 28.
6. von Boehn, *op. cit.*, pp. 487–8.
7. The term 'bizarre' was first coined by W. Sloman, *Bizarre Designs in Silks*, Copenhagen 1953.
8. *Historical Memoirs of the Duc de Saint-Simon*, ed. and trans. L. Norton, London 1972, p. 123. The order was that of Saint Andrew, the first Russian order, founded by Peter the Great in 1699 to celebrate victory over Sweden.
9. Saint-Simon, *op. cit.*, p. 326.
10. H. Walpole, *Reminiscences written in 1788 for the Amusement of Miss Mary and Miss Agnes Berry*, London 1805, p. 6. The blue ribbon was the sash of the Order of the Garter.
11. J. Macky, *A Journey through England*, London 1722, p. 238.
12. C. de Saussure, *A Foreign View of England in the Reigns of George I and George II*, ed. and trans. M. van Muyden, London 1902, p. 112.
13. C. L. von Pöllnitz, *Travels from Prussia thro' Germany, Italy, France, Flanders, Holland, England etc.*, 3rd. ed., London 1745, III, p. 289.
14. J. Gay, *Trivia; or the Art of Walking the Streets of London*, London 1716, p. 4.
15. D. Defoe, *A Tour Thro' the Whole Island of Great Britain*, London 1724, I, p. 93.
16. T. Campbell, *Frederick the Great, his Court and Times*, London 1842, IV, p. 459.
17. *Diaries of a Duchess, Extracts from the Diaries of the first Duchess of Northumberland, 1716–1776*, ed. J. Greig, London 1926, p. 173.
18. M. Swain, *Nightgown into Dressing Gown, A Study of Men's Nightgowns*, in *Costume*, 1972, pp. 14–15.
19. Pöllnitz, *op. cit.*, III, p. 200.
20. Baretti, *op. cit.*, I, p. 326.
21. The word 'cravat' has attracted some attention; one theory regarding its origin is that it represents the adoption of a central European style (worn by Croats) by French

soldiers in the Thirty Years War. However, it seems likely that this kind of neckcloth was already in use in western Europe, and it is more probable that the name comes from the French 'rabat' lace collar.

22. *The Present State of the Court of France, and City of Paris*, London 1712, p. 36.
23. Mrs Delany, *op. cit.*, I. p. 193.
24. de Saussure, *op. cit.*, p. 112.
25. A. de La Motraye, *Voyages . . . en Diverses Provinces et Places de la Prusse Ducale et Royale, de la Russie, de la Pologne, etc.*, The Hague 1732, p. 108.
26. *The Present State of the Court of France, op. cit.*, p. 16.
27. *Letters from Liselotte, Elizabeth Charlotte, Princess Palatine and Duchess of Orléans, 'Madame', 1652–1722*, ed. and trans. M. Kroll, London 1970, p. 235.
28. 'Madame', *op. cit*, p. 238.
29. Mrs Delany, *op. cit.*, II, p. 452.
30. P. de Marivaux, *Pièces détachées écrites dans le goût du Spectateur François*, Paris 1728, II, p. 510.
31. *Mercure de France, op. cit.*, p. 611.
32. *Purefoy Letters, 1735–1753*, ed. G. Eland, London 1931, II, p. 303.
33. R. Halsband, *Lord Hervey, Eighteenth Century Courtier*, London 1973, p. 219.
34. *An Inventory of Margaret Cavendishe, Duchess of Portland's weding cloaths and linen, July 11th, 1734*, in Calendar of MSS of the Marquis of Bath, Longleat, Historical Manuscripts Commission, London 1904, I, p. 361.
35. Mrs Delany, *op. cit.*, II, pp. 27–8.
36. *Ibid.*, I, pp. 427–8.
37. *Ibid.*, I, p. 198. On the subject of lace-patterned silks, it has been noted that there was also some influence of silk designs on lace itself; 'bizarre' elements, for example, can be traced in some Brussels laces. See S. Levey, *Lace and lace-patterned silks: some comparative illustrations*, in *Studies in Textile History in memory of H. B. Burnham*, ed. V. Gervers, Royal Ontario Museum, 1977.
38. Mrs Delany, *op. cit.*, I, p. 99.
39. N. Rothstein, 'God Bless this Choye', in *Costume*, 1977, p. 67.
40. Mrs Delany, *op. cit.*, I, p. 428.
41. *Mercure de France, op. cit.*, p. 611.
42. *Chronique de la Régence et du Règne de Louis XV (1718–1763) ou Journal de Barbier, Avocat au Parlement de Paris*, Paris 1857, II, p. 37 *et seq.*
43. Pöllnitz, *op. cit.*, III, p. 287.
44. R. Nisbet Bain, *The Pupils of Peter the Great*, London 1897, p. 109.

45. T. Smollett, *Memoirs of a Lady of Quality* (included in *Peregrine Pickle*, London 1751, III, p. 108).
46. *The Present State of the Court of France, op. cit.*, p. 16.
47. *The Art of Dress*, London 1717, p. 25.
48. Gay, *op. cit.*, p. 14.
49. Pöllnitz, *op. cit.*, V, pp. 221–2.
50. *Mercure de France, op. cit.*, pp. 613–4.
51. *The Complete Letters of Lady Mary Wortley Montagu*, ed. R. Halsband, Oxford 1965–7, I, p. 265.
52. *The Prose Works of Jonathan Swift*, ed. T. Scott, London 1897, II, p. 285.
53. Saint-Simon, *op. cit.*, p. 230.
54. D. de Marly, *The Vocabulary of the female headdress 1678–1713*, in *Waffen und Kostümkunde*, 1975.
55. *Mercure de France, op. cit.*, p. 615.
56. de Saussure, *op. cit.*, p. 204. Ribbons were associated with French hairdressing, Mrs Delany remarking in 1729 that the Duchess of Richmond had returned from Paris in the French mode: 'her head was yellow gauze and lappets tied with puffs of scarlet ribbon' (I. p. 224).

Chapter Two

1. *The Present State of the Court of France, and City of Paris*, London 1712, p. 45.
2. N. M. Karamzin, *Travels from Moscow through Prussia, Germany, Switzerland, France and England*, London 1803, II, p. 223.
3. W. H. Pyne, *Wine and Walnuts*, London 1823, I, p. 89.
4. *Ibid*, pp. 90–1.
5. L. S. Mercier, *Tableau de Paris*, Amsterdam 1788, VI, p. 112.
6. C. de Saussure, *A Foreign View of England in the Reigns of George I and George II*, ed. and trans. M. van Muyden, London 1902, p. 74, p. 79.
7. *Sophie in London 1786, being the Diary of Sophie von la Roche*, trans. C. Williams, London 1933, p. 262.
8. T. Nugent, *Travels through Germany*, London 1768, II, p. 316.
9. In some countries Jews were obliged to wear yellow badges; Nugent's travel book for those undertaking the Grand Tour (1778) stated that along with other cities in Germany, the Frankfurt Jews 'are obliged to wear a piece of yellow cloth to distinguish them from the other inhabitants'. In the territories of the Holy Roman Empire, the badge was abolished

by order of Joseph II in 1765, but it was worn in Italy until 1816. In eastern Europe the Jews adopted as another distinguishing mark the caftan and fur-trimmed hat, which had been traditional Russian costume until abolished by Peter the Great; but in western Europe most Jews wore versions of fashionable dress. In Holland and England there were no restrictions on dress, but many Jews wore long beards; Francis Place (*Place Collections*, B.M. Add. MS 27827, p. 144) recalled that Jewish sellers of old clothes were easily recognizable by their shabby clothes and beards and were often baited in the streets until Daniel Mendoza set up *c.* 1787 a boxing school where they could learn to defend themselves.

10. P. Thornton, *Baroque and Rococo Silks*, London 1965, p. 80.
11. A. M. W. Stirling, *Annals of a Yorkshire House*, London 1911, I, p. 325.
12. *Livre-Journal de Madame Eloffe, Marchande de Modes, Couturière Lingère Ordinaire de la Reine et des Dames de sa Cour*, ed. le comte de Reiset, Paris 1885, I, p. 319.
13. For information about Rose Bertin's life and clients, see E. Langlade, *La Marchande de Modes de Marie Antoinette, Rose Bertin*, Paris 1911. As with all translations where dress and textile terms are concerned, the English version (A. S. Rappoport, *Rose Bertin, The Creator of Fashion at the Court of Marie Antoinette*, London 1913) should be read in conjunction with the original.
14. The book in the Victoria and Albert Museum (T.219.1973) contains samples of fabrics purchased throughout Barbara Johnson's long life (1738–1825).
15. Preliminary work on the Barbier letters has been done by Mary Schoeser in her M.A. report for the University of London, Courtauld Institute of Art, entitled *Letters to M. Barbier, Parisian Silk Merchant, 1755–97* (1979).
16. *Letters and Journals of Lady Mary Coke*, ed. J. A. Home, Edinburgh 1889, II, p. 117.
17. T. Smollett, *Travels through France and Italy*, London 1766, I, p. 60.
18. T. Smollett, *Ferdinand, Count Fathom*, London 1753, I, p. 215.
19. Coke, *op. cit.*, II, p. 288.
20. Mercier, *op. cit.*, II, p. 125.
21. *Selections from the Letters of De Brosses*, trans. Lord Ronald Sutherland Gower, London 1897, p. 69.
22. M. Vaussard, *Daily Life in Eighteenth Century Italy*, trans. M. Heron, London 1962, p. 202. A rough translation would be: 'You will see them flocking before you, scrutinizing piece by piece, the andrienne, the cap, the ribbons, the vast hoop, and casting their eager looks even to the inside and underneath of each petticoat.'

23. Quoted in the *Diary of Anna Green Winslow, 1771–3*, ed. A. M. Earle, Boston 1894, p. 115. One such doll was thrown into the sea at the Boston Tea Party in 1773, and is now in the collection of the Bostonian Society. Most dolls were used thoroughly by metropolitan and local dressmakers and then passed to children; consequently only a small number have survived.
24. *Lady's Magazine* 1773, p. 199.
25. H. Fielding, *Joseph Andrews*, 1742, ed. M. C. Battestin, Oxford 1967, p. 108.
26. J. Russel, *Letters from a Young Painter abroad to his Friends in England*, London 1750, I, p. 4.
27. D. Yarwood, *Robert Adam*, London 1970, p. 53.
28. R. Campbell, *The London Tradesman*, London 1747, p. 192.
29. See M. Ginsburg, *The Tailoring and Dressmaking Trades 1700–1850*, in *Costume*, 1972, p. 64, p. 67.
30. *Purefoy Letters, 1735–1753*, ed. G. Eland, London 1931, I, p. 297.
31. Langlade, *op. cit.*, p. 36.
32. *Memoirs of the Baroness d'Oberkirch*, ed. Count de Montbrison, London 1852, II, p. 102.
33. A. Varron, *Great Paris Fashion Artists*, in *Ciba Review*, vol. XXV, 1939, p. 898.
34. *Journal d'une Femme de 50 ans, 1778–1815*, by the marquise de la Tour du Pin, Paris 1951, p. 40.
35. Coke, *op. cit.*, II, p. 57, p. 61.
36. Campbell, *op. cit.*, p. 207.
37. See P. Clabburn, *A Provincial Milliners's Shop in 1785*, in *Costume*, 1977. This article lists some of the goods in an inventory made when the owner went bankrupt; they include a wide range of fabrics and some ready-made items like stays and shirts, cloaks and cardinals which might have been made up on the premises from stock.
38. R. Campbell, *op. cit.*, pp. 224–5.
39. *Ibid.*, p. 147.
40. M. de Saint-Aubin, *L'Art du Brodeur*, Paris 1770, p. 10.
41. *Chronique de la Régence et du Règne de Louis XV (1718–1763) ou Journal de Barbier, Avocat au Parlement de Paris*, Paris 1857, I, p. 200.
42. *Autobiography and Correspondence of Mary Granville, Mrs Delany*, ed. Lady Llanover, London 1861–2, II, pl 72.

43. S. Richardson, *Clarissa Harlowe*, 1748, 1768 ed., III, p. 28

44. *Banks Collection*, British Museum.

45. See J. Arnold, 'A mantua *c.* 1708–9', in *Costume*, 1970, p. 27.

46. For information on the trousseaux of German princesses, see M. von Boehn, *Deutschland im 18 Jahrhundert*, Berlin 1921, II, p. 498. It was customary for members of the Austrian royal family to donate their wedding clothes to religious foundations; the silver brocade wedding dresses of the archduchesses Maria Josepha (1720) and Amalie (1723) were given to the Heimsuchung Mariae Cloister in Vienna, for a set of vestments, with gold embroidery by professional embroiderers. See D. Heinz, *Meisterwerke Barocker Textilkunst*, Österreichisches Museum für angewandte Kunst, Vienna 1972.

47. H. L. Piozzi, *Observations and Reflections made in the course of a Journey through France, Italy and Germany*, London 1789, I, p. 102.

48. Mrs Delany, *op. cit.*, III, p. 400.

49. Sir N. Wraxall, *Memoirs of the Courts of Berlin, Dresden, Warsaw and Vienna in the years 1777, 1778 and 1779*, London 1799, I, p. 109.

50. Nugent, *op. cit.*, II, p. 295.

51. Smollett, *Travels, op. cit.*, I, p. 98.

52. M. Grosley, *A Tour to London*, London 1772, I, p. 106.

53. *Memoirs of William Hickey*, ed. A. Spencer, London 1913, II, p. 253.

54. Smollett, *Travels, op. cit.*, p. 97.

55. Eloffe, *op. cit.*, I, p. 136.

56. *The Memoirs of Jacques Casanova de Seingalt, 1725–1798*, trans. A. Machen, Edinburgh 1940, III, p. 192. Casanova, who was in gaol at the time in Venice (1756), was able from this to make a lamp to lighten his captivity.

57. Grosley, *op. cit.*, I, p. 45.

58. T. Smollett, *Humphry Clinker*, London 1771, I, p. 84.

59. E. McClellan, *A History of American Costume 1607–1870*, New York 1904, reprinted 1969 with intr. by R. Riley, p. 154.

60. See A. Mansfield, 'Dyeing and cleaning clothes in the late eighteenth and early nineteenth centuries', in *Costume*, 1968, pp. 26–7.

61. *Memoirs of the Private Life of Marie Antoinette, Queen of France*, by Madame de Campan, First Lady of the Bed-Chamber to the Queen, London 1823, I, p. 284.

62. An extra and valued source of income for servants was the money raised from the sale of their masters' or mistresses' clothes when they were dispensed with; Longprix's shop in the rue Saint-Honoré was famous for a wide range of such clothes. No doubt this was where some of the clothes in the nine trunks left by Madame de Pompadour to her servants (1764) ended up.

63. Campbell, *op. cit.*, p. 301.

64. *Letters of Mrs Adams*, intr. C. F. Adams, Boston 1848, p. 221.

65. *Ibid*, p. 107.

66. S. Richardson, *Pamela*, London 1740, I, p. 60.

67. Mrs Delany, *op. cit.*, III, p. 371.

68. Such gowns were almost a uniform, worn by clergymen and schoolmasters; in the latter category, Smollett's novel *Roderick Random* (1748) describes a poor schoolmaster 'dressed in a nightgown of plaid, fastened about his middle with a serjeant's old sash'. John Holker's sample book *c.* 1750 (Musée des Arts Décoratifs, Paris) has a collection of checks in line and cotton, and Scotch plaid (shades of red, blue and green predominate) of twilled worsted, used both for Scottish regiments and for men's dressing gowns.

69. Lord Macartney, *An Account of Russia, 1767*, London 1768, p. 42.

70. See, for example, the archives of the 'Florida' parishes (the name given in the eighteenth century to a section of Louisiana which from 1779 to 1810 was under Spanish rule), transcribed copies of which are deposited at the Louisiana State University, Baton Rouge.

71. K. F. du Bocage, *Letters Concerning England, Holland and Italy*, London 1770, I, p. 61.

72. T. Smollett, *Sir Lancelot Greaves*, London 1762, 4th ed. 1767, p. 35.

73. *Place Collections*, vol. XXXIX, Add. MS 27827, pp. 50–52.

74. For a discussion of short gowns, see C. Kidwell, *Short Gowns*, in *Dress*, 1978.

75. Sir F. Eden, *The State of the Poor*, London 1797, I, p. 557.

76. R. Cobb, *Death in Paris, 1795–1801*, Oxford 1978, p. 73 *et seq.*

Chapter Three

1. T. Campbell, *Frederick the Great, his Court and Times*, London 1842, I, p. 90.

2. M. von Boehn, *Deutschland im 18 Jahrhundert*, Berlin 1921, II, p. 486.

3. *Memoirs of Frederica Sophia Wilhelmina, Princess Royal of Prussia, Margravine of Bareith, Written by Herself*, 1812, I, p. 119.

4. *Idée de la personne, de la manière de vivre et de la Cour du roy de Prusse*, London 1752, p. 4.

5. A. de La Motraye, *Voyages ... en Diverses Provinces et Places de le Prusse Ducale, de la Russie, de la Pologne*, etc., The Hague 1732, p. 107.

6. T. Nugent, *Travels through Germany*, London, 1768, I, p. 58.

7. T. Nugent, *The Grand Tour, or a Journey through the Netherlands, Germany, Italy and France*, London 1778, II, p. 56.

8. *Ibid.*

9. *The Complete Letters of Lady Mary Wortley Montagu*, ed. R. Halsband, Oxford 1965–7, I, p. 255.

10. W. H. Bruford, *Germany in the Eighteenth Century: The Social Background of the Literary Revival*, Cambridge 1935, p. 220.

11. Nugent, *Travels, op. cit.*, p. 61.

12. von Boehn, *op. cit.*, p. 506.

13. J. G. Keysler, *Travels through Germany, Hungary, Bohemia, Switzerland, Italy and Lorrain*, London 1758, I, p. 126.

14. H. L. Piozzi, *Observations and Reflections made in the course of a Journey through France, Italy and Germany*, London 1789, II, p. 279.

15. Nugent, *Travels, op. cit.*, p. 122.

16. For detailed account of Swiss sumptuary legislation, see J. M. Vincent, *Costume and Conduct in the Laws of Basel, Bern and Zurich, 1370–1800*, Baltimore 1935.

17. Keysler, *op. cit.*, I, p. 4.

18. N. M. Karamzin, *Travels from Moscow through Prussia, Germany, Switzerland, France and England*, London 1803, II, p. 9.

19. J. Moore, *A View of Society and Manners in France, Switzerland and Germany*, London 1779, I, p. 322.

20. *Ibid.*

21. E. Vehse, *Memoirs of the Court and Aristocracy of Austria*, trans. F. Demmler, London 1856, II, p. 308.

22. Nugent, *The Grand Tour, op. cit.*, II, p. 255.

23. Piozzi, *op. cit.*, II, p. 318.

24. A useful summary of Hungarian costume can be found in the catalogue of an exhibition held at the Whitworth Art Gallery, University of Manchester, June–August 1979, *Historic Hungarian Costume from Budapest*.

25. Montagu, *op. cit.*, I, p. 303.

26. Keysler, *op. cit.*, IV, p. 73.

27. N. Wraxall, *Memoirs of the Courts of Berlin, Dresden, Warsaw and Vienna in the years 1777, 1778, and 1779*, London 1799, I, p. 377.

28. *Ibid*, II, p. 10 *et seq*.

29. *Ibid.*, I, p. 396.

30. R. Nisbet Bain, *The Last King of Poland and his Contemporaries*, London 1909, p. 33.

31. Wraxall, *op. cit.*, II, p. 113.

32. J. Perry, *The State of Russia under the Present Czar*, London 1716, p. 197.

33. *Ibid.* Caftans, of embroidered or woven silks (damasks, brocades), were still worn by members of the court and nobility; some belonging to Peter the Great still survive in The Hermitage, Leningrad.

34. R. Nisbet Bain, *The Pupils of Peter the Great*, London 1897, p. 196.

35. Lord Macartney, *An Account of Russia, 1767*, London 1768, p. 50.

36. *Ibid.*, p. 147.

37. J. G. Korb, *The Diary of an Austrian Secretary of Legation, at the Court of Czar Peter the Great*, trans. C. MacDonnell, London 1863, II, p. 206.

38. Mrs Ward, *Letters from a Lady who resided some Years in Russia*, London 1777, p. 39. The author, a clergyman's daughter, married first Thomas Ward, Consul General to Russia (1728), and secondly Claudius Rondeau, the English resident at the Russian Court (1731).

39. A. Swinton, *Travels into Norway, Denmark and Russia in the Years 1788, 1789, 1790 and 1791*, London 1792, p. 227.

40. W. Coxe, *Travels into Poland, Russia, Sweden and Denmark*, London 1790, I, p. 488.

41. Swinton, *op. cit.*, p. 195.

42. J. Bell, *A Journey from St Petersburg to Pekin, 1719–22*, ed. and intr. J. L. Stevenson, Edinburgh 1965, p. 66 *et seq*.

43. Coxe, *op. cit.*, I, p. 253, II, p. 95.

44. J. Marshall, *Travels through Holland, Flanders, Germany, Denmark, Sweden, Lapland, Russia, the Ukraine and Poland in the Years 1768, 1769 and 1770*, London 1772–6, III, p. 98.

45. Coxe, *op. cit.*, II, p. 527.

46. Nugent, *The Grand Tour, op. cit.*, I, p. 41.

47. *Letters of Mrs Adams*, ed. C. F. Adams, Boston 1848, p. 303.

48. P. V. Fithian, *Journal and Letters, 1767–1774*, ed. J. R. Williams, Princeton 1900, p. 58.

49. E. Burt, *Letters from a Gentleman in the North of Scotland to his Friend in London*, London 1754, p. 100.

50. G. Miège, *The Present State of Great-Britain and Ireland*, London 1715, II, p. 38.

51. T. Smollett, *Humphry Clinker*, London 1771, III, p. 20.

52. L. Melville, *Lady Suffolk and her Circle*, London 1924, p. 147.

53. Miège, *op. cit.*, III, p. 5.

54. J. Baretti, *An Account of the Manners and Customs of Italy*, London 1769, II, p. 208.

55. Nugent, *The Grand Tour, op. cit.*, III, p. 17.
56. *Ibid.*, III, p. 79.
57. Baretti *op. cit.*, II, p. 206.
58. *Selections from the Letters of De Brosses*, trans. Lord Ronald Sutherland Gower, London 1897, p. 31.
59. Piozzi, *op. cit.*, I, p. 184.
60. Keysler, *op. cit.*, III, p. 274.
61. P. Molmenti, *Venice: Its Individual Growth from the Earliest Beginnings to the Fall of the Republic*, trans. H. F. Brown, Part III, *The Decadence*, London 1908, I, p. 215.
62. Baretti, *op. cit.*, II, p. 206.
63. De Brosses, *op. cit.*, p. 69.
64. P. Labat, *Voyages en Espagne et en Italie*, Paris 1730, V, pp. 206–7.
65. J. Houel, *Voyage Pittoresque des Isles de Sicile*, Paris 1782, I, p. 3.
66. Piozzi, *op. cit.*, II, p. 31.
67. *Ibid.*, I, p. 40.
68. *The Courts of Europe at the Close of the Last Century* (from the travels of H. Swinburne), ed. C. White, London 1841, II, p. 265.
69. Piozzi, *op. cit.*, I, p. 306.
70. Labat, *op. cit.*, II, p. 271.
71. J. Townsend, *A Journey through Spain in the Years 1786 and 1787*, London 1791, I, p. 333.
72. P-A. C. de Beaumarchais, *Le Barbier de Séville*, Paris 1775.
73. H. Swinburne, *Travels through Spain in the Years 1775 and 1776*, London 1779, p. 334.
74. J. Baretti, *A Journey from London to Genoa, through England, Portugal, Spain and France*, London 1770, II, p. 92.
75. Townsend, *op. cit.*, I, p. 335.
76. Baretti, *A Journey, op. cit.*, II, p. 103.
77. *Ibid.*
78. *Ibid.*, II, p. 410.
79. R. Twiss, *Travels through Portugal and Spain in 1772 and 1773*, London 1775, p. 33.

Chapter Four

1. *Boswell in Holland, 1763–4*, ed. F. A. Pottle, New York 1952, p. 270.
2. *Autobiography and Correspondence of Mary Granville, Mrs Delany*, ed. Lady Llanover, London 1861–2, III, p. 250.
3. H. Fielding, *Joseph Andrews*, London 1742, ed. M. C. Battestin, Oxford 1967, p. 108.
4. T. Smollett, *Roderick Random*, London 1748, Bell and Sons ed., London 1895, p. 239.
5. *Ibid.*, p. 311.
6. *The Letters and Journals of Lady Mary Coke*, ed. J. A. Home, Edinburgh 1889, III, p. 176. On the subject of fur trimming and lining in eighteenth-century dress, see A. Ribeiro, 'Furs in Fashion', in *Connoisseur*, December 1979.
7. Boswell, *op. cit.*, pp. 395–6.
8. *The World*, London 1753, vol. XVII, p. 101.
9. *Gray's Inn Journal*, quoted in C. W. & P. Cunnington, *Handbook of English Costume in the Eighteenth Century*, London, revised ed. 1972, p. 17.
10. F. A. de Garsault, *L'Art du Tailleur*, Paris 1769, p. 9, p. 18.
11. *Boswell on the Grand Tour 1764*, ed. F. A. Pottle, London 1953, p. 217.
12. *London Chronicle*, 1762, vol. XI, p. 167.
13. E. McClellan, *A History of American Costume, 1607–1870*, New York 1904, reprinted 1969, intr. R. Riley, p. 228.
14. *Place Collections*, vol. XXXIX, British Museum Add. MS 27827, p. 167.
15. George, Prince of Wales, later George IV, had a number of perfume merchants from whom he ordered huge quantities of perfumed powder; see C. Hibbert, *George IV, Prince of Wales*, London 1972, p. 175.
16. Quoted in F. W. Fairholt, *Satirical Songs and Poems on Costume*, London 1849, p. 233.
17. J. Moore, *A View of Society and Manners in France, Switzerland and Germany*, London 1779, II, p. 246.
18. W. H. Pyne, *Wine and Walnuts*, London 1823, I, p. 30.
19. *Memoirs and Recollections of Count Ségur*, London 1835, III, p. 463.
20. N. M. Karamzin, *Travels from Moscow through Prussia, Germany, Switzerland, France and England*, London 1803, III, p. 212.
21. *London Chronicle, op. cit.*, p. 167.
22. J. G. Keysler, *Travels through Germany, Hungary, Bohemia, Switzerland, Italy and Lorrain*, London 1758, IV, p. 103.
23. S. Richardson, *Clarissa Harlowe*, London 1748, 1768 ed., III, p. 28.
24. Mrs Delany, *op. cit.*, II, p. 200.
25. *Ibid.*, II, p. 447.
26. *Ibid.*, II, p. 487.
27. *The British Magazine*, London 1746, I, p. 257.
28. Mrs Delany, *op. cit.*, III, p. 300.
29. O. Goldsmith, *The Bee*, London 1759, II, p. 39.
30. *The Female Tatler*, London 1761, p. 439.
31. *Inventaire des Biens de Madame de Pompadour*, intr. J. Cordrey, Paris 1939.
32. *Ibid.*, p. 75. Madame de Pompadour had, in the same trunk, a dress with fashionable Turkish embroidery, 'une robbe de chambre et son tablier, broderie de Turquie, fond blanc, bordé d'un petit lizeré d'or' (p. 75).

33. H. Walpole, *Letters*, ed. Paget Toynbee, Oxford 1903–15, V, pp. 167–8.

34. *The Memoirs of Catherine the Great*, trans, M. Budberg, London 1955, p. 181.

35. *Letters of Baron Bielfeld*, trans. Mr Hooper, London 1768–70, p. 190.

36. O. Goldsmith, *The Vicar of Wakefield*, London 1766, p. 121.

37. Mrs Delany, *op. cit.*, III, p. 321.

38. Ribeiro, 'Furs in Fashion', *op. cit.*, p. 229.

39. *Mrs Montagu, Her Letters and Friendships, 1762–1800*, ed. R. Blunt, London 1923, I, p. 218.

40. J. Russel, *Letters from a Young Painter abroad to his Friends in England*, London 1750, I, p. 3.

41. Mrs Ward, *Letters from a Lady who resided some Years in Russia*, London 1777, p. 31.

42. F. C. Weber, *The Present State of Russia*, London 1723, I, p. 148.

43. A. Le Camus, *Abdeker, or The Art of preserving Beauty*, London 1754, p. 151.

44. T. Nugent, *The Grand Tour, or a Journey through the Netherlands, Germany, Italy and France*, London 1778, III, p. 16.

45. *The Art of Dress*, London 1717, p. 18.

46. Budberg, *op. cit.*, p. 113. Even the ladies from the city had to wear black perukes when they appeared at court; they wore them over their own hair, which 'pushed the perukes upwards', in contrast to those worn by the court which at least 'were better fitted to their heads'.

47. *Ibid.*, p. 67.

48. *The Female Spectator*, London 1744, III, p. 161.

49. *Life and Letters of Lady Sarah Lennox*, ed. Countess of Ilchester and Lord Stavordale, London 1901, p. 178.

50. T. Smollett, *Travels through France and Italy*, London 1766, I, p. 105.

51. *Oxford Gazette and Reading Mercury*, No. 456, 29 July 1754.

52. Mrs Delany, *op. cit.*, III, p. 300.

53. Walpole, *op. cit.*, III, p. 314.

54. *London Chronicle*, *op. cit.*, II, p. 167.

55. W. Hogarth, *The Analysis of Beauty*, 1753, ed. J. Burke, Oxford 1955, p. 174.

56. Lennox, *op. cit.*, I, p. 177.

57. *Letters from Lady Jane Coke to her friend Mrs Eyre, 1747–1758*, ed. A. Rathbone, London 1899, p. 123.

58. For a complete list of the jewellery belonging to the Dauphine, see the 1767 *Inventaire de Marie-Josèphe de Saxe, Dauphine de France*, ed. G. Bapst, Paris 1883.

59. *Memoirs of Frederica Sophia Wilhelmina, Princess Royal of Prussia, Margravine of Bareith,* Written by Herself, London 1812, I, p. 43.

60. D. Jeffries, *A Treatise on Diamonds and Pearls*, London 1750. 'Diamonds,' he says in his introduction, 'are the chief ornaments of great and distinguished personages.' For a further discussion of the part played by jewellery in dress, see A. Ribeiro, 'Eighteenth-century Jewellery in England', in *Connoisseur*, October 1978.

61. Mrs Delany, *op. cit.*, III, p. 400.

62. Walpole, *op. cit.*, III, p. 264.

63. S. Richardson, *Pamela*, London 1740, I, p. 61.

64. J. T. Smith, *Nollekens and his Times*, London 1829, I, pp. 16–17.

Chapter Five

1. *Chronique de la Régence et du Règne de Louis XV, ou Journal de Barbier*, Paris 1857, I, p. 379.

2. W. Coxe, *Travels into Poland, Russia, Sweden and Denmark*, London 1784, I, p. 247.

3. *Goethe's Travels in Italy*, trans. A. J. W. Morrison & C. Nisbet, London 1892, p. 495.

4. J. Baretti, *A Journey from London to Genoa through England, Portugal, Spain and France*, London 1770, I, p. 43.

5. T. Smollett, *Humphry Clinker*, London 1771, II, p. 202.

6. S. Richardson, *Clarissa Harlowe*, London 1748, 1768 ed., IV, p. 92.

7. O. Goldsmith, *The Citizen of the World*, London 1762, I, p. 235.

8. B. de Mandeville, *The Fable of the Bees*, London 1714, p. 105.

9. *Ibid.*, p. 106.

10. Smollett *op. cit.*

11. *Ibid.*, I, p. 198.

12. 'Say what she would, protest, argue, and harangue, sacks were left off, ostrich-feathers worn, and a thousand fantastic dresses invented . . . the hoop vanished after the sack, and like Tilburina's confidante, everybody ran mad in white linen' – *Lady Louisa Stuart, Selections from her Manuscripts*, ed. J. A. Home, Edinburgh 1899, p. 143.

13. H. L. Piozzi, *Observations and Reflections made in the course of a journey through France, Italy and Germany*, London 1789, II, p. 280.

14. Goethe, *op. cit.*, p. 238.

15. *Memoirs of Frederica Sophia Wilhelmina, Princess Royal of Prussia, Margravine of Bareith*, 'Written by Herself', London 1812, I, p. 347.

16. *The Art of Dress*, London 1717, p. 21.

17. *Lady's Magazine*, London 1773, pp. 140–1.

18. J. Andrews, *An Account of the Character and Manners of the French*, London 1770, II, p. 36.
19. *The Connoisseur*, London 1754, p. 5.
20. M. Grosley, *A Tour to London, or New Observations on England and its Inhabitants*, trans. T. Nugent, London 1772, p. 253.
21. P. C. de Laclos, *Les Liaisons Dangereuses*, Paris 1782, English trans. London 1784, I, p. 19.
22. *The Female Spectator*, London 1744, I, p. 241.
23. *The Present State of the Court of France, and City of Paris*, London 1712, p. 36.
24. Nash, said Goldsmith, 'was the first who difused a desire of society and an easiness of address among a whole people'; this he achieved at Bath by a series of regulations regarding conduct and clothing, and by his own example. See A. Barbeau, *Life and Letters at Bath in the Eighteenth Century*, London 1904.
25. *London Magazine*, London 1774, p. 213. So much were the bag-wigs and swords an essential part of formal dress that they were worn even in hot climates for 'state' occasions; Hickey in Bengal in 1777 found that on the king's birthday, 'everybody, malgré the extreme heat, appeared in full dress with bags and swords'.
26. L. M. Hawkins, *Gossip about Dr Johnson and Others*, 1824, ed. F. H. Skrine, London 1926, p. 32. In all fairness to Dr Johnson, infirmity helped to produce his peculiar gait.
27. Andrews, *op. cit.*, I, p. 78. Goethe found when he went to university at Strasbourg in 1770 that there were a number of aristocrats from all over Europe who 'have come to "perfect" themselves before they can be allowed on the floor of the great metropolis, where every step, every gesture, every slightest trait is observed and ridiculed'. See R. Friedenthal, *Goethe, his Life and Times*, London 1965.
28. E. Topham, *Letters from Edinburgh, Written in the Years 1774 and 1775*, London 1776, p. 262 *et seq.*
29. A. Young, *Travels during the Years 1787, 1788 and 1789*, London 1793, I, p. 53.
30. *Letters of Baron Bielfeld*, trans. Mr Hooper, London 1768–70, IV, p. 162.
31. *The Present State of the Court of France, op. cit.*, p. 48.
32. L. Fusil, *Souvenirs d'une Actrice*, Brussels 1841, p. 102 *et seq.*
33. T. Smollett, *Travels through France and Italy*, London 1766, I, p. 114.
34. Fusil, *op. cit.*, p. 109.
35. H. Walpole, *Letters*, ed. Paget Toynbee, Oxford 1903–15, III, p. 13.
36. H. Fielding, *Joseph Andrews*, London 1742, ed. M. C. Battestin, Oxford 1967, p. 204.
37. *Memoirs and Correspondence of Madame d'Epinay*, trans. J. H. Freese, London 1897, II, p. 305.
38. K. F. du Bocage, *Letters Concerning England, Holland and Italy*, London 1770, I, p. 37.
39. J. T. Smith, *Nollekens and his Times*, London 1829, II, p. 402.
40. J. Moore, *A View of Society and Manners in France, Switzerland and Germany*, London 1779, II, p. 287. When the Prussians came to Dresden during the Seven Years War, they found his huge wardrobe, which included 200 pairs of shoes, 800 dressing gowns, and 1500 wigs, the latter calling forth from Frederick the Great the comment 'Wieviel Perrüquen für einen Menschen, der keinen Kopf hat!'
41. Comte F. d'Hézecques, *Souvenirs d'un Page de la Cour de Louis XVI*, Paris 1873, p. 164 *et seq.*
42. J. L. H. Campan, *Mémoires sur la vie privée de Marie Antoinette*, Paris 1822, trans. and publ. London 1823, I, p. 308 *et seq.*
43. *Archives de France*, No. AE 16, no. 2.
44. R. Nisbet Bain, *Gustavus III and his Contemporaries*, London 1894, I, pp. 213–15. For the influence of French taste on Gustavus, see B. Scott, *Gustave III's Love of Paris*, in *Connoisseur*, November 1970.
45. V. Cronin, *Catherine, Empress of all the Russias*, London 1978, p. 289 *et seq.*
46. J. M. Beattie, *The English Court in the Reign of George I*, Cambridge 1967, p. 51 *et seq.*
47. *Diary and Letters of Madame d'Arblay*, ed. by her niece, London 1842, III, p. 28.
48. See H. Brocher, *Le Rang et l'Etiquette sous l'ancien Régime*, Paris 1934.
49. F. A. de Garsault, *L'Art du Tailleur*, Paris 1769, p. 55.
50. *Livre-Journal de Madame Eloffe, Marchande de Modes*, ed. le comte de Reiset, Paris 1885, I, p. 98.
51. H-L. de la Tour du Pin, *Journal d'une Femme de 50 ans, 1778–1815*, Paris 1951, p. 45 *et seq.*
52. Comtesse de Genlis, *Dictionnaire critique et raisonné des Etiquettes de la Cour et des Usages du Monde*, Paris 1818, II, p. 40.
53. *The Memoirs of Jacques Casanova de Seingalt, 1725–1789*, trans. A. Machen, Edinburgh 1940, I, p. 270.
54. *Magazine à la Mode*, London 1777, p. 4.
55. *Letters of Mrs Adams*, intr. C. F. Adams, Boston 1848, p. 254.
56. *d'Arblay, op. cit.*, II, pp. 190–1.
57. S. Siddons, *Reminiscences, 1773–1785*, ed. W. van Lennep, Cambridge, Mass., 1942, p. 21.
58. E. Vehse, *Memoirs of the Court and Aristocracy of Austria*, trans. F. Demmler, London 1856, II, p. 122 *et seq.*

59. J. G. Keysler, *Travels through Germany, Hungary, Bohemia, Switzerland, Italy and Lorrain*, London 1758, IV, p. 28.
60. L-J-A. de Bouillé, *Souvenirs et Fragments pour servir aux Mémoires de ma Vie et de mon Temps*, ed. P-L. de Kermaingant, Paris 1906–11, I, p. 72.
61. *The Letters and Journals of Lady Mary Coke*, ed. J. A. Home, Edinburgh 1889, III, p. 344.
62. d'Hézecques, *op. cit.*, p. 189. All the French orders of chivalry, including the Saint-Esprit (but excepting the Order of Saint-Louis, for bravery) were abolished in 1791.
63. This survives in the Livrustkammaren in Stockholm.
64. S. Sitwell, *German Baroque Art*, London 1927, p. 18.
65. Barbier, *op. cit.*, IV, p. 484.
66. See O. Morshead, *The Windsor Uniform*, in *Connoisseur*, April 1935.
67. *Letters of Lady Louisa Stuart*, ed. R. Brimley Johnson, London 1926, p. 100.
68. Coxe, *op. cit.*, II, p. 328.
69. A. de La Motraye, *Voyages ... en diverses provinces et places de la Prusse Ducale et Royale, de la Russie, de la Pologne, etc.*, The Hague 1732, p. 399.
70. *Extracts from the Diaries of the First Duchess of Northumberland, 1716–1776*, ed. J. Greig, London 1926, p. 31.
71. Frederica Sophia Wilhelmina, *op. cit.*, I, p. 351.
72. de la Tour du Pin, *op. cit.*, p. 38 *et seq.*
73. F. Burney, *Early Diary, 1768–1778*, ed. A. R. Ellis, London 1889, I, p. 16.
74. Walpole, *op. cit.*, IV, p. 265.
75. S. Richardson, *Pamela*, London 1740, II, p. 420.
76. E. M. Graham, *The Beautiful Mrs Graham*, London 1927, p. 92.
77. J. T. Smith, *op. cit.*, I, pp. 16–17.
78. Barbier, *op. cit.*, IV, p. 234 *et seq.*
79. *Ibid.*, p. 326.
80. Walpole, *op. cit.*, IV, p. 457.
81. *The Complete Letters of Lady Mary Wortley Montagu*, ed. R. Halsband, Oxford 1965–7, I, p. 268.
82. Coke, *op. cit.*, III, p. 317.
83. *Autobiography and Correspondence of Mary Granville, Mrs Delany*, ed. Lady Llanover, London 1861–2, II, p. 478.

Chapter Six

1. See M. Delpierre, *Marie Antoinette, reine de la mode*, in *Versailles*, 1975.
2. *Magazine à la Mode*, London 1777, p. 49.
3. L. M. Hawkins, *Gossip about Dr Johnson and Others*, 1824, ed. F. H. Skrine, London 1926, p. 32.
4. *The Waiting City: Paris 1782–88* (from Mercier's *Tableau de Paris*), ed. & trans. H. Simpson, London 1933, p. 88.
5. *The Pantheonites*, London 1773, p. 17.
6. *Town and Country Magazine*, London 1772, p. 242. See also A. Ribeiro, 'The Macaronis', in *History Today*, July 1978.
7. *Memoirs of William Hickey*, ed. A. Spencer, London 1913, I, p. 139.
8. *Fashionable Magazine*, London 1786, p. 43.
9. In 1768 Goldsmith bought a coat of 'Tyrian bloom satin' (what the colour was is not clear, but he ordered the coat to wear with 'garter blue silk breeches' – see Prior's *Life of Goldsmith*). Boswell records in his *Life of Johnson*, that when Goldsmith bragged of his coat, he was crushed by Dr Johnson, whose description of the offending garment was 'strange-colour'!
10. E. McClellan, *History of American Costume, 1607–1870*, New York 1904, reprinted 1969 with intr. by R. Riley, p. 234.
11. Hickey, *op. cit.*, II, p. 261.
12. *Travels of Carl Philipp Moritz in England in 1782*, intr. P. E. Matheson, London 1924, p. 83.
13. N. M. Karamzin, *Travels from Moscow through Prussia, Germany, Switzerland, France and England*, London 1803, III, p. 217.
14. Hickey, *op. cit.*, II, p. 261.
15. *Petit Dictionnaire de la Cour et de la Ville*, Londres, 1788, no pagination.
16. *The Autobiography of Francis Place*, ed. & intr. M. Thale, Cambridge 1972, pp. 62–3.
17. A. R. d'Allemagne, *Les Accessoires du Costume et du Mobilier depuis le treizième jusqu'au milieu du dixneuvième siècle*, Paris 1928, I, p. 40. In 1776 a French jeweller, Dauffe, obtained the monopoly of making cut-steel jewellery, and selling it.
18. Quoted in *Livre-Journal de Madame Eloffe, Marchande de Modes*, ed. le comte de Reiset, Paris 1885, I, p. 48.
19. H. L. Piozzi, *Observations and Reflections made in the course of a Journey through France, Italy and Germany*, London 1789, I, p. 93.
20. 'I am to be drawn of the size of life, enveloped in a white mantle, and sitting on a fallen obelisk viewing the ruins of the Campagna di

Roma' – *Goethe's Travels in Italy*, trans.
A. J. W. Morrison & C. Nisbet, London 1892,
p. 141.

21. *Sir Joshua's Nephew, Being letters written
1760–1778 by a young man to his sisters*, ed.
S. M. Radcliffe, London 1930, p. 40.

22. F. Burney, *Evelina*, London 1778, III, p. 256. In
the same year that *Evelina* was published
Benjamin Franklin was received at the French
court wearing a simple brown suit, and his
own unpowdered hair. In a previous period
the lack of a wig would have horrified the
French, but by this date they accepted it as an
amiable eccentricity; some were, in any case,
sympathetic to the struggle of the American
colonists against English power, and Franklin
seemed to typify all that was noble in the New
World as against the artificialities of the Old.

23. H. Angelo, *Reminiscences*, London 1828, II,
p. 379.

24. E. Langlade, *La Marchande de Modes de Marie
Antoinette, Rose Bertin*, Paris 1911, p. 92.

25. *Diaries of a Duchess, Extracts from the Diaries of
the first Duchess of Northumberland, 1716–1776*,
ed. J. Greig, London 1926, p. 204.

26. *Ibid.*, p. 174.

27. *Extracts from the Correspondence of Georgiana,
Duchess of Devonshire*, ed. Earl of Bessborough,
London 1955, p. 95.

28. *Magazine à la Mode, op. cit.*, p. 416.

29. Devonshire, *op. cit.*, p. 91.

30. *Lady's Magazine*, London 1787, p. 331.

31. H. Walpole, *Letters addressed to the Countess of
Ossory, 1769–1797*, ed. R. V. Smith, London
1848, p. 379.

32. *Cabinet des Modes*, Paris 1786, p. 4.

33. *Diary and Letters of Madame d'Arblay*, ed. by
her niece, London 1842, III, p. 170.

34. See A. Jardine, *Letters from Barbary, France,
Spain, Portugal etc.*, London 1788, where the
author urges women to ride side-saddle. 'They
ought to wear drawers under their present, or
some more graceful, long dress . . . the sex
would certainly gain by shewing a little more
of their legs' (I, p. 321).

35. *Mrs Montagu, 'Queen of the Blues', Her Letters
and Friendships from 1762–1800*, ed. R. Blunt,
London 1923, II, p. 82.

36. In Mary Russell Mitford's famous account of
Our Village: Sketches of Rural Scenery,
1824–32, she recalled 'early in the present
century' two old ladies whose style of dress
dated from the 1770s: 'Their motion out of
doors was indescribable; it most nearly
resembled sailing.' It was probably rather like
that of the French emigrées whom Miss

Mitford mentions later in the book, 'with the
peculiarly bad, unsteady walk, something
between a trip and a totter, that Frenchwomen
of rank used to acquire from their high heels
and the habit of never using their feet'. (I,
p. 38, and II, p. 213).

37. Quoted in C. W. and P. Cunnington,
*Handbook of English Costume in the Eighteenth
Century*, revised ed., London 1972, p. 297.

38. J. T. Smith, *Nollekens and his Times*, London
1829, I, p. 17.

39. The Warner Collection of textile patterns
(part of the Warner Archive in the Victoria
and Albert Museum) of the 1770s and 1780s
shows a wide range of silk designs, many on
dark grounds like the fashionable cottons. In
the 1770s (T. 374–1972) there are small laurel
wreaths surrounding spots (e.g. f. 137 1777),
loops of 'frogspawn' on light and dark
grounds (f. 158^v, f. 159 1777), flowers in
medallions, and tiny florals and garlands. In
the 1780s (T. 377–1972 and T. 378–1972)
patterns include random spots, various kinds
of doodles, checks, stripes and bands, and, by
the end of the decade, large circles, perhaps
copying the large buttons in vogue in
costume. By this time, there appear to be far
more winter patterns, possibly because in the
spring and summer months, muslin and
printed cottons/linens were dominating the
market.

40. Devonshire, *op. cit.*, p. 91.

41. d'Arblay, *op. cit.*, III, p. 368.

42. *Letters of Mrs Adams*, intr. C. F. Adams, Boston
1848, pp. 182–3.

43. J. P. Brissot de Warville, *Nouveau Voyage dans
les Etats Unis*, trans. J. Barlow, Paris 1791, I,
p. 134.

44. *Sophie in London in 1786, being the Diary of
Sophie von la Roche*, trans. C. Williams,
London 1933, p. 208, p. 95.

45. *Diary of Anna Green Winslow, 1771–3*, ed.
A. M. Earle, Boston 1894. p. 71, *et seq.*

46. Mrs Fay, *Original Letters from India*, Calcutta
1821, p. 142.

47. *The Waiting City, op. cit.*, p. 239.

48. M. Grosley, *A Tour to London; or New
Observations on England and its Inhabitants*,
trans. T. Nugent, London 1772, I, p. 255.

49. J. T. Smith, *op. cit.*, I, p. 218.

50. Winslow, *op. cit.*, p. 17.

51. J. Baretti, *A Journey from London to Genoa,
through England, Portugal, Spain and France*,
London 1770, I, p. 95.

52. T. 4588.

53. Place, *op. cit.*, pp. 62–3.

54. Mrs Papendiek, *Court and Private Life in the Time of Queen Charlotte*, ed. V. D. Broughton, London 1887, II, pp. 230–1.

Chapter Seven

1. K. F. du Bocage, *Letters Concerning England, Holland and Italy*, London 1770, I, p. 140.
2. J. Moore, *A View of Society and Manners in Italy*, London 1781, II, p. 81.
3. J. Russel, *Letters from a Young Painter abroad to his Friends in England*, London 1750, I, p. 44.
4. *Goethe's Travels in Italy*, trans. A. J. W. Morrison & C. Nisbet, London 1892, p. 509.
5. See F. Boucher, 'Les Dessins de Vien pour la Mascarade de 1748 à Rome', in the *Bulletin de la Société de l'Histoire de l'Art Français*, 1963, pp. 69–76, and, by the same author, 'An Episode in the Life of the Académie de France à Rome', in *Connoisseur*, October 1961.
6. *The Courts of Europe at the Close of the Last Century* (from the travels of H. Swinburne), ed. C. White, London 1841, II, p. 202.
7. H. Carré, *Jeux, Sports et Divertissements des Rois de France*, Paris 1937, p. 231.
8. *Ibid.*, p. 230.
9. J. Townsend, *A Journey through Spain in the Years 1786 and 1787*, London 1791, I, p. 39.
10. J. Baretti, *A Journey from London to Genoa, through England, Portugal, Spain and France*, London 1770, II, p. 104.
11. See A. Ribeiro, 'The Exotic Diversion, the Dress worn at Masquerades in Eighteenth Century London', in *Connoisseur*, January 1978.
12. H. Walpole, *Letters*, ed. Paget Toynbee, Oxford 1903–15, II, p. 369.
13. *Ibid.*, p. 371.
14. On the taste for chinoiserie in the eighteenth century, see O. Impey, *Chinoiserie – The Impact of Oriental Styles on Western Art and Decoration*, Oxford, 1977.
15. See A. Ribeiro, 'Mrs Cornelys and Carlisle House', in *History Today*, January 1978.
16. Walpole, *op. cit.*, VIII, p. 162.
17. Mrs Ward, *Letters from a Lady who resided some Years in Russia*, London 1777, p. 99.
18. This fête champêtre was so popular that there are many accounts of it, most notably in the letters of both Walpole and Mrs Delany; there was also a play, by J. Burgoyne, entitled *The Maid of the Oaks*, performed at the Theatre Royal, Drury Lane (1774), with Mrs Abington as the female lead. See A. Ribeiro, 'Rural Masquerades', in *Antique Collector*, September 1983.

19. W. Coxe, *Travels into Poland, Russia, Sweden and Denmark*, London 1784, 1790, I, p. 178 *et seq.*
20. See G. H. Lewes, *Goethe's Life at Weimar, 1775–9*, 1854, London 1904.
21. W. H. Bruford, *Germany in the Eighteenth Century*, Cambridge 1935, p. 89.
22. A. S. Levetus, *Imperial Vienna*, London 1905, p. 96.
23. J. Moore, *A View of Society and Manners in France, Switzerland and Germany*, London 1779, II, p. 379.
24. *Ibid.*, II, p. 80.
25. *Letters and Journals of Lady Mary Coke*, ed. J. A. Home, Edinburgh 1889, II, p. 350, IV, p. 10.
26. A. de La Motraye, *Voyages . . . en Diverses Provinces et Places de la Prusse Ducale et Royale, de la Russie, de la Pologne, etc.*, The Hague 1732, p. 231.
27. Coxe, *op. cit.*, I, p. 497.
28. *Memoirs of Frederica Sophia Wilhelmina, Princess Royal of Prussia, Margravine of Bareith, Written by Herself*, London 1812, II, p. 280.
29. P. de Bretagne, *Réjouissances et Fêtes Magnifiques qui se sont faites en Bavière l'an 1722 . . .*, Munich, 1723.
30. *Journal Historique des Fêtes que le Roi a données à Potsdam . . .*, Berlin 1750.
31. H. Swinburne, *Travels through Spain in the Years 1775 and 1776*, London 1779, p. 348.
32. Baretti, *op. cit.*, I, p. 88.
33. See the exhibition catalogue *Le Style Troubadour*, Bourg-en-Bresse, June–October, 1971.
34. A comprehensive account of the theatre under Gustavus III is to be found in *Gustaviansk Teater*, Malmö 1947 (Skrifter utgivna av Föreningen Drottningholmsteaterns Vänner V). The Drottningholms Teatermuseum (Stockholm) has a collection of theatre designs by a number of artists, and some surviving theatre costumes, including carrousel costumes worn by Gustavus III at tournaments. See also A. Beijer, 'Les Théâtres de Drottningholm et de Gripsholm', in *Revue d'Histoire du Théâtre*, Paris 1956.
35. C. L. von Pöllnitz, *Travels from Prussia thro' Germany, Italy, France, Flanders, Holland, England, etc.*, 3rd. ed., London 1745, II, p. 187.
36. P. Martin, 'Les Costumes de fêtes portés à l'occasion de l'entrée du roi Louis XV à Strasbourg en 1744', in *Waffen und Kostümkunde*, 1970.
37. E. Clark, *Letters Concerning the Spanish Nation, Written at Madrid during the Years 1760 and 1761*, London 1763, p. 322.

38. R. Nisbet Bain, *The Daughter of Peter the Great*, London 1899, pp. 152–4.

39. Lewes, *op. cit.*, p. 35.

40. Pöllnitz, *op. cit.*, V, p. 66 *et seq.* The marriage of the Elector, Augustus II, in 1719, was the occasion for many pageants and festivities. Keysler, when visiting Dresden in 1730, saw the royal wardrobes crammed with costumes including that worn by the Elector at his 'nuptial feast', when 'he represented the element of water'.

41. See A. Ribeiro, 'Hussars in Masquerade', in *Apollo*, February 1977.

42. *Memoirs of William Hickey*, ed. A. Spencer, London 1913, I, p. 280.

43. *Letters of Baron Bielfeld*, trans. Mr Hooper, London 1768–70, II, p. 235. He was referring to a masquerade held at the opera house in Hanover, and the Elector's costume, 'a Turkish dress, the turban of which was ornamented with a magnificent egret of diamonds'.

44. Frederica Sophia Wilhemina, *op. cit.*, I, p. 104.

45. J. G. Keysler, *Travels through Germany, Hungary, Bohemia, Switzerland, Italy and Lorrain*, London 1758, IV, p. 118.

46. See G. Chapman, *Beckford*, London 1937, pp. 104–6. As a child, William Beckford had been interested in the Orient, and on his return from the Grand Tour (1781) he became immersed in the study of the East, working on manuscripts once in the possession of Edward Wortley Montagu who was himself a strange character, the rogue son of the well-known traveller Lady Mary Wortley Montagu, and also prone to wearing Turkish costume.

47. See A. Ribeiro, 'The King of Denmark's Masquerade', in *History Today*, June 1977.

48. *The Complete Letters of Lady Mary Wortley Montagu*, ed. R. Halsband, Oxford 1965–7, I, p. 326.

49. J. Arbuthnot, *The Ball, Stated in a Dialogue betwixt a Prude and a Coquet*, London, 1724, p. 1, p. 3.

50. *Autobiography and Correspondence of Mary Granville, Mrs Delany*, ed. Lady Llanover, London 1861–2, II, p. 185.

51. *The Oxford Magazine*, 1768, p. 161.

52. See above, note 5.

53. J-L. Vaudoyer, 'L'Orientalisme en Europe au XVIIIᵉ Siècle', in *Gazette des Beaux Arts*, Paris 1911, p. 98. 'Liotard le dessine, et c'est Mlle Raymond qui l'execute.' Many of Liotard's famous sitters are dressed in oriental costumes which look observed from life, either made for them, or taken from dresses which the artist had in his studio.

54. *Magazine à la Mode*, London 1777, p. 367. For the influence of Turkish dress on high fashion, see A. Ribeiro, 'Turquerie: Turkish Dress and English Fashion in the Eighteenth Century' in *Connoisseur*, May 1979.

55. Mrs Delany, *op. cit.*, II, p. 487.

56. *Mrs Montagu, 'Queen of the Blues', Her Letters and Friendships from 1762–1800*, ed. R. Blunt, London 1923, II, p. 103.

57. C. R. Leslie & T. Taylor, *The Life and Times of Sir Joshua Reynolds*, London 1865, I, p. 398.

58. *Ibid.*

59. E. Malone, *The Works of Sir Joshua Reynolds*, London 1798, I, p. 237; this is from Reynolds's *Seventh Discourse*, delivered to the students of the Royal Academy in 1776.

60. Romney was rather more successful than Reynolds in painting 'classical' costume, though he had equal trouble with his sitters. In 1790 Lady Newdigate went to London to sit to him for her portrait, taking with her a borrowed white satin dress which he had requested her to wear; the artist, however, was not satisfied with this gown, and 'insists upon my having a rich white Sattin with a long train made by Tuesday & to have it left with him all summer' (Lady Newdigate-Newdigate, *The Cheverels of Cheverel Manor*, London 1898, p. 101).

61. *The Memoirs of Mme Elisabeth Louise Vigée-Lebrun, 1755–1789*, trans. G. Shelley, London 1926, p. 74.

62. By the end of the 1780s some French writers were anticipating the curious hybrid 'classical' costumes advocated during the French Revolution, and depicted by, among others, J. L. David. J. F. Sobry, for example, in *Le Mode François* (1786) urged that officials should wear the long cassock or 'simarre', and gentlemen would be advised to wear a short tunic; both sexes, on grounds of health, would be advised to wear sandals.

63. Goethe, *op. cit.*, p. 199.

64. J. W. Tischbein, *Aus Meinem Leben*, 1956, pp. 296–7, quoted in *Van Dyck in Check Trousers, Fancy Dress in Art and Life, 1700–1900*, Scottish National Portrait Gallery, Edinburgh 1978.

65. *Covent Garden Magazine*, London 1773, II, p. 245.

66. Bielfeld, *op. cit.*, II, p. 235.

67. S. Richardson, *Sir Charles Grandison*, London 1753–4, I, p. 43.

68. *Report on the MSS of the late Reginald Rawdon Hastings*, ed. F. Bickley, Historical Manuscripts Commission, London 1928, III, p. 150.

69. Mrs Montagu, *op. cit.*, I, p. 171.

70. Sir Ashton Lever's house in Leicester Fields, for example, housed in the 1770s and 1780s a collection of historic costumes, including 'the dress worn in Charles 1rst's time', according to Fanny Burney.

71. For a discussion of the growth in accuracy in theatre costumes, see R. J. Pentzell, *New Dress'd in the Ancient Manner: The Rise of Historical Realism in Costuming the serious Drama of England and France in the Eighteenth Century*, Yale University Ph.D., 1967.

72. Walpole, *op. cit.*, VIII, p. 251, pp. 262–3.

73. E. Langlade, *La Marchande de Modes de Marie-Antoinette, Rose Bertin*, Paris 1911, p. 138. In the 1780s Marie Antoinette ordered from Mme Eloffe a number of 'cherusques en fraise', vandyke collars either pleated or embroidered.

74. *Vertue Notebooks*, III, p. 57, Walpole Society, London 1933–4.

75. See J. Steegman, 'A Drapery Painter of the Eighteenth Century', in *Connoisseur*, June 1936.

76. Walpole, *op. cit.*, I, p. 182. For a general discussion of the causes and the spread of Vandyke dress in England, see J. L. Nevinson, 'Vandyke Dress', in *Connoisseur*, November 1964.

77. *Elizabeth Montagu, Correspondence 1720–61*, ed. E. J. Climenson, London 1906, I, p. 264.

78. *Lady's Magazine*, London 1759, p. 128.

79. *The Diary of Silas Neville*, 1767–1788, ed. B. Cozens-Hardy, London 1950, p. 82.

80. Walpole, *op. cit.* (Supplement to the *Letters*), p. 233.

81. See J. L. Nevinson 'The Vogue of the Vandyke Dress', in *Country Life Annual*, 1959.

82. *Letters of Thomas Gainsborough*, ed. M. Woodall, London 1963, p. 52.

83. Malone, *op. cit.*, I, p. 234. Unlike his rival, Reynolds' style was not suited to the rendering of the rich glowing satins and spiky, gauzy lace of Vandyke costume; 'Sir Joshua's draperies represent clothes, never their materials,' noted Walpole with reference to Reynolds *Eleventh Discourse* in 1782, when the artist quoted 'Vandyck, who at least specified silks, satins, velvets' (*Letters*, XII, p. 403).

Conclusion

1. A. Young, *Travels in France and Italy during the Years 1787, 1788 and 1789*, London 1915, p. 325.

2. See the *Journal d'une Femme de 50 ans, 1778–1815* by the marquise de la Tour du Pin, written in 1820, and published in Paris, 1951. In 1789 her father-in-law was made Minister of War, the War Department being at Versailles, and the marquise was responsible for the entertaining of government officials and delegates from the Assembly. Full dress was demanded at Versailles, and court presentations continued until 1790; even after that date the queen continued to order clothes from Rose Bertin (who had supplied many of the presentation dresses). Rose Bertin's accounts end on August 7, 1792; three days later the Tuileries was besieged and the mob pillaged the queen's wardrobe. Both the king and queen's wardrobes were later sold.

3. N. W. Wraxall, *Historical Memoirs of His Own Times*, revised ed. London 1836, I, p. 142.

A note on European currencies in the eighteenth century

It is difficult to establish an exact exchange rate in the eighteenth century, and to estimate what money would have purchased. However, the following notes may serve as a very approximate guide when prices of clothes or textiles are mentioned in the text.

In *France*, the value of money was fixed by a decree of 1726, and remained virtually unaltered until the Revolution. The basic unit was the livre tournois or franc; a louis d'or was 23 livres, and an écu was 6 livres. In *c.* 1760 an artisan might earn 500 livres, a country gentleman might have an income of 10,000 livres, and a grand seigneur or rich city merchant might have revenues of considerably more than 10,000 livres.

In *England*, the pound sterling was, in *c.* 1760, roughly worth a louis d'or or 23 livres. Arthur Young's table of conversion in 1788 was:

$$50 \text{ livres} = £2 \text{ 3s. 9d.}$$
$$100 \text{ livres} = £4 \text{ 7s. 6d.}$$
$$500 \text{ livres} = £21 \text{ 17s. 6d.}$$
$$1,000 \text{ livres} = £43 \text{ 15s. 0d.}$$

By the end of our period, less than 15 per cent of British families had an income of more than £50 a year; of this 15 per cent only one quarter, approximately, earned more than £200 a year.

Outside France and England, the situation with regard to currency is very confused. In *America*, for example, the various states had not only different currencies (American dollars, Spanish pesos, English and French money), but within one currency, the exchange could vary. Brissot de Warville found on his American journey that a French écu of 6 livres was worth 8s. 9d. in New York, 6s. 8d. in Massachusetts and Connecticut, and only 5s. 5d. in Georgia and South Carolina. An English guinea varied in price from its face value (£1 1s. 0d.) to almost £2.

In *Italy*, Thomas Nugent found that 'every little state and principality . . . coins its own money', but perhaps the most common currency was the Florentine scudo (of 7 lire, each lira worth 20 soldi) worth (*c.* 1760) 5.68 livres.

In *Germany*, the situation was as confused as in Italy; states had their own currencies, based usually on the thaler and mark, and, in addition, the imperial currency, the reichsthaler (worth twice the value of the thaler). This was valued (*c.* 1760) at 1 écu.

Finally, we should note that Wraxall, visiting *Russia* in 1774, states that 1 rouble was worth 4s. 6d.

A chronology of significant events in politics and culture, 1713–1789

1713 Peace of Utrecht ends the War of the Spanish Succession, and French political predominance in Europe.

1714 Accession of the Hanoverian dynasty in England, with George I. Alexander Pope's *The Rape of the Lock*.

1715 Death of Louis XIV; Philippe, duc d'Orléans, Regent during the minority of Louis XV.

1718 Publication of Voltaire's first tragedy, *Oedipus*. Quadruple Alliance formed by Britain, France, Holland and the Austrian Empire against Spanish aggrandisement, and to defend the Utrecht settlement.

1719 Daniel Defoe's *Robinson Crusoe*.

1720 Collapse of speculative financial schemes in France and England.

1721 In England, Robert Walpole winds up the South Sea Bubble, restoring national credit, and begins a 21-year tenure as principal Minister of State.
Treaty of Nystadt ends Swedish claims to predominance in northern Europe, with the ceding of territory to Russia. Montesquieu's *Lettres Persanes*.

1723 Death of the Regent in France; Louis XV assumes full control. J. S. Bach becomes music director in Leipzig.

1725 Death of Peter the Great in Russia.

1726 Cardinal Fleury becomes principal adviser to Louis XV.
Dean Swift's *Gulliver's Travels*.

1731 Prévost's *Manon Lescaut*.

1733 Voltaire's *Lettres Philosophiques*.

1738 Treaty of Vienna ends the War of the Polish Succession. Augustus III, Elector of Saxony, confirmed as ruler of Poland, Stanislas Leszcynski given in compensation the duchy of Lorraine, which is to revert to the French crown on his death. Austria cedes Naples

and Sicily to Spain and is awarded in exchange Parma, Piacenza, and the Grand Duchy of Tuscany.

1739 David Hume's *Treatise of Human Nature*.

1740 Accession of Maria Theresa to Habsburg throne. Accession of Frederick the Great in Prussia. Prussian invasion of Silesia begins the War of the Austrian Succession; the main protagonists are Prussia and France versus Austria and England.
Samuel Richardson's *Pamela*.

1742 First peformance of Handel's *Messiah* in Dublin.

1743 Battle of Dettingen, an English victory over the French.

1744 Anglo-French hostilities spread to North America and India.

1745 Maria Theresa's husband Franz Stephan of Lorraine crowned Emperor.

1746 Rebellion of the 'Young Pretender', to restore the Stuarts to the English throne, crushed at the battle of Culloden.

1748 Treaty of Aix-la-Chapelle ends War of Austrian Succession; Prussia keeps Silesia, and France and England reciprocally restore all colonial conquests.

1750 Accession of Joseph I of Portugal; the real ruler of the country for the next quarter of a century is the Marquês de Pombal.

1751 Voltaire's *Le Siècle de Louis XIV*. Diderot's *Encyclopédie* begins to appear in instalments.

1755 Dr Johnson's *Dictionary*. Lisbon earthquake.

1756 Re-arrangement of European alliances; an Anglo-Prussian agreement is followed by the diplomatic alignment of France and Austria, the latter the work of Kaunitz, Maria Theresa's main adviser on foreign affairs. Seven Years War begins.

1757 In England, the ministry of William Pitt the Elder begins.
At the battle of Rossbach, the Prussians defeat the French army. In India, Clive is victorious over the French at the battle of Plassey.

1759 English capture Quebec from the French.
Accession of Charles III of Spain.
Voltaire's *Candide*.
The British Museum in London opens.

1760 Accession of George III in England.

1762 Accession of Catherine II in Russia.
Rousseau's *Du Contrat Social* and *Emile*.
Gluck's *Orfeo ed Euridice* performed in Vienna.

1763 Treaty of Paris ends Seven Years War. Prussian conquest of Silesia finally acknowledged, as is British supremacy in the New World and India.
Winckelmann's *Geschichte der Kunst des Altertums*.

1765 Joseph II becomes Emperor and Co-Regent of the Habsburg possessions with Maria Theresa; his brother Leopold becomes Grand Duke of Tuscany.

1768 James Cook begins his circumnavigation of the globe in the *Endeavour*.

1771 Accession of Gustavus III of Sweden.

1772 First Partition of Poland by Russia, Prussia and Austria.

1774 Accession of Louis XVI of France.
Goethe's *Die Leiden des Jungen Werther*.

1776 Americans issue Declaration of Independence.
Adam Smith's *Wealth of Nations*.
First volume of Gibbon's *The History of the Decline and Fall of the Roman Empire*.

1781 Emperor Joseph II frees the serfs in the Habsburg dominions.
Kant's *Critik der reinen Vernunft*.

1783 Peace of Versailles. American independence achieved.
Russia annexes the Crimea.

1784 First performance of Beaumarchais' *The Marriage of Figaro*.

1787 Mozart's *Don Giovanni*.

1788 Necker becomes Director-General of Finance in France.

1789 The meeting of the Estates General sets in train the events which lead to the storming of the Bastille and the French Revolution.

Glossary

Terms which appear in the text without explanation

Armosin/Armazeen   taffeta.
Bag   'an ornamental purse of silk tied to men's hair' (Johnson's *Dictionary*, 1755).
Bas de robe   detachable court train.
Bazin/Basin (Fr.)   dimity (q.v.).
Beaver   amphibious broad-tailed soft-furred rodent of genus Castor, chief raw material for hats in the eighteenth century; the fur fibres were combed out of the skin and made a glossy waterproof fabric.
Bombazine   cloth of silk and worsted.
Broadcloth   best woollen cloth.
Bristol stone   kind of colourless quartz used for buckles and buttons.
Brocade   'a stuff of gold, silver or silk, raised and enriched with flowers, foliages and other ornaments' (*A New and Complete Dictionary of Arts and Sciences, 1754–5*).
Brocatelle   'a kind of coarse brocade, chiefly used for tapestry' (*A New and Complete Dictionary of Arts and Sciences, 1754–5*).
Buckram   'a sort of coarse cloth made of hemp, gummed, calendered, and dyed several colours. It is put into those places of the lining of a garment, which one would have stiff and to keep their forms' (*A New and Complete Dictionary of Arts and Sciences, 1754–5*).
Buckskin   leather made from the skin of a buck, or sheepskin prepared in a particular way.
Buffskin   velvety dull-yellow ox leather, or any leather of a similar buff colour.
Bugles   tube-shaped glass beads.
Calico   cotton cloth with patterns printed in one or more colours; the name comes from Calicut, a port on the west coast of Malabar, south of Madras.
Calimanco   'a sort of woollen stuff manufactured in England and in Brabant. It has a fine gloss . . . Some calamancos are quite plain, others have broad stripes adorned with flowers;

some with plain broad stripes, some with narrow stripes, and others watered' (*A New and Complete Dictionary of Arts and Sciences, 1754–5*).
Cambric   fine white linen from Cambrai.
Camlet   'a kind of stuff originally made by a mixture of silk and camel's hair; it is now made with wool and silk' (Johnson's *Dictionary*, 1755). According to the *New and Complete Dictionary of Arts and Sciences, 1754–5*, camlets could be made of all silk, all wool, or mixtures such as goat's hair and silk, silk and thread, and 'some are striped, some waved or watered, and some figured'.
Cardinal   hooded cloak, originally made of scarlet wool.
Cashmere   very soft fine wool or woollen material made from the fleece of the Kashmir goat.
Chenille   velvety cord with short threads or fibres of silk woven standing out at right angles from a core of thread or wire, like the hairs of a caterpillar. The technique was invented by a tailor Scheling, in the reign of Louis X V; it decorated women's dresses and men's waistcoats.
Chintz   printed or painted calico.
Chip   wood or woody fibre split into thin strips for making hats.
Crêpe/Crape   thin silk gauze; or a silk and worsted fabric used for mourning.
Damask   'a silk stuff with a raised pattern so that the right side of the damask is that which hath the flowers raised or sattined' (*A New and Complete Dictionary of Arts and Sciences, 1754–5*). Damasks could also be made of wool and were manufactured in France and Flanders.
Dimity   fine cotton, usually white, with a raised woven design, also white.
Ermine   the winter fur of the northern stoat; its black tail tip was used to 'powder' the white fur at regular intervals.
Floss   untwisted silk.
Frieze   a coarse woollen napped cloth.

Furbelow 'a piece of stuff plaited and puckered together, either below or above, on the petticoats or gowns of women' (Johnson's *Dictionary*, 1755).

Fustian cloth with a linen warp and cotton weft.

Galloon ribbon of thread, or gold or silver tissue.

Gauze very fine, open-weave silk.

Harden coarse fabric made from the hards of flax or hemp.

Indiennes name given in France to all Eastern painted and printed stuffs, whatever their country of origin.

Kersey coarse woollen cloth, possibly from Kersey in Suffolk.

Lawn very fine linen.

Linsey-woolsey cloth made with linen warp and wool weft.

Lutestring/Lustring plain weave silk with glossy finish; very popular for summer wear.

Marten members of the weasel family with much-valued fur.

Mechlin fine bobbin lace from Mechlin (Malines) in Flanders.

Meroquin Morocco leather.

Mob a woman's cap with gathered crown and frill.

Mohair 'the hair of a kind of goat, frequent about Angoura in Turky; the inhabitants of which city are all employed in the manufacture of camblets, made of this hair. Some give the name Mohair to the camblets or stuffs made of this hair' (*A New and Complete Dictionary of Arts and Sciences, 1754–5*).

Muslin very fine, semi-transparent cotton.

Nankeen plain closely woven cotton, usually buff colour.

Paduasoy a strong silk, often figured.

Paillettes, paillons spangles.

Parements 'sont des garnitures dont on décore le devant des robes & des jupons, sous le nom de falbala, volans, etc.' (*Encyclopédie Méthodique*, 1785).

Persian thin, plain silk.

Point d'Espagne metal lace.

Pomatum scented ointment, in which apples are said to have been originally an ingredient, used to dress the hair.

Poplin mixture of silk and worsted.

Rateen thick twilled cloth, usually friezed.

Russet coarse woollen homespun, usually brown or grey.

Sable small fur-bearing animal of the marten family; the best sable came from Russia.

Serge hard-wearing twilled worsted.

Shalloon a light-weight woollen worsted.

Stuff plain or twilled woollen stuff.

Swanskin closely woven flannel.

Tabby a thick silk of taffeta weave with a slight nap, calendered by passing it in folds under a hot cylinder, which produced an uneven or moiré effect on the surface of the material.

Taffeta plain weave flossy silk.

Tambour a circular frame formed of one hoop fitting within another, in which silk, muslin or other material is stretched for embroidering.

Tammy a twilled worsted.

Tissue a woven textile of gold, silver or silk thread.

Toupet elevated front section of the wig or natural hair.

Warehouse a large shop selling goods not made on the premises.

Bibliography

This includes most of the works referred to in the footnotes (except where they are of specialist interest, such as certain articles, or newspapers and magazines), and other, more general works. It does not claim to be a comprehensive list.

Adams, A., *Letters*, intr. C. F. Adams, Boston 1848.

Andersen, E., *Danske Dragter: Moden i 1700-årene*, Copenhagen Nationalmuseet, 1977.

Andrews, J., *An Account of the Character and Manners of the French*, 2 vols., London 1770.

Angelo, H., *Reminiscences*, 2 vols., London 1828.

Archenholz, F. W. von, *A Picture of England*, 2 vols., London 1789.

—*A Picture of Italy*, 2 vols., London 1791.

Barbeau, A., *Life and Letters at Bath in the Eighteenth Century*, London 1904

Barbier, E. J. F., *Chronique de la Régence et du Règne de Louis XV, ou Journal de Barbier*, 8 vols., Paris 1857.

Baretti, J., *An Account of the Manners and Customs of Italy*, 2 vols., London 1769.

—*A Journey from London to Genoa, through England, Portugal, Spain and France*, 2 vols., London 1770.

Besant, W., *London in the Eighteenth Century*, London 1902.

Bielfeld, J. F., Baron von, *Letters of Baron Bielfeld ... containing original Anecdotes of the Prussian court for the last Twenty Years*, trans. Mr Hooper, 4 vols., London 1768–70.

Bocage, K. F. du, *Letters Concerning England, Holland and Italy*, 2 vols., London 1770.

Boehn, M. von, *Deutschland im 18 Jahrhundert*, 2 vols., Berlin 1921.

Boswell, J., *Boswell in Holland, 1763–4*, ed. F. A. Pottle, New York 1952.

—*Boswell on the Grand Tour, 1764*, ed. F. A. Pottle, New York 1953.

—*The Life of Samuel Johnson*, 3 vols., London 1791.

Boucher, F., *Le Costume Français vu par les artistes, XVIIᵉ, XVIIIᵉ, XIXᵉ siècles*, Paris 1949.

—*A History of Costume in the West*, London 1967.

Brissot de Warville, J. P., *Nouveau Voyage dans les Etats Unis*, trans. J. Barlow, 3 vols., Paris 1791.

Brocher, H., *Le Rang et l'Etiquette sous l'ancien Régime*, Paris 1934.

Brosses, C. de, *Selections from the Letters*, trans. Lord Ronald Sutherland Gower, London 1897.

Bruford, W. H., *Germany in the Eighteenth Century: The Social Background of the Literary Revival*, Cambridge 1935.

Buck, A., & Cunnington, C., *Children's Costume in England, 1300–1900*, London 1965.

—*Dress in Eighteenth-Century England*, London 1979.

Burney, F., *Evelina*, 3 vols., London 1778.

—*Cecilia*, 5 vols., London 1782.

—*Early Diary, 1768–1778*, ed. A. R. Ellis, 2 vols., London 1889.

—*Diary and Letters of Madame d'Arblay*, edited by her niece, 7 vols., London 1842–6.

Byrde, P., *The Male Image: Men's Fashion in Britain, 1300–1970*, London 1979.

Campan, J. L. H., *Memoires sur la vie privée de Marie Antoinette*, 3 vols., Paris 1822.

Campbell, T. (ed.), *Frederick the Great, his Court and Times*, 2 vols., London 1842.

Caraccioli, L. A. de., *Voyage de la Raison en Europe*, Paris 1772.

Carré, H., *Jeux, Sports et Divertissements des Rois de France*, Paris 1937.

Casanova, J., *The Memoirs of Jacques Casanova de Seingalt, 1725–1798*, trans. A. Machen, 8 vols., Edinburgh 1940.

Catherine II, *The Memoirs of Catherine the Great*, trans, M. Budberg, London 1955.

Cherry, D. & Harris, J., 'Eighteenth-century portraiture and the seventeenth-century past: Gainsborough and Van Dyck', *Art History*, vol. 5, no. 3, 1982.

Chesterfield, P., Earl of, *Letters to his son*, ed. & intr. C. Strachey, 2 vols., London 1901.

Clarke, E., *Letters concerning the Spanish Nation, Written at Madrid during the Years 1760 and 1761*, London 1763.

Coke, Lady J., *Letters from Lady Jane Coke to her friend Mrs Eyre, 1747–1758*, ed. A. Rathbone, London 1899.

Coke, Lady M., *Letters and Journals*, ed. J. A. Home, 4 vols., Edinburgh 1889.

Coventry, F., *Pompey the Little*, London 1751.

Coxe, W., *Travels into Poland, Russia, Sweden and Denmark*, 2 vols., London 1784, and 3rd. vol. 1790.

—*Memoirs of the Kings of Spain from the Accession of Philip the Fifth to the Death of Charles the Third, 1700–1788*, 3 vols., London 1813.

Coyer, Abbé, *Voyages d'Italie et de Hollande*, 2 vols., Paris 1775.

Cronin, V., *Catherine, Empress of all the Russias*, London 1978.

Cunninton, C. W. & P., *Handbook of English Costume of the Eighteenth Century*, revised ed., London 1972.

Davenport, M., *The Book of Costume*, New York 1948.

Decremps, M., *Le Parisian à Londres, ou Avis aux Français qui vont en Angleterre*, 2 vols., Amsterdam 1789.

Defoe, D., *A Tour Thro' the whole Island of Great Britain*, 3 vols., London 1724.

Delany, M., *Autobiography and Correspondence of Mary Granville, Mrs Delany*, ed. Lady Llanover, 6 vols., London 1861–2.

Delpierre, M., *Robes de Grande Parure du Temps de Louis XVI*, in *Bulletin du Musée Carnavalet*, June 1966, no. 1.

—*Marie Antoinette, reine de la mode*, in *Versailles*, no. 59, 1975.

—*L'élégance à Versailles au temps de Louis XV*, in *Versailles*, no. 55, 1974.

Devonshire, G., Duchess of, *Extracts from the Correspondence of Georgiana, Duchess of Devonshire*, ed. Earl of Bessborough, London 1955.

Dickens, A. G. (ed.), *The Courts of Europe, Politics, Patronage and Royalty, 1400–1800*, London 1977.

Eden, Sir F., *The State of the Poor*, 3 vols., London 1797.

Eloffe, Mme., *Livre-Journal de Madame Eloffe*, ed. le comte de Reiset, 2 vols., Paris 1885.

Fairholt, F. W., *Satirical Songs and Poems on Costume*, London 1849.

Fielding, J., *Joseph Andrews*, 2 vols., London 1742.

—*Tom Jones*, 6 vols., London 1749.

—*Amelia*, 4 vols., London 1751.

Fithian, P. V., *Journal and Letters, 1767–1774*, ed. J. R. Williams, Princeton 1900.

—*Journal, 1775–1776*, ed. R. G. Albion & L. Dodson, Princeton 1934.

Forster, R. & E., *European Society in the Eighteenth Century*, London 1969.

Friedenthal, R., *Goethe – His Life and Times*, London 1965.

Fusil, L., *Souvenirs d'une Actrice*, 2 vols., Brussels 1841.

Gallerie des Modes et Costumes Français, Dessinés d'après Nature, 1778–1787, intr. P. Cornu, Paris 1911–1914.

Garsault, F. A. de, *L'Art du Perruquier*, Académie Royale des Sciences, Descriptions des Arts et Métiers, Paris 1767.

—*L'Art du Tailleur*, Académie Royale des Sciences, Descriptions des Arts et Métiers, Paris 1769.

Garsault, F. A. de, *L'Art de la Lingerie*, Académie Royale des Sciences, Descriptions des Arts et Métiers, Paris 1771.

Gay, J., *Trivia; or The Art of Walking the Streets of London*, London 1716.

Genlis, S. F., comtesse de, *Dictionnaire critique et raisonné des Etiquettes de la Cour et des Usages du Monde*, 2 vols., Paris 1818.

—*Mémoires Inédits*, 8 vols., Paris 1825.

George, M. D., *London Life in the Eighteenth Century*, London 1925.

—*England in Transition*, London 1931.

Goethe, J. W. von, *Travels in Italy*, trans. A. J. W. Morrison & C. Nisbet, London 1892.

Goldsmith, O., *The Citizen of the World*, 2 vols., London 1762.

—*The Vicar of Wakefield*, London 1766.

—*She Stoops to Conquer*, London 1773.

Goncourt, E. & J. de, *La Femme au dix-huitième siècle*, Paris 1862.

—*L'Amour au dix-huitième siècle*, Paris 1875.

Grosley, J., *New Observations on Italy and Its Inhabitants*, trans. T. Nugent, 2 vols., London 1769.

—*A Tour to London, or New Observations on England and Its Inhabitants*, trans. T. Nugent, 2 vols., London 1772.

Hamilton, M., *Letters and Diaries, 1756–1816*, ed. E. & F. Anson, London 1925.

Haumant, E., *La Culture Française en Russie, 1700–1900*, Paris 1913.

Hawkins, L. M., *Gossip about Dr Johnson and Others*, ed. F. H. Skrine, London 1926.

Hedley, O., *Queen Charlotte*, London 1975.

d'Hézecques, F., comte, *Souvenirs d'un Page de la Cour de Louis XVI*, Paris 1873.

Hickey, W., *Memoirs*, ed. A. Spencer, 4 vols., London 1913.

Hutton, C., *Reminiscences of a Gentlewoman of the last century*, ed. C. H. Beale, Birmingham 1891.

Johnson, S., *Sir Joshua's Nephew, being Letters written 1760–1778 by a Young Man to his Sisters*, ed. S. M. Radcliffe, London 1930.

Kalm, P., *Kalm's Account of his Visit to England on his way to America in 1748*, trans. J. Lucas, London 1892.

Karamzin, N. M., *Travels from Moscow through Prussia, Germany, Switzerland, France and England*, 3 vols., London 1803.

Keysler, J. G., *Travels through Germany, Hungary, Bohemia, Switzerland, Italy and Lorrain*, trans. from 2nd German ed., 4 vols., London 1758.

Labat, P., *Voyages en Espagne et en Italie*, 8 vols., Paris 1730.

Lacroix, P., *The Eighteenth Century: Its Institutions, Customs and Costumes; France 1700–1789*, London 1876.

La Motraye, A., *Voyages . . . en diverses provinces et places de la Prusse Ducale et Royale, de la Russie, de la Pologne, etc.*, The Hague, 1732.

Langlade, E., *La Marchande de Modes de Marie Antoinette, Rose Bertin*, Paris 1911.

la Tour du Pin, H–L., marquise de, *Journal d'une Femme de 50 ans, 1778–1815*, Paris 1951.

Le Camus, A., *Abdeker, or The Art of preserving Beauty*, London 1754.

Leinster, E., Duchess of, *Correspondence*, ed. B. Fitzgerald, 3 vols., Dublin 1949.

Leroy, A., *The Portraits of Madame de Pompadour*, in *Connoisseur*, June 1939.

Lennox, Lady S., *Life and Letters*, ed. Countess of Ilchester & Lord Stavordale, 2 vols., London 1901.

Levron, J., *Daily Life at Versailles in the Seventeenth and Eighteenth Centuries*, trans, C. E. Engel, London 1968.

Lowe, A., *La Serenissima: The Last Flowering of the Venetian Republic*, London 1974.

Macartney, Lord, *An Account of Russia, 1767*, London 1768.

Malcolm, J. P., *Anecdotes of the Manners and Customs of London during the Eighteenth Century*, London 1808.

Marshall, J., *Travels through Holland, Flanders, Germany, Denmark, Sweden, Lapland, Russia, The Ukraine and Poland, in the Years 1768, 1769 and 1770*, 4 vols., London 1772–6.

McClellan, E., *History of American Costume, 1607–1870*, New York 1904, reprint 1969.

Melville, L., *Lady Suffolk and her Circle*, London 1924.

Mercier, L. S., *Tableau de Paris*, 8 vols., Amsterdam 1782–88.

—trans. & abridged by H. Simpson as *The Waiting City: Paris, 1782–1788*, London 1933.

Miège, G., *The Present State of Great-Britain and Ireland*, London 1715.

Mingay, G. E., *English Landed Society in the 18th Century*, London 1963.

Molmenti, P., *Venice: Its Individual growth from the Earliest Beginnings to the Fall of the Republic*, trans. H. F. Brown, Part III, *The Decadence*, 2 vols., London 1908.

Montagu, E., *Elizabeth Montagu: Correspondence, 1720–61*, ed. E. J. Climenson, 2 vols., London 1906.

—*Mrs Montagu, 'Queen of the Blues': Her Letters and Friendships from 1762–1800*, ed. R. Blunt, 2 vols., London 1923.

Montagu, Lady M. W., *Town Eclogues*, London 1747 (originally published, in an unauthorized edition, as *Court Poems*, 1715).

—*The Complete Letters of Lady Mary Wortley Montagu*, ed. R. Halsband, 3 vols., Oxford 1965–7.

Montgomery, F. M., *Printed Textiles: English and American Cottons and Linens, 1700–1800*, New York 1970.

Moore, J., *A view of Society and Manners in France, Switzerland and Germany*, 2 vols., London 1779.

—*A View of Society and Manners in Italy*, 2 vols., London 1781.

Moritz, C. P., *Travels in England in 1782*, intr. P. E. Matheson, London 1924.

Neville, S., *Diary, 1767–1788*, ed. B. Cozens-Hardy, London 1950.

Nisbet Bain, R., *Gustavus III and his Contemporaries, 1746–92*, 2 vols., London 1894.

—*The Pupils of Peter the Great: A History of the Russian Court and Empire from 1697 to 1740*, London 1897.

—*The Last King of Poland and his Contemporaries*, London 1909.

Nivelon, F., *The Rudiments of Genteel Behavior*, London 1737.

Northumberland, Duchess of, *Diaries of a Duchess: Extracts from the Diaries of the first Duchess of Northumberland, 1716–1776*, ed. J. Greig, London 1926.

Nugent, T., *Travels through Germany*, 2 vols., London 1768.

—*The Grand Tour, or A Journey through the Netherlands, Germany, Italy and France*, 4 vols., London 1778. This is a compendium of contemporary information on the life and customs of these countries, taken from various sources such as Pöllnitz (*q.v.*) and Keysler (*q.v.*).

Oberkirch, H. L., Baroness d', *Memoirs*, ed. Count de Montbrison, 3 vols., London 1852.

Orléans, E. C., duchesse d', *Letters from Liselotte, Elizabeth Charlotte, Princess Palatine and Duchess of Orléans, 'Madame', 1652–1722*, trans. & ed. M. Kroll, London 1970.

Papendiek, C. L. H., *Court and Private Life in the Time of Queen Charlotte, being the Journals of Mrs Papendiek, Assistant Keeper of the Wardrobe and Reader to Her Majesty*, ed. V. D. Broughton, 2 vols., London 1887.

Paston, G., *Side-Lights on the Georgian Period*, London 1902.

—*Social Caricature in the Eighteenth Century*, London 1905.

Perry, J., *The State of Russia under the Present Czar*, London 1716.

Pilon, E., & Saisset, F., *Les Fêtes en Europe au XVIIIᵉ siècle*, Saint-Gratien 1943.

Piozzi, H. L., *Observations and Reflections made in the course of a Journey through France, Italy and Germany*, 2 vols., London 1789.

Place, F., *Place Collections*, British Museum, Add. MS. 27827.

—*Autobiography*, ed. & intr. M. Thale, Cambridge, 1972.

Pöllnitz, C., Baron von, *Travels from Prussia thro' Germany, Italy, France, Flanders, Holland, England, etc.*, 5 vols., London 1745. This is a 'kind of glorified Baedeker for the Grand Tour'; Pöllnitz worked up the book from his notes, and did not, in fact, make the journeys as described either in time or sequence. See E. Cuthell, *A Vagabond Courtier*, 2 vols., London 1913.

Powys, Mrs P. L., *Passages from the Diaries of Mrs Philip Lybbe Powys, 1756–1808*, ed. E. J. Climenson, London 1899.

Prussia, Princess Royal of, *Memoirs of Frederica Sophia Wilhelmina, Princess Royal of Prussia, Margravine of Bareith*, 2 vols., London 1812.

Purefoy Letters, 1735–1753, ed. G. Eland, 2 vols., London 1931.

Pyne, W. H. ('Ephraim Hardcastle'), *Wine and Walnuts*, 2 vols., London 1823.

Retif de la Bretonne, *Tableaux de la Bonne Compagnie*, 2 vols., Paris 1787.

Ribeiro, A., *A Visual History of Costume: The Eighteenth Century*, London 1983.

Richardson, S., *Pamela; or Virtue Rewarded*, 4 vols., London 1740.

—*Clarissa Harlow*, 8 vols., London 1748.

—*Sir Charles Grandison*, 7 vols., London 1753–4.

Roche, S. von la, *Sophie in London, 1786, being the Diary of Sophie von la Roche*, trans. C. Williams, London 1933.

Rochefoucauld, F. de la, *A Frenchman in England, 1784, Being the Mélanges sur l'Angleterre of*

François de la Rochefoucauld, ed. & intr. J. Marchand, Cambridge 1933.

Roland de la Platière, J-M., *Encyclopédie Méthodique*, Paris 1785.

Rudé, G., *Hanoverian London, 1714–1808*, London 1971.

—*Europe in the Eighteenth Century*, London 1972.

Russel, J., *Letters from a Young Painter abroad to his Friends in England*, 2 vols., London 1750.

Saint-Simon, L. de R., duc de, *Historical Memoirs*, ed. & trans. L. Norton, London 1967–72.

Saussure, C. de, *A Foreign View of England in the Reigns of George I and George II*, trans. & ed. M. van Muyden, London 1902.

Ségur, J. A., comte de, *Memoirs and Recollections*, 3 vols., London 1825.

Shennan, J. H., *Philippe, Duke of Orléans, Regent of France, 1715–1723*, London 1979.

Sheridan, R. B., *The Rivals*, London 1775.

—*School for Scandal*, Dublin 1777.

Smith, J. T., *Nollekens and his Times*, 2 vols., London 1829.

Smollett, T., *Roderick Random*, 2 vols., London 1748.

—*Peregrine Pickle*, 4 vols., London 1751.

—*Ferdinand, Count Fathom*, 2 vols., London 1753.

—*Travels through France and Italy*, 2 vols., London 1766.

—*Humphry Clinker*, 3 vols., London 1771.

Sobry, J. F., *Le Mode François: Discours sur les Principaux Usages de la Nation Françoise*, Paris 1786.

Spink, J. S., *Woman and Society in Eighteenth-Century France: Essays in Honour of John Stephenson Spink*, ed. E. Jacobs, W. H. Barber, J. H. Bloch, F. W. Leakey and E. Le Breton, London 1979.

Stirling, A. M. W., *Annals of a Yorkshire House, from the papers of a macaroni and his kindred*, 2 vols., London 1911.

Stuart, Lady L., *Gleanings from an old Portfolio, containing some Correspondence between Lady Louisa Stuart and her sister Caroline, Countess of Portarlington, and other friends and relations*, ed. Mrs Godfrey Clark, 3 vols., Edinburgh 1895.

—*Letters*, ed. R. Brimley Johnson, London 1926.

Swinton, A., *Travels into Norway, Denmark and Russia in the Years 1788, 1789, 1790 and 1791*, London 1792.

Talbot Rice, T., *Elizabeth, Empress of Russia*, London 1940.

Thornton, P., *Baroque and Rococo silks*, London 1965.

Topham, E., *Letters from Edinburgh, Written in the years 1774 and 1775: Containing some Observations on the Diversions, Customs, Manners and Laws, of the Scotch Nation*, London 1776.

Toth, K., *Woman and Rococo in France*, trans. R. Abingdon, London 1931.

Townsend, J., *A Journey through Spain in the years 1786 and 1787*, 3 vols., London 1791.

Turberville, A. S. (ed.), *Johnson's England*, 2 vols., London 1933.

Twiss, R., *Travels through Portugal and Spain in 1772 and 1773*, London 1775.

Vaussard, M., *La Vie Quotidienne en Italie au XVIIIe siècle*, Paris 1959.

Vehse, E., *Memoirs of the Court and Aristocracy of Austria*, trans. F. Demmler, 2 vols, London 1856.

Vigée-Lebrun, E. L., *Memoirs, 1755–1789*, trans. G. Shelley, London 1926.

Walpole, H., *Letters*, ed. Paget Toynbee, 16 vols., Oxford 1903–15, & suppl. vol. 1918.

Wansey, H., *Journal of an Excursion to the United States of America*, Salisbury 1796.

Ward, Mrs, *Letters from a Lady who resided some Years in Russia, to her Friend in England*, London 1777.

Warwick, E., *Early American Dress*, New York 1965.

Waugh, N., *The Cut of Men's Clothes, 1600–1900*, London 1964.

— *The Cut of Women's Clothes, 1600–1930*, London 1968.

Weber, F. C., *The Present State of Russia*, 2 vols., London 1723.

Weigert, R-A., *Textiles en Europe sous Louis XV: Les Plus Beaux Spécimens de la Collection Richelieu*, Fribourg 1964.

White, C. (ed.), *The Courts of Europe at the Close of the Last Century*, 2 vols., London 1841.

Winslow, A. G., *Diary, 1771–3*, ed. A. M. Earle, Boston 1894.

Woodforde, J., *The Diary of a Country Parson, 1758–1802*, ed. J. Beresford, 5 vols., London 1924–31.

Wraxall, N. W., *A Tour through some of the Northern Parts of Europe*, London 1776.

— *Memoirs of the Courts of Berlin, Dresden, Warsaw and Vienna in the Years 1777, 1778 and 1779*, 2 vols., London 1799.

— *Historical Memoirs of His Own Time*, revised ed., 4 vols., London 1836.

Young, A., *Travels during the Years 1787, 1788 and 1789, to which is added, the register of a Tour into Spain*, 2 vols., London 1793.

Exhibition catalogues and museum publications

Of the large numbers of publications dealing with eighteenth-century art and costume, the following list is of necessity very limited, but it may serve as a starting point for further research. Publications are listed by *place*.

Bristol, Museum and Art Gallery
Bennett, H., & Witt, C., *18th Century Women's Costume at Blaise Castle House*, Bristol City Museum, Blaise Castle House (n.d.).

Brussels, Musées Royaux d'Art et de Costume
Coppens, M., *Le Costume au XVIIIe siècle*, 1978.

Chertsey, Chertsey Museum
Rowley, C., *Costume in Chertsey Museum, 1700–1800*, Runnymede District Council, 1976.

Chicago, Art Institute
Painting in Italy in the Eighteenth Century, ed. J. Maxon & J. J. Rishel, The Art Institute of Chicago, Chicago, 1970.

Florence, Palazzo Pitti
Curiosità di una reggia Vicende della Guardaroba di Palazzo Pitti, Palazzo Pitti, Firenze, 1979.

The Hague, Nederlands Kostuummuseum
de Jong, M.C., *Waaiers & Mode, 18e eeuw tot heden*, Dienst voor Schone Kunsten, Den Haag, (n.d.).

London, Greater London Council, Iveagh Bequest, Kenwood
Einberg, E., *The French Taste in English Painting during the first half of the 18th century*, Greater London Council, 1968.
Stainton, E., *British Artists in Rome, 1700–1800*, Greater London Council, 1974.
Goodreau, D., *Nathaniel Dance, 1735–1811*, Greater London Council, 1977.
Miles, E., & Simon, J., *Thomas Hudson, 1701–1779*, Greater London Council, 1979.
Bowron, E. P., *Pompeo Batoni and his British Patrons*, Greater London Council, 1982.

London, Museum of London
Halls, Z., *Women's Costumes, 1600–1750*; *Women's Costumes, 1750–1800*; *Men's Costumes, 1560–1750*; *Men's Costumes, 1750–1800*, HMSO, London, 1969–73.
Fox, C. & Ribeiro, A., *Masquerade*, 1983.

London, National Portrait Gallery
Kerslake, J., *Early Georgian Portraits in the National Portrait Gallery, 1714–1760*, HMSO, 1978.

Webster, M., *Johan Zoffany, 1733–1810*, National Portrait Gallery, 1976.

London, Royal Academy of Arts
Sutton, D., *France in the Eighteenth Century*, 1968.

London, Tate Gallery
Gowing, L., & Paulson, R., *William Hogarth*, Tate Gallery, 1971.
Hayes, J., *Thomas Gainsborough*, Tate Gallery, 1980.

Los Angeles, County Museum of Art
An Elegant Art: Fashion and Fantasy in the Eighteenth Century, 1983.

Melbourne, National Gallery of Victoria
Clark, J., *The Great Eighteenth Century Exhibition*, 1983.

New Haven, Yale Center for British Art
Plumb, J. H., *The Pursuit of Happiness, A View of Life in Georgian England*, 1977.
D'Oench, E. G., *The Conversation Piece: Arthur Devis and His Contemporaries*, 1980.

New York, Metropolitan Museum of Art
Russian Costume from the Eleventh to the Twentieth Century, from the collections of the Arsenal Museum, Leningrad, Hermitage, Leningrad, Historical Museum, Moscow, Kremlin Museums, Moscow, and Pavlovsk Museum, Metropolitan Museum of Art, New York, 1976.
The Eighteenth-Century Woman, Costume Institute 1981–2.

Paris, Musée du Costume de la Ville de Paris
Costume Français du XVIIIᵉ siècle, 1715–1789, Musée Carnavalet, 1954–5.
Elégances du XVIIIᵉ siècle: Costumes Français, 1730–1794, Musée Carnavalet, 1963–4.

Paris, Musée de L'Histoire de France
Babelon, J-P., & Duboscq, G., *La Cour de France au XVIIIᵉ siècle*, Archives Nationales, 1971–2.

Paris, La Réunion des musées nationaux
La peinture française au XVIIIᵉ siècle à la cour de Frédéric II, Louvre, 1963.
L'Art Européen à la Cour d'Espagne au XVIIIᵉ siècle, Grand-Palais, 1979.

Stockholm, Nationalmuseum
Dahlbäck, B. (and others), *1700-tal Tanke och form i rokokon*, Nationalmuseum, Stockholm, 1979–80.

Vienna, Schloss Schönbrunn
Maria Theresa un ihre Zeit, Bundesministerium für Wissenschaft und Forschung, Vienna, 1980.

Index

Figures in italic type refer to pages on which illustrations appear.